Flashback, Eclipse

Flashback, Eclipse

The Political Imaginary
of Italian Art in
the 1960s

Romy Golan

ZONE BOOKS · NEW YORK

2021

Printed in the United States of America.

Distributed by Princeton University Press,
Princeton, New Jersey, and Woodstock, United Kingdom

Library of Congress Cataloging-in-Publication Data
Names: Golan, Romy, author.
Title: Flashback, eclipse : the political imaginary of Italian art in
    the 1960s / Romy Golan.
Description: New York : Zone Books, 2021. | Includes bibliographical
    references and index.| Description based on print version record
    and CIP data provided by publisher; resource not viewed.
Identifiers: LCCN 2020041739 (print) | LCCN 2020041740 (ebook) |
    ISBN 9781942130505 (hardcover) | ISBN 9781942130512 (ebook)
Subjects: LCSH: Arts and history—Italy—History—20th century. | Arts—
    Political aspects—Italy—History—20th century. | Arts, Italian—
    20th century—Themes, motives. | Imagery (Psychology) in art.
Classification: LCC NX180.H57 G65 2021 (print) | LCC NX180.H57 (ebook) |
    DDC 709.45/0904—dc23
LC record available at https://lccn.loc.gov/2020041739

For my mother, Esther Golan,

and her *anni romani*

Contents

Flashback, Eclipse

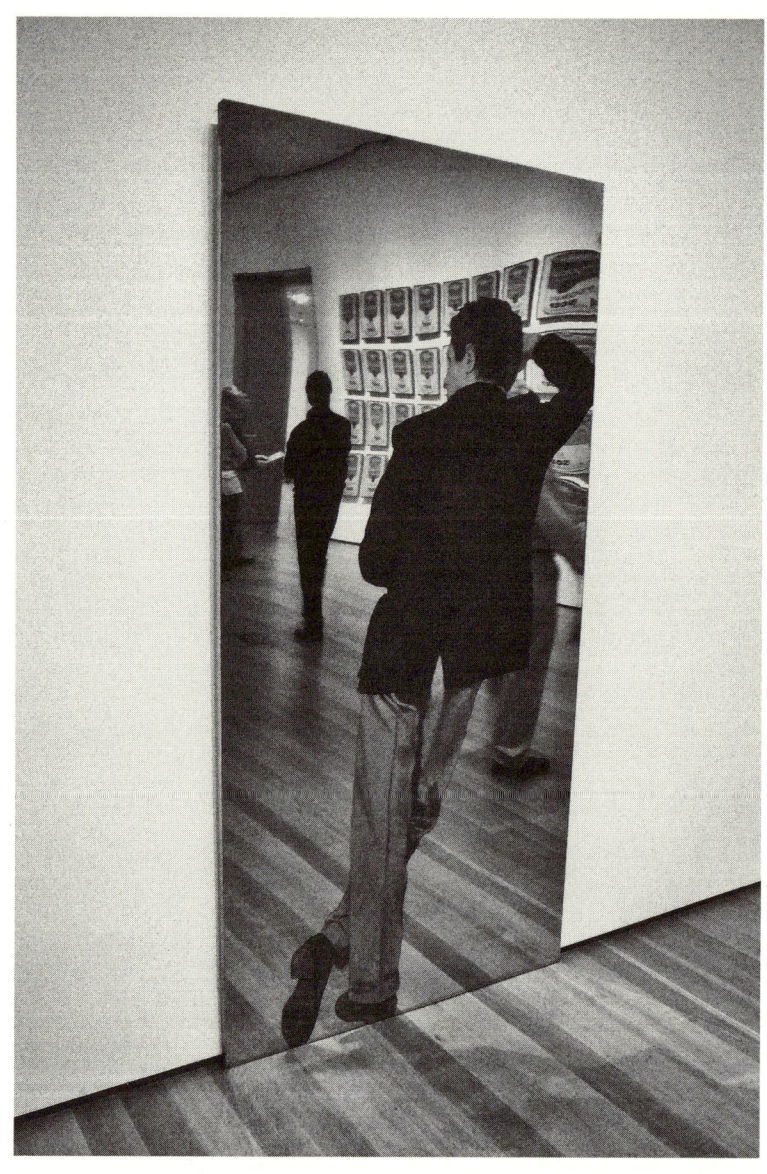

Figure I.1. Michelangelo Pistoletto, *Uomo con pantaloni gialli* (Man with yellow pants, 1964). Painted tissue paper on polished stainless steel, 200 × 120 cm. Museum of Modern Art, New York. Photograph: the author.

Introduction

This book is about 1960s Italian art and its troubled, but also resourceful relation to the history and politics of the first part of the century and the aftermath of World War II. It rewrites the history of Italian art of that decade, exploring, but also reproducing the ambiguities and temporal switchbacks that the artists themselves performed — my method adopts and adapts strategies that I identify in the works. My account is mostly structured by the flashback and the eclipse — two forms of nonlinear and decidedly nonpresentist forms of temporality — as well as by flashbacks within flashbacks in the form of a *mise en abyme*. Although some of the flashbacks might appear fanciful, my method is fundamentally archival. Both flashbacks and eclipses are, without fail, historically specific. They are efforts to recover what the established, more linear narratives have left out. At the same time, these temporal models complicate chronology. What are being recalled in flashbacks and at other moments occluded in the art of the 1960s are not only episodes of Italian nationalism and Fascism, but also various liberatory moments of political and cultural resistance: the political imaginary of 1960s Italian art.

The word "imaginary" appears in the subtitle as a noun, rather than an adjective. It signifies ways in which a social group images its history, its nation, its geography, its institutions, its laws, its symbols, and its place in the world. Here, I hope to offer a model to those

11

cultural and political historians who are increasingly thinking about how the past is processed *in* images. The book achieves its revision of existing accounts through analysis not only of artworks, but also of the images that mediated these artworks, including photo books and shots of exhibitions. Some images are culled from films. I also attend to works' critical and often poetic reception.

The book is full of images virtually unknown to English-language readers. It is centered geographically and mnemonically on Italy, but some of its imaginaries are not: they include, notably, those of Paris and New York. Thus, even though it deals with just one decade and one country, it is resonant with European and American postwar culture at large. It is Italian, but also concerned, at moments, with geopolitics. Italian art, with its political preoccupations, invites such an approach, but this book more broadly aims to offer a general paradigm of how artworks and images redouble or even triple their artistic and political contexts.

My main protagonists are, in order of appearance, the artists Michelangelo Pistoletto and Giosetta Fioroni, the photographer Ugo Mulas, Ettore Sottsass (as a critic, rather than a designer), the graphic designer Bruno Munari, the curators Luciano Caramel and Achille Bonito Oliva, the architect Piero Sartogo, Carla Lonzi (as an artist, rather than a critic), the filmmakers Michelangelo Antonioni and Bernardo Bertolucci, and, in flashback among the departed, the Novecento painter Felice Casorati, the writer Massimo Bontempelli, the art historian Aby Warburg, the architect Giuseppe Terragni, and the Renaissance friar-philosopher-mathematician Giordano Bruno (as patron saint of the sixty-eighters).

My project began somewhat serendipitously with what became this book's first chapter: the detection of narrative plots in images of Pistoletto's *Mirror Paintings* — life-size cutouts of people and mundane objects made of thin, translucent paper and placed on the reflective surface of polished stainless steel — when they appeared on the pages of art magazines, exhibition leaflets or catalogues, and books during the 1960s. In the *Mirror Paintings*, the viewer and anything that happens to be placed in front of the sheet of steel become part of the scene.[1] Creating an image of these artworks required a specific technique. In order to photograph these paintings without being included in the picture, one would have to move sideways and shoot at an angle. Any images one sees of the *Mirror Paintings* unencumbered by glimpses of the photographer himself or herself have been airbrushed, as they have been in most color reproductions featured in Pistoletto's post-1960s publications. When I told Pistoletto himself that I was interested in what was captured in the 1960s photographs of his works, he was attentive, but ultimately perplexed; he protested that "the *Mirror Paintings* are impossible to photograph: you lose the dynamic of the present. The photos are nothing but a collateral effect." But this "collateral effect"[2] and its relation to what is omitted in "the dynamic of the present" were precisely what interested me, and it became paradigmatic of my approach to the Italian 1960s as a whole via the flashback and the eclipse.

While the flashback reveals something that has been omitted, the eclipse reveals by omission. The two can be seen as opposites, but also as complementary. Constantly flipping between the two, the format of this book functions like a device or *dispositif.*

A flashback refers to the intervention of the past in the present flow of a narrative. Flashbacks are used in literature and film to recount events that happened before the story's primary sequence of events, to fill in crucial backstory. As Maureen Turim explains in *Flashbacks in Film: Memory and History,* "The flashback is a privileged moment in unfolding that juxtaposes different moments of temporal reference. A juncture is wrought between present and past and two concepts are implied in this juncture: memory and history. The analysis of flashbacks in film is first of all a history of formal changes in storytelling techniques."[3] Citing Leslie Halliwell's *Filmgoer's Companion,* Turim calls flashback "a break in chronological narrative during which we are shown events of past time which bear on the present situation."[4] In film, various camera techniques and special effects have been employed to alert the viewer that the action shown is from the past; the edges of the picture may be deliberately blurred, the cinematography may become jarring or choppy, or unusual coloration may be used. There are, moreover, various types of flashbacks: multiple flashbacks, embedded flashbacks, disruptive or abrupt modernist flashbacks, all of which exemplify the self-reflexivity of the medium.[5] Key to the flashback is the collapse of the distinction made between history (a generic linear narrative) and story or plot (the inscription of events as they appear in the personal, subjective narrative of an artwork). The flashback is simultaneously historical and subjective.[6]

Often associated with 1960s Italy due to the title of Michelangelo Antonioni's most famous film, *L'eclisse*, made in 1962, the eclipse is less readily discernable as a visual and temporal device. A solar eclipse (such as that in Antonioni's film) is a planetary alignment in which the moon blots out the sun from the perspective of those on earth. But even at the moment of total occlusion, a trace of the sun's glow remains visible behind the dark disk of the moon. This vestige of what lies behind the moon draws attention to what is being momentarily hidden. It is dangerous to stare at an eclipse: although one isn't immediately aware of it, the solar rays that escape around the edges of the moon can excoriate the eye. Eclipses have been regarded as bad omens. Observers experience unease at the untimely disappearance of sunlight and the eerie light that remains. Difficult to photograph, an eclipse also mimics, in cosmic terms, the movement of a camera's shutter opening and closing as it captures its subject. In doing so, eclipses seem to turn the world into an image-making apparatus.[7] This photographic (and filmic) nature of the flashback and eclipse is why my analysis is largely mediated by black-and-white photographs: those culled from art, design, and architecture magazines such as *Domus*, those of photo books, and shots of exhibitions already installed, in contrast to exhibition catalogues, which are almost always produced beforehand.

An eclipse, once it is recognized as such, can mask a flashback. And a flashback can include, nested in it, either another flashback or an eclipse. When nested, they produce an effect of a *mise en abyme*. The reduplication of the same image within the image itself — be it a painting within a painting, a film within a film, or a text within a text — *mise en abyme* is also common in dreams, as when we dream that we are dreaming. In an article published in *Art International* in 1975, the art historian Valentina Anker and the literary critic Lucien Dällenbach proposed the *mise en abyme* as a key strategy of recent art. They noted that most artists, rather than manually and painstakingly replicating an image in paint, opted for the mirrored surface as a shortcut.[8] Dällenbach went on to propose that the *mise en abyme* and the mirror are interchangeable.[9]

Dällenbach posits that not only do the stories within the stories produced by the *mise en abyme* necessarily disrupt the development of chronology, but the *mise en abyme* also produces either a semantic compression or a semantic dilation of the thematic content of the main story and that of the story contained within it.[10] Although fleeting, the flashbacks and eclipses produced by the works in this book triggered such a response on the part of art critics. They loosened fingers upon typewriter keys. Hence the many quotes that I include from contemporary reviews, translated here into English for the first time. The quotes themselves perform some of the flashbacks and eclipses that structure the book.[11]

A number of the connections I make between artists and events, especially in the longer flashbacks, might appear to be a stretch, the result of associative thinking, and indeed, many of the flashbacks and eclipses in this book are mine, but a degree of speculation is within the logic of the visual thinking on which this study is founded. Flashbacks and eclipses are by nature investigative. They complicate narrative. They do not merely deliver meaning, but also generate it. The images know more than we do. The artworks and the images thereof generate both real and imagined narratives about the connection between the present and the past that historians cannot grasp with documents alone. Flashbacks and eclipses are mostly involuntary — each realization hit me, visually, in an unexpected manner, a testament to the power that artworks and images of artworks have to attract one another. I thus capture mental images that are visually vivid, momentary, and fleeting — hence the elliptical quality of some of this book's passages. Some degree of decontextualization and elliptical writing is necessary for a flashback to remain a flashback and for an eclipse to remain an eclipse.

As a result, while each chapter in this book involves discrete episodes, they resolutely do not constitute "case studies." This is because flashbacks, eclipses, and the resulting *mises en abyme* at work in each chapter end up rearranging and enfolding the overall narrative in ways that make the chapters overlap with one another, thus constituting the book as a whole. This introduction provides a prequel explaining *why* Italian artists, critics, gallerists, and curators wanted to revisit their recent past obliquely, through flashbacks and eclipses, and why this should have happened during the 1960s.

That impulse derived from the fact that the artistic avant-gardes of the 1910s and 1920s — in other nations associated with progressive or oppositional politics — were in Italy deeply imbricated first with nationalism and then with Fascism. The Futurists are emblematic of this artistic entanglement with rightist politics, but they were by no means alone. During the *ventennio*, Fascism's two decades in power, the regime managed to maintain an insidious combination of tolerance and censorship regarding art. As many have noted, it was not so much that any tendency in art was accepted, but rather that everything was instrumentalized, and each tendency reflected a different facet of what Fascism was: Futurism, Magic Realism, Neoclassicism, Neo-Etruscanism, Neo-Byzantinism, and even abstraction.[12] Mussolini's hands-off art policy during the *ventennio* had the effect of dividing and conquering the intellectual community, making opposition particularly difficult.[13]

Consequently, around 1960, the protagonists of this book found themselves uncertain about their own relation to their twentieth-century pasts. In the aftermath of the war, the newly minted Italianate lineage of abstraction was made to square with the postwar myth of the "zero hour," an absolute break with the past and a rebooting of history. Many were happy to echo the philosopher Benedetto Croce's claim that the Fascist *ventennio* was only a historical "parenthesis" in the country's steady path to liberalism since unification in the 1860s. Croce's concept of a parenthesis was one that allowed for both a rhetoric of historical continuity — minus twenty years — with an idealized parliamentary democratic past and, alternatively, one of rupture with totalitarianism.[14]

This triumphant abstraction was pitted by artists, critics, curators, and politicians against a pictorial Socialist Realism similarly defended by artists, critics, curators, and politicians aligned with the USSR. In 1948, under the aegis of the two postwar priestesses of pictorial and sculptural abstraction — the American expat collector Peggy Guggenheim and Palma Bucarelli, the new director of Rome's Galleria Nazionale d'Arte Moderna — the first postwar Venice Biennale and the first postwar Rome Quadriennale, respectively, were both dominated by the democratizing agenda of pictorial and sculptural abstraction.[15] This agenda coincided, in 1948, with Italy's first postwar elections and the victory of the Christian Democrats, who would dominate Italian governments throughout the period covered by this book. But in a country with the largest communist party outside of the Eastern Bloc, the polarizing geopolitics of the Cold War locked artistic discourse in Italy into years of tenacious and acrimonious debate about the merits of abstraction versus figuration well into the 1960s.[16] Although staunchly ideological in tone, this all-absorbing debate — one that, in Italy, was mostly an affair *within* the political Left — was itself a form of amnesia, absolving those involved from a reflection on Italy's recent Fascist past.

Concomitant with this was a key theme in the historiography of the Italian postwar: the celebration, verging on myth, of a string of minor victories against Fascism after the long stain of collaboration with and occupation by the German Nazis. This was the equivalent of what Henri Rousso, in his study of the French Resistance during the years of Vichy, called "Résistantialisme."[17] Paradoxically, it was the turn to a Pop type of figuration in Pistoletto's *Mirror Paintings* in the early 1960s that brought back the past lost in the rebooting of history from year zero or under erasure in Croce's parenthesis, in part serendipitously, as we will see.

Chapter 1 uncovers the narrative plots reflected in both the *Mirror Paintings* of the Turinese artist Pistoletto and in the images made of them. The pent-up body language of the figures profiled on his steel plates and the gallery installations of these works portray a bourgeoisie transitioning out of the political engagement of the immediate postwar decade to the psychological disaffection of the Italian economic miracle.[18] Like the protagonists in Michelangelo Antonioni's famous tetralogy of *L'avventura* (The adventure, 1960), *La notte* (The night, 1961), *L'eclisse* (The eclipse, 1962), and *Deserto rosso* (Red desert, 1964), which single-handedly closed off the political engagement of Italian cinema that characterized the immediate postwar Neorealist decade, Pistoletto's figures are those of anomie. They embody the troubling situation of Italy in 1962 and 1963, the starting point of this book. This moment, known as *la congiuntura*, the conjuncture, was an economic inflection point in which the optimism of the postwar reconstruction, followed by the Italian economic miracle begun in 1954, showed the first signs of inversion. Inflation and a slowdown in productivity pointed to the gap between real salaries and the mirage of possibilities offered by the "boom."

However, key to rethinking the geopolitics of Pop outside the United States and Britain is viewing it in terms of a history of circulation, not merely of artworks, but of images that appeared in magazines. Photographed in the magazine *Domus* (a true institution on the Italian cultural landscape from the time of its founding in 1928), the images of Pistoletto's *Mirror Paintings* reaffirm a complicity, so totally Italian, with the world of design, but more significantly, appearing as they did in the pages of a magazine relentlessly and successfully intent on Italy's *aggiornamento* (catching up) with its European neighbors and the United States, they reveal the nonsynchronisms of what some historians have called *il lungo dopoguerra Italiano*, the protracted Italian postwar.

Assessments of the geopolitics of Pop have varied greatly. Until recently, American critics and scholars have largely dismissed Pop art as a derivative and doomed option for European artists. Embracing Pop also was seen by 1960s critics and subsequently by scholars as surrendering to America and to the amnesiac pleasures of the postwar economic boom. In contrast, studies of the Nouveaux Réalistes, the French counterparts of the Pop artists, have stressed their confrontational, anticonsumerist resistance to America. The Americanophilia of English Pop has conversely been interpreted as an ironic, deflationary stance. The German artist Gerhard Richter's photo paintings have been viewed, meanwhile, both as a response to Andy Warhol and, in German terms, as the by-product of a traumatic history.

In fact, as the *International Pop* exhibition at the Walker Art Center in Minneapolis (the museum that gave Pistoletto his first solo show abroad in 1966) and *The World Goes Pop* exhibition at the Tate Gallery in London (both in 2015) showed, Pop art was a phenomenon that emerged almost simultaneously in industrialized and industrializing nations across the globe in the early 1960s. In contrast to the other Pop artists in Italy and elsewhere, however, Pistoletto's attitude cannot be grasped as fascination, deflation, or hostility toward American Pop and American-style consumerism. Many of the photos in *Domus* of Pistoletto's *Mirror Paintings* show other artists' paintings in reflection, revealing how the reflective surface selected by Pistoletto is a device to enter into a dialogue, obliquely, with British, French, and, most importantly, American Pop. With his *Mirror Paintings*, Pistoletto, I propose, was the only Pop artist to thematize what it felt like to be on the receiving end not just of an American economic but also cultural dominance that had become virtually absolute by the early 1960s.

By reflecting the works of others, Pistoletto's *Mirror Paintings* have a tendency to eclipse themselves. As such, they are the only Pop works to interrogate how American artists and critics in the 1960s perceived European and other foreign "Popisms" as mere reflections of themselves. Until 2019, for example, Pistoletto's *Uomo con pantaloni gialli* (Man with yellow pants, 1964), a cutout of his Turinese dealer Gian Enzo Sperone, whose gallery brought American Pop to Italy, forced the other — all American — Pop works hanging in the main Pop room at MoMA into a compelling scenario that brought all these questions — artistic, existential, and geopolitical — to the fore. The viewer saw Sperone from the back, standing while leaning an elbow against the edge of the mirror, one leg crossed in front of the other. His pose reads as one of observation, reflection, and relaxation, but also of passivity toward whatever happened to hang on the gallery wall diagonally or in front of him — in this case, Andy Warhol's Campbell's Soup silk screens (Figure I.1; Plate 1). Was Sperone — or his alter ego, Pistoletto — a key player, a witness, or an intruder who has infiltrated a room in which peripheral figures do not really belong?

The reception of Pop was of course not the only element of the Italian art scene in the 1960s. In anglophone art history, the account of Italian art of the early 1960s has been fixated on the figure of Piero Manzoni and especially on the movement known as Arte Povera.[19] Spearheaded by Germano Celant, this movement finally placed postwar Italian art on the international map. Arte Povera has been valued as a process-oriented art. While some have interpreted it as fraudulently antitechnological and nostalgic, it has been redeemed in other accounts that stress its militant political activism and its desire to dissolve sculpture into performance. More recent studies have widened its purview to include other art movements,[20] as did an issue of the journal *October* dedicated to postwar Italian art.[21]

However, this focus on Arte Povera itself reflects in the current presentist approach to Italian art a loss of interest in the past and uncertainty about the future, as the French historian François Hartog posited in *Regimes of Historicity: Presentism and Experiences of Time*.[22] That presentism actually began in the 1960s with the events of 1968, when students declared, "Tout, tout de suite" (Everything, right now). The presentist approach harks back most significantly to two major exhibition catalogues: Germano Celant's *Identité italienne: L'art en Italie depuis 1959* (Italian identity: Art in Italy since 1959) at the Centre Georges Pompidou in 1981 and *Roma anni '60: Al di là della pittura* (Rome in the '60s: Beyond painting) at the Palazzo delle Esposizioni in Rome in 1990.[23] More recent studies by a younger generation of Italian scholars and curators have focused on the Italian version of Pop (namely, the Roman Pop movement known as the Scuola di Piazza del Popolo), the history of exhibitions, and the reorientation of practices toward the extramural trespass of art into its surroundings in an art of participation.[24]

These detailed and archive-based reconstructions of the feverish 1960s, book-length studies, have all been written in the form of reportage. Their intent is always to recapture the urgency of what Fabio Belloni has called an "impegno nel presente," that is, a militant political commitment in the present tense. All these authors seem to covet the 1960s and want us to relive rather than revisit them. They do not address the ways in which what occurred before year zero affected postwar Italian art, a past that, precisely because it was then being eclipsed, appears only obliquely and tangentially, as in Pistoletto's *Mirror Paintings*.

Chapters 2 and 3 therefore look at artists, participatory events, and exhibitions that have remained for the most part off the radar. The second chapter centers on a participational event, *Campo urbano: Interventi estetici nella dimensione collettiva urbana* (Urban field: Aesthetic interventions in the collective urban dimension), a series of interventions by forty artists (among them Bruno Munari and the collectives of the younger generation, Gruppo N and Gruppo T) who, joined by musicians, architects (Ugo La Pietra), art critics, local firemen, electricians, and the general public, took over the northern city of Como, as well as part of its lake, for a single day, on September 1, 1969 (Figure I.2). *Campo urbano* belongs to a number of urban "sorties" that took place, some semiofficially, others almost anarchically, in provincial towns across the peninsula from 1967 to 1969, none of which had previously been host to contemporary art. Many of these events had fallen into obscurity before being revived

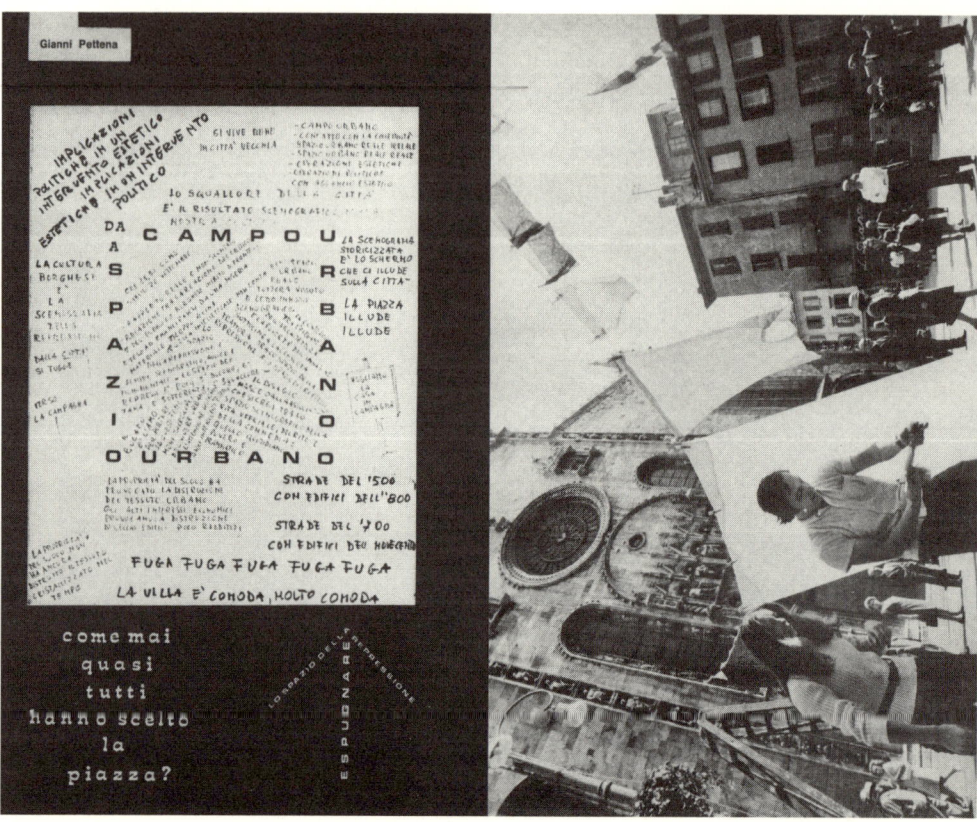

Figure I.2. Gianni Pettena, *Come mai quasi tutti hanno scelto la piazza?* (How come almost everyone has picked the main square?). *Campo urbano,* 1969. Photography: Ugo Mulas. Design: Bruno Munari.

by Alessandra Acocella in *Avanguardia diffusa: Luoghi di sperimentazione artistica in Italia, 1967–1970* (Pervasive avant-gardes: Sites of artistic experimentation in Italy, 1967–1970). These include *Parole sui muri* (Words on walls), which took place in Fiumalbo in the province of Modena (August 8 to 18, 1967); *Un paese + l'avanguardia artistica* (A country + the artistic avant-garde), in Anfo in the province of Brescia (August 25 to September 3, 1968); *Al di là della pittura* (Beyond painting), in San Benedetto del Tronto, a small resort town near Ascoli Piceno (July 5 to August 18, 1969); *Nuovi materiali nuove tecniche* (New materials new techniques), in Caorle, a town on the Adriatic coast close to Venice (July 20 to August 20, 1969); and *Meno 31: Rapporto estetico per il 2000* (Minus 31: Aesthetic report for 2000), in Varese (September 13 to 21, 1969). Best known was *Arte povera + azioni povere* (Poor art + poor actions), which took place in the resort town of Amalfi. There, Germano Celant and the publisher-collector Marcello Rumma convened an international cast of artists for three days of actions, performances, and debates in early October 1968.[25] The organizers of these events sought sponsorship — often successfully — from the municipality, the local tourist agency, the chamber of commerce, and other institutions, rather than from a cumbersome or incompetent central governmental art bureaucracy. In doing so, the organizers inadvertently highlighted the reality of the constant removal of regulations in Italy, where rules are often taken lightly.

What distinguishes *Campo urbano* from the others in this list is the self-conscious way in which its artists and its organizer, the art historian Luciano Caramel, used the historical center of the city of Como as their frame. What also distinguishes it, even more importantly for my account, is the way it was recorded by means of a photo book. Other late 1960s event-based artistic interventions used the printed page as their documentary platform. But the *Campo urbano*'s photo book — shot by Ugo Mulas, otherwise known for his reportage of the Venice Biennales, with a layout by Bruno Munari, Italy's foremost book designer — is unique. Nothing could be more "event based" and "in the moment" than *Campo urbano* photographed by Mulas with a single handheld Olympus camera, without which no trace of that day would remain. And yet, designed by Munari, whose long career (he was born in 1907) bridged both halves of the past century, the *Campo urbano* photo book summons — breathlessly — a series of episodes in Italy's all-too-brief historical avant-garde.

For example: the moment when the first phase of Italian Futurism had an impact on Dada, or the little-known and hardly ever recorded exhibitions of "scatter pieces" by Munari in Milan galleries that marked the sporadic emergence of an Italian neo-avant-garde in the 1950s. Moving from *campo* to *campo* (square to square), the Mulas/Munari *Campo urbano* photo book telescopes, in one of the furthest flashbacks in this book, almost four centuries, back to Giordano Bruno, and from there forward to the sojourn of the art historian Aby Warbug in Rome in 1929. With the artists of *Campo urbano* avoiding Como's most famous building, Giuseppe Terragni's Casa del Fascio, Chapter 2 includes one of this book's most eminent eclipses. The building is Como's modernist landmark, built in 1934, when the architect had designated Como as the Fascist regime's model city.

The book's third chapter changes gears and atmosphere by moving from the pent-up body language of the *Mirror Paintings* and the free movement in the city streets of *Campo urbano* to an exhibition held in a city where everything feels historically overdetermined: Rome.[26] It centers on *Vitalità del negativo nell'arte Italiana 1960/70* (Vitality of the negative in Italian art 1960/70), an exhibition that occupied the ground floor of the monumental Palazzo delle Esposizioni on Via Nazionale in the winter of 1970, reviving an ideologically loaded Neoclassical venue under the mantle of contemporary art. Curated by the rising star of the moment, Achille Bonito Oliva (the principal competitor of Celant), it was designed by the architect Piero Sartogo (Figure I.3). Bonito Oliva is known in the Anglo-American art world primarily for his later work as a champion of Transavanguardia and as a protagonist of 1980s postmodernism. It is his first two years as curator that are of interest here, however. *Vitalità*'s closest reference points appeared to be the Tuscan and Umbrian

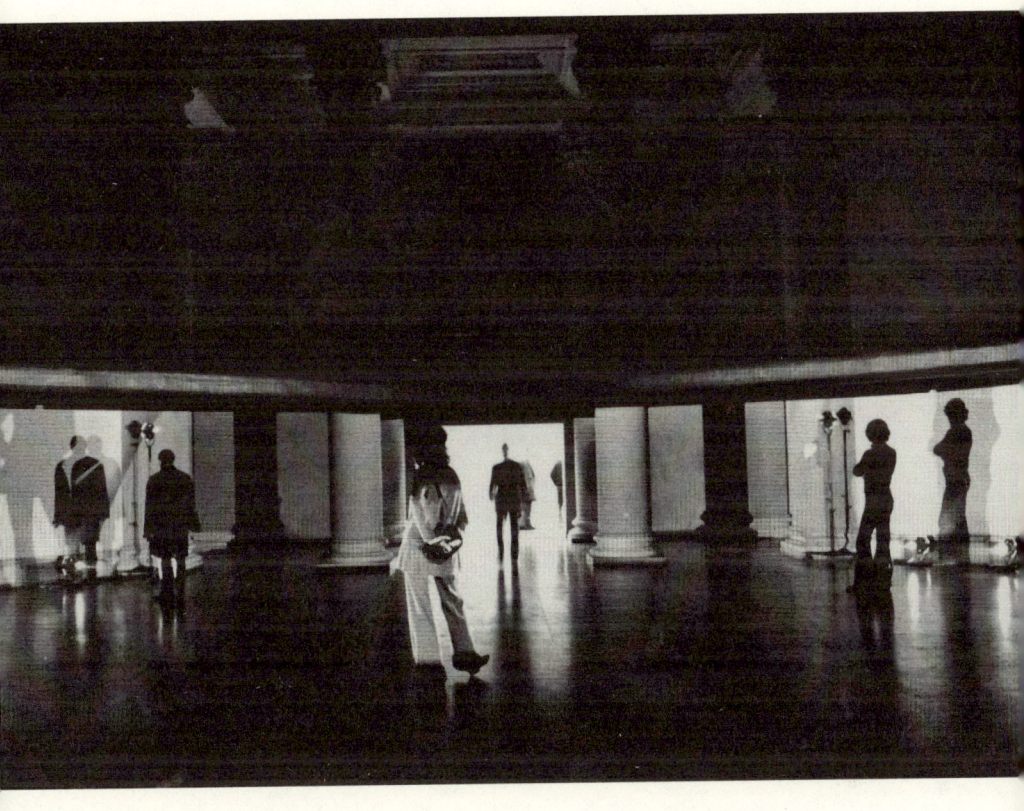

Figure I.3. Piero Sartogo, entrance to *Vitalità del negativo*, 1970. Photograph: Ugo Mulas. Courtesy of the Piero Sartogo Archive.

towns that had just hosted similar avant-garde exhibitions. And yet its atmosphere recalled that of the many exhibitions that had taken place in those same rooms during the 1930s. Nowhere, one could argue, did exhibitions (as distinct from permanent museum displays) play such a cardinal role as in Italy.[27]

Exhibition design rose to prominence in the post-Fascist, postwar reconstruction years, when Italy resumed its status as an avant-garde project. Yet in a curious mirror image, such had already been the case with exhibition design during Mussolini's *ventennio*. So central were exhibitions to the regime that the art historian and media theorist Jeffrey Schnapp, the historian Marla Stone, and, most recently, Germano Celant himself, with his blockbuster *Post Zang Tumb Tuuum: Art Life Politics Italia 1918-1943* at the Fondazione Prada in 2018 in Milan, were able to recount the course of Italian Fascism via its exhibitions.[28]

Too little attention has been paid in exhibition histories to the way in which exhibitions related to their architectural containers and to how exhibitions may function as palimpsests, that is, a superimposition (mostly as mental images) of other exhibitions that have taken place in the same space. Although half of Italy's museums were founded after 1945, Italian curators, architects, and exhibition designers still found themselves endlessly revisiting preexisting interiors, some of which were ideologically toxic. It is significant in this regard that the essay on exhibition design in the multivolume *Storia dell'architettura Italiana* (History of Italian architecture) published in 1997 should describe it as first and foremost an art of prosthetics. "In designing an exhibition," writes its author, Sergio Polano, "one constructs a set of relationships with a space that welcomes, includes, hosts — relationships that can in turn negate, hide, conceal, occlude, veil the 'container' in the process of attempting to read that space, comment upon it, enhance it, but also deform it, modify it, estrange it."[29] A key protagonist in this chapter is thus the nineteenth-century Beaux Arts Palazzo delle Esposizioni, refurbished in 1931 to house the Rome Quadriennali, the main showcase for the display of painting and sculpture produced not just during but in celebration of Fascist rule, as well as other major propaganda exhibitions of the regime.[30] The somber mood of *Vitalità*, set in the premier space of Fascist exhibitions, provoked some critics to accuse Bonito Oliva of reviving the Fascist seduction.

Taking place at the threshold of the *anni di piombo* (years of lead), *Vitalità* can also be seen in retrospect as a harbinger of the violence of the coming decade, when Italian cities would be rocked by bombings in the bitter struggle between the extreme Right and the extra-parliamentary Left. Key to my interpretation of *Vitalità* are the dual concepts of "mimetic subversion" (a strategy that engages the enemy, but obliquely) and that of the likelihood of the betrayal of fellow artists and the solidarity of the avant-garde.[31] Here I propose a filmic reading of the exhibition: the date of its opening coincided with the moment when *Il conformista* (The conformist), Bernardo Bertolucci's own revisitation of the *ventennio*, a film where treason is all-important to the narrative, hit Italy's movie screens. As evidenced by the photographs shot by Mulas on its opening night and the reviews of the time, *Vitalità* produced in its visitors a sensation of entrapment. It is with this scenario of a cul-de-sac as phenomenological as it was political, rather than with a separate conclusion, that this book intentionally reaches its frustrating denouement.

This being a book on the 1960s, I was able to interview some of its main protagonists: Pistoletto, Fioroni, Caramel, Bonito Oliva, and Sartogo. Others unfortunately died before I was able to speak with them. Sottsass, the author of the two longest and most extraordinary quotations in this book, died in 2007, just as I was beginning this project. Carla Lonzi died in 1982 at the age of fifty-one. Mulas, the one figure who traverses all three chapters of this book, also died prematurely, in 1973 at the age of forty-five. In the little book *La fotografia* (Photography) published just after his death, Mulas reminisces about the beginning of his career at the Venice Biennales:

> I was photographing without any intention to understand what was going on, and there was always something happening.... I was photographing

everything: not only the most important artists and the most important events: it's not that I was lacking the will to choose, but I felt that I could not take on the attitude of a critic — there was nothing in particular to understand, there was nothing to do but to report.[32]

My approach to Mulas's photographs contradicts his assertion: it is Mulas who conveyed, better than any art critic, the deep meaning of the artworks described in this book.

Largely inhabited by men, this book is traversed in a significant but not always obvious way by a number of female figures.[33] Present in the first chapter but not in the events surrounding 1968 recounted in Chapter 2, women reappear in Chapter 3. In Chapter 1, in the most spectacular installation of Pistoletto's *Mirror Paintings* in Milan, we encounter working-class girls. They stand at the center of the lineup of anonymous figures in *Ragazze alla balconata* (Girls at the balcony, 1964), in one of the three mirrors lined up on a plinth in a showroom in Milan in 1965. We see them, as always with Pistoletto's cutouts, from the back looking outward, toward the void, or more prosaically, toward whatever happens to be reflected in the mirror, in this case, an elegant commercial street (see Figure 1.7). Sottsass, in some of his more wonderful lines on the *Mirror Paintings*, imagines them coming to Milan from Turin or perhaps coming from Carmagnola, a small town some thirty kilometers away from Turin, to Italy's second-largest industrial hub, dressed in their Sunday best. Later in the chapter, Giosetta Fioroni appears, in a photo by Mulas, as the only woman artist standing among her cohort of Italian Pop artists at the 1964 Venice Biennale (see Figure 1.11). The men all look in different directions, oblivious to the feminine silhouette appearing behind them in the photograph of one of Fioroni's paintings. Six years later, in the 1970s, and now in Chapter 3, Fioroni reappears. She is again the only woman in the otherwise all-male cast of Bonito Oliva's *Vitalità del negativo*. Her faint but mural-sized images are among the historically and politically most haunting works in that exhibition. It is the silhouette of Fioroni standing in front of her mural installation on opening night in a photo shot again by Mulas that opens the door toward my cinematic reading of that show (see Figure 3.18). Later in that chapter enters Italy's most influential female critic at that moment, Carla Lonzi, now turned militant feminist (see Figure 3.24). She appears in the last pages of this book in another one of those all-male situations, the one set up by *Amore mio* (My love), a smaller exhibition curated by Bonito Oliva a few months before *Vitalità* in the Palazzo Ricci in the town of Montepulciano. Technically uninvited, Lonzi takes her stand not through her presence in the Palazzo that hosted *Amore mio*, but by being introduced by a third party only into the pages of its catalogue. Betraying a betrayer who had betrayed another betrayer, Lonzi's intrusion creates, in the last paragraphs of the book, an unexpected narrative twist.

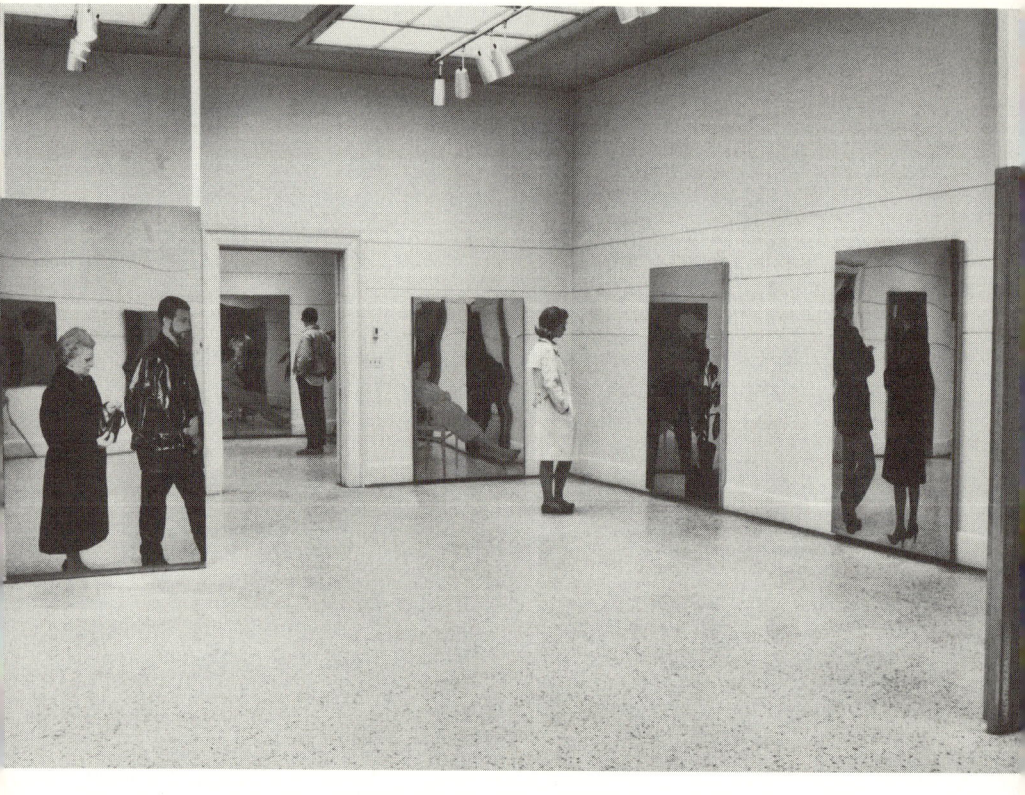

Figure 1.1. *Michelangelo Pistoletto: A Reflected World*, Walker Art Center, 1966.

CHAPTER ONE

Inside/Outside:

Michelangelo Pistoletto's

Mirror Paintings

Steel Plates: An Occasion for Reflections

In 1962, Michelangelo Pistoletto, a young Turinese artist later identified with Arte Povera, began making life-size cutouts of friends and
mundane objects out of translucent painted tissue paper and placing
these on the reflective surfaces of highly polished stainless steel. The
Mirror Paintings, as they were known, instantly confounded pictorial
and viewing space, making the act of looking an active phenomenological experience. The format also allowed for a nearly endless variety
of effects with the simplest of means; he often used the same images
in different groupings (Figure 1.1).[1] While the figures that Pistoletto
adhered to these surfaces evolved over the course of the series, from
drawn to photographic and from quasi-monochromatic to full color,
the basic concept remained remarkably constant.

The same can be said of the critical response that the *Mirror Paintings* have generated, which has focused on their "presentness" as
viewers encounter them when walking into a room. The reviews
written by the critic Tommaso Trini, who repeatedly addressed the
ideas underlying Pistoletto's work, exemplify this interpretation:
"His paintings reproduce exactly the portion of space, of objects, of

movement in front of which they are placed. That is, all that we can see around us without him, and yet with an added presence: our own. We had almost forgotten it, this presence that needs to be accounted for. . . . What is one to do? Hide behind the silhouettes?"[2] Three years later, Trini pressed this point again: "Ultimately, there is no subject matter, since it cannot be any different from the reality that is being reflected."[3] Umberto Eco made a similar argument in a 1985 essay in which he argued that since the mirror stubbornly registers what comes into contact with it "as is," while the sign is predicated, conversely, on absence, mirrors by definition can only denote and never connote. He writes:

> The reflected image is present, it is in the presence *of a referent that cannot be absent*. It never takes us to remote meanings. The relation between object and image is the relation between two presences without any mediation. The image is *causally produced by the object* and cannot come into being in its absence. As such the mirror image *cannot be used to lie*. One can lie *about* and *around* specular images (by passing off as specular images that are not), but you cannot lie *with* and *through* an image in the mirror. . . . The mirror image *is not interpretable*. What is interpretable, if anything, is the object to which it refers, that is, the activated field of which it is the double.[4]

But what happens when we are not in front of them in a gallery, and instead look at the reflections in Pistoletto's *Mirror Paintings* when they are fixed by the camera in the pages of a magazine or book? While most of the photographs in Pistoletto's post-1960s monographs, especially those reproduced in color, have been airbrushed, in these 1960s photographs, ambient figures and objects that happen into the mirror's field become impossibly entangled with the cutout figures and objects previously affixed by Pistoletto to his metal surfaces (Figure 1.2). Only two critics writing on Pistoletto at the time (or any time after that), both American, addressed the questions raised by these photographs. While Italian critics described the *Mirror Paintings* only in their presentness, as if we were ourselves standing in the room, the Americans, neither writing for an Italian journal, seem to have had

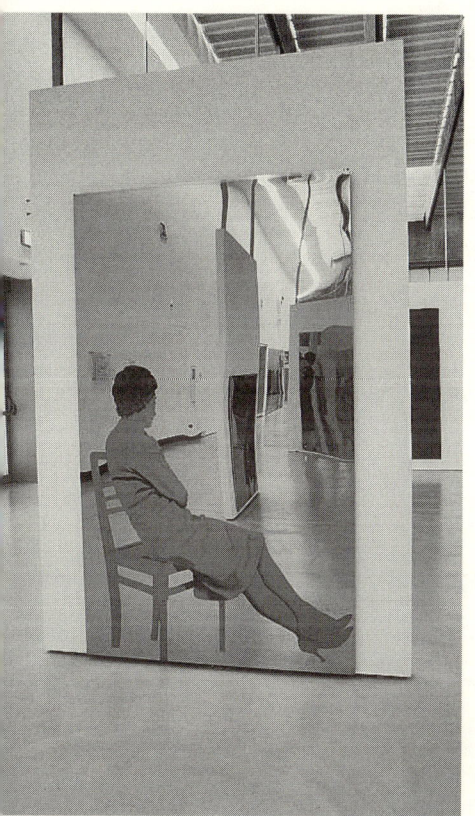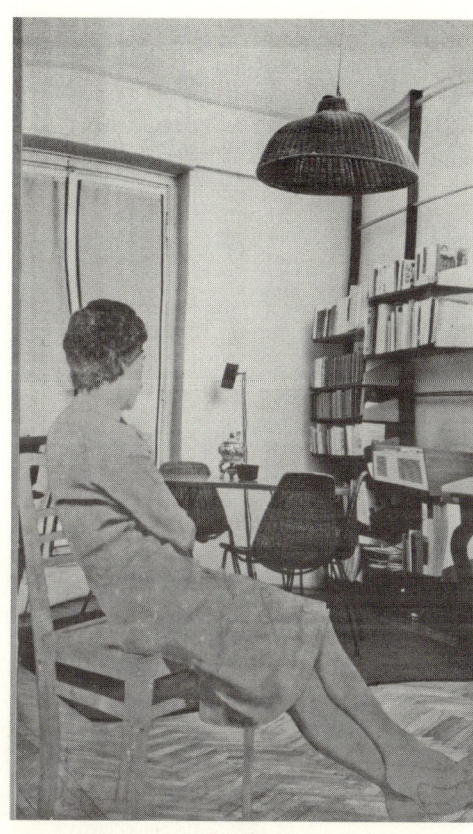

Figure 1.2. Michelangelo Pistoletto, *Donna seduta di spalle* (Seated woman from behind, 1963). Painted tissue paper on polished stainless steel, 200 × 120 cm. The Sonnabend Collection. *left:* In *Michelangelo Pistoletto: From One to Many*, MAXXI, 2011. *right:* As reproduced in Alberto Boatto, *Pistoletto: Dentro/fuori lo specchio* (Rome: Fantini, 1970). Photography: Paolo Bressano. Courtesy of the Cittadellarte–Fondazione Pistoletto, Biella, Italy.

the necessary degree of separation required to perceive the strategies at work in Pistoletto's deceptively simple mirror conceit. Writing for journals intended for an international readership, these critics knew that their readers would see the works only in print, the platform through which most works were circulated and consumed.

Reviewing Pistoletto's 1964 show at Ileana Sonnabend's gallery in Paris for the *New York Herald Tribune*, the poet John Ashbery wrote: "Simpleminded as it sounds, Pistoletto's art is fascinating and even haunting. For one thing, the mirror surfaces automatically pick up the rest of the room, including you, who suddenly find yourself, like it or not, the subject of a Pop picture. Not the main subject, either, but somewhere in the background — the foreground being taken up by your anonymous two-dimensional companions."[5] Returning to the mirrors two years later on the occasion of *Pistoletto: A Reflected World*, an exhibition held in 1966 at the Walker Art Center in Minneapolis, Ashbery noted the disparity between his experience of the photographs and his physical encounter with the *Mirror Paintings*:

> The figures and the decor that are the symptoms of today's strange new disease of alienation are the raw material, and perhaps the end product, of Pistoletto's art [....] The decor is that of a gallery, or your own home if you own a Pistoletto, or whatever surroundings the mirrored surface happens to reflect. Chances are there will be white walls, modern furniture (Knoll, if the picture is in a gallery) and potted plants — probably the ubiquitous philodendron.[6]

Annette Michelson also immediately caught on to the game, writing about the 1964 Sonnabend Paris show for *Art International*: "Pistoletto ... makes traps and teasers. ... Supposing one wishes to choose a photograph for illustration, the hide and seek with the self is arrested, deprived of the opening onto infinity, and is impoverished in a mere image. Neither object nor image, really, Pistolettos are Occasions for Reflection."[7] The accompanying photograph shows the painting *Uomo seduto* (Seated man, 1962) next to the future art dealer Annina Nosei sitting, looking a little despondent, at the front desk at Sonnabend's gallery. She appears reflected twice, once from the back in a *profil perdu* similar to that of many of Pistoletto's cutout figures, and again frontally, with her head resting, distracted, slightly bored perhaps, on her hand.

Reading for the Plot in Early 1960s Turin

No sooner were the *Mirror Paintings* photographed than they began to suggest narrative plots.[8] The interior of the brochure produced for the first exhibition of these works features four shots of another version of *Uomo seduto* (Figure 1.3). Apparently taken only minutes apart, the photos show what was reflected in the mirror at each moment and thus create, in combination with the cutout figure of the seated man wearing a dark suit, different tableaus. Four different men appear in the photographs, all wearing suits. Two of the men are younger (Pistoletto and his fellow artist Aldo Mondino), while the other two are older (Paolo Bressano and Renato Rinaldi); the latter were the photographers responsible for most of the cutouts used by Pistoletto for his 1960s *Mirror Paintings* and the shots of the finished paintings, as well. In all of them, Rinaldi is represented by his cutout, sitting on a wooden stool, and the others strike a variety of poses. Here we already encounter a disconnect between the game captured by the photographs and the ponderous statement on the mirrors themselves written by Luigi Carluccio, the in-house gallery curator. His essay muses about solitude, human fragility, and the existential void.[9]

While these first images of the *Mirror Paintings* allude to the photographer's studio, those reproduced in the brochures for Pistoletto's second and third exhibitions the following year — at the Sonnabend Gallery in Paris and at Gian Enzo Sperone's gallery in Turin — allude to cinema. The Sonnabend brochure featured three sequential shots of *Due persone* (Two people, 1963–64) showing, as cutouts, Pistoletto standing next to Marzia Calleri, his wife at the time. The one produced for Sperone's gallery a few months later featured, on one page, a photograph of a version of *Uomo seduto*, showing a cutout of Pistoletto in white jeans kneeling next to the reflection of one of Marcel Breuer's tubular-steel-and-black-leather "Wassily" armchairs in the

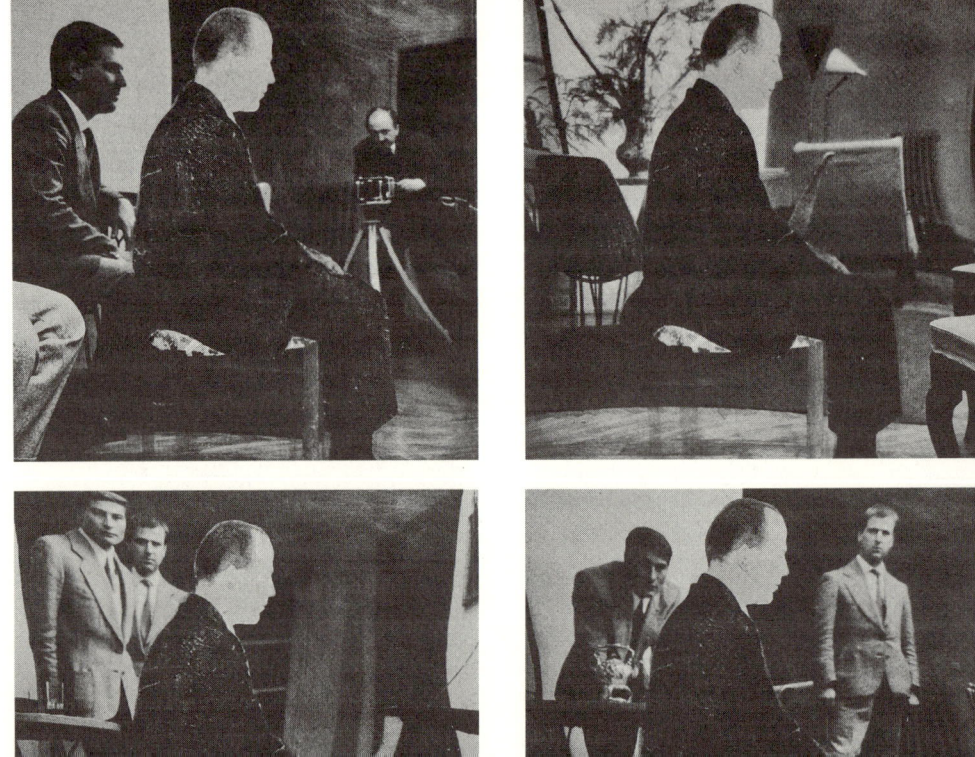

Figure 1.3. Michelangelo Pistoletto, *Uomo seduto* (Seated man, 1962). As reproduced in the exhibition catalogue *Michelangelo Pistoletto: Opere recenti* (Turin: Galleria Galatea, 1963). Photographs: Paolo Bressano. Courtesy of the Cittadellarte–Fondazione Pistoletto, Biella, Italy.

streamlined gallery space, and on the other page, *Marzia con la bambina* (Marzia with child, 1963) showing a cutout image of his wife and baby daughter, radically truncated by the edge of the mirror (Figure 1.4).

It could be argued that because he was working in a nonfilmic medium, Pistoletto was able to stage what Gilles Deleuze has identified in Italian cinema of the 1960s, and particularly in the films of Michelangelo Antonioni, as the crisis of the "movement-image" and its shift to the "time-image." Deleuze introduces a new category of sign that he calls the "opsign," in which the image breaks with the sensory-motor schema of film to become first and foremost an optical sign — a "cinema of vision," as Antonioni called it.[10] As Pistoletto told Germano Celant: "In the mirror painting, we have the ephemerality of the moment, which is, however, detained in the duration of time. The figure that I fix endures in the present; in this case, it is the ephemeral that makes the static, the past, endure."[11] One might also say that Pistoletto's *Mirror Paintings* function like freeze-frames. As the film theorist Raymond Bellour wrote in his essay "The Film Stilled," no image seems more immobile than the freeze-frame. Dramatized by implied movement, it is a species of still image that exists only in cinema. Bellour argues: "There is one category of time not considered by Gilles Deleuze in his dynamic taxonomy of images: the interruption of movement. The often unique, fugitive, yet perhaps decisive instant when cinema seems to be fighting against its very principle, if this is defined as the movement-image."[12] The freeze-frame might point to the essence of the film as photographic: not the still frame torn out of the film, but the still frame surging. As Bellour contends, "The history of the freeze-frame remains to be written."[13]

The visual parallels between Pistoletto's *Mirror Paintings* and Antonioni's films abound (Figure 1.5): the way the main characters/actors are cut out as if pinned to the wall; the lack of communication between couples; their withdrawn body language with their slouched shoulders and passive, pensive demeanor; the disconnected space and the way some of the figures appear to be not just walking

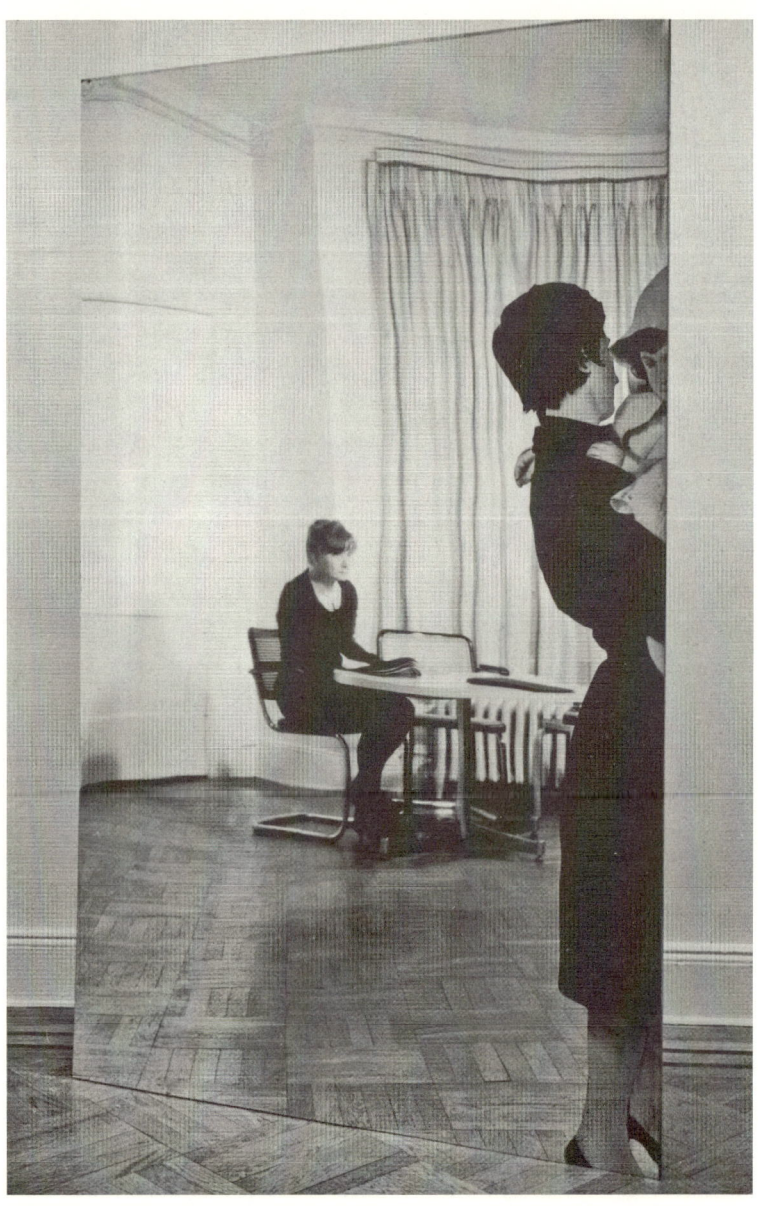

Figure 1.4. Michelangelo Pistoletto, *Marzia con la bambina* (Marzia with child, 1963). As reproduced in Alberto Boatto, *Pistoletto: Dentro/fuori lo specchio* (Rome: Fantini, 1970). Photograph: Paolo Bressano. Courtesy of the Cittadellarte–Fondazione Pistoletto, Biella, Italy.

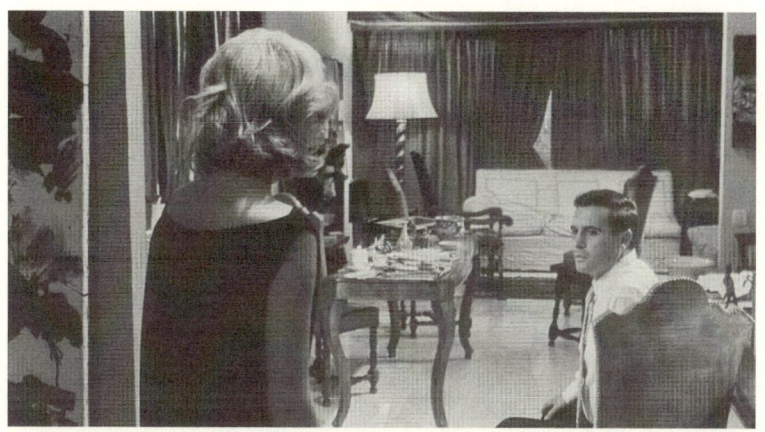

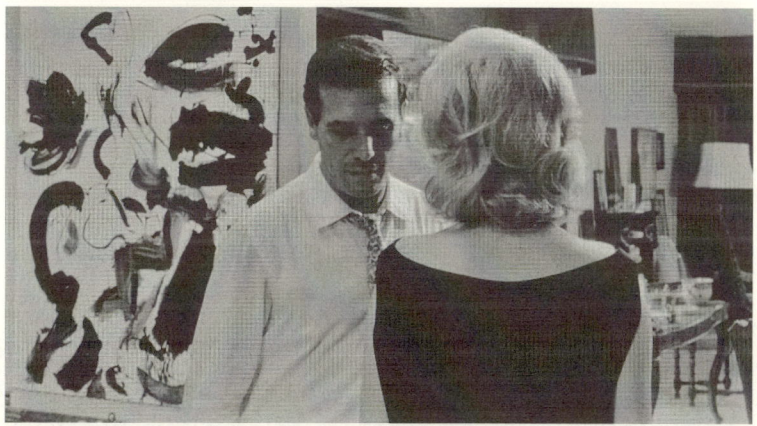

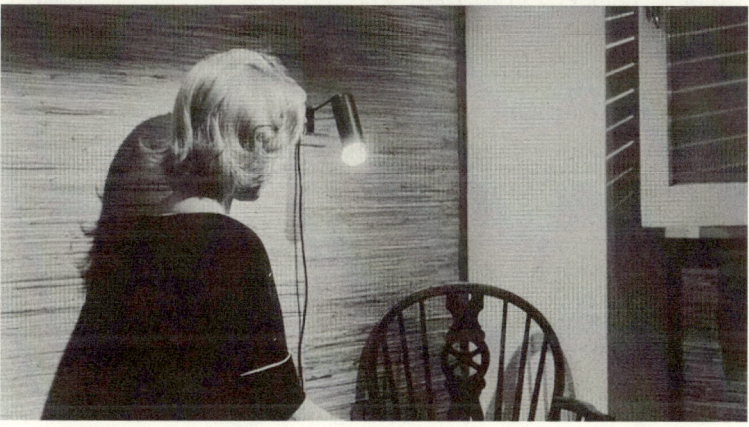

Figure 1.5. Michelangelo Antonioni, dir., *L'eclisse*, 1962.

out of the frame, but passing into the void. We may read these exits as a removal from the scenes of dreariness of Neorealism into a world where these figures would find themselves transfixed, almost inadvertently, by the phantasmagoria of Italy's (as well as Europe's) economic miracle.[14] Most perplexing is how elusive Pistoletto's figures tend to be, offering us only a *profil perdu*, or their backs. We are looking at them as reflected cohabitants, facing them in their space, but, as with zombies, we will never see their faces. "Not only are the figures exceedingly flat," writes Michelson, "they have been bled of color, contaminated by their entrance into the mirror world."[15]

Ettore Sottsass's Vertiginous Flashbacks

The first extensive essay about Pistoletto in *Domus*—and the first to reach a wide Italian readership—was written by the designer Ettore Sottsass Jr.[16] Entitled "Pop e non Pop: A proposito di Michelangelo Pistoletto" (Pop and not Pop: About Michelangelo Pistoletto) and published in *Domus* in May 1964, Sottsass's essay was illustrated by photographs of the *Mirror Paintings*, most of them culled from the Sonnabend catalogue in a sequential format that once again emphasized their cinematic quality (Figure 1.6). The series begins with a photograph of *Donna in verde e due personaggi* (Woman in green with two figures, 1963), featuring cutouts of Marzia, Pistoletto, and the Turinese poet Piera Oppezzo. The reflective surface of the work produces an illusion that the three figures are standing in Sonnabend's gallery (recognizable by the floor tiles) and looking at an *informale* painting (the Italian equivalent of Abstract Expressionism); the photograph was evidently taken just prior to the deinstallation of the works from an earlier show.[17] The next page of the *Domus* article features a photograph of *Persona di schiena* (Man from the back, 1962) showing a cutout of a man seen from the back who appears to be facing the reflection of an unidentified man in the gallery. The pair of photographs on the following page moves us back in time to Pistoletto's studio/apartment in Turin. The first shows *Bottiglia sul pavimento* (Bottle on the ground, 1963) reflecting the contents of the artist's studio. The second photo is taken from the same perspective, but with Pistoletto's *Due persone* (Two people, 1963–64; featuring cutouts of Pistoletto and Marzia) inserted into the composition, so that one painting reflects another. In a similar dynamic, the two photographs on the facing page show the latter painting straight on with two different backgrounds. On the left, they stand, presumably on the landing of Pistoletto's studio, and on the right, the sequence ends with the most confounding of the four shots, with Pistoletto and Marzia standing, as if they had themselves stepped out of the mirror into *real* space, in front of a young man who is looking back at them from what looks like the space of a mirror painting.

These scenes of couples and threesomes seen from the back, looking at artworks, appear almost as if lifted from two sequences in Antonioni's *Le amiche* (The friends), Sottsass's constant underlying reference. In the film, we constantly look at characters in twos or threes either in three-quarter view or from the back, looking at artworks. In the first scene, Lorenzo, a failed painter played by Gabriele Ferzetti, stands next to his companion, a ceramicist named Nene, played by Valentina Cortese (who appears to have resembled Pistoletto's wife, slim with cropped hair). The two are shown staring at a portrait of Rosetta, a suicidal girl in love with Lorenzo. A few scenes later, we see Lorenzo and Nene's gallerist taking a call from a New York dealer asking him to send her (not his!) works to the United States. Setting aside the possible feminist touch it might have had in the film, the dealer's preference must have induced a pang in the contemporary Italian viewer, because it reflected the postwar infatuation of American collectors and museum curators with the talent of Italian artists as ceramicists, rather than as painters.[18]

After a short digression on how American Pop art had lost its initial shock value after being domesticated by the society ladies of New York who hung Warhols as trophies on the walls of their Park Avenue apartments, Sottsass's essay abruptly changes tack. The essay's title, "Pop e non Pop," was clearly intended to stem the flood of articles written by the Italian critics — including Sottsass himself,

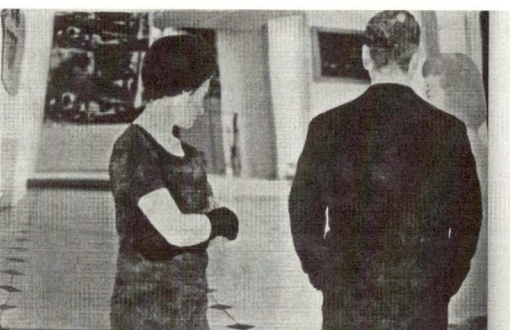

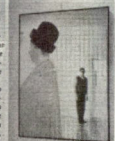

Figure 1.6. Michelangelo Pistoletto, *Donna in verde e due personaggi* (Woman in green with two figures, 1963); *Persona di schiena* (Man from the back, 1962); *Bottiglia sul pavimento* (Bottle on the ground, 1963); *Bottiglia sul pavimento* and *Due persone* (Two people, 1963–64); two views of *Due persone*. From Ettore Sottsass Jr., "Pop e non Pop: A proposito di Michelangelo Pistoletto," *Domus*, no. 414, May 1964.

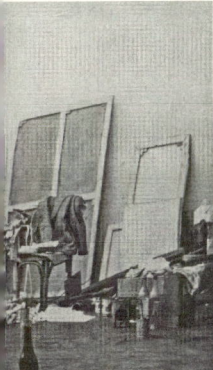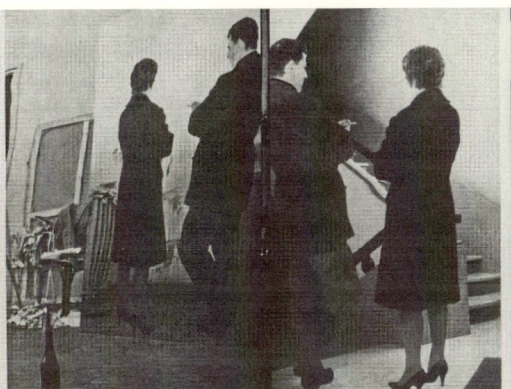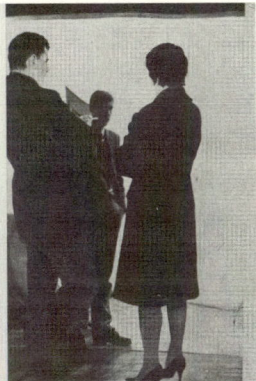

sulla lastra di acciaio è dipinto soltanto la bottiglia: tutto il resto è riflesso, sia l'ambiente che il secondo quadro, con le due «persone di schiena» quadri di Michelangelo Pistoletto il fondo cambia, riflesso nella lastra di acciaio, dietro le due, dipinte, «persone di schiena»

saprà mai niente e tutto si muoverà in una ambigua atmosfera di cose non capite o di cose che non si sono volute capire.
Ad ogni modo questa storia l'ho raccontata per dire che ormai i pittori POP sono trionfalmente installati negli appartamenti di Park Ave e ormai i quadri di Lichtenstein si pagano fino a 4000 dollari — dice «Life» — cioè due milioni e mezzo di lire e questo non significa altro se non che piacciono a gente che ha 4000 dollari da spendere per un quadro: «fascinating», dicono i collezionisti, «forceful», «starkly beautiful». In altre parole è il gusto e quello POP. È di buon gusto il POP, caro ed entusiasta amico Rasham che mi hai mandato gli auguri di Natale con sotto scritto «È il gusto — W il POP.
È terribilmente di buon gusto il POP, il brivido POP.
E ormai, dal momento che questo fenomeno è successo, da tutte le parti escono piano piano i misconosciuti pittori POP che erano stati pittori POP da sempre e che loro s'eravano sempre detto «la tal cosa è POP», eccetera. Qualcuno anche se non s'l'aveva sempre detto, però è riuscito ad abbancarsi al tram della pittura POP all'ultimo momento, con un piccolo colpo di ance ecc. ecc. e ha la sensazione che sia in questa atmosfera POP, non figurativa, e ritorna l'uomo questo eterno protagonista che mi sono venuti tra le mani le foto dei quadri di Pistoletto e mi è stato chiesto di scrivere un articolo su questo giovane pittore che si chiama Michelangelo Pistoletto è nato a Biella nel 1933, che ha una faccia robusta e vive a Torino in un appartamento di via Cibrario, vecchia strada 1910, arredato con mobili di serie tipo Rinascente 1958 di biodino di ferro sono con vinioli marrone sulle sedie, kblicosa e ripiani lucidi agganciati a tubi di alluminio anodizzato (sato?), lampade Arteto e giradischi Braun e dipinge su lastre di acciaio inossidabile, dette inox, ombre o silhouettes di gente, «persona di schiena», dice il titolo, «persona in piedi», «persona che guarda», «persona appoggiata». Lasciando l'acciaio lucido dove

non c'è il personaggio dipinto, l'ambiente e le persone che circondano il quadro si specchiano nella lastra come attraverso una nebbia: sol, spettatori, fantasmi per trovarsi nel quadro, lasbarno ecci e infantiliti di mettere insieme a quei personaggi silenziosi, ciechi, immobili e sconosciuti che non ti degnano di alcuna attenzione, non ci guardano, gente che non si girerà mai. Potremo de via Cibrario sparse per il mondo e nelle continua di miglia operosamente chiamata, lavorerà, supplicarà quella gente, non girerà, non ci sorriderà, non ci racconterà la sua storia, non ti lavorerà in alcun modo comunicare.
Di solito quei personaggi sono girati di spalle come se si voltassero dai loro grossi peccati o semplicemente della loro vita; e come se non volessero sapere dei peccati nostri o della loro stessa vita, di noi che stiamo loro inseguendo di viaggio destra allo spazio inox, immobile, di centimetri 120 per 200, centimetri 125 per 180, centimetri 100 per 170, o centimetri 125 per 180, e aspettassero insieme a noi l'arrivo di un treno felice annunciando di fischio all'orizzonte, un treno felice che in realtà non arriva mai apparenti non'è delle mallcomie, dai dentoli, dai cadaveri, dalle miglia e miglia di via Cibrario sparse nel mondo, risontonti in vecchi treni nei pomeriggi di domenica, il scarpe buone del pomeriggio di domenica, di faticoso dipenderti di cardi, aghi vino peuante nei pomeriggi di domenica, di sestera ululanti, col fumor di atance, di caramelle, di chewing-gum nei pomeriggi domenica al Cinema Statuto. Quel treno felice non arriva mai i personaggi di questi quadri aspettano insieme a noi, immobili. Mi pare di vedere, mi ricordo molte bene la gente aspettare nei corridoi degli ospedali che il chirurgo esca dalla porta bianca e dica l'operazione è riuscita e poi la gente aspettare in silenzio chiacchierando ancora i pomodori, il fumo ancora queste cose. Al salato che si sveglia, e poi la gente aspettare che passi la febbre, Torino, in piazza San Carlo, si beve il Punt e Mes seduti su e poi la gente aspettare che gli ritorni la febbre, e poi la prossente sedie stile barocco e si mangia poco gelato, voglio dire, aspettare che arrivi la notte, e poi la gente aspettare che così loro moto gelato ma poco ice cream, pochi fiori di plastica in respiro e, altro non si fa che aspettare: si aspettano sempre treni

non arrivano mai, si guardano cose che non si vedono mai, rendo breve i giorni che la gente passa nelle miglia e miglia di anni e per 3, dove la luce arriva grigia e polverosa le miglia e miglia di via Cibrario sparse per il mondo.
e non si può dire che sia un pittore POP, come qualcuno ha detto, è meglio sia chiaro che questo ragazzo Torino non c'entra niente coi pittori POP e cosa mai piattoolo opening le immagini dei suoi quadri restano su un fulcro statico, e si realizzano per un istante e si cancellano per sempre, la quando traccia la cui origine è quasi irriconoscibile e indetermina- ma il POP non c'entra. Anche se sono sicuro che le foto- de delle cose di Pistoletto mi sono venute tra le mani traspor- da questo nuovo filone di materiale che c'è nella pittura POP, un certo che il POP non c'entra perché a Torino e forse in tutta talt non ci sono le premesse per diventare pittori POP: non c'è quella pensione soffocante e invincibile, il Coca-Cola ameri- non c'è il vermouth e Perfino », non c'è la corruzione post- industre, non c'è la violenza post-cowboys, non ci sono vampe, non ci sono neanche sirene, si pratica per il Hirth neutrol, si gioca non gli anticonformisti, si usano poco i deodoranti e invece si gioca la camicia da appartare le boote, ci si mette ancora il pigiama e la camicia da per andare a dormire, si cuoce ancora la pasta asciutta, si chiacchierano ancora queste cose

si ribellano ancora alle mamme, il mondo delle chiacchiere, come una volta, ha ancora il suo fulcro nella storia della famiglia del padrone della città, nel fotografo che ne fa i ritratti, nella mantenuta che aprirà la boutique e nella Lancia che è la macchina che finisce bene». Così con ci sono ancora le ragioni per l'arte POP a Torino e — lo spero (con perché con questi l'arte POP, ma perché spero che son misteriosi mai le sue premesse: — non ci saranno mai e invece piano piano si sono create per un giovane pittore come Pistoletto le ragioni per quella sua pittura, che si comunica con le immagini un'angoscia già profondamente stabilita nei petti dei giovani dell'Europa, dai tempi di Metropolis, di Kafka, di Schlemmer, di Céline, anche di Maserel, di Quesena e così via, l'angoscia della solitudine, l'angoscia dell'anonimità, l'angoscia per la drammatica attesa della realizzazione individuale, la pietrificazione dei gesti e dei movimenti, delle parole e dei pensieri, quando gesti, movimenti, parole e pensieri si svolgono in uno spazio senza misure, senza gravità, senza suoni, senza echi; quella sua pittura che si comunica con le immagini il rapporto tra il peso di pietra della nostra storia e i movimenti ridicoli, nebbiati, inutili che la circondano.
Così lo direi che questo ragazzo di Torino è un poeta più serio; anche se forse meno preciso e caustico che non siano i ragazzi di New York, i Lichtenstein, i Rosenquist, i Rauschenberg, gli Olden- burg, i Chamberlain nel raccontarci la situazione del nostro dramma, il caso della nostra storia. Forse questo ragazzo di Torino, come scrisse qualcuno a Parigi, usa colori che confericono alla sua pit- tura «den crédits crépusculaires» e questi riflessi non sono senza ragione e un'aria crepuscolare c'è, forse anche al di là dei colori: l'aria di Torino e le stasi annidate nei suoi giorni. Il che non toglie che Pistoletto ci racconti bene e fino in fondo le storie che che ha da raccontarci.

Ennio Salomo Jr.

22 febbraio 1964

but with the notable exception of Trini — who had traveled to New York the previous year to report on the Pop art phenomenon.[19] Sottsass decided to concentrate instead on what was happening in Italy — specifically, on what he termed "the atmosphere of Turin and the boredom of its days." He extemporized on Turin as a one-factory town huddled at the foot of the Alps, a city that had remained provincial, on the periphery, cut off from the hub of nearby Milan, which, like Rome and Naples, was regarded as a European cultural and economic crossroads. This is the postwar city described by the sociologist Luciano Gallino in an interview with the leftist militant art historian Mirella Bandini entitled "Torino 1960/1973."[20] It is also the city described by another of its famous natives, the philosopher Norberto Bobbio, who wrote: "The old Turin was dead and a new one had not yet been born."[21] Sottsass's essay is worth quoting at some length, not only because of his unusual gift as a prose stylist, but also because it brings the poignant question of anachronism to the fore in the pages of a *Domus* that was otherwise devoted to its readers' insatiable desire to keep up with the latest trends in design:

I happened to receive some photographs of the *Mirror Paintings*, and I was asked to write about this young man born in Biella in 1933 who has a tough face and lives in Turin in an apartment on the Via Cibrario, an old and dark street of 1910, furnished with mass-produced furniture like what one might buy at La Rinascente department store, wrought iron and wicker chairs, bookshelves with shiny anodized surfaces hung with stainless steel metal, spotlights and Braun record players, everything reflected into the mirrors as if enveloped by fog. These characters . . . it is as if they were waiting along with us for a train to a future that in truth will never come, waiting for something, burdened by the melancholy fates, the corpses, the thousands and thousands of Via Cibrarios that exist around the world, resonant of old tramways on those Sunday afternoons, heavy digestions of garlic and wine, howling Westerns, the smell of orange peels and chewing gum at the Cinema Statuto. This youngster named Michelangelo Pistoletto, one cannot say that he is a Pop painter, as someone has said, and if someone hasn't said it, we'd better be clear that this guy has nothing to do with Pop, because in Turin, as probably in all of Italy, the premises for Pop painting do not exist, there is only this oppressive and invincible weight, no American Coke, no Vermouth Perlino, no vamps, not much use of deodorant, people still sleep in their pajamas, people still cook pasta, squeeze the tomatoes, people still do all those things. At the Bar Torino on Piazza San Carlo, you sit on little baroque chairs to eat lots of gelato, but not much ice cream. Thus, I would say that this boy from Turin is a true poet, even if perhaps less incisive and caustic than the boys from New York, the Lichtensteins, the Rosenquists, the Rauschenbergs, the Oldenburgs, and the Chamberlains, in recounting to us the conditions of our own drama, our own story.[22]

One may well wonder what triggered such a long-winded account. Perhaps it is the fact that Sottsass wrote his piece after having been handed, as he remarks, a group of photographs — a few more than those reproduced in his article and in the Sonnabend catalogue — rather than seeing Pistoletto's *Mirror Paintings* in person. Roland Barthes and others have famously meditated upon the mnemonic power of the photograph.[23] And there is no doubt that, for the reader, the temporal gap between then and now, the gray area between the "Pop" and "non-Pop" of Sottsass's title, was widened by the appearance of the black-and-white *Mirror Paintings* photographs — the customary format for the illustration of all the articles in *Domus* dedicated to "high" art — sandwiched between large glossy color photographs and ads brimming with plastic furniture ensembles and *elettrodomestici*, the new buzzword for domestic appliances.[24] It contrasted with the obstinately upbeat presentism of the large majority of its articles, as well as those of other journals such as *Metro*, a new, large-format journal founded in 1960 by the critic and publisher Bruno Alfieri. Tightly connected to and probably partly financed by Leo Castelli's gallery in New York, it was filled with ads relating to that gallery's commerce with Sonnabend in Paris and Sperone in Turin.[25] It also contrasted with the large color photographs lavished upon Pop art, especially American Pop art, by an infatuated Italian press, in the pages of popular weeklies such as *Epoca*, *L'Espresso*, and *L'Europeo*.[26]

Most striking about Sottsass's response to the melancholy, grainy photographs is its strongly novelistic quality, a style that dramatically departed from that of the other writings found in *Domus* and one that pointed again to the plotted quality of Pistoletto's *Mirror Paintings*. Sottsass's writing is reminiscent of one of Italy's foremost young writers at the time, Italo Calvino, particularly his story *La nuvola di smog* (Smog, 1958), which is written in a style midway between the realism of Cesare Pavese and the witty absurdism of Franz Kafka. It follows a nameless protagonist who works for a scientific journal called *La Purificazione (dell'Aria dal Fumo, dalle Esalazioni Chimiche e dai Prodotti della Combustione)* (Purification [of air from smoke, of chemical exhalations, and of combustion products]), based in Turin. The city is described as perennially enveloped in fog, its facades black, its windows opaque, the silhouettes of its denizens turned into mere ideograms with nearly effaced faces — a place where every single object is coated in a film of dust, leaving open the question of whether all this gray is a result of depressive loneliness, inclement weather, or chemical pollution.[27]

The photographs of the *Mirror Paintings* that illustrate Sottsass's *Domus* article appear immediately after a series of pages presenting portraits of new dealers in contemporary art. These photographs blend almost seamlessly with the Antonioni film stills and the images of the *Mirror Paintings*. They include a candid shot of Beatrice Monti, director of the Galleria dell'Ariete in Milan, hobnobbing with Robert Rauschenberg at the Leo Castelli Gallery in New York, where Monti looks like the actress Monica Vitti in one of her brunette incarnations. Another shot of Monti shows her with her arms lifted and her hands behind her head (a typical Vitti pose), conversing with Sam Francis in the garden of his house in Santa Barbara, California.[28]

In all of these, the sequential interaction between couples often seen from the back recalls the most popular magazine format of those years: the *fotoromanzo* or "photo novel," itself an anachronism by 1964. In the 1940s and immediate postwar years, it became common to publish sequences of actual film stills mixed in with others that looked like ones in magazines. With pipe-dream titles such as *Grand Hotel*, *Bolero Film*, *Il Mio Sogno* (My dream), and *Luna Park*, these cheaply printed magazines were the quintessential mass medium of postwar Italy. Also known as "pocket films" (*cinematografici tascabili*), they extended the reach of cinema culture to rural towns without movie theaters. Aimed mostly at women of modest standing, they would be passed from hand to hand, and their readers would often cut out images from them.[29] Antonioni openly acknowledged, in a number of interviews, the impact of the *fotoromanzo* on his own films. Indeed *L'amorosa menzogna* (Lies of love, 1949), one of Antonioni's earliest shorts, follows a group of provincial young women rushing to the local newsstand to get their favorite *fotoromanzo*, which they then circulate among themselves.[30]

One may read the first photograph in Sottsass's 1964 article in *Domus*, showing Pistoletto's three cutout figures looking at an *informale* painting, as the signal of a shift from the postwar world of *Le amiche* to the early 1960s world of *L'eclisse*. At the end of the above-mentioned opening scene, Vittoria (Monica Vitti) and her boyfriend Riccardo (Francisco Rabal) are shown standing, looking bored and alienated, in front of a large gestural painting. This shot is immediately followed by another of Riccardo standing alone, after Vittoria has left, in front of an even larger *informale* canvas. In another parallel with Pistoletto, a few minutes earlier in the film there is a startling shot of Riccardo sitting motionless, as if nailed to his armchair.[31]

The title of Ashbery's 1966 *ARTnews* piece, "Talking of Michelangelo," positioned Pistoletto and Antonioni (who share the same first name) as mirror images of one another. The phrase came from a famous line in T. S. Eliot's "Love Song of J. Alfred Prufrock" — "In the room the women come and go / Talking of Michelangelo" — a sentence that takes us back to Ashbery's first piece on Pistoletto, in the *Herald Tribune* two years earlier, where he made reference to *Le amiche*, a relatively early and little-known film shot by Antonioni in 1955. Based on a short novel by Pavese entitled *Tra donne sole* (Among women only, 1949), this film follows four women from different

47

walks of life, all of whom aspire to a higher status by partaking in the life of Turin's bourgeoisie.[32] Ashbery writes: "These figures have a peculiarly oppressive quality. Well dressed in a white-collarish way, they remind you of the languid countesses and business executives in Antonioni's movies (Pistoletto is from Turin, where *Le Amiche* was filmed). They either turn away from you gazing listlessly into the mirrored depths of the picture, or slump in modern chairs, fixing an unexpectedly pale and unsettling gaze on the viewer."[33]

In 1966, Ashbery began his second review of Pistoletto's work with a detailed description of the first scene of *L'eclisse* (1962), which has a markedly "sixties" flavor:

> In the opening scene of Antonioni's *The Eclipse* we see Monica Vitti, alienated as usual, cowering on a sofa in a pleasant, livable apartment that apparently belongs to someone of intelligence and means — probably an architect. But somehow the soothing decor has turned on Miss Vitti and driven her up the wall — that at least is the impression we get during the long wordless scene in which she circulates in her prison, fingering pieces of modern sculpture and striped slipcovers. It seems as though the more we attempt to cushion ourselves from the realities of alienated life with a buffer-state of objects, art and the people and attitudes that go with them, the more we expose ourselves to these dangers.[34]

Thus by the time Trini wrote his second piece about Pistoletto in 1966, the parallel with *cinema d'autore* had been made more than once. But it is significant that Trini, adhering to a fundamental tenet of modernist art criticism, appears to want to dissociate Pistoletto from the possibility of a cinematic narrative, while Ashbery, the poet, had gone the opposite way. Trini writes:

> These images have reminded some of the cinema of Fellini, Antonioni, Resnais, and the phenomenology of the *école du regard*. Of course there is a kind of iconography of contemporary life, one can find it anywhere, it is enough to look at oneself in the mirror. And this is what happened with Pistoletto's work. But in fact it is cinematic technique that is implicit in his work. Pistoletto likes going to the movies: "The story interests me, of course, but what really fascinates me is the mechanism of the images."[35]

A more unexpected theme in both Ashbery's and Sottsass's articles on Pistoletto is that of suicide. After a paragraph commenting on objects as ostensible providers of comfort and yet not necessarily being sufficient to bring personal happiness, Ashbery's paragraph about *L'eclisse* segues into the following observation: "Scandinavia, where questions of interior decoration, architecture, city planning and public welfare in general are taken more seriously than in most countries, has a famous suicide rate, and its principal artistic contributions are the tormented works of Ibsen, Strindberg, Munch, Bergman and Dreyer."[36] This detour to the North in fact takes us back to Turin, since *Le amiche* revolves, as does Pavese's novel, around Rosetta's attempted suicide early in the narrative. This occurs in a generic Turin hotel room.[37] In her second attempt, a successful one, she jumps off a bridge.

Sottsass's second essay on Pistoletto was published as a leaflet in February 1965 to accompany Pistoletto's installation of four of his largest *Mirror Paintings* behind the large glass windows of Sala Espressioni, the showroom of Ideal Standard, a producer of bathroom appliances, on Via Hoepli, one of Milan's most elegant streets. Four different versions of *Persone alla balconata* (People on a balcony, all dated 1964) were placed on shallow platforms designed by Gio Ponti, who described the space in *Domus* as "a store, not of objects, but of expressions, of ideas" (Figure 1.7). The showroom space had previously been handed over to other designers and artists, including Bruno Munari, Enrico Castellani, and Achille and Pier Giacomo Castiglioni. Following Pistoletto, Sottsass himself was given the space for his own installation.[38]

At Pistoletto's installation, Sottsass approached the seamless lineup of figures as if it was a large narrative fresco, a format that had become taboo after Fascism's embrace of mural painting. In a tour de force of prose, Sottsass telescopes the two decades that had elapsed since the fall of the Fascist regime into a breathless flashback. This second extraordinary excerpt from Sottsass is from a piece originally published as a two-page leaflet. Kept in a file in the *Domus* archive,

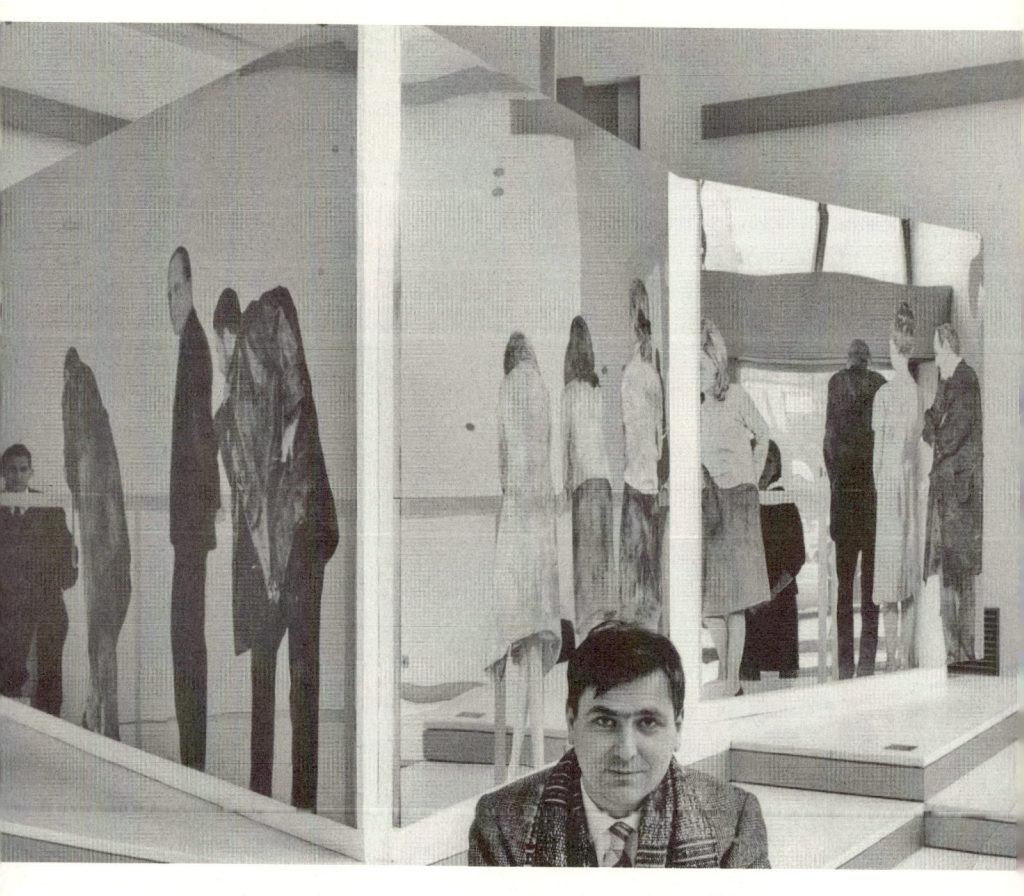

Figure 1.7. Michelangelo Pistoletto in Sala Espressioni, Milan, 1965. Photograph: Ugo Mulas. Courtesy of the Cittadellarte–Fondazione Pistoletto, Biella, Italy.

this liminal piece of art writing has never been published since. Sottsass writes:

> The story began with Trini Castelli, the guy on the right with the beard and the black shiny raincoat like the one worn by cod fishermen on the North Sea, leaning on the railing [. . . .] He came over to me and so now there are two characters; and the third one enters the story almost at once because Trini Castelli showed me the photos of the Pistoletto mirrors and told me the story of Pistoletto, a friend of his who was showing his stainless steel plates at the Sonnabend Gallery in Paris and who was, in any case, as you can see in the photo, a guy who looks at the world in his own way. He, too, is leaning on that railing looking down into a pit — at what, no one really knows. A snake pit? A marble quarry? A soccer game? An anatomy lesson? The funeral of Marilyn Monroe? Our own funeral? The entry of the troops? The retreat of the troops? A gored bullfighter? The consecration of bishops? I showed the photos to *Domus*, and *Domus* published them. Thus they were seen by Ponti, who then asked Pistoletto to do a show for the store window on Via Hoepli, and so Pistoletto came to me to ask if I would write what we now call a "presentation." The circle of characters seems to be closed. But meanwhile, other people had entered the story, others who were looking down into the pit, including Sperone, the one from the gallery in Turin who shows Pop painters, in a way of speaking — a skimpy young man who never seems to find the solution and is always a bit feverish and lives with his ailing mother in the small town of Carmagnola on the outskirts of Turin and whose part in this story is that of a merchant, a rare kind of merchant who doesn't sell to make money, but because he feels he belongs to this story whose characters are leaning on the railing and looking down into the pit. And then there are the girls. I don't know who they are, these lovely young girls, with their little sweaters and overcoats, with ribbons in their hair, leaning against the railing. Are they maybe the young girls from Via Cibrario, where Pistoletto lives, or the ones from Carmagnola who walk up and down Main Street on Sunday morning? Here the story becomes a little bit more mysterious. Who are they? How come they, too, are involved in this story of people looking down into the pit? I would have preferred if the girls weren't there [. . . .] But Pistoletto is right. There must be girls looking down into the pit, girls in their Sunday best, their knee-highs and lovely

shoes from the factories of Varese, girls who wait. And there also needs to be that guy who turned to look me in the face, like the one who, on the morning he was to be shot, when they made him sit on a chair facing the wall, turned around just before they shot him, to see where death was coming from. Inside and out, on either side of the mirror, there is nothing but a long wait to see how the spectacle will end, the suspense that stretches all the way to the end, the only reality that keeps us going. Pistoletto has understood all this, damn it, so that one never knows whether he is standing on this side or that side of his stainless steel filters, or on both sides.[39]

A series of resonant images and themes, some of them disturbing, are evoked in intermittent flashes in Sottsass's text: the allusion to troops, referring to the invasions by the Germans and then the Allies; the fall of the Fascist regime, with its murky tales of collaboration and resistance; the executed prisoner (a cryptic reference, perhaps, to the end of Roberto Rossellini's film *Roma città aperta* (Rome open city), when the priest, a member of the Underground Resistance during the last days of the Nazis' control of Rome, is executed by the Fascists while seated on a chair facing the camera); the bullfight (a likely reference to the extraordinary impact that Picasso's *Guernica* had on Italian artists as an anti-Fascist statement when it toured Europe in 1953); the hopeful girls and boys, displaced by Italy's imperfect and incomplete modernization, which forced millions of uprooted provincials to toil in the cities. Sottsass's text also recalls the last seven minutes of *L'eclisse* — one of the most chilling sequences of postwar Italian cinema. In a series of silent freeze-frames, Antonioni recapitulates his entire film, as in that instant of "total recall" before dying when one's entire life flashes before one's eyes. Each freeze-frame is reminiscent, I believe, of an episode in history.[40]

More importantly for us, each is reminiscent of a particular episode in Italian art. Antonioni shows us a trash barrel in a fenced-in pit, suggesting the aesthetic of Neo-Dada and unknowingly foreshadowing Pistoletto's corrugated cardboard *Pozzo* (Well, 1965), one of his mid-1960s *Ogetti in meno* (Minus objects) (Figure 1.8a); streets in

Mussolini's EUR (Esposizione Universale Roma, Mussolini's ideal city) and the survival of its ghostly monumental cityscape south of Rome, side by side with its post-Fascist architectural aftermath; a building covered with scaffolding, suggesting Giacomo Balla's pre-Futurist painting *La giornata dell'operaio* (The worker's day, 1904) (Figure 1.8b); a man on a horse-drawn cart and a nanny pushing a baby carriage, subjects painted by the Macchiaioli, a group of Italian artists in the mid- to late nineteenth century; crosswalks echoing the style of geometric abstraction; and, the very last shot, of a streetlamp, a substitute for both atomic glare and solar eclipse, much the way the glaring light bulb in Picasso's *Guernica* symbolizes the first experiments in saturation bombing (Figure 1.8c).

Most interesting, because we glimpse it as furtively as in a Pistoletto *Mirror Painting*, is the way the camera dwells for a few seconds, in the first scene of *L'eclisse*, on a pile of magazines and newspapers on the desk in Riccardo's living room. The Communist *Rinascita* appears in the middle of the pile, while on top is an issue of its monthly supplement, *Il Contemporaneo*. Its cover features a reproduction of the painting *La fucilazione in campagna* (Execution in the countryside), Renato Guttuso's 1939 homage to Federico García Lorca, the Spanish anti-Fascist poet killed in 1936 at the beginning of the Spanish Civil War, very likely by Nationalist militia siding with General Franco. The first issue of the journal, in 1954, was devoted, appropriately enough, to the shift from the political commitment of Neorealism to the indifference personified in *L'eclisse* by Riccardo. The last sentence in Sottsass's text echoes the phrases used by the left-leaning philosopher Norberto Bobbio in his essay "Intellettuali e vita politica in Italia," published in *Nuovi argomenti* in 1954, to describe the subject position of Italian intellectuals vis-à-vis politics the year Italy entered the period of its economic miracle: "Above the fray, neither here nor there, both here and there, aiming at synthesis."[41] Here was a bourgeois intellectual who, like the men in suits in the *Mirror Paintings* and like Pistoletto and Antonioni themselves, subscribed to the Left while embracing the comforts of the new object world.

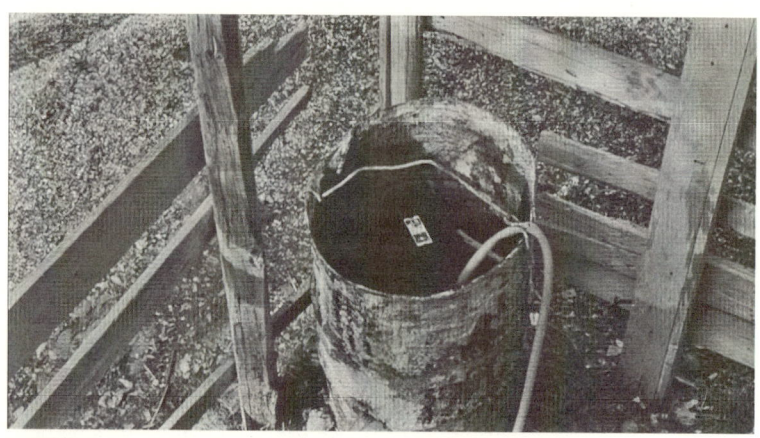

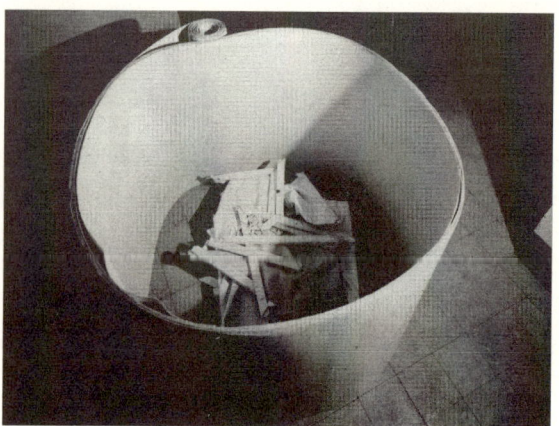

Figure 1.8a. *Top:* Michelangelo Antonioni, dir., *L'eclisse*, 1962. *bottom:* Michelangelo Pistoletto, *Pozzo* (Well, 1965). Corrugated cardboard, canvases, and broken frames, 100 × 140 cm. Courtesy of the Cittadellarte—Fondazione Pistoletto, Biella, Italy.

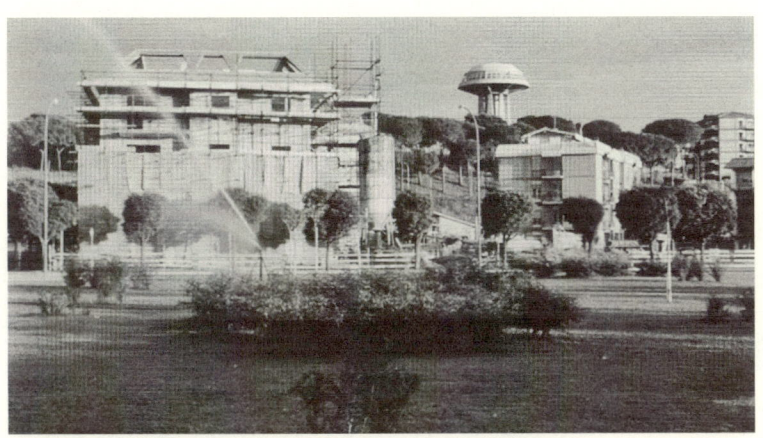

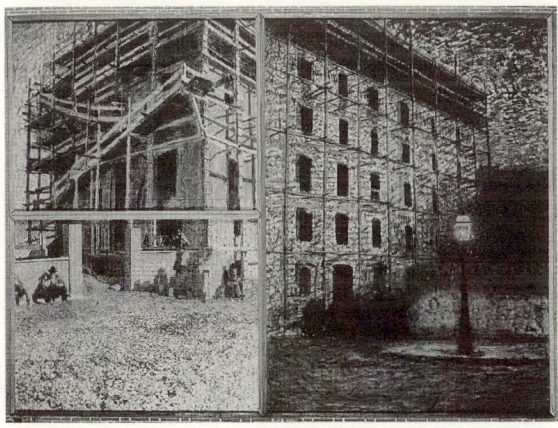

Figure 1.8b. *Top:* Michelangelo Antonioni, dir., *L'eclisse*, 1962. *bottom:* Giacomo Balla, *La giornata dell'operaio* (A worker's day, 1904). Oil on coardboard, 135 × 100 cm. Private collection.

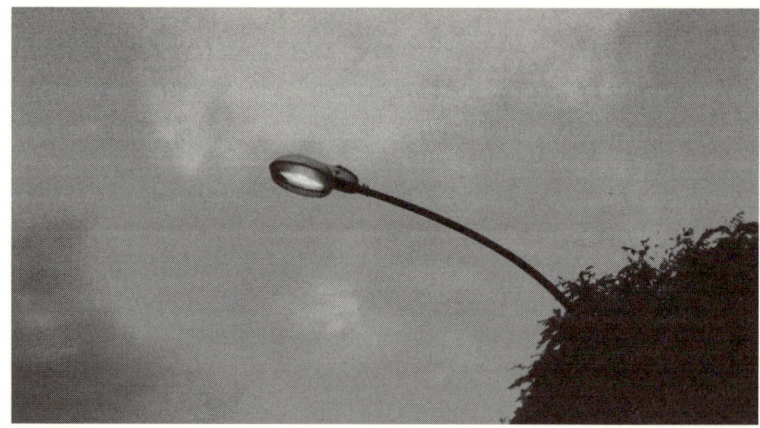

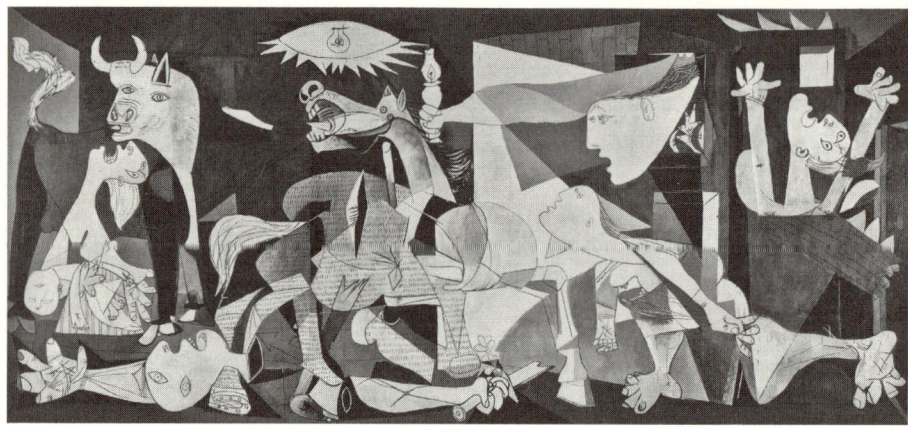

Figure 1.8c. *top:* Michelangelo Antonioni, dir., *L'eclisse*, 1962. *bottom:* Pablo Picasso, *Guernica*, 1937. Oil on canvas, 3.49 × 7.76 m. Museo Reina Sofia, Madrid.

While the flashbacks in Sottsass's first essay on Pistoletto were prompted by photographs of the *Mirror Paintings* sent to him by Sonnabend, the vertiginous flashbacks of his second text might have been sparked by seeing the actual objects at Ideal Standard. On Via Hoepli, one saw the figures on the *balconata* first through the shop window from the street, then between two reflective surfaces once inside the gallery. In this case, the two large mirroring surfaces must have created, as in a hall of mirrors, an acute sensation of *mise en abyme*. Here we have the maximal example of what Lucien Dällenbach describes in *The Mirror in the Text* when he writes that one can "distinguish three sorts of *mises en abyme* corresponding to the three forms of dissonance between the time of the narrative and the time of the figure: the first (prospective) reflects the story to come; the second (retrospective) reflects the story already completed; and the third (retro-prospective) reflects the story by revealing events both before and after its point of insertion in the narrative."[42] In his review of Pistoletto in *Domus*, the critic Guido Ballo described a similar sensation of giddiness, writing that "even though its feet rest on the ground, the humanity portrayed [in *Persone alla balconata*] appears provisional, suspended in a limitless void."[43]

Much like the illustrations accompanying "Pop e non Pop" the year before, the grainy black-and-white photographs of *Persone alla balconata* illustrating Ballo's article existed in a different temporality from the rest of the issue: the former (Italian Pop) fuzzy and disorienting, the latter (American Pop) slick, massive, and already purchased for a high price.[44] Meanwhile, in color, gracing the magazine's cover, was a detail of another, more spectacular, mural-sized painting, James Rosenquist's wraparound *F-111* (1964–65), named for the new American fighter bomber soon to be used in Vietnam. "The largest 'Pop' painting in the world," read the caption of the accompanying article in the journal, announcing that the painting, just sold to Robert and Ethel Scull, was about to go on a tour of European museums.[45]

While Sottsass and Ballo both expressed a sense of giddiness and even of historical vertigo, Ashbery experienced no such thing when he saw *Tre ragazze alla balconata* (Three girls on a balcony) a year later on the landing of a staircase at the Minneapolis Museum of Art. He wrote: "Pistoletto's girls, their backs turned to the viewer, are gazing at something that turns out to be you and the room you are in."[46] Instead of its projecting anxiously into the void, Ashbery experienced the piece as a tautology that grounded you back on your feet. How are we to interpret this disconnect? Are we to read it, again, as an American sense of groundedness and stability, being at the center of the world, as opposed to the European sense of precariousness?

Looking Askance at (International) Pop

Just a few weeks later, American Pop art took the 1964 Venice Biennale, and Europe, by storm. The controversial awarding of the coveted grand prize in painting to Robert Rauschenberg's *Combines* — signaling the obsolescence of any such prize for a work in the medium of painting — elicited international coverage that ranged from fascination to outrage. As Alberto Boatto wrote in his review of the 1964 Biennale: "That this is a good Biennale is evident from the light it throws on a situation that goes beyond artistic matters."[47] He understood that Pop had created a no-win situation for Italian artists. The curators of the Italian section at the Biennale, among them the art historian and critic Maurizio Calvesi, had placed their bets on their own contingent of Pop artists: Franco Angeli, Tano Festa, Titina Maselli, Concetto Pozzati, Antonio Recalcati, and Mario Schifano.[48] But while Calvesi had been happy to place Angeli, Lucio Del Pezzo, and Festa within what he called "the neometaphysical pole" of Pop — meaning paintings that looked like those of Giorgio de Chirico and his epigones — and thus to link them to the strategies of appropriation used by de Chirico, Boatto saw citationality as a dead end for his conationals. Facsimiles of Old Master paintings, which read as camp when embedded in a Rauschenberg combine or silk screen, were fated to fall flat in an Italian Pop piece.

Moreover, as Boatto noted, "instead of directly absorbing objects and images," these neometaphysical artists were "still transcribing, and by traditional pictorial means." Examples of this were the series created in 1963–64 by Tano Festa in which the artist lifted entire paintings by Jean-Auguste Dominique Ingres and *The Creation of Man* in Michelangelo's Sistine Chapel ceiling, both of which proved, in Boatto's intimation, "how difficult the art of citation really is." Boatto ended with a dire conclusion: "It would seem that everyone is burdened by a culture whose symbols and obligations hinder any strong grasp of or straightforward relation to the world. In the case of older artists, this culture reveals itself to be nothing but an out-moded world, a suffocation long since institutionalized."[49] His colleague Giorgio de Marchis was hardly more charitable in his review of the Biennale for *Art International*. After declaring it an unmitigated success for the Americans, he, too, noted the dangerous tendency toward neometaphysical painting on the part of the Italian Pop artists. Schifano, whose participation was particularly anticipated after his stay in New York, disappointed with his slovenly workmanship and impoverished imagery. Here again, the critic's conclusion was unforgiving: "The young Italian neometaphysical school seems to suffer from a lack of urgency, a lack of images, of myths — evidence of a narcissistic and necrophile culture where everything is known and where nothing happens anymore."[50]

One may argue that the best words to describe the surface of the paintings produced by the Italian Pop artists are "recalcitrant" and "refractive." Pale and ill-defined images, they seem to pull away from the viewer, to be drained out, as if out of fear of the empire of the sign and a desire to distill the stream of Pop images emitted by Italy's overly charismatic transatlantic counterpart. In his 1963 article "La giovane scuola di Roma" (The young school of Rome), Cesare Vivaldi, a critic closely identified with the movement, described Italian Pop in terms of a disappearance. He noted that the flashy, mass-media repertoire of American Pop — Coca-Cola bottles, tin cans, ads, labels, tabloids, comic strips — found previously in the works of the Roman Mario Schifano and his cohort had by that point all but disappeared, replaced by more modest, subdued landscapes, people,

still lives, and symbols. Perceiving objects and landscapes via photography involved the reconstruction of data no longer perceptible
to the naked eye, Vivaldi also noted, and this pointed to a sensibility
that Italian critics found lacking in American Pop.[51] Emblematic of
this recoil from American signage and mottos is *Tutta propaganda* (All
propaganda, 1963) by Schifano, an enamel painting that shows (very
much indebted to Warhol's 1961 paintings) signage for Coca-Cola and
other products dissolving into a quasi-monochromatic landscape
(Figure 1.9; Plate 2). No wonder, perhaps, that Schifano titled one of
his own series *Paesaggi anemici* (Anemic landscapes, 1964–65).[52] But
one can also argue that this recalcitrance, like Pistoletto's distancing
via the mirror, was strategic.

By all accounts, the intense political infighting between nations
produced by the system of awarding prizes at the Biennale reached a
climax that year. When the dust settled, Leo Castelli and his ex-wife,
Ileana Sonnabend, the American doyenne of Pop in Paris, divided
among themselves the spoils of Europe. The most spirited photo
reportage on the events of that opening week was by Ugo Mulas
for *Domus*. This coverage more closely resembled a film by Fellini
than one by Antonioni. Full-page portraits of Rauschenberg and
Lucio Fontana appeared on facing pages, showing both enthroned in
matching Venetian gilded chairs. Another page presents a somewhat
silly upside-down juxtaposition of two photographs of a celebratory
toast (*brindisi*) between Rauschenberg and Andrea Cascella (whether
the toast was genuine or contrived is unclear), the latter being the
much lesser-known Italian artist who received the sculpture prize.[53]

Mulas's photographs did little to dispel the sinking feeling that
after the feasting and diplomatic pageantry at the Biennale, the Euro-
peans were somewhat bereft. The most widely reproduced photograph of that Biennale, taken by Mulas for the same Restany review
in *Domus*, shows canvases by Rauschenberg being carefully loaded
onto a motorboat so that they could be whisked from the US Consul-
ate to the grounds of the Giardini, a move that allowed the artist to
be eligible for the Gran Premio after the fact (Figure 1.10).[54] While the

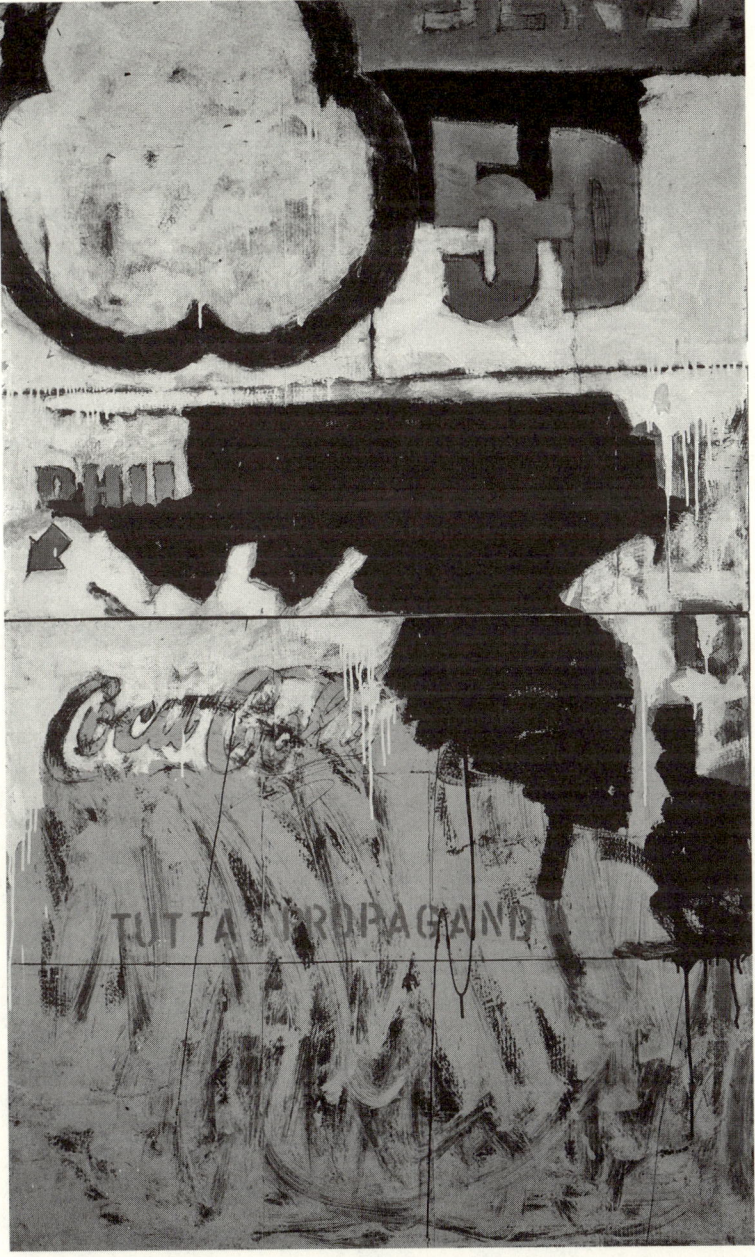

Figure 1.9. Mario Schifano, *Tutta propaganda* (All propaganda, 1963). Enamel on cardboard mounted on canvas, 198 × 118 cm. Fondazione Marconi, Milan.

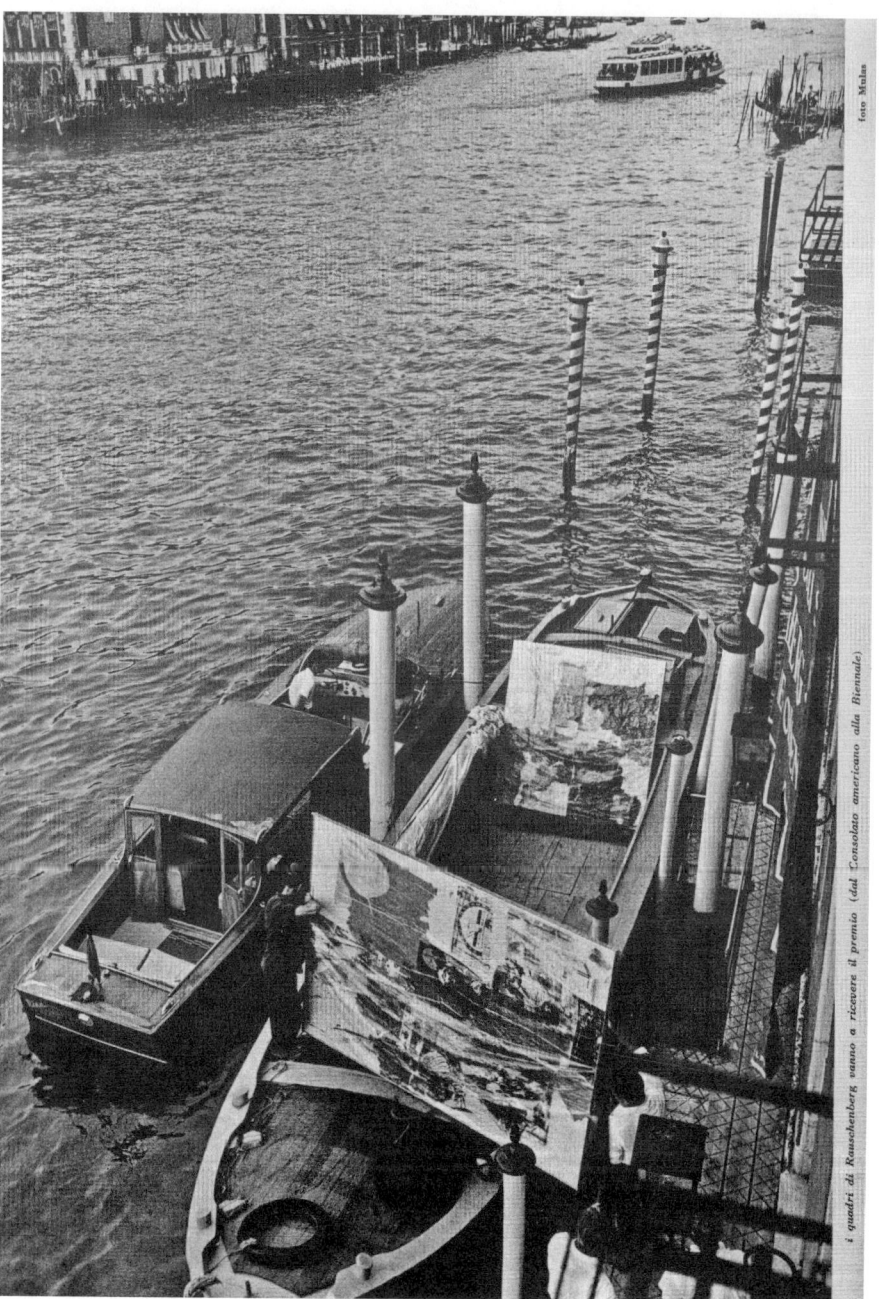

Figure 1.10. Robert Rauschenberg's works being loaded aboard motorboats on the Grand Canal, Venice, *Domus*, no. 417, August 1964. Photograph: Ugo Mulas.

boat provided a logistical solution for the Americans, from an Italian standpoint, the published images of these vessels exemplified Italy's problem. This view of the Grand Canal perpetuated the perception of Italy, decades after the Futurists' vituperations against foreigners' morbid love for Venice, as the perennial land of touristic kitsch, visual clichés, and *passatismo* (pastism).[55]

One of the most intriguing photographs that Mulas took at that year's Biennale was not included in his *Domus* reportage. It shows (from left to right) Festa, Schifano, the gallerist Gian Tomaso Liverani (the owner of La Salita, which competed with Giorgio de Marchis's La Tartaruga for the representation of Pop art in Rome), and Fioroni standing in front of Fioroni's painting *L'immagine del silenzio* (The image of silence, 1964) (Figure 1.11). A camera hangs around Fioroni's neck, indicating her experimentation with photography. But perhaps most noticeable, as remarked in the Introduction, is the photograph's decenteredness: each of the protagonists is looking in a different direction at something outside the picture frame, oblivious to the feminine silhouette appearing behind them. Calvesi included *L'immagine del silenzio* in the Biennale's Italian pavilion, which was dedicated to the Roman artists of the Scuola di Piazza del Popolo. An interview between Calvesi and Fioroni, published in September 1964 in the journal *Marcatrè*, opens with the following exchange:

> [Calvesi]: I saw your four panels with an image that recurs in more or less the same pose, but with different values of contour, light, etc. Could you explain your procedure?
>
> [Fioroni]: I don't agree with the word *panels*. What interests me is very simple, it's a certain type of narration linked to a cinematographic image that repeats itself. I insist on calling it narrative because for almost a year now I have been looking for ways to recount certain things.[56]

Taking note of Fioroni's pointed response to Calvesi, the critic Gillo Dorfles later elaborated, in the brochure for the artist's 1965 solo show at the Galleria del Cavallino in Venice, that "the repetition—at

times insistent — of the same figure, of a silhouette, sometimes mag-
nified or shrunken, sometimes overlapping, and then, like a cinemat-
ographic fade out, vanishing into nothingness, truly has the effect
of an ectoplasmic apparition in which we perceive an impalpable
presence while recognizing in it improbability or threat."[57] Although
the filmmaker's name never appears in the literature on Fioroni,
every one of Dorfles's key phrases — "vanishing into nothingness,"
"apparition," "improbability," and "threat" — conspires, as with Pistoletto, to project us into the universe of Antonioni. Everything in
Mulas's image, from its decentered composition to the clothes worn
by the four subjects on that summer day at the Biennale — Festa's
black polo shirt, Schifano's white rolled-up sleeves, Liverani's light
summer suit and straw hat, and Fioroni's polka-dotted dress — makes
it look like a still from the first of Antonioni's tetralogy: *L'avventura* of
1960. It evokes, notably, the scene in which the film's lead characters
search for their lost companion, Anna, among the deserted rocks of
the Lisca Bianca in the Aeolian Islands (Figure 1.12). The four artists
appear to be searching for the ghostly figure just behind them.

The passage that best describes the arc of Fioroni's artistic production was, in fact, penned not by an art critic, but by the film
critic Pascal Bonitzer in "Il concetto di scomparsa" (The concept of
disappearance), an essay on Antonioni's *L'avventura* published in 1985.
Bonitzer seems to outline the trajectory of Fiorini's work — from her
1961 drawing *La fidanzata* (Girlfriend), which shows a loose-limbed
young woman in sunglasses, a T-shirt, and a skirt walking along the
bottom edge of the paper (a drawing Fioroni would recycle in 1966 and
1967 in two different formats); to *La ragazza sulla spiaggia* (Beach girl,
1965), depicting a young woman in a sarong walking, head down along
a beach, as though searching for something; to her spectral landscapes
and cityscapes of 1970–71, from which all figures have vanished. The
original, Italian title of Bonitzer's piece, "Il concetto di scomparsa"
involves a wordplay between the word *comparsa*, meaning "extra" in
a play or film, and *scomparsa*, meaning "disappearance," which points
to something Fioroni's work shared with Pistoletto's cinematic *Mirror*

Paintings. The mirrors allow us to position our own image next to his
cutout figures, but during this encounter, we come to realize that we
are taking part in a situation where everyone — cutout and reflected
figures alike — is performing not as protagonists so much as extras.
Here is the third long quote in this chapter, elicited this time not by a
mise en abyme but an eclipse. Bonitzer writes:

> Antonioni is a painter in the sense that, for him, white, black, grey, and the
> various colors of the spectrum are not merely ornamental, atmospheric, or
> emotional, but are veritable ideas which envelop characters and events. [. . .]
> White connotes the absence, the disaffection, the emptiness that paralyzes
> Antonioni's characters. [. . .] *L'avventura* is ostensibly the story of a disappear-
> ance, but a disappearance whose importance and density evaporate little by
> little, until the very structure and form of the narrative are perilously contami-
> nated and impaired; what happens in reality is *the disappearance of the disap-*
> *pearance* of Anna. [. . .] We note that many of Antonioni's other films have for
> their argument an inquest, a police-style investigation. [. . .] In many Antonioni
> films something or someone disappears, but this disappearance is such that
> the tension appropriate to the police investigation, to the chase, to suspense,
> tends to vanish, as well. Thus, in *L'avventura*, the disappearance of Anna under-
> lines, insidiously, another disappearance, more secret and harder to make out,
> which haunts and misleads the remaining characters, preventing them from
> concentrating on the search for the missing woman. . . . Plastically, narratively,
> and ontologically, Antonioni's is a world in pieces, and "putting the pieces back
> together" [. . .] is precisely the operation abandoned by Antonioni's derailed,
> alienated characters. [. . .] We find, in his perambulating characters (people
> walk a lot in Antonioni's films), an insistent fascination with the amorphous,
> the formally abstract, the self-hidden, self-erased figure slipping into nondif-
> ferentiation. [. . .] To overturn an inkwell on a half-finished sketch is to destroy
> the sketch, but it is also to splatter on the paper, in place of the sketch (the
> dry academic copy), a wild ink-flower. In the same way, the art of the cinema
> inextricably contains a priori forms (the *mental object* which the *mise-en-scène*
> must bring forth on the screen) and raw images offered by the real world. The
> sketch disappears, but this disappearance is not a simple erasure; we shall never
> recover in its primal freshness the virgin page defended by its whiteness.[58]

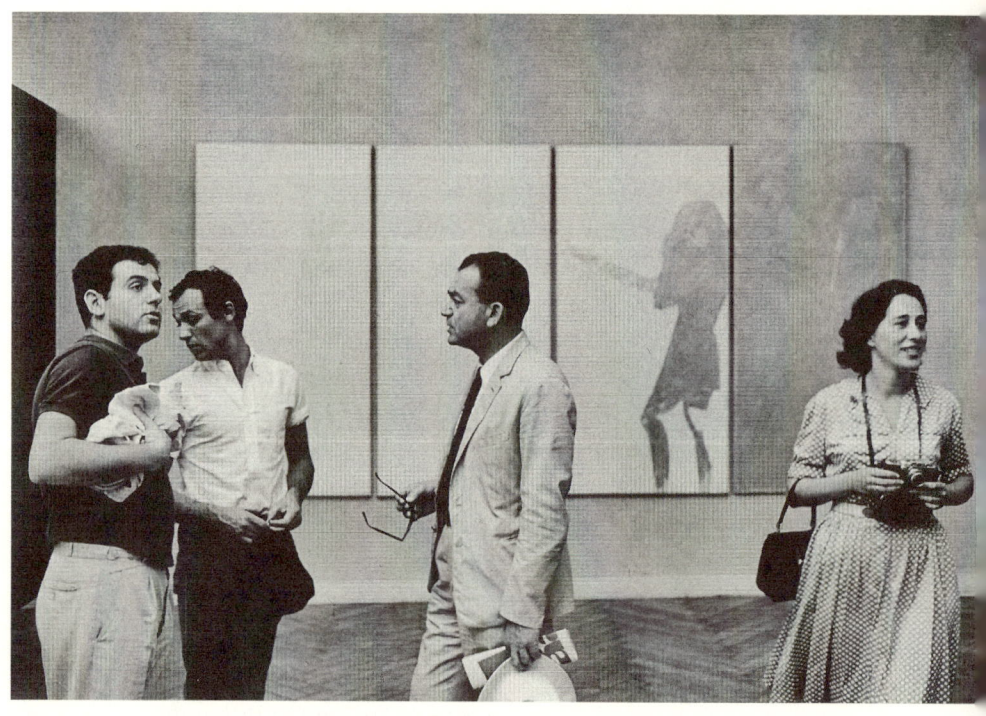

Figure 1.11. Tano Festa, Mario Schifano, Gian Tomaso Liverani, and Giosetta Fioroni at the opening of the 1964 Venice Biennale, in front of Fioroni's *L'immagine del silenzio* (The image of silence, 1964). Photograph: Ugo Mulas. Courtesy Ugo Mulas Heirs.

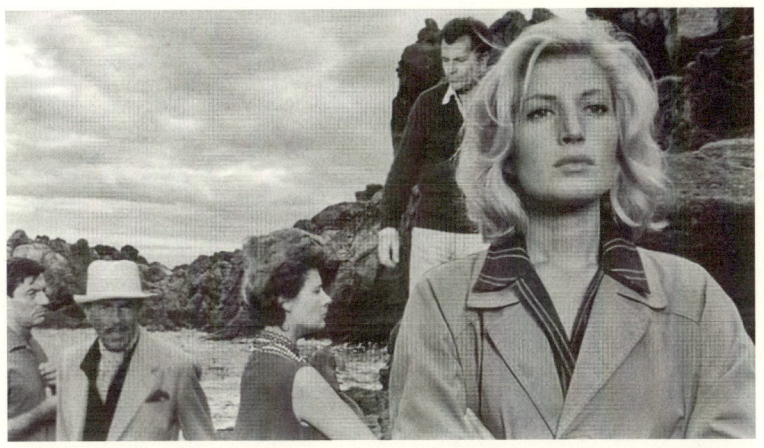

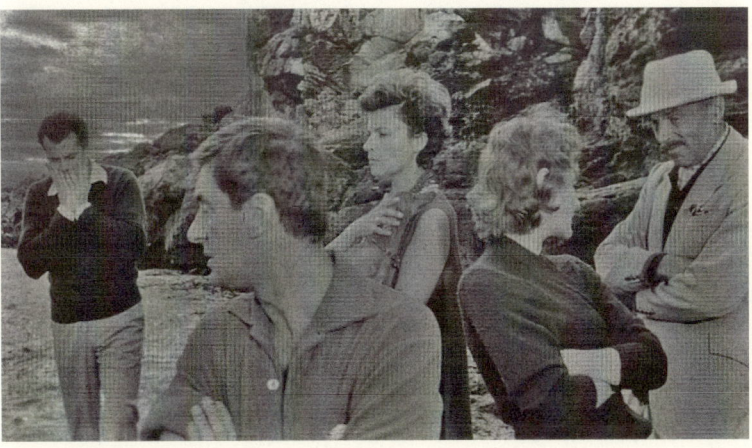

Figure 1.12. Michelangelo Antonioni, dir., *L'avventura*, 1962.

Pistoletto had no works in the 1964 Biennale, and the two *Mirror Paintings* he subsequently based on Pop works that he saw there — one featuring a cutout of Oldenburg's *Stove*, the other a cutout of a crushed-metal sculpture by John Chamberlain — can be read as his way of absenting himself from all the commotion and stating: "I came, I saw, but I did not participate. These are souvenir pictures."

"Paintings that one doesn't see at first, this is how Pistoletto captures us, he operates by transparency": these were Trini's words when he first encountered the *Mirror Paintings*.[59] It is this gift of invisibility that allowed the *Mirror Paintings* to slip by unnoticed among other artists' works. Once photographed, they functioned almost like cameras themselves, producing a whole set of exhibitional scenarios that emblematized the ambivalence and misgivings felt by a European artist often (mis)labeled as "Pop." Indeed, from 1964 onward, a remarkable number of photographs of Pistoletto's *Mirror Paintings* published in 1960s art magazines cast his lonely cutout figures (sometimes the artist himself) thoughtfully, yet passively examining iconic works by their transatlantic and European Pop counterparts. His nomadic figures appeared among — or rather, superimposed themselves on — a variety of works by more or less famous Pop artists from both sides of the Atlantic during and after that year's Biennale.

This being said, the story has a somewhat comical prelude with the publication of Sottsass's "Pop e non Pop" in *Domus* in May 1964, just days before the opening of the Biennale. The article included a photograph of *La signora Lichtenstein* (Mrs. Lichtenstein, 1964), a small mirror painting featuring a cutout of Roy Lichtenstein's mother in the form of a portrait bust, wearing a close-fitting hat and looking incongruously like Britain's Queen Mother. In the photograph, this figure is apparently being ogled by the reflection of a young man in the gallery (see Figure 1.6). The cutout was in fact based on a photo taken by Sottsass himself to illustrate his review of a show at the Sidney Janis Gallery in New York for *Domus* the year before.[60] The reappearance of Lichtenstein's mother in *Domus* in the context of Sottsass's review of the Pistoletto show at Sonnabend is one of the many amusing examples of the critic's use of his own photographic reportages.

In the November 1964 issue of *Domus*, Pierre Restany's review of the myriad Pop art shows that had taken place that summer and fall ended with a photograph of a version of Pistoletto's *Uomo seduto* taken at the exhibition *Pop etc.*, curated by Werner Hofmann at the Museum des 20. Jahrhunderts in Vienna (Figure 1.13). In the photograph, the cutout man appears to be deep in thought in front of a 1962 painting by British Pop artist Derek Boshier, aptly titled *Rethink/Re-Entry*, installed not far from an ominously suspended *Tire* by Lichtenstein. The slight spatial deformation produced by the *Mirror Paintings*' undulating surface of stainless steel lends a disorienting dizziness to the atmosphere of the exhibition. Also exhibited were Lichtenstein's ubiquitous *Whaam!*, also owned by Sonnabend, and *Tire*, shown in a Lichtenstein exhibition in Italy, curated by Sperone for Turin's Galleria Il Punto (December 1963).[61] Continuing this theme, *Uomo con pantaloni gialli* (Man with yellow pants, 1964), featuring a cutout of Sperone (now at MoMA; see Figure I.1) appeared that summer staring at a painting by Francis Bacon, one of Pistoletto's most important formative influences, in the catalogue of the exhibition *The Object Transformed*, curated by Arthur Drexler at MoMA. Meanwhile, *Donna seduta di spalle* (Woman seated from behind, 1963) was included, as an interloper, in *Mythologies quotidiennes* curated by Gérald Gassiot-Talabot — Restany's nemesis — at the Musée d'Art Moderne de la Ville de Paris that same year. That exhibition, which was planned as a counteroffensive to Europe's colonization by the Americans, launched a militantly anticonsumerist and anti-imperialist homespun movement known in French as Figuration Narrative. The *Mirror Paintings*' gift of invisibility might also explain, in retrospect, why Pistoletto was one of the first European artists of his generation to be given a solo exhibition in the United States, at the Walker Art Center in 1966 (his first museum show).[62] The editors of *ARTnews* chose to illustrate Ashbery's review of that show with a photo of Pistoletto's *Persona appoggiata* (Person leaning, 1964),

69

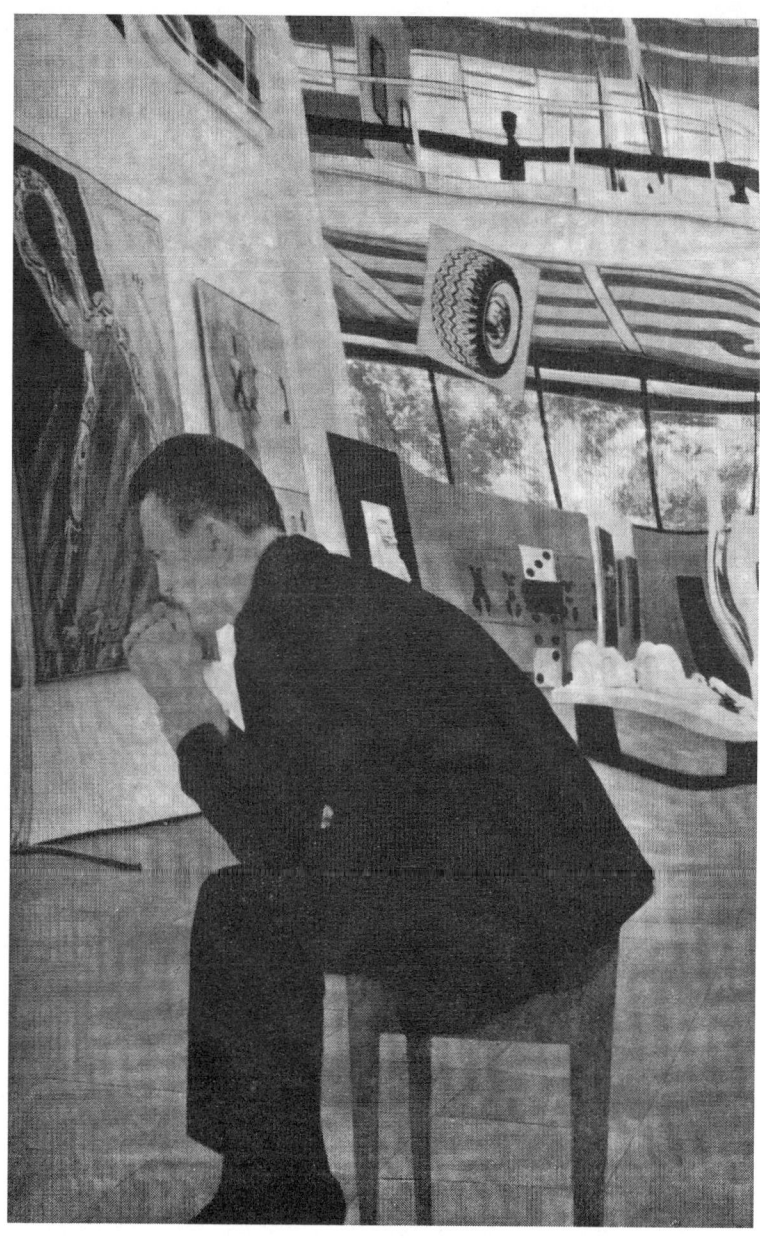

Figure 1.13. Michelangelo Pistoletto, *Uomo seduto* (Seated man, 1963). As reproduced in Pierre Restany, "Estate 1964: La 'nuova' figurazione è Pop," *Domus*, no. 420, November 1964.

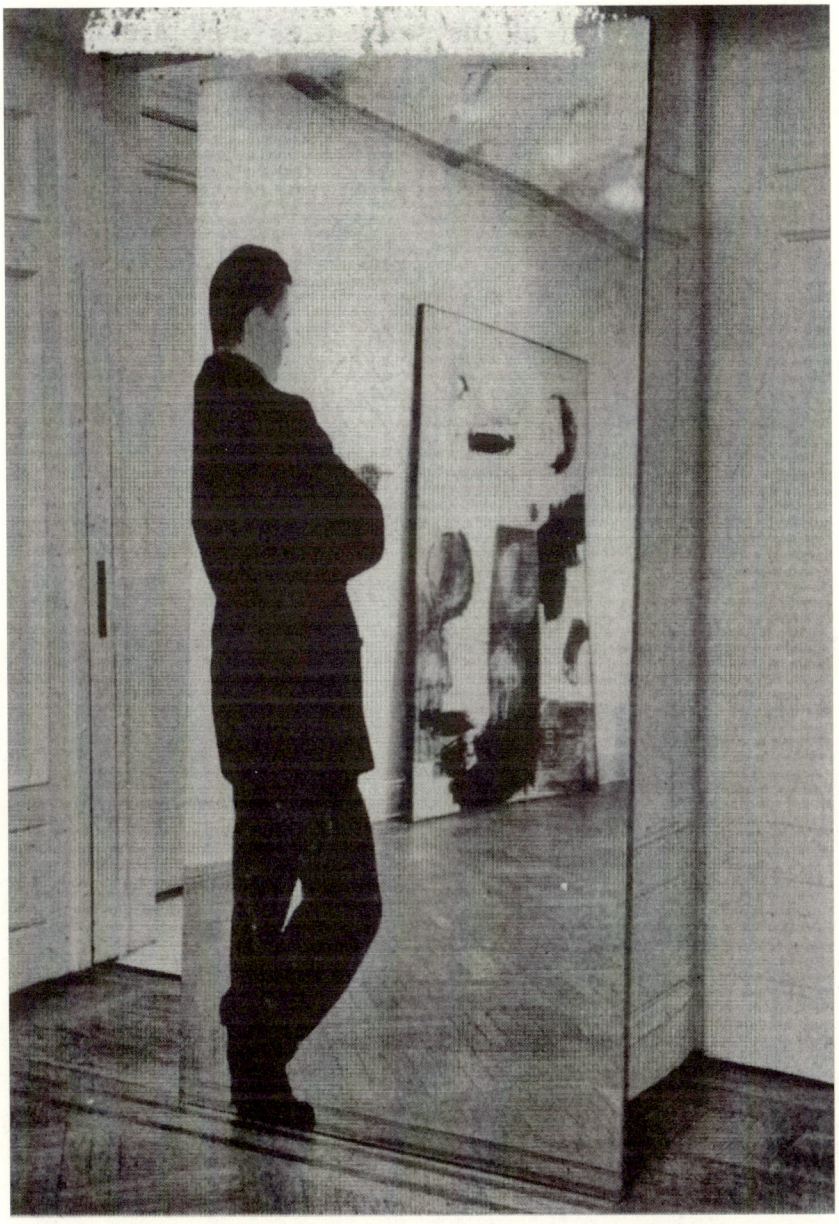

Figure 1.14. Michelangelo Pistoletto, *Persona appoggiata* (Person leaning, 1964). As reproduced in John Ashbery, "Talking to Michelangelo," *ARTnews* 65.4 (Summer 1966).

in which his own silhouette appears to stand in Castelli's gallery in New York, casting a sidelong glance at a silk screen by Rauschenberg (Figure 1.14).

The Many Wars of Pistoletto's Alpino

Most revealing, and a case of maximal compression functioning almost as an allegory of Italy's embrace of and resistance to American Pop is the itinerary taken by *Alpino* (Alpine soldier), one of Pistoletto's first *Mirror Paintings*. The piece exists in two slightly different versions — one, with the tissue paper particularly bleached, dated 1962, and the other, more colored and with more detail, dated 1963. Both show a young man in uniform, a member of Italy's battalion of mountain soldiers known as Alpini, seen from behind and embracing his girlfriend (Figure 1.15; Plate 3).

The story of this work's reception begins with an attempt by Calvesi to bring a New York gallery show, Sidney Janis's *Environments by 4 New Realists*, into the ambit of Italian art. In his review, Calvesi mentions Pistoletto as a hypothetical addition to the roster of artists included in the 1964 exhibition: Jim Dine, Claes Oldenburg, James Rosenquist, and George Segal.[63] A year later, as if to fulfill Calvesi's wish, Sperone included Pistoletto as the sole Italian artist in his *Pop*, the first gallery show to bring the majority of the American Pop contingent — Dine, Lichtenstein, Oldenburg, Rauschenberg, Rosenquist, Warhol, and Tom Wesselmann — to Italy from June 11 to the end of July of 1965.[64] Installation shots show Pistoletto's *Alpino* leaning against the wall alongside Rosenquist's *Trophies of an Old Soldier* (1962); a vitrine with plaster food sculptures by Oldenburg, including a little homage to Italy entitled *Vitello tonnato*; and a silk screened *Car Crash* painting by Warhol (Figure 1.16). *Alpino* does not appear among the Pistoletto works listed in the exhibition's leaflet, but it may not be happenstance that this particular painting was chosen — apparently at the last minute given its omission from the leaflet — to hang across from Lichtenstein's comic-book war diptych *Whaam!* (1963). As a result, the two appear superimposed in many photographs of

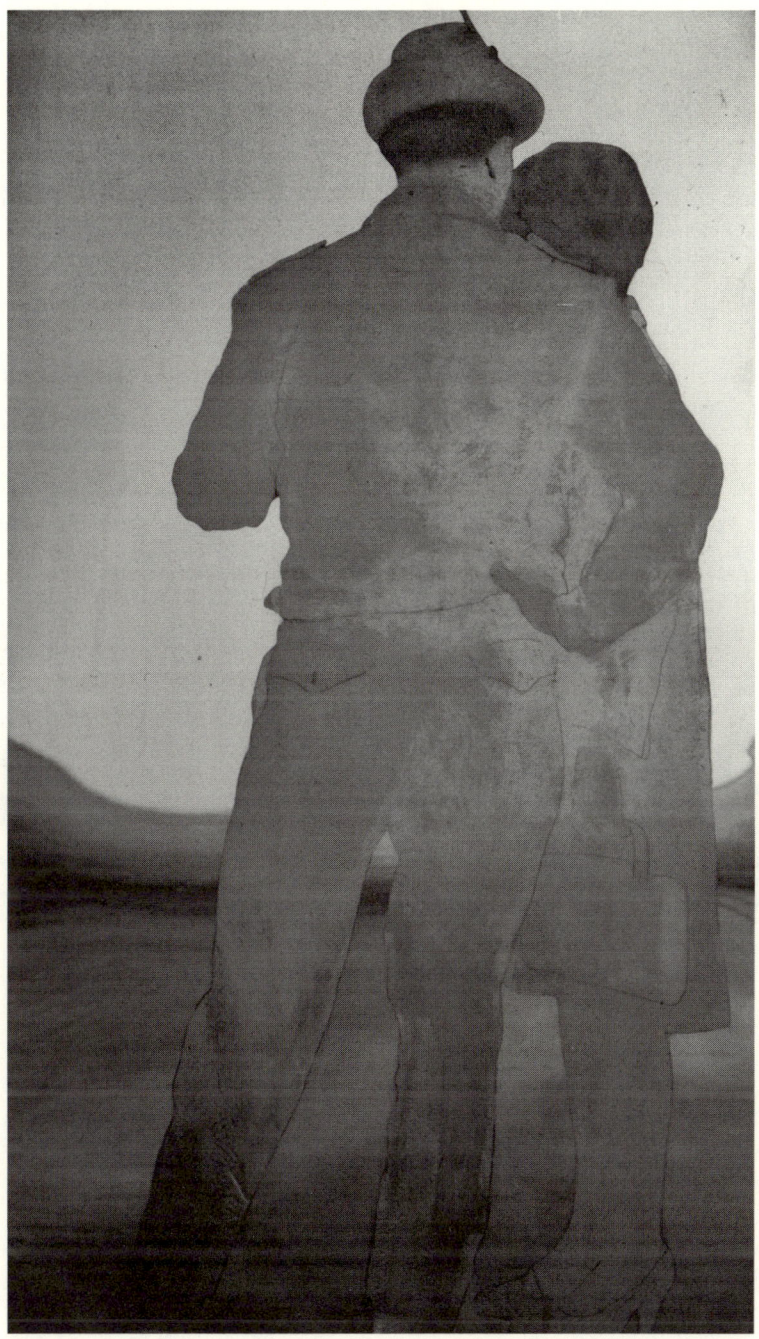

Figure 1.15. Michelangelo Pistoletto, *Alpino* (Alpine soldier, first version, 1962). Painted tissue paper on polished stainless steel, 200 × 120 cm. Courtesy of the Cittadellarte–Fondazione Pistoletto, Biella, Italy.

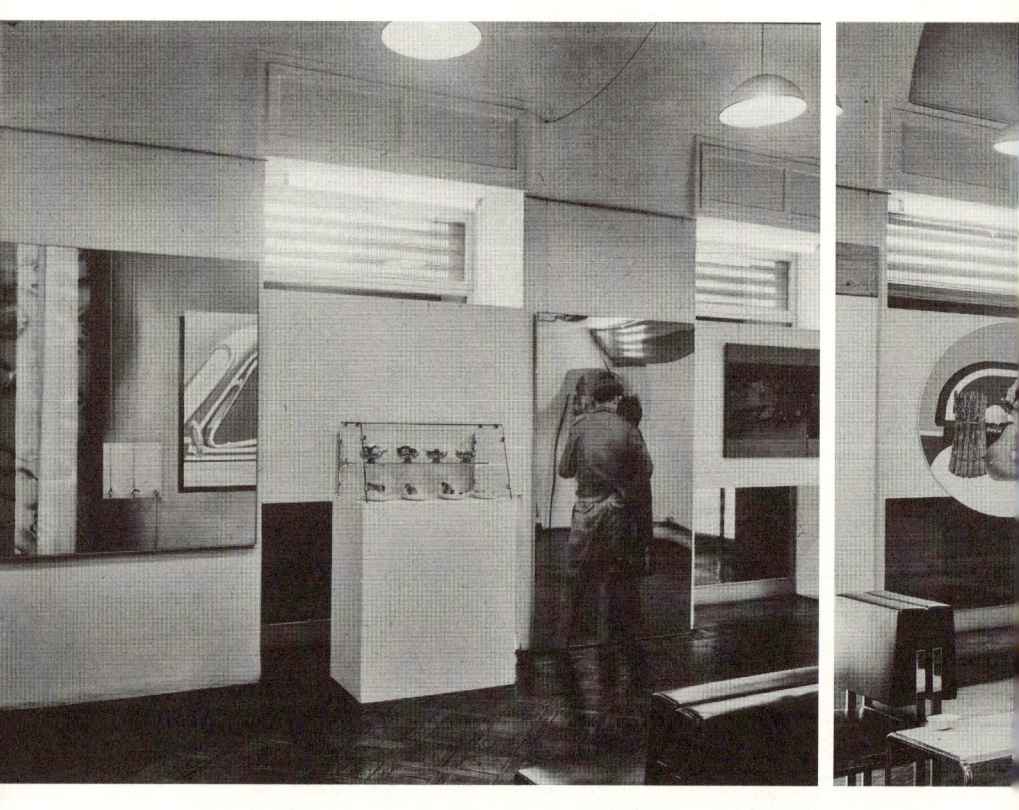

Figure 1.16. Views of the installation at *Pop*. Gian Enzo Sperone's gallery, Turin, 1965. Courtesy of the Cittadellarte–Fondazione Pistoletto, Biella, Italy.

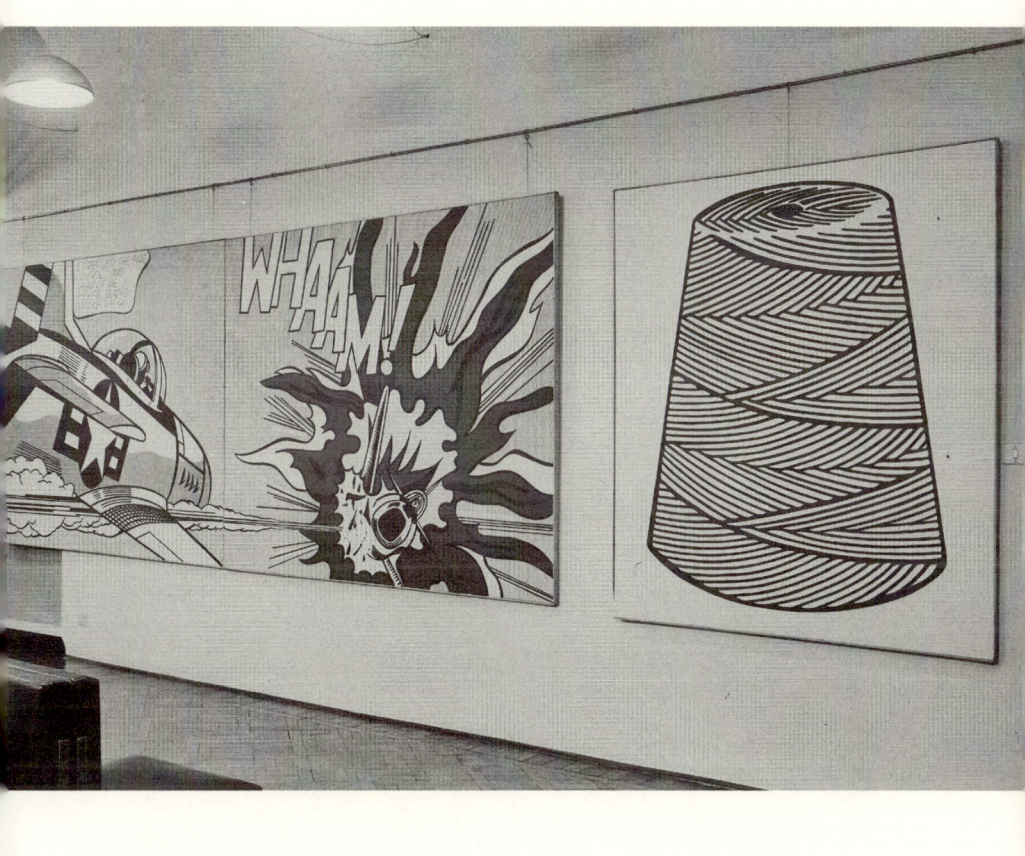

the exhibition, with the onomatopoeia reversed by the effect of the mirror.[65] By means of reflection, one of these exhibition photographs telescopes the history of the two World Wars and Italy's participation in them.

The original 1872 mission of the Alpini was to protect Italy's northern border with France and Austria. Yet Pistoletto's soldier is wearing a uniform that could belong to either of the two World Wars. The reference here, at least for an Italian gallery visitor, may have been to the Futurist artists. Galvanized by *irredentismo*, the revanchist movement to regain the northeastern portion of the Italian peninsula from Austria during World War I, many Futurists enlisted in the army's Lombard Battalion of Volunteer Cyclists and Motorists and went to Peschiera, on the shores of Lake Garda, to receive training as Alpini (Figure 1.17, top). Umberto Boccioni, Antonio Sant'Elia, Mario Sironi, and Filippo Tommaso Marinetti — the first two of whom eventually died in that war — all appear together in a photograph from 1913, valiantly uniformed in their Alpine surroundings.[66]

In 1943, in the midst of another war, after the aerial bombardments of Turin, Pistoletto's family had taken refuge in Val di Susa, where they stayed until 1946. At that time, the Alpini played an important role along with the Partisans in anti-Fascist insurrections in the Piedmont. In the spring of 1945, the Alpine divisions descended from the Alps to fight the German Wehrmacht in the streets of Turin. As general accounts of postwar Italian history make clear, it was in Turin that the national insurrection against Fascists and then against the Germans in the spring of 1945 was intensely dramatic. Fearing that too slow an insurrection would lead to, after an Allied victory, the occupation of Italy by foreign armies, as was the case for Germany, the Partisans sped to precede the Allies in the liberation of Piedmont (Figure 1.17, bottom).[67] The strike that took place in Turin on April 18 — in the struggle organized by clandestine committees in the industrial centers of the North — was popular and insurrectional in character. The following week, on April 24, the Germans surrendered in Biella, Pistoletto's hometown. *Alpino* thus

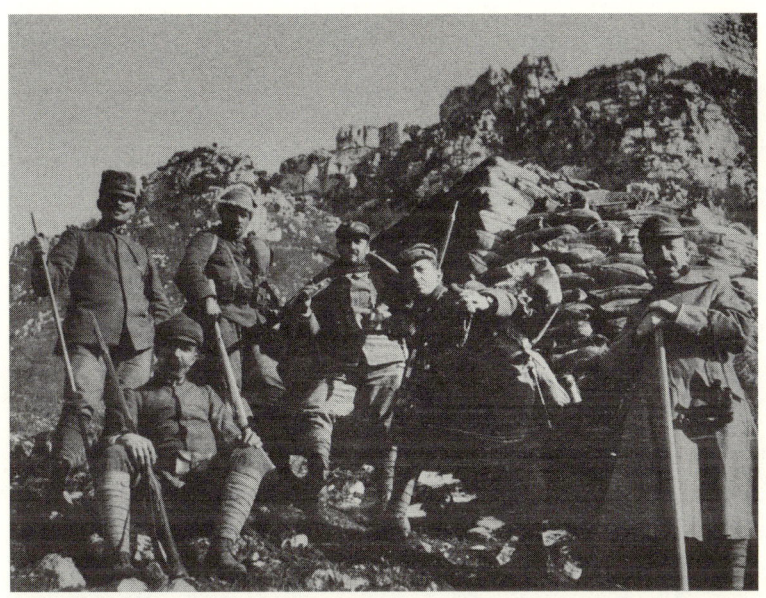

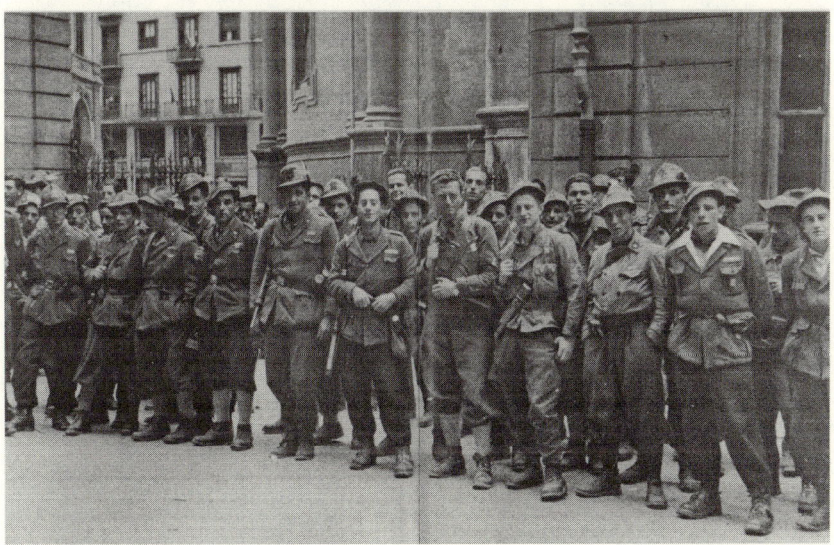

Figure 1.17. *Top:* Futurists on the front, 1915. *bottom:* Partisans of the Alpini division Stellina on the day of the liberation of Turin, May 6, 1945. Courtesy of Filippo Tommaso Marinetti Papers, General Collection, Beinecke Rare Books and Manuscript Library, Yale University.

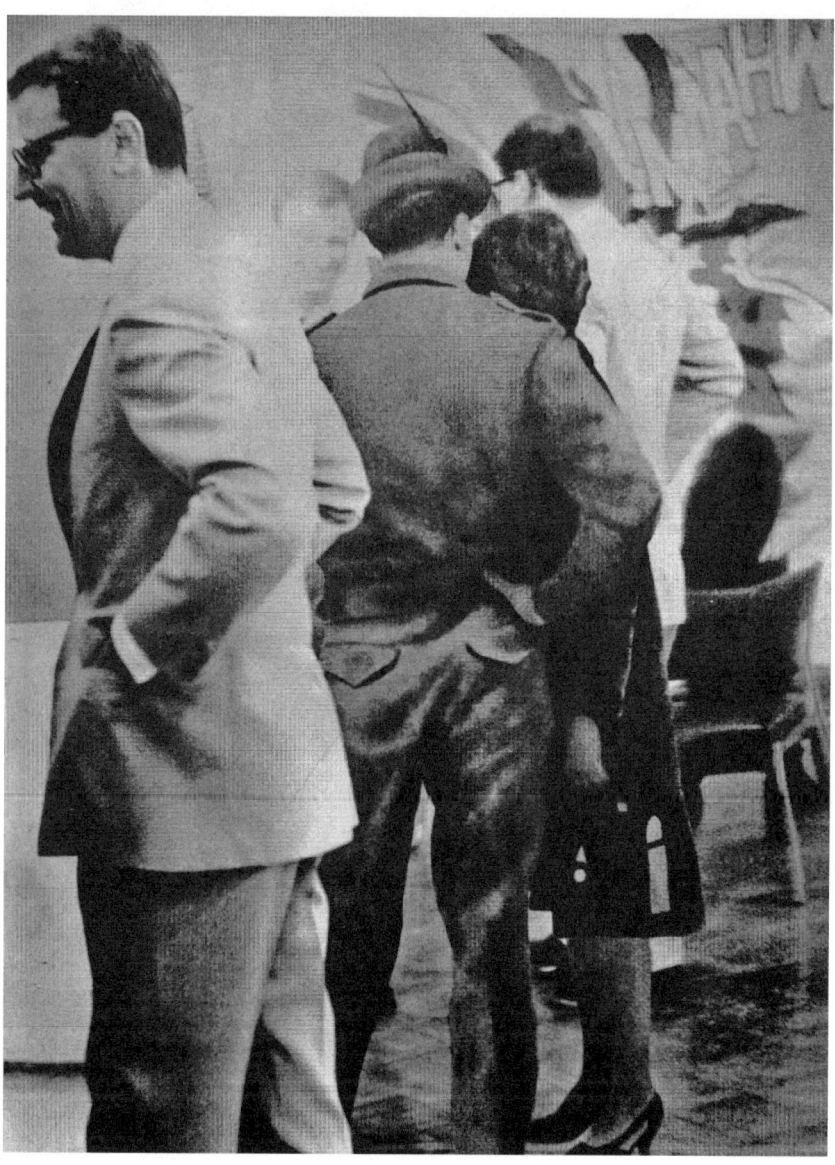

Figure 1.18. Michelangelo Pistoletto, *Alpino* (Alpine soldier, 1963). As reproduced in Alberto Boatto, *Pistoletto: Dentro/fuori lo specchio* (Rome: Fantini, 1970). Photograph: Paolo Bressano. Courtesy of the Cittadellarte–Fondazione Pistoletto, Biella, Italy.

flashed back to a key theme in the Italians' postwar embrace of the resistance *epos*.[68] Meanwhile, the reference to more than one war was already there in *Whaam!* and in fact was already present in Lichtenstein's comic-book source, the DC classic *All-American Men at War*, illustrated by cartoonist Irv Novik. *Whaam!* was culled from issue number 89 (February 1962) of that magazine, which featured three stories, each involving the air force in a different war: World War I, World War II, and the Korean War.[69]

Pistoletto's *Alpino* subsequently appeared, as if in two film frames, in two contiguous photos in an anthology of Calvesi's writings entitled *Le due avanguardie* (The two avant-gardes) published in 1966. In the first photograph, *Whaam!* appears reflected in the mirror portion of the work, but in the second, *Whaam!* is eliminated and the soldier and his girlfriend now face a blank wall and a door that has been left ajar.[70] It is as if, in a single stroke, Calvesi has wished away American Pop, the Cold War, and the concomitant culture wars.

Boatto — whose views on the geopolitics of Pop were quite different from Calvesi's, judging from his reaction to the 1964 Venice Biennale — opted for a different tactic in his choice of photographs for his 1969 book *Pistoletto: Dentro/fuori lo specchio* (Pistoletto inside outside the mirror) (Figure 1.18).[71] As a topical late-1960s anti-Vietnam War gesture, Boatto reproduced a shot of *Alpino* at Sperone's gallery, where the charged field between the young man in uniform and *Whaam!* is traversed by the laughing figure of Pistoletto himself. The artist appears twice — directly in front of the camera and reflected in the surface of his work — thus illustrating the title of Boatto's book.[72]

Eclipse of the Object at the 1964 Milan Triennale

In the early photographs of the *Mirror Paintings*, we find a narrative of objects — mostly chairs, but also lamps — both in the photographic reflections and in the actual cutouts, as in *Lampadina* (Light bulb) and *Riflettore* (Spotlight), both of 1964, in which light fixtures are the only items affixed to the surface. In Antonioni's *L'eclisse*, we are similarly shown, scene after scene, an entire catalogue of lamps — from nineteenth-century pastiches to the widely acclaimed midcentury modern lighting fixtures produced during the postwar economic miracle (see Figure 1.5). Such fixtures were designed by Gio Ponti, the Castiglioni brothers, Marco Zanuso, Vittoriano Viganò, Joe Colombo, and others for design firms including Arredoluce, Oluce, Fontana Arte, Flos, Stilnovo, and Artemide. The fixation on lamps in Italian design at midcentury led the designer and theorist Andrea Branzi to infer that the numinous glow emanating from them and the absorption they elicited in the figures perambulating around them could be read as an unwitting philosophical meditation, in the midst of the frenzy produced by the economic boom, on the mysterious, dark side of technology.[73]

With Italy enjoying a full-blown postwar "economic miracle" (spurred by the Marshall Plan), the 1954 Triennale made the famous stairway of the Milan Triennale, built in 1933 by Giovanni Muzio, almost unrecognizable in an attempt to generate excitement (Figure 1.19). This Triennale was impressive indeed. Two decades of mural decoration and sometimes extravagant ceilings were eclipsed by a cinematic vista offered by the glass wall at the top of the stair- case, which allowed visitors immediate visual access to the *Mostra dell' industrial design*. Placed on low-lying bases, the products dis- played were dramatically exhibited in galleries painted black, lit with enormous hanging lamps of white canvas that hovered over them like celestial disks, designed by the brothers Achille and Pier Giacomo Castiglioni. This epiphanic exhibition design earned the tenth Trien- nale the popular nickname "Miracolo a Milano."[74] Given the hyper- consumerist nature of this "miracle," the sobriquet — which refers to Vittorio De Sica's 1951 film of the same title — must have had a wry or even bitter touch, for as Milan was entering its miracle years, it was not only the memory of Fascism, but the postwar social pieties of De Sica's late Neorealism that were left behind. In 1954, a new com- petition — *Il compasso d'oro* (The golden compass) — was instituted to reward the best design for industrial products. And among the winners, we find Ettore Sottsass with his Lettera 22 typewriter for

Olivetti. As Guido Crainz reminds us in his *Storia del miracolo italiano* (History of the Italian miracle), in 1954, the vision offered by the objects under the glowing lamps was still very much a promise in a nation with low individual revenue and a low consumer index, compared with France, Britain, and Germany.[75]

Ten years later, the audience at the 1964 Triennale was confronted with an incongruity: a thirteenth Milan Triennale, nicknamed "la triennale Pop," characterized by the eclipse of the object. In view of economic numbers, it was indeed a paradox. From 1954 to 1964, the national revenue had doubled, and so had per capita income. During that decade, industrial productivity rose a staggering 84 percent.[76] Featured back to back with the Venice Biennale in *Domus* in the summer of 1964, this Triennale was the first since it began in the 1930s (first as the Monza Biennale) to be organized around a theme, and its chosen topic was "free time" (*tempo libero*).[77] As Umberto Eco, its co-organizer with architect Vittorio Gregotti, stated in an interview, this was the first Milan Triennale to deliver a message, rather than merely decorate a setting for the display of objects.

It was also the first where painters, sculptors, designers, and filmmakers were asked to address a topical issue.[78] In an all-out attempt to locate design within an increasingly media-saturated culture, Gregotti and Eco foregrounded the total environment over the display of singular commodities, alternately presenting visitors with a barrage of visual and auditory sensations (most culled from cinema and television) and empty spaces. In their desire to counter the Triennale as a mere trade show in a city where no fewer than forty design magazines sprang up between 1945 to the 1970s (nine from 1960 to 1966 alone), Gregotti and Eco placed their bets on ambience.[79] Most daunting was the monumental entrance staircase (Figure 1.20; Plate 4). Since 1933, it had welcomed visitors into the Palazzo dell'Arte to see the Triennale's national displays of product design. This time, as we see in the photograph, the entryway was entirely covered, from floor to ceiling, with a reflective silvery material. It was left empty except for eight protruding containers, each with a pulsating neon sign: two

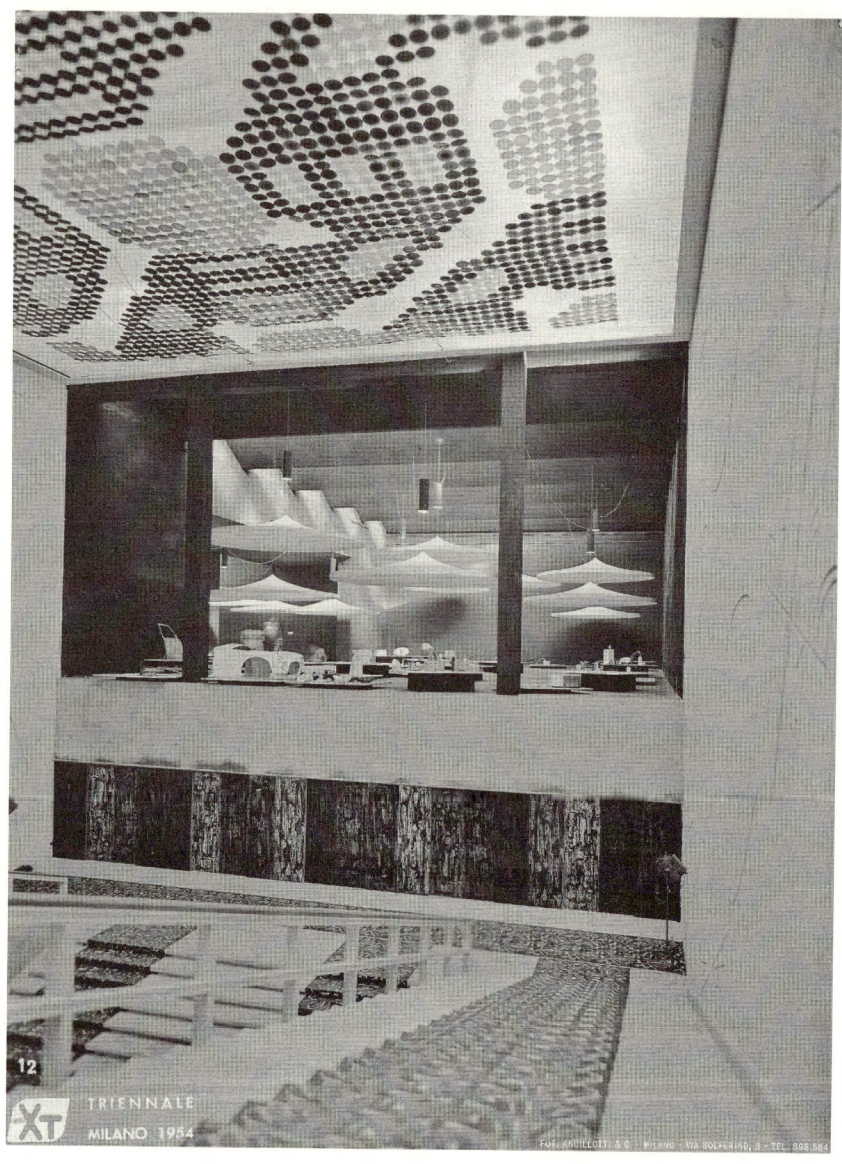

Figure 1.19. Main staircase of the Milan Triennale, 1954. Photograph courtesy of the Historical and Photo Archive, La Triennale di Milano.

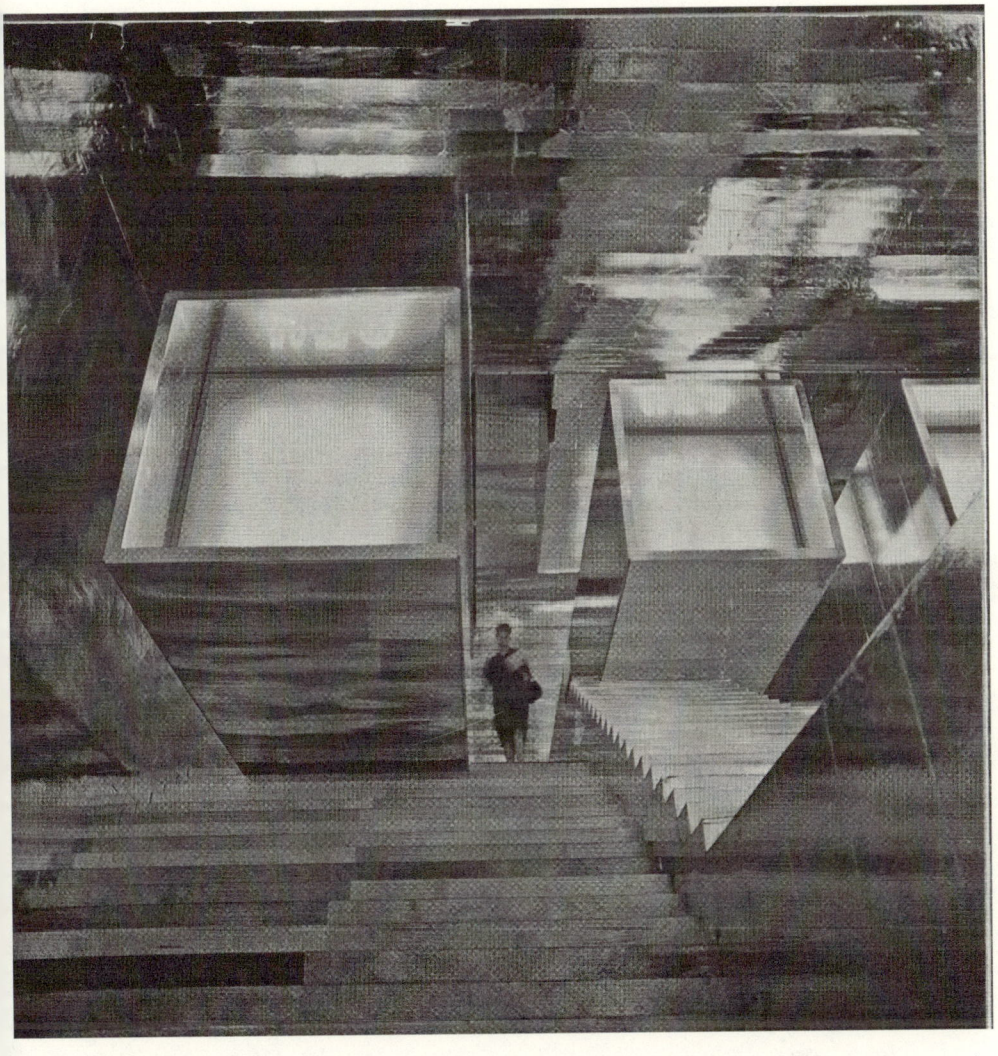

Figure 1.20. Main staircase of the Milan Triennale, 1964. As reproduced in *Domus*, no. 418, September 1964.

with the letter *I* for *Illusione*, two with the letter *T* for *Tecnica*, two with *I* again for *Integrazione*, and two with *U* for *Utopie*. Everywhere the design object was replaced by an image world.[80]

Like the Venice Biennale that summer, the 1964 Triennale elicited an unprecedented flurry of reviews. Many critics were puzzled by the mixture of highbrow and lowbrow. From the other end of the political spectrum, the reviewer of *Corriere della Sera*, Milan's most important and business-oriented daily, wrote: "It is not clear what the Triennale is about, since it dwells on what it is not."[81] The headline of another review in the *Corriere della Sera*, published the following day, was "Eight Hours to Play: The 13th Triennale Is More Amusement Park than Trade Show."[82] The review published in the *Corriere Lombardo*, titled "Delirious Things at the Triennale," lamented that "the conduits [that is, the aforementioned containers] feel like interrogation rooms, bunkers of desperation,"[83] while that in the trade magazine *Italia Moderna Produce* complained of "intellectual games in a tormenting and chaotic atmosphere."[84] In the Milan fashion magazine *Bellezza*, Isa Vercelloni wrote: "This Triennale is no longer a trade fair for housewives to inform themselves about the latest trends in furnishing and design, the way one goes to a fashion show. It is a highbrow fun fair, with its slot machines, halls of mirrors, papier-mâché mannequins, tinfoil staircases, and even a striptease and a tunnel of horrors."[85] "Those 'Hidden Persuaders' [from the eponymous book of 1957 by Vance Packard, translated by Einaudi in 1958 as *I persuasori occulti*] are the real authors of the Triennale," wrote the reviewer of *Letture d'Italia* before launching into a disquisition on the work of French and American sociologists.[86] "Here we are again, climbing the triumphal staircase of Milan's good old Palazzo dell'Arte, into the enchanted world of the Folies Bergère, but seen from backstage," wrote a reviewer from Turin.[87] "Nightmares, Suffocation, and Delirium in the Prison of Free Time," proclaimed the headline in Trieste's *Il Piccolo*.[88]

More charitable were the articles in *Casabella*. "The Triennale has emerged from its coma," declared Ernesto Rogers, its chief editor, expressing relief after what he considered to have been the botched eleventh and twelfth iterations of the fair.[89] "In contrast to the stale, academic seriousness of the Triennali that preceded it," wrote Gillo Dorfles in the same issue of the journal, "this one declares itself ephemeral and even parodic: it managed to turn Pop against itself."[90] "A surrealist funhouse with philosophical overtones," wrote Ashbery for his Anglophone readers in the *New York Herald Tribune*, "its endless Piranesian staircase covered with silver foil wanders upwards towards a mirrored ceiling suggesting the finale of a Busby Berkeley musical.... Although fourteen nations, including the US, have exhibits, this is obviously an Italian affair from start to finish. None of the other countries can compete with the Italians' decorative flair and it apparently never occurred to them to do so."[91]

Most damning, as he often was in his reviews of the Triennales, was Bruno Zevi, Italy's most vocal architectural historian from the 1950s well into the 1970s. In a piece entitled "The Triennale on Trial: The Sad Carnival of Architects" (one of no fewer than three reviews on the Triennale he wrote for the illustrated weekly *L'Espresso*), he expressly alluded to the Fascist venue being obscured by the decorative blitz:

> The ideological void is matched by a senseless architectonic program. One wastes 250 to 300 million lira by giving a group of artists (all of them, it goes without saying, "politically engaged") the chance to vent their repressed desire for escapism. Every three years, the Milanese architects find themselves in the same quandary: how to mask Giovanni Muzio's historicist palazzo. Every three years a new device: laminated sheets or banners to hide the arcades and the columns.... The images — brilliant, sophisticated and abstruse — communicate the void, and the state of being they impart to the viewer is that of torpor. If nausea is the outcome of leisure, then the performance was a success.[92]

A full-page color photograph of the Triennale's 1964 *scalone* was published in the September issue of *Domus*, a few pages away from Mulas's upbeat photographs of the events taking place in Venice.[93] The photo features a diminutive figure of a woman descending the staircase in a space suffused by a sulfuric light. The image projects us once again into the realm of an Antonioni film, specifically that of *Il deserto rosso*, about to be presented at the Venice Film Festival in September that year and the director's first in color.

Antonioni's view of industrial progress is filtered through the mental state of the film's female protagonist. In the film, the camera follows the agoraphobic and neurotic Giuliana, played by Monica Vitti, as she wanders the toxic industrial landscape of the Po delta near Ravenna. In one of the last and truly Dantean scenes in the film, Giuliana drifts among the corroded metal hulls of colossal containerships. Like the typical visitor to the Triennale, she is a bourgeois housewife. In the opening sequence, as the film credits roll, Giuliana is shown walking, holding the hand of her young son, across the desolate wasteland of the petrochemical factories near Ravenna. The scene is immersed, as are many that come after it, in a choking yellow fog. When the credits end, the image sharpens into a series of cuts showing different views of a slate-gray tableau of factories in the rain. Giuliana looks out across the undulating expanse of oily puddles and refuse. The only touches of color are her mint-green coat, her child's ochre duffel coat, and the orange petroleum flares emitted by the power plant in the background.

While Antonioni is never mentioned by Eco and Gregotti or by any of the Triennale's many reviewers, an essay in *Casabella* by the three young architects responsible for the initial design of the Triennale had a subtitle that read — cryptically — "Class Struggle Is Worth the Mystery of the Gender Relations in the Style of Antonioni."[94] One of the preparatory drawings shows the tiny figure, a woman holding the hand of a child in front of a barren landscape; as in *Deserto rosso*, she is wearing an olive-green coat. As Antonioni stated just prior to the film's release: "Color has, in modern life, a meaning and a function that it never had in the past. I am convinced that before long, black and white will truly become the stuff of museums. This is also the least autobiographical of my films. The one in which I have kept my eye turned most to external things."[95]

The malaise exuding from *Deserto rosso* and the 1964 Triennale sig-naled the end of Italy's economic boom as strikes against low wages and growing unemployment began to besiege factories, beginning with that of Fiat in Turin. Meanwhile, imperturbable, Pistoletto's *Uomo seduto* continued his rounds, accompanied by another of the *Mirror Paintings* entitled *Ficus* (1965). It appeared — courtesy of Ileana Son-nabend — in *Présences d'Italie* (Presences of Italy), a design trade show held in the spring of 1967 in the Galeries Lafayette department store in Paris, where two *Mirror Paintings* were included in a section curated by Gio Ponti entitled "*Domus*: Formes Italiennes." This being the first time that the *Mirror Paintings* penetrated a true temple of commerce, rather than the display windows of a producer of bathroom appliances, it was also the first time that works by Pistoletto were reproduced in color in *Domus*. As Ponti gloated in his magazine's editorial: "Italian avant-garde art was included in the exhibit, and it always appeared next to serial industrial products. For the first time, works usually exhibited in art galleries were placed in direct contact with the mass public of the department store."[96]

By that time, however, Pistoletto had moved on. The early pho-tographs of the *Mirror Paintings* captured the private space of his "studio/abitazione" on Via Cibrario. In early 1966, as if to counter their recent presence in a department store, Pistoletto exhibited his new work, the *Oggetti in meno* (Minus objects) in a new studio where he had moved to live among his works; the space tripled as home, studio, and gallery space. The ambiguous objects, midway between sculpture and mock furniture, did not let one decide whether they belonged to the simulacra of Pop or the "specific objects" of Mini-malism, to the artisanal or the manufactured. Among them was *Pae-saggio* (Landscape), a crèche with clay and cardboard figures; *Quadro da pranzo* (Lunch painting), a framed table and chairs; and the afore-mentioned *Pozzo*, all dated 1965 or 1966. Like the *Mirror Paintings*, the *Oggetti in meno* were rooted in a strategy of subtraction that, for Pistoletto, had become something closer to a refusal: refusal to be branded as a "maker of mirrors" by producing a series of works that defied his signature style; refusal to move to New York, despite Leo Castelli's invitation to join his stable of artists; and a refusal to surrender to Milan's near obsession with industrial design, even as his Turin-based dealer, Sperone, opened a gallery there.

Pistoletto, however, was responding to a fraught yet fluid situation symptomatic of postwar Italian art. Pistoletto's *Oggetti in meno* have often been described as a prelude to the emergence of Arte Povera, whose spokesman, Germano Celant, would famously claim in 1967, in the new Milanese magazine *Flash Art*, that its "poverty" of materials represented a guerilla strike against conspicuous consumption.[97] Arte Povera in fact imagined spaces where the relation between art and design was more generative and dialectical than the oft-told story of total recoiling from commodification. Sperone, one of Arte Povera's earliest and most important gallerists, dedicated no fewer than three shows, from 1965 to 1967, to Sottsass's furniture and ceramic designs, while the new Milanese Galleria Toselli opened with a show of Ponti's furniture and immediately followed it with one on Arte Povera.[98] *Arte abitabile* (Habitable art), curated by Pistoletto and Piero Gilardi, along with Gianni Piacentino, in the summer of 1966, turned the gallery into a "live-in" environment whose sculptures were conceived as hybrids between Minimalist, Postminimalist, and basic furniture pieces. Similarly, *Inventory 1* and *Inventory 2*, held in Sperone's Deposito d'Arte Presente in 1967 and 1969, looked very much like the countless design showrooms of nearby Milan.[99]

This was exactly the moment Trini chose to join Sottsass and Restany as the third art critic on *Domus*'s masthead. Asked some years later what it was like to work for such a publication, the critic answered: "The city stood for the opposite of what we thought art ought to be. It was dominated by design. The consumerist production of housewares has always been at the core of Milanese aesthetic sensibility. For us, art in Milan had sold its soul to upholstery. None of the designers' lights would ever reach the spiritual intensity of a single neon by Flavin."[100]

But Trini would not find it so easy to escape those light fixtures, and it is in Pistoletto's work that he encountered them first. His initial piece for *Domus* — a review of a series of Pistoletto shows in the spring of 1967 in Milan, Genoa, New York, and Brussels — was illustrated by a photograph of Pistoletto at the Galleria Notizie in Milan, standing next to a couple of gallery visitors and a man with a tripod, all reflected in one of his own *Mirror Paintings*: *Riflettore* (Spotlight). This work isolates a profile image of a stylish wall-mounted lamp, and its enigmatic space is traversed, twice, in the space of the photograph, by Trini's wife, Ciaccia, looking rather like Monica Vitti (Figure 1.21; see also Figure 1.5).[101]

Italian design was simply a given. Going back full circle to the first set of photographs discussed in this chapter, we find Pistoletto, in one of the images in the exhibition leaflet, in the company of the photographer Bressano (Figure 1.22). They are peering into the round mirror at the bottom of *Well*, one of Pistoletto's *Minus Objects*, a cylindrical pit made out of cardboard, on the cover of the Genoa exhibition's leaflet. They appear to be watching an eclipse. The only two objects that share the circular space with the two men are the tip of the Rolleiflex camera that captured the image, which projects over the edge of the cardboard wall (it is on a tripod, and Bressano probably activated a cable release), and, on the ceiling above them, a single neon light.

Magic Realism Redux: Pistoletto and Felice Casorati

In March 1963, just as he was preparing the first show of Pistoletto's *Mirror Paintings*, scheduled to open at the Galleria Galatea in April, the critic and curator Luigi Carluccio penned an obituary for Felice Casorati.[102] A painter most often identified with the 1920s Novecento group, Casorati was arguably the most important artist working in Turin from the interwar years to the 1950s, until Pistoletto appeared on the scene. There is no trace of Casorati in Pistoletto's archive in Biella, and it is hard to imagine Pistoletto wanting to cite the work of a painter seen by some of his contemporaries as an outmoded and even reactionary figure. The Novecento painters had been championed by two preeminent Fascists: Margherita Sarfatti, the éminence

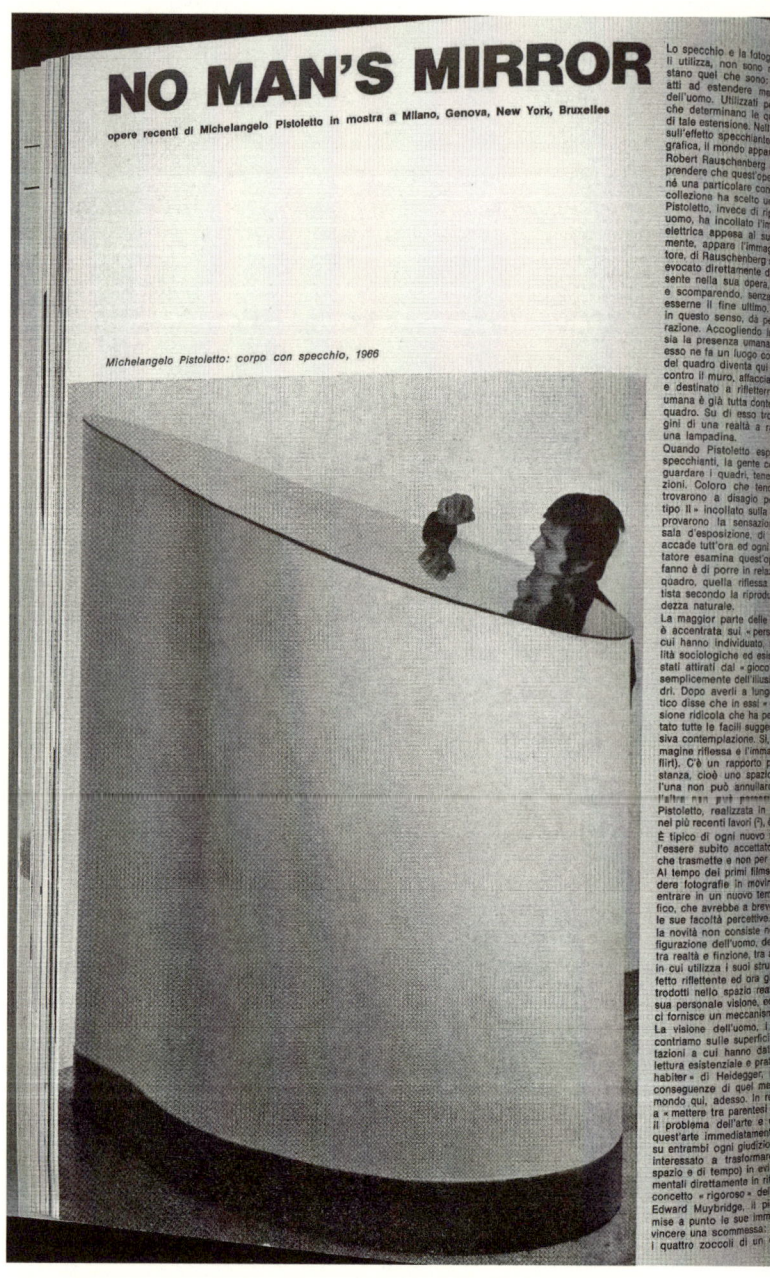

Figure 1.21. Michelangelo Pistoletto, *Riflettore* (Spotlight, 1966). As reproduced in Tommaso Trini, "No Man's Mirror," *Domus*, no. 449, April 1967. Photograph: Manfredi Bellati.

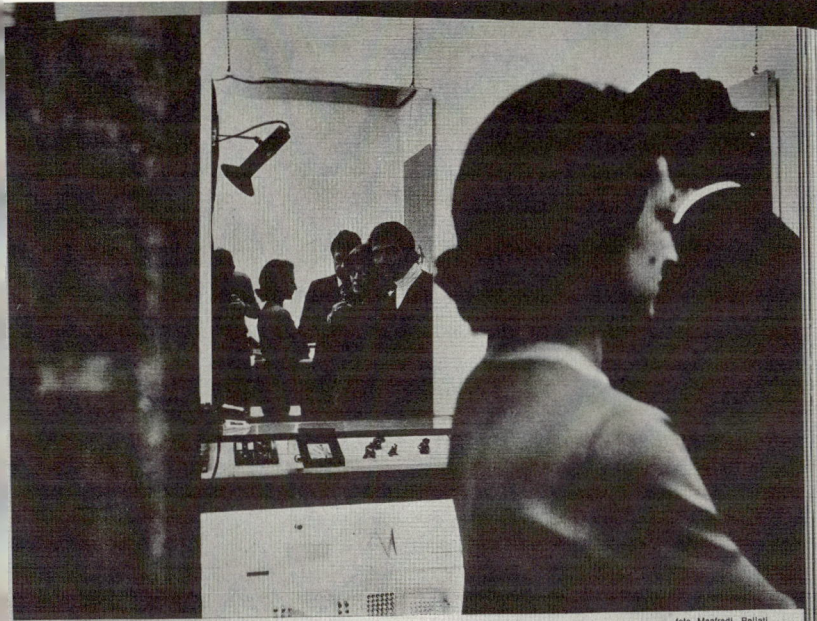

Michelangelo Pistoletto: *veline su acciaio inox, 1966*

foto Manfredi Bellati

tutti, ad un dato momento e simultaneamente, staccati dal terreno. Le due immagini visibili nei quadri di Pistoletto, quella dipinta e quella riflessa, sono anch'esse entrambe svincolate dal terreno in cui opera questo artista. Più volte egli ha detto di voler occupare quel luogo (impercorribile) che sta tra il contorno della silhouette ed il contorno dell'immagine in movimento. Tutta la sua opera sembra essere stata messa a punto per dimostrare che quel luogo, non solo esiste, ma si può abitare. All'inizio, lo ha messo tra parentesi mediante queste due immagini. Per realizzare la silhouette ha utilizzato fotogrammi della vita quotidiana. È ricorso anche al libro di Muybridge, *The Figure in Motion*. Con la fotografia, che ha il potere di isolare l'attimo nel tempo, ha visibilmente introdotto questa dimensione nei suoi lavori: il tempo, vissuto con immediatezza attraverso il movimento dell'immagine riflessa, è formulato mediante il particolare segnale della silhouette fotografica. Qui è un'esperienza mediata, diretta dall'artista. Il nuovo luogo-tempo era individuato. In seguito, Pistoletto ha esplorato le possibilità di agire in esso. Con i suoi lavori in plexiglass, ha eliminato l'effetto riflettente e scomposto i vari elementi, simboli e strumenti che compongono il quadro e che significano l'arte. Da questo sondaggio meccanico è derivato l'attuale ribaltamento del suo processo creativo. Non troviamo più superfici d'acciaio che riflettono la realtà a raso terra, ma oggetti che riflettono il soffitto o il cielo; noi non siamo più riportati fotograficamente sulle superfici o presentati nel fondo specchiante, ma giriamo intorno all'oggetto, nel suo stesso spazio-tempo. Nel riflesso dei quadri c'era ancora la presenza prospettica, come fatto ottico e non come legge: il punto di fuga era costituito da un « uomo di fuga ». I nuovi lavori c'introducono oltre il punto di vista tridimensionale quando constatiamo che ogni lavoro è diverso dall'altro. Lo spazio appare occupato da una pluralità di tempi singoli. La proposta veramente nuova offertaci dall'opera di Pistoletto appare essere questo spazio-tempo unico dapprima rappresentato nei suoi quadri riflettenti, come estensione delle nostre intuizioni,

ed ora occupato dai suoi oggetti in modo da estendere fisicamente le nostre azioni. Nel vuoto dello specchio Pistoletto ha mutato la passività in attività. Il dentro è stato ribaltato in fuori. In questa terra di nessuno nata dallo specchio, in questo *no man's mirror*, muta anche il nostro senso del tempo. Se nei quadri c'era una rappresentazione del tempo, visibile nelle relazioni tra le due immagini, nei nuovi oggetti questa dimensione diventa un'esperienza diretta ed immediata. Là era lineare ed uniforme, qui diventa un'idea globale e ciclica. I nuovi lavori di Pistoletto si possono spiegare solo pezzo per pezzo; ognuno rappresenta un secondo, un presente immobile, che può contenere tutti i secoli passati, e indicare quelli futuri.

Nell'estate '66 Pistoletto dispose nel suo studio una mostra privata dei suoi ultimi lavori. Gli amici che la visitarono furono colpiti dal fatto che quei pezzi non avevano quasi niente in comune ». La novità rispetto ai vecchi quadri appare naturale. Essi reagivano secondo il normale senso del tempo, lineare ed evolutivo. Pistoletto invece stava agendo nel suo studio, una mostra per lui, è un ostacolo al senso della comunità. Dove gli oggetti non hanno interrelazioni, almeno apparenti, gli uomini possono fare a meno di strutture intercomunicative. Pistoletto ha sempre mostrato una spiccata attitudine a condizionare gli altri con le sue opere, dapprima attirandoli nel riflesso, ed ora trasportandoli oltre il riflesso. Ciò naturalmente, vale anche per lui. In un recente « happening sonoro » da lui organizzato al Piper Club di Torino, egli coperse con la propria immagine fotografica i visi dei trenta suonatori che facevano vibrare i suoi strumenti d'acciaio. Apparvero così trenta Pistoletto che unificavano ancor più il tempo-ritmo creato nel locale dalle vibrazioni metalliche. Il solo presupposto che unisce nella loro eterogeneità i nuovi lavori di Pistoletto è quello di liberarsi da ogni meccanismo che non sia quello di realizzare, singolarmente, al di fuori dello schema storico e della concezione evolutiva in arte, i loro stimoli percettivi. « Non costruzioni ma liberazioni », e libe-

razioni di esperienze visive isolate, li ha definiti l'artista. Le nuove opere saranno tante e diverse quanto lo saranno le esperienze di Pistoletto. La sua idea globale e ciclica del tempo è in armonia con il senso acquistato oggi dall'uomo di scienza. Marshall McLuhan scrive: « [Il fisico e lo scienziato moderno] non cercano più di contenere gli eventi nel tempo, ma hanno di ogni cosa l'idea che faccia il suo proprio tempo e il suo proprio spazio. Inoltre, ora che viviamo elettricamente in un mondo istantaneo, lo spazio e il tempo si compenetrano totalmente l'un l'altro in un mondo spazio-temporale ». Alcuni dei più recenti lavori di Pistoletto, come la serie dei « Pozzi » con il fondo costituito da uno specchio che situa i singoli pezzi in altrettanti e diversi singoli mondi istantanei, sembrano illustrare quella compenetrazione e renderci coscienti della sua azione sui nostri sensi.

Tommaso Trini

(¹) L'opera di Pistoletto costituita dai quadri-specchio è attualmente esposta alla Kornblee Gallery di New York.
(²) I nuovi lavori di Pistoletto, mostrati in Italia dalle gallerie La Bertesca di Genova e Il Naviglio di Milano, sono attualmente esposti al Musée des Beaux-Arts di Bruxelles.

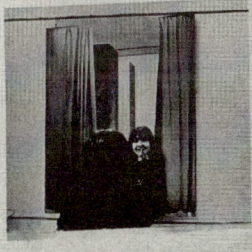

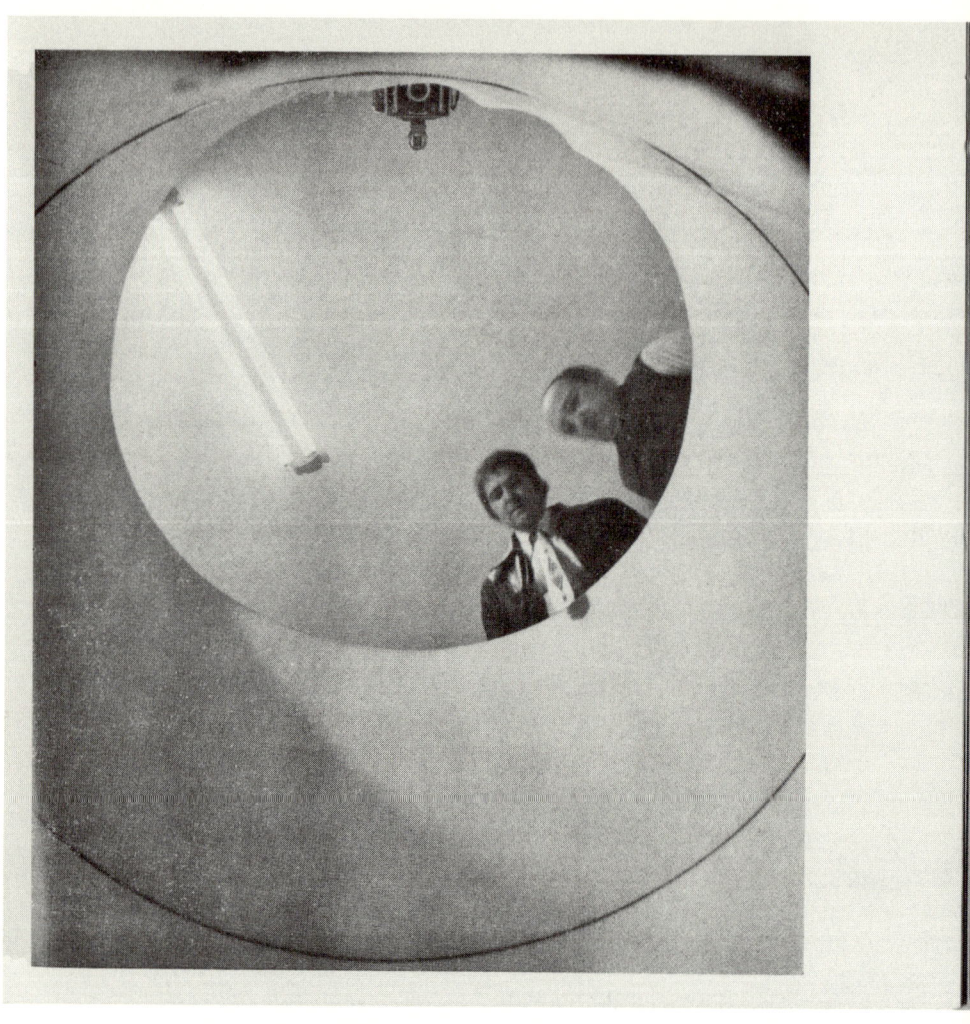

Figure 1.22. Michelangelo Pistoletto, *Pozzo* (Well, 1965). As reproduced in the catalogue of Galleria La Bertesca, Genoa, 1967. Photograph: Paolo Bressano.

grise of Italian art (and Mussolini's paramour), and the critic and writer Massimo Bontempelli. And yet when asked, a few decades later, what it was like to run a gallery of contemporary art in Turin in the 1950s, the art dealer Luciano Pistoi had this to say: "It was a tough call. What we would now call cultural politics were dominated by Casorati. His shadow was longer than one might have thought, and it was cast on artists one might not have expected. If I had to nominate the real heir of Casorati, I would say Michelangelo Pistoletto. I am thinking of his mirrors, the same frozen world as Casorati's."[103]

Carluccio's concomitant investment in the works of both artists from 1958, the year he also discovered Pistoletto, to 1964, when he curated the large Casorati retrospective (269 works) for Turin's Galleria Civica d'Arte Moderna in 1964, is revealing.[104] As Pistoletto was preparing his first show, he must have been aware, simply by perusing the Casorati obituaries in Turin's local dailies, of the similarity between the descriptions of Casorati's paintings and his own mirrors. "The Painter of Metaphysical Solitude," *Stampa Sera* labeled Casorati on March 2, 1963, the day after his death, while others wrote of "Casorati's eloquent silence" and "Casorati the detached one," claiming that over the last decades, the names of Casorati and Turin had become almost synonymous.[105]

There is indeed a parallel between Pistoletto's return to the figure after the dominance of abstraction and his own brushings with *Informale* in the 1950s and Casorati's own return to figuration in the 1920s in the context of the so-called Rappel à l'ordre (Call to order) after the experimentation with abstraction and photomontage before the war. "Magic Realism" is the oxymoron coined by the German critic and art historian Franz Roh in 1925 to describe paintings that endowed realism with an uncanny effect,[106] and I would go as far as to say that Pistoletto's *Mirror Paintings* constituted a Magic Realism redux in the 1960s.

The similarities between Pistoletto's *Mirror Paintings* and Casorati's paintings of the mid-1920s (those that most interested Carluccio) are many: the near life-size figures that appear to be collaged on backdrops; the recurrence of the same individuals in different artworks; the reduced color palette, pointing to the impact of the photographic; the painted or reflected presence of thresholds, stairs, and partitions; an almost suffocating silence. The works of Pistoletto and Casorati share a hypnotic poetry. While only some of Casorati's paintings feature actual mirrors as a motif, what interests me is how all the paintings produced by this artist during the 1920s produce the peculiar sensation that their subjects have been placed in front of mirrors, even when none are depicted. A number of his portraits involve a specular doubling. For instance in his *Ritratto di Hena Rigotti* (Portrait of Hena Rigotti, 1924), a woman wearing a low-cut black dress looms in the darkened space behind the sitter. And in the larger painting *Meriggio* (Noon, 1923), the same nude, or one similar to the point of looking like a double, appears twice, perhaps thrice.

In his essay for *Michelangelo Pistoletto: From One to Many, 1956–1974*, the most recent retrospective of the early *Mirror Paintings* (2010), the curator Carlos Basualdo describes the space created by the paintings as "enchanted."[107] This same effect is produced by Casorati's paintings when hung together in an exhibition. It happened in the retrospective of 1964, which Pistoletto most probably saw, and it had happened forty years earlier, when fourteen paintings by Casorati were exhibited as a solo show in an octagonal room in 1924 in Venice (Figure 1.23).[108] In both cases, the effect is that of a *mise en abyme*. In *Doppio ritratto* (Double portrait, 1924), two figures — as in the *Domus* photographs of the *Mirror Paintings* exhibited at Sonnabend in 1964 — stand in front of what Carluccio described in 1958 as a "quadreria di famiglia," a family portrait gallery (Figure 1.24; Plate 5). That same *quadreria* reappears in the background of *Ritratto di Hena Rigotti*.[109] In Venice, across the room hung the still life *Mannequins*, whose background reveals Casorati's *Maternità* (Maternity, 1923–1924), a painting we know from the catalogue also to have been in that room, reversed as in a mirror. Next to it in the painting, also as if in reflection, is Casorati's only known self-portrait. The most striking painting in Casorati's room at the Biennale, next to the portraits of his parents, was *Ritratto di*

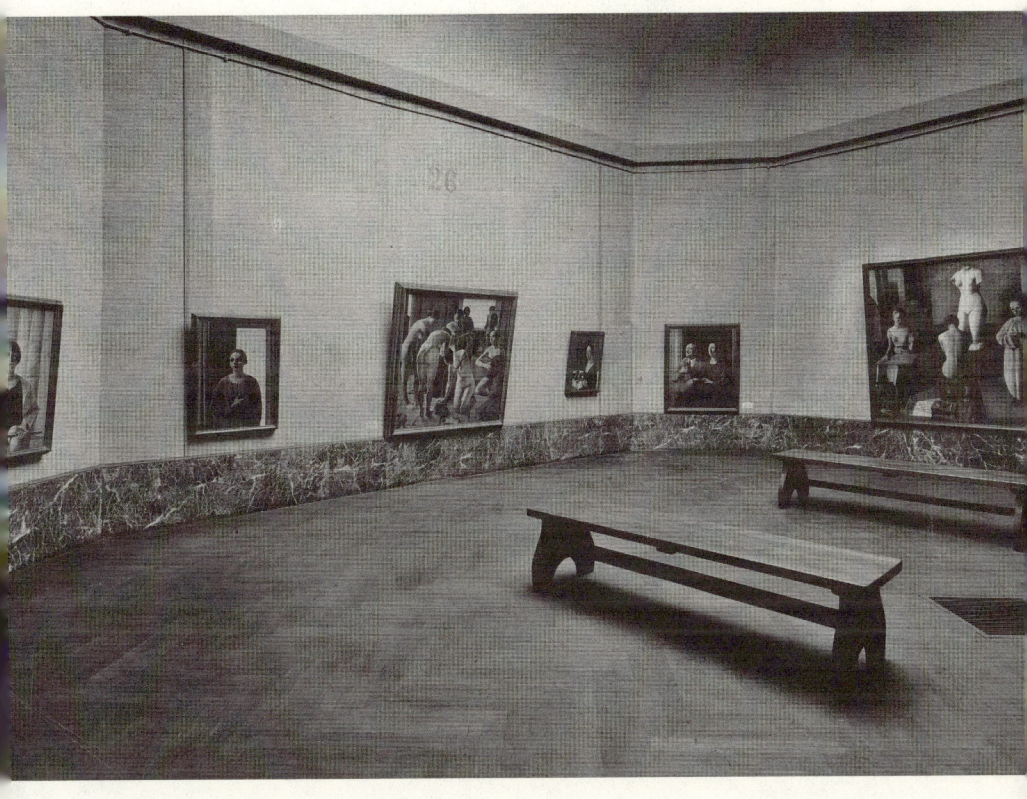

Figure 1.23. Felice Casorati, Room 26, Fourteenth Venice Biennale, 1924. Photograph: Courtesy of ASAC, Venice.

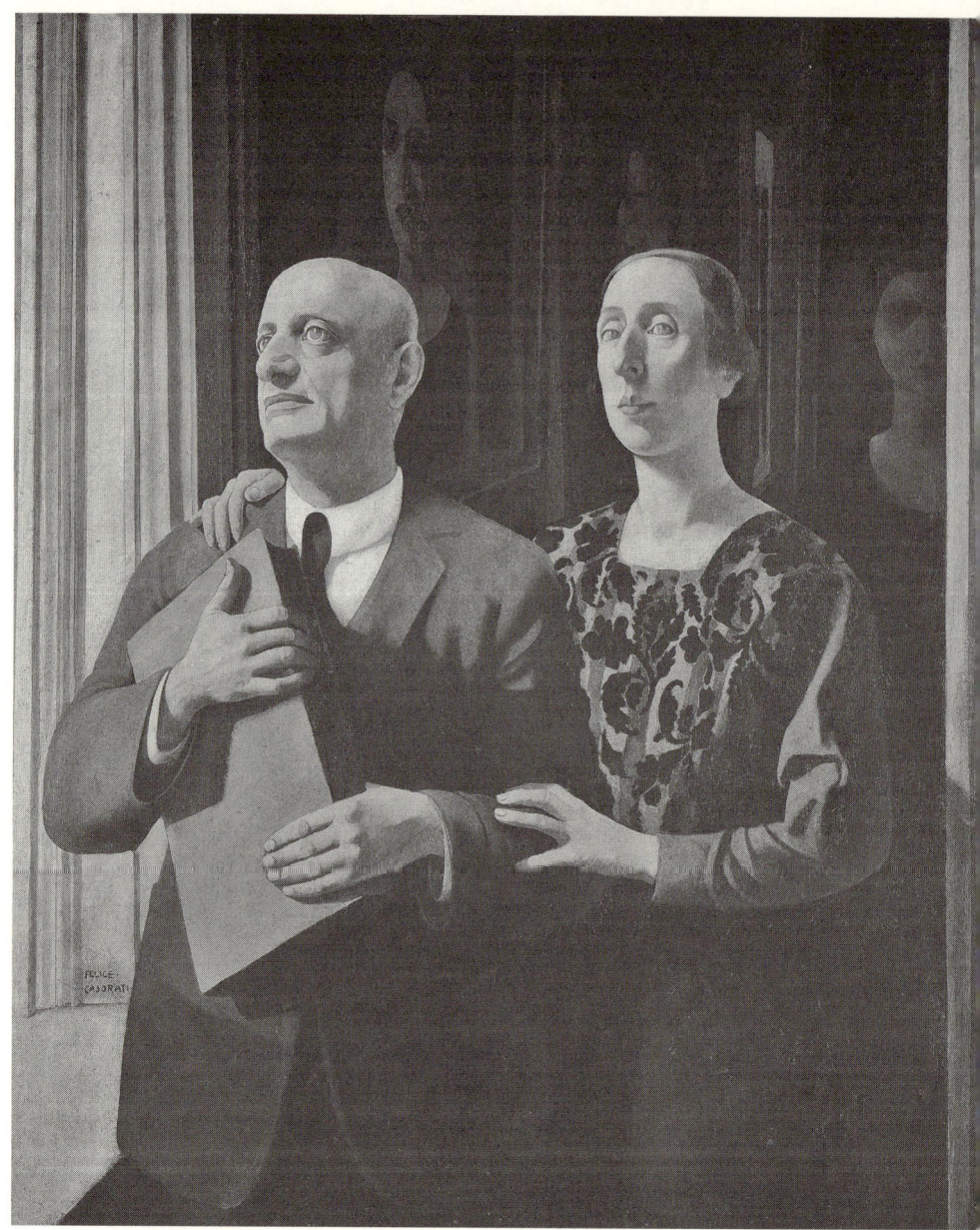

Figure 1.24. Felice Casorati, *Doppio ritratto* (Double portrait, ca. 1924). Tempera on plywood, 120 × 100 cm. Private collection.

Renato Gualino (Portrait of Renato Gualino, 1924) (Figure 1.25), a work that must have held a special place for Carluccio, since it was included in every one of the Casorati shows that he curated in the 1950s and 1960s.[110] As befits the scion of Riccardo Gualino — Turin's foremost financier, art patron, and collector, hailed as an heir to the munificent patrons of the Renaissance — Renato is depicted in the manner of Domenico Ghirlandaio's portraits of the young sons of Lorenzo de' Medici. His father, known as "the self-made man from Biella," Pistoletto's hometown, made his fortune in the founding of SNIA Viscosa, at the time the largest artificial silk factory in Europe. Donning a cape and a pageboy haircut, Renato sits upright in front of a sharply creased pink backdrop that parts like a theater curtain. He is staring, almost transfixed, at the viewer. "The crimson stick resting on his knees, on which rest in turn the boy's delicately painted hands, is both a material object and something allusive," wrote Carluccio the first time he exhibited the painting.[111] In a self-reflexive act, Renato is presented to us as a surrogate for the artist-magician. What he is performing in the 1920s, a decade that witnessed the emergence of photography as a major and ineluctable protagonist, is painting as a magic act.

It was after visiting the 1924 Venice Biennale that Franz Roh set out to write *Nach-Expressionismus: Magischer Realismus; Probleme der neuesten europäischen Malerei* (Postexpressionism: Magical Realism; Problems in the newest European painting) and that Gustav Hartlaub decided to organize his 1925 exhibition *Neue Sachlichkeit: Deutsche Malerei seit dem Expressionismus* (New Objectivity: German painting after Expressionism) at the Kunsthalle in Mannheim.[112] From his 1925 exhibition until Hartlaub's *Zauber des Spiegels: Geschichte und Bedeutung des Spiegels in der Kunst* (Magic of the mirror: History and meaning of the mirror in art), published in 1951, the mirror was central to Magic Realism: "Properly installed or combined with other mirrors, it 'sees' more, it extends our vision, and thus becomes a spyglass or a device that lets us see ourselves as others see us." In magic, "practical uses of the mirror are turned into attributes and powers of the instrument itself. The mirror becomes animated and is regarded as a being

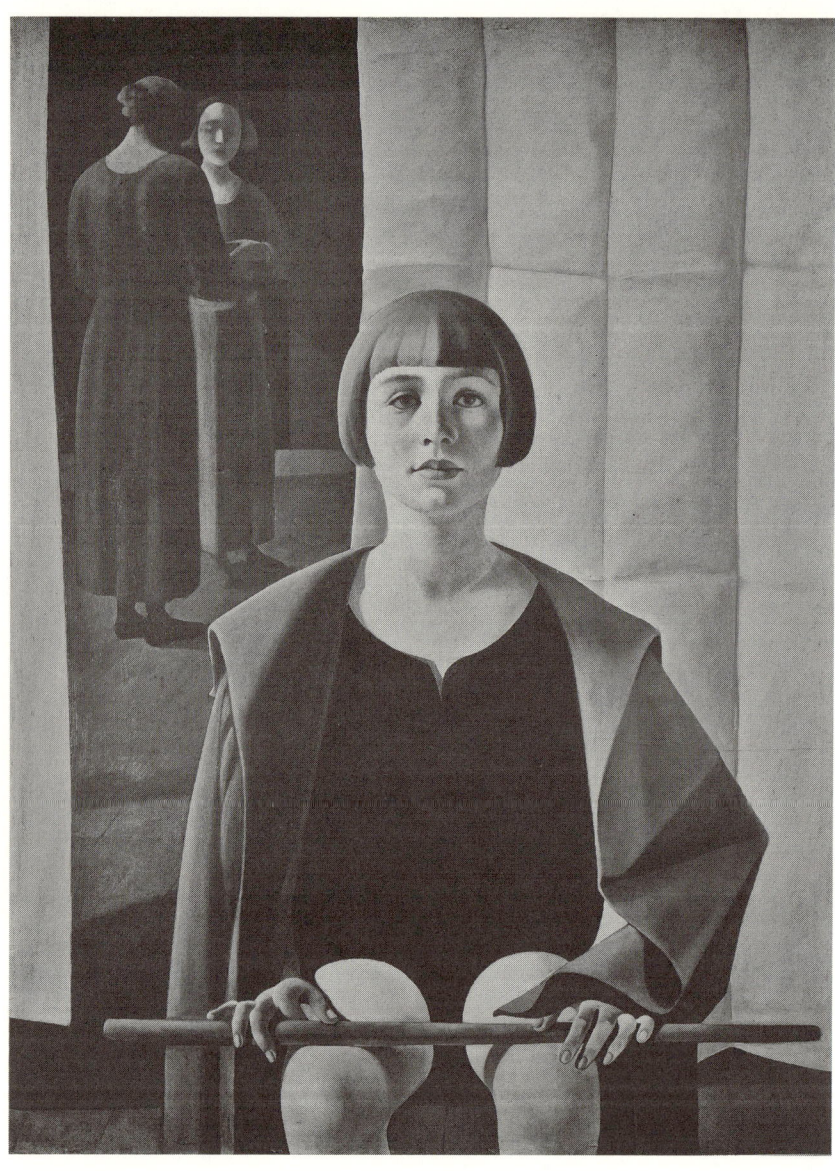

Figure 1.25. Felice Casorati, *Ritratto di Renato Gualino* (Portrait of Renato Gualino, 1924). Oil on plywood, 97 × 74.5 cm, Istituto Matteucci, Viareggio, Italy. Photograph: Courtesy Istituto Matteucci.

endowed with the capacity to know and to act."[113] In the last chapter of his book, Hartlaub explores the representation of mirrors or mirroring surfaces in occult sciences of divination such as catoptromancy (divination using a mirror) and crystal gazing and the mirror as the attribute of seers, fortune-tellers, soothsayers, and alchemists. Similarly, in the essay that accompanied the first exhibition of Pistoletto's *Mirror Paintings* at the Galleria Galatea in 1963, Carluccio came close to describing them as activations of the beyond. He writes:

> When I say that Pistoletto's work is disconcerting, I am mostly thinking about the striking impact of the material he uses: stainless steel polished until it is a mirror.... One can meet and match with his characters, and one has the sensation of being at the center of a world that overturns right in front of us what is in fact right behind us, tipping us over, planting eyes in the backs of our heads.... Deceived by the trickery of the mirror, we try to speak to Pistoletto's characters. They don't answer, they don't listen to us. The game remains, precisely, a game of mirrors, which takes place on the margins, feeding upon itself and dissolving in its own infinite void.... Fragility, solitude, emptiness, existence, in the sense of an actual "presence," more than an existential agitation—a reason for wonderment, rather than anguish.[114]

Pistoletto's *Mirror Paintings* came out of a series of self-portraits dated from 1960 to 1961, painted on monochrome grounds of black, silver, and gold, in which the artist confronts us, as does Renato, with the stare of a hypnotist (Figure 1.26). In this series, Pistoletto applied a thick layer of varnish, a finish rarely used by modern painters, except, notably, by the Novecentisti and their European peers in the 1920s, who were competing with or in fact mimicking photography. The shift in medium took place when Pistoletto realized that he could capitalize on the mirror effect produced by varnish by using reflective panes of steel. As Valentina Anker and Lucien Dällenbach noted in their article about *mise en abyme* in *Art International*, most artists in the 1960s, rather than manually and painstakingly replicating an image in paint, opted for the mirrored surface as a shortcut.[115]

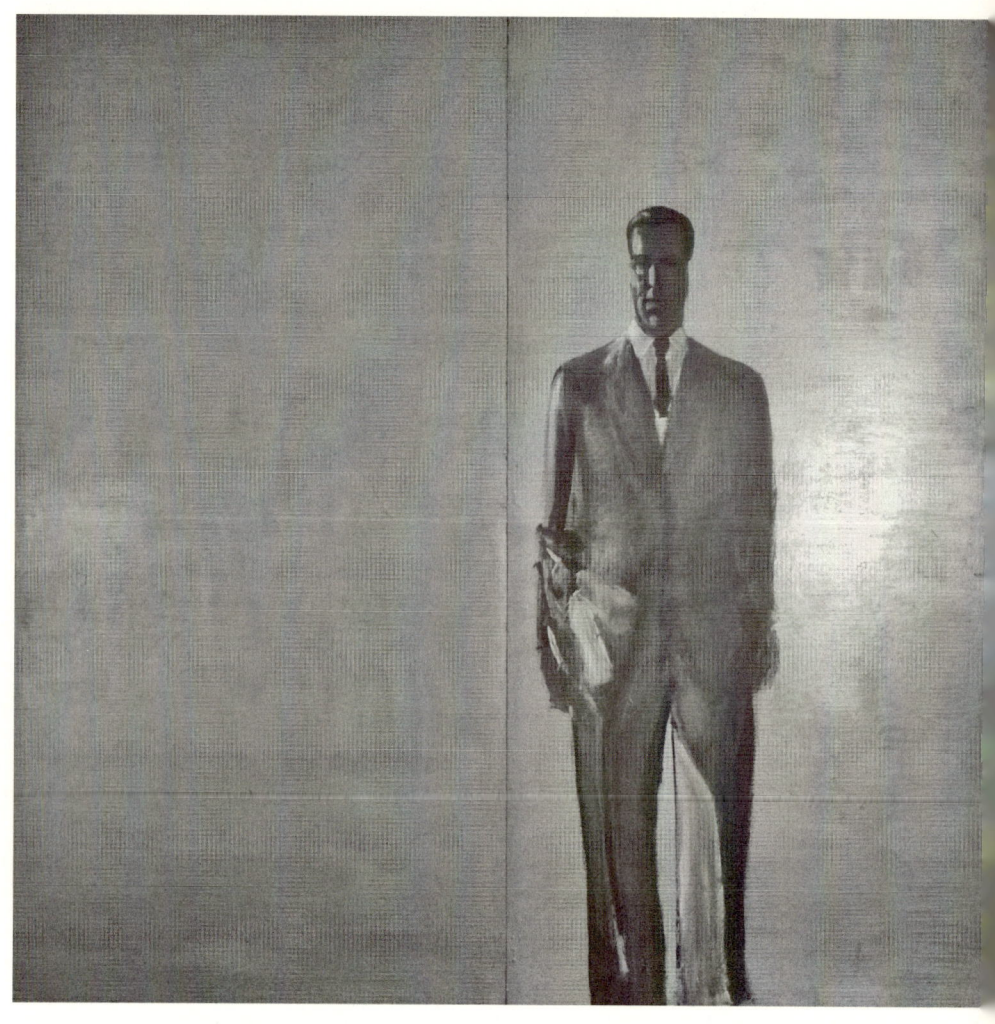

Figure 1.26. Michelangelo Pistoletto, *Autoritratto argento* (Silver self-portrait, 1960). Oil, acrylic, and silver on wood, 200 × 200 cm. Collection of the artist.

It is this shortcut that allowed Pistoletto to forsake his self-depiction as artist-magician. In a typical 1960s move, the magic of the *Mirror Paintings* was now ready-made. "A gimmick," wrote a sarcastic reviewer for the *Minneapolis Star* at the time of Pistoletto's show at the Walker Art Center in 1966, titling his piece "Mirror, Mirror."[116] "You can be part of the painting, several paintings, without sitting for your portrait. How? Merely by attending the Michelangelo Pistoletto opening Monday at the Walker Art Center," quipped the reviewer of the *Minneapolis Tribune*, titling his review "Now You Can Put Yourself . . . in the Picture." Printed on facing pages, the two photographs of the review read like a magic act (Figure 1.27).[117]

Pistoletto and Casorati both depict frozen figures belonging to a Turinese upper class impervious to the massive proletarianization of their city. In his 1963 obituary of Casorati, however, Carluccio maintained that this imperviousness was only apparent, for while the class tensions in the metropolis were was repressed, the class anxiety was there. This was one reason why Casorati was ready, in the critic's view, for reconsideration.[118] As with Pistoletto's *Alpino*, it is — between the lines — the secretive history of Turin's anti-Fascist resistance that runs like a red thread through the pairing of Pistoletto with Casorati.

In an interview with the art historian and critic Mirella Bandini published in a 1973 issue of *NAC* (*Notiziario Arte Contemporanea*) devoted to Turin in the 1960s, sociologist Luciano Gallino noted that while the political impact of famous Turinese such as the Marxist philosopher Antonio Gramsci and the journalist Piero Gobetti registered on the outside, it was largely ignored by the Turinese themselves. Gramsci's reflection on the working class in the particular case of advanced industrialization in Italy represented by Turin was little known in his hometown during his lifetime and in the years after was known only to a small group of intellectuals. This was due, in Gallino's view, to Turin's historical isolation from other Italian cities and international events, a situation resulting in part from its being a one-factory town.[119] In postwar Turin, where Pistoletto grew up, it was Gobetti, the author

Now You
Can Put
Yourself...

YOU CAN BE part of a painting—several paintings—without sitting for your portrait. How? Merely by attending the Michelangelo Pistoletto show opening Monday at Walker Art Center. The exhibition, the first of Pistoletto works in the United States, continues through May 8.

Pistoletto is a young Italian artist who creates startling illusion by painting life-size human figures and objects on mirrored surfaces. He applies photographic collage images on polished, unoxidized steel which reflects the figures of onlookers as well as the room in which the painting is placed. Thus the viewers and their surroundings in effect become part of the painting's composition, as shown on these pages and on the cover. This startling result has been compared with the experience of "happenings" in which the spectator is an active participant.

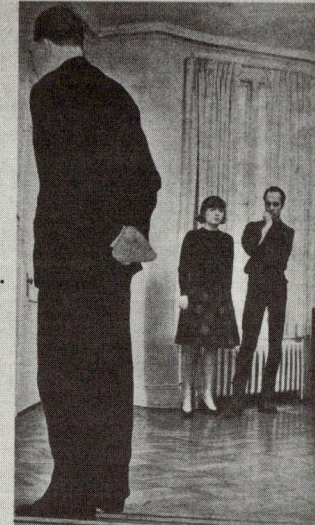

Viewers contemplate "Standing Man in Black."

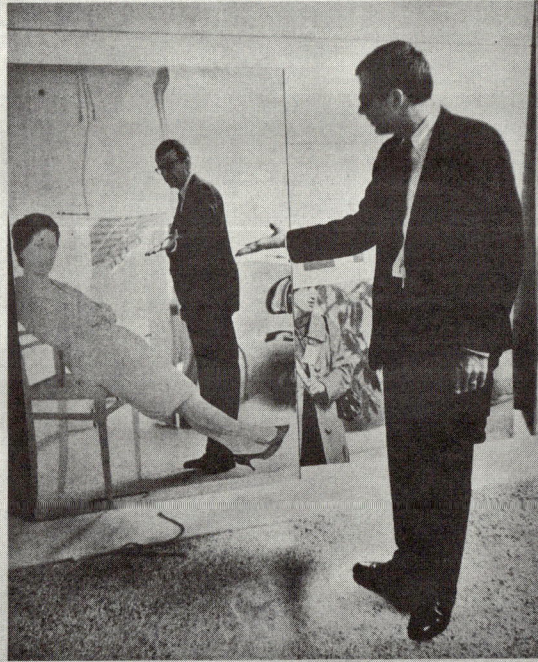

"Seated Woman" gives viewer a chance to "ham it up" as part of picture.

...in the Picture

Some 30 works by Pistoletto have been lent from American and European collections for the one-man show. It was organized by Martin Friedman, Walker's director.

Pistoletto's figures appear either in relaxed, contemplative attitudes or are shown as part of processions frozen in motion. Figures and objects are based on actual photographs and are mildly distorted "actual" color produced with crayon and other means. Such selective use of the photographic process, frequently used in American pop art, implies a "cool," detached manner of direct presentation—with immediately recognizable images whose presence in the painting remains enigmatic and rather mysterious.

Composition is a critical element in Pistoletto's work. His figures are carefully located on the picture surface and great attention is given to their contour. The background of the composition is deliberately left incomplete so that the room in which the picture is shown becomes the background. This often includes the viewers.

Pistoletto was born in Biella, Italy, in 1933. Until 1957 he worked with his father as a restorer of paintings. He now lives and works in Turin, Italy.

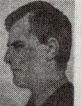

Pistoletto, self-portrait

Figure 1.27. Review of *Michelangelo Pistoletto: A Reflected World*, *Minneapolis Tribune*, April 3, 1966.

of the first Casorati monograph in 1923, who became the model for a younger generation of Turinese intellectuals such as Norberto Bobbio, not the likes of Gramsci.[120] And in 1976, it was Carluccio who was asked to write the first essay about the relation between Gobetti and Casorati.[121]

Closing the Temporal Gap

In 1965, for his *Comizzi* (Demonstrations) series, Pistoletto for the first time made cutouts from photographs taken outdoors. As he explained: "Through Rinaldi, I started to use . . . images from the social world from outside the family and friends. He was a kind of an eye that went on the street."[122] That year, workers from Fiat and other large factories all over Italy were protesting the lowering of wages that signaled a shrinking economy, with the suspension of one hundred thousand metalworkers and a salary block signaling the end of the economic boom. In August 1964, there had been large processions at the funeral of Palmiro Togliatti, the leader of the Italian Communist Party. Exhibited in a room together at the Walker Art Center in 1966, it was as if the figures in *No all' aumento del Tram* (No to the raising of the tram fare), *Persone che guardano* (People looking), *Due persone che passano* (Two people passing by), and *Bandiera rossa (comizio 1)* (Red flag [demonstration 1]), in unison with the museum viewers, were demonstrating on Turin's Piazza del Statuto, knocking, militantly, at the invisible glass door of the earlier *Mirror Paintings* (Figure 1.28). Pistoletto's *Mirror Paintings* were no longer shatterproof.

And yet the *Comizzi* series still retains a bit of the mystery of Pistoletto's previous *Mirror Paintings* in that the source images of the cutouts are difficult to date. Although the figures were presumably photographed by Rinaldi in the 1960s, the marchers' worn, baggy, ill-fitting jackets and coats and the men's hairdos and mustaches recall images of crowds in the streets of Turin on the days following the Armistice of September 1943—in which case, the pensive boy in shorts and knee-highs in *Ragazzo* (Boy) (Figure 1.28, center) could

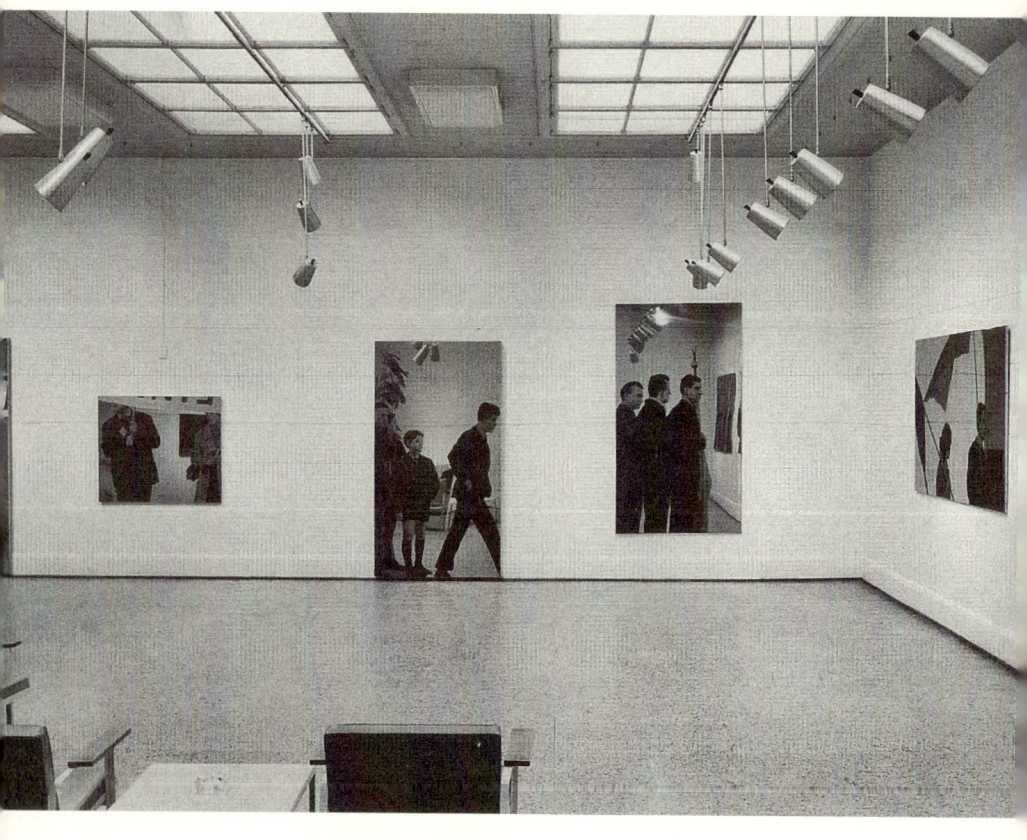

Figure 1.28. *Michelangelo Pistoletto: A Reflected World*, Walker Art Gallery, 1966. Photograph: Courtesy of the Walker Art Center, Minneapolis.

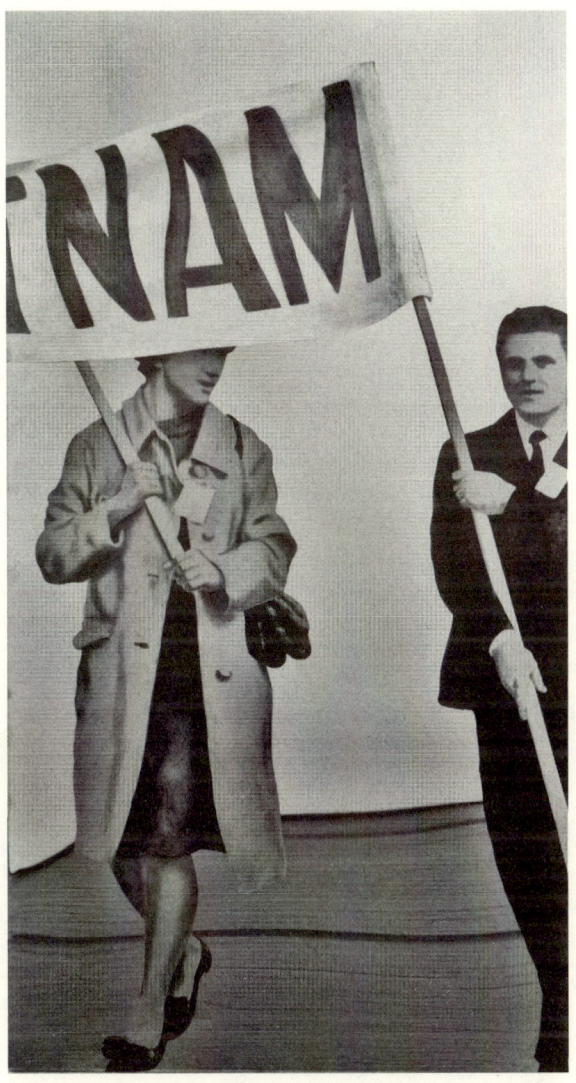

Figure 1.29. Michelangelo Pistoletto, *Vietnam*, 1965. Graphite and oil on paper mounted on stainless steel, 220 × 120 cm. The Menil Collection, Houston.

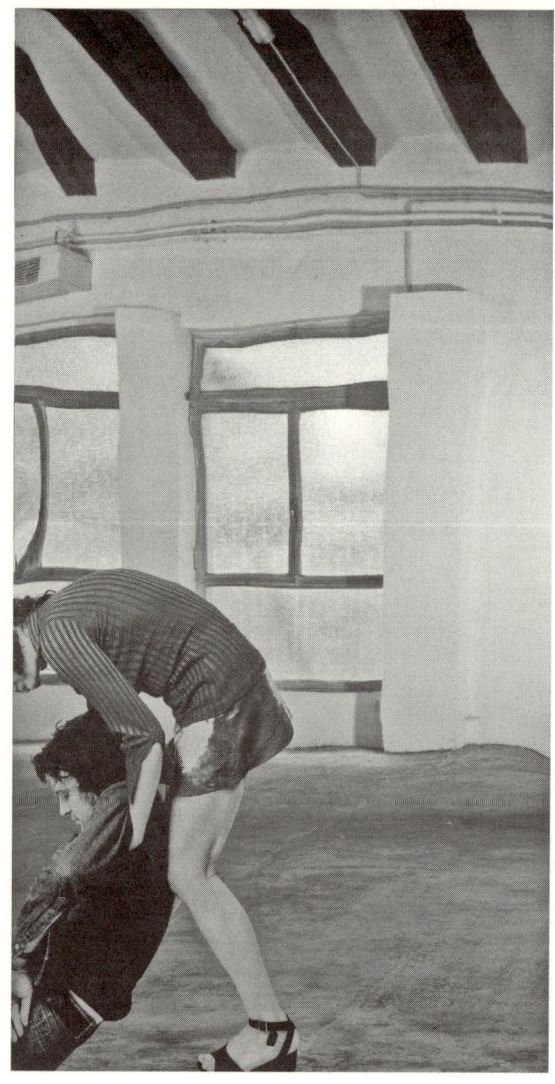

Figure 1.30. Michelangelo Pistoletto, *Deposizione* (Deposition, 1973). Silk screen on polished stainless steel, 230 × 120 cm. Collection of the artist. Photograph: Courtesy of the Cittadellarte–Fondazione Pistoletto, Biella, Italy.

be a ten-year-old Pistoletto. This temporal oscillation was pushed aside in *Vietnam*, also of 1965, in which a woman, wearing a pink 1960s raincoat and a man in jacket and tie demonstrate holding a banner featuring the half word "nam" that gave the work its title (Figure 1.29).[123] Combining it textually with *No all' aumento del tram*, Pistoletto extricates the work from its local context and transforms it into one about current global events — which is no doubt why among the *Mirror Paintings*, *Vietnam* is the one most often reproduced. Student mobilization by those whom the journal *Rinascita* called "la generazione del Vietnam" began in earnest in 1966.[124] Meanwhile, the peak of labor agitation came, as it often did in Italian labor history, with the demonstrations of the workers in the Fiat factories of Turin in the summer of 1969.

The narrowing of the temporal gap in Pistoletto works and the exiting of his figures from their claustrophobic interiors into the street brings us to the next chapter, one in which art became almost impossible to distinguish from countless "movimenti di piazza" that shook every Italian city in the wake of 1968. By 1973, when Pistoletto made *Deposizione* (Deposition) (Figure 1.30), a painting of another demonstration, in which a young man is dragged off the street by his female companion, Italy had entered its *anni di piombo* (years of lead). Here, as in all the others at this point in Pistoletto's career, the clothing has become unmistakably contemporary: the young man's tightly fitting jeans, the young woman's ribbed sweater, leather miniskirt, and wedge sandals, even the rusty red of the sweater and the Bordeaux-colored skirt are vintage 1970s. What such details betray is Pistoletto's desire from then on to connect directly with the viewer in time and space. The result runs close to turning the mirror into a photojournalist's camera and the artwork into a chronicling of current events. This closure of the temporal gap in the outfits, the gestures, and the context of the cutout figures in Pistoletto's *Mirror Paintings* as the decade wore on are symptomatic of the pressure exerted by the urgent presentness of 1968. Hence, this is also the moment when this book moves on from Pistoletto's work.

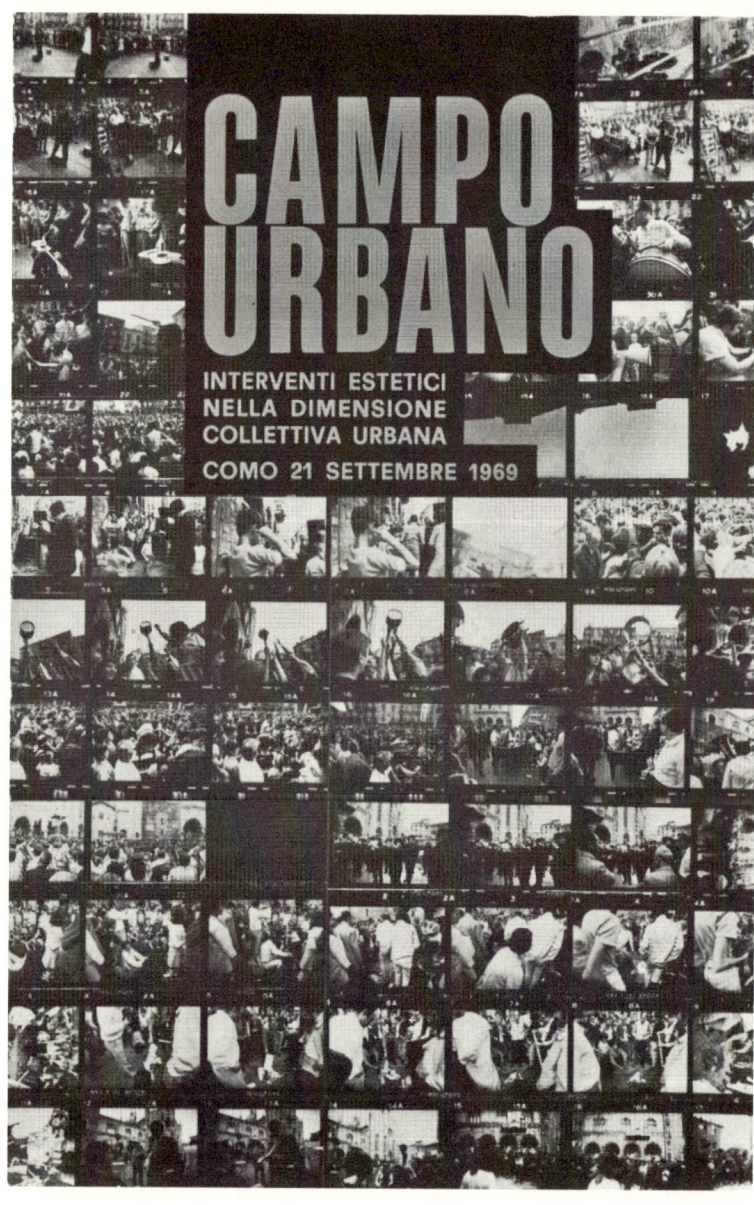

Figure 2.1. *Campo urbano: Interventi estetici nella dimensione collettiva urbana* (Urban field: Aesthetic interventions in the collective urban dimension), 1969, cover.

CHAPTER TWO

Campo urbano:

A Late Summer Festival

Como: The City as Frame

"Ultimately what Bruno Munari has been continuously proposing is a kind of *dérèglement des procédés*," wrote Enrico Crispolti in November 1969 in his cameo piece, "Il caso Munari," published in *NAC*.[1] Munari had kept to this modus operandi when he designed the splendid photo book *Campo urbano: Interventi estetici nella dimensione collettiva urbana* (Urban field: Aesthetic interventions in the collective urban dimension) which took place in Como on September 21, 1969 (Figure 2.1).[2] The *Campo urbano* "interventions" — actions by forty artists, coordinated by the historian of art and architecture Luciano Caramel and publicized through the distribution of leaflets — were documented by the photographer Ugo Mulas.

In the book, Mulas's full-page photographs alternate between contact sheets, bird's-eye views, and panoramic shots, with many of the images rotated vertically to create a jolting collage effect and with some actions spilling across multiple pages. The shifts in spatial and temporal registers capture the way the photographer, the artists, and the public moved across the city to partake in the events, which often took place simultaneously in different locations. Some of the images taken from Mulas's black-and-white negatives were printed as if bathed in a solution of metallic cerulean blue, making them reflective and difficult to read, simulating an act of erasure.

According to Caramel, the use of the colored *viraggi* (veering) was Munari's idea, which the book designer executed by putting two different inks in the offset print: "This was a gesture against art photography, very much in the spirit of *Campo urbano*, something Munari understood better than anyone else," Caramel said.[3] The previous year, Munari had similarly tampered with a Xerox machine, using red ink to produce a series of "Xerografie" for a small show at the appropriately named Serendipity 54 gallery in Rome.[4] In the case of *Campo urbano*, according to Camillo Vittani, the book was printed in offset with an Itek Platemaster, a low-cost system. This machine printed simultaneously in two colors, two pages at a time, switching from black and white to blue and white.[5] As the photography historian and curator Clément Chéroux argued in *Fautographie*, a book dedicated to the conceit of failure in the history of photography, to err means to make a mistake, but also to wander, to stray.[6] By flashing back to moments in nineteenth-century amateur photography, as when the fixer failed to stabilize the image and other such accidents, Munari was capitalizing on serendipity, but also on intermedial effects.

Some of Mulas's photographs of *Campo urbano* were initially published in small format (5.5 × 5.5 cm) in a compendium of reviews of the event put together by Caramel as a supplement for Como's local *Quadrante Lariano*, a journal we will return to many times in this chapter.[7] A larger selection of the photographs was concomitantly shown at Galleria La Colonna, a space in Como owned by Enrica Vittani; according to Caramel, the intention of the exhibition was to show as many of the photographs as possible in the order in which they were shot.[8] "There was no money," Caramel says, "so the idea for a photo book came a bit later." For the book's design, Caramel turned to his friend Bruno Munari because he had been a participating artist in the *Campo urbano* event itself and, as Caramel put it, "was at home in Como."[9] The photo book was produced pro bono in 1970 by Camillo Vittani, a local printer (and the brother of gallery owner Enrica Vittani), and Cesare Nani, a local publisher.[10]

Munari arranged Mulas's photographs into sequences of about four or five images per "action," creating a photo book of 146 pages. In order not to interrupt the visual flow of the images, Munari's design embeds the artists' written statements about their actions on the first pages of these photographic sequences. However, the year-long lapse between the original happenings and Munari's selection and arrangement of the images documenting them would prove significant to his own understanding of *Campo urbano* itself as an event.

As Caramel said, "It was essential" to the spirit of *Campo urbano* "that everything be ephemeral, without any sculptures around the city."[11] To use artist/critic Piero Gilardi's term, it was a *mostra aperta* (open-ended exhibit). It illustrates the reorientation of contemporary art practice toward the dematerialization of the art object, as well as trespassing into its surroundings.[12] The closest precedent was *Une journée dans la rue* (A day in the street), orchestrated by the recently disbanded French collective Groupe de Recherche d'Art Visuel (GRAV) in 1966. On April 19 of that year, the members of GRAV solicited audience participation in various parts of Paris by handing out small gifts at the entrance of the Metro at Châtelet, assembling and disassembling kinetic structures on the Champs-Élysées for the public to manipulate, building a giant kaleidoscope in the Tuileries Gardens, and inviting people to walk on movable paving slabs on Boulevard du Montparnasse and to play with balloons on the Boulevard Saint-Germain. They ended the day with a promenade from the Seine to the Luxembourg Gardens with handheld flashing electric lights. There was no accompanying publication.[13]

Closer to home were the sorties in Italian provincial towns discussed in my Introduction. Among the first and one of the more well-known was *Con/temp/l'azione*, organized in Turin by the art critic Daniela Palazzoli on December 4, 1967.[14] Connecting the city's three most progressive art galleries — Christian Stein, Sperone, and

Il Punto — she transformed the opening night into a street festival. That evening, Michelangelo Pistoletto sent one of his *Oggetti in meno* (Minus objects), a large ball made of newspaper, rolling out of the gallery and through his hometown's famed arcades.[15] A few months later, he took to the streets of small provincial towns to perform impromptu theatrical pieces with fanciful props and neomedieval clothes, along with a troupe of artists he called Lo Zoo.

Then came *Arte povera + Azioni povere* (Poor art + Poor actions) in Amalfi, the only international event among these — three days of actions, performances, and debates in early October 1968.[16] More inclusive, with up to sixty-eight artists participating and without any of the better-known international artists who participated in *Arte povera + Azioni povere*, was *Nuovi materiali nuove tecniche* (New materials new techniques) in Caorle and *Al di là della pittura* (Beyond painting) in San Benedetto del Tronto. As with *Campo urbano*, many of their artists belonged to Arte Programmata (that is, kinetic art). As with *Arte povera + Azioni povere*, on both occasions, the actions and performances spilled from emptied interiors — in this case, a vacated high school — into the streets all the way down to the waterfront: in Caorle to a pier and in San Benedetto del Tronto down to partially abandoned boatyards.[17] Both sought to communicate with a wider public. In San Benedetto del Tronto, Ugo Nespolo used a paint roller to draw a huge sun on a vacant lot near the boatyards. Mario Nanni, an artist from Bologna, created a two-part work. In the school, he filled his allotted space from floor to ceiling with plated steel rings of different diameters, but in *Progetto per una esplorazione ed automis-urazione psicologica* (Project for a psychological exploration and self-measurement), he took youngsters to the beach to aim the rings at cylindrical poles. The Roman artist Eliseo Mattiacci sent his *Zat-teronmarante*, a wooden raft covered in black industrial paint, into the water. The maritime locations gave these summer events an amusing quality, with Nanni's beach game the most popular with the local crowd and most often illustrated in the local press. "A marvelous formula," proclaimed the *Cronaca di Fermo e San Benedetto*.[18]

Ugo Mulas: One Camera, One Day

The year 1968 lived up to its reputation for dissent and contention in the art world as in the political one. The fourteenth Milan Triennale experienced violence on May 30, when its displays were trashed by art, design, and architecture students, forcing the Triennale to close its doors just hours after opening. As if in the hope of forestalling an impending disaster, three of its organizers — the architect Giancarlo de Carlo, the filmmaker Marco Bellocchio, and the artist Bruno Caruso — decided to mount, in extremis, an impromptu spectacle: an anticonsumerist diorama in which furniture, lamps, and TV sets were stacked in huge heaps in front of photomurals depicting student demonstrations in the streets of Paris, with mounds of cobblestones, the symbol of the barricade, in the foreground. As with Campo urbano a year later, real and mock vandalism, revolution and art installation, were wrapped together.[19]

The thirty-fourth Venice Biennale a few weeks later also turned into a battlefield. Jolted by the havoc of the students' and artists' occupation of the Triennale, the police overreacted in Venice, charging at demonstrators. Many of the city's galleries, shocked by the situation, showed their solidarity with the demonstrators by closing on June 22, the day of the Biennale's official opening (also perhaps in order to avoid having their gallery windows smashed). In the Giardini, a handful of organizers sided with the rioters, boycotting the event by temporarily shutting down some of the Biennale's national pavilions. As the critic Lea Vergine wrote, "In Venice, there were more policemen than artworks."[20] Referring to the color of police and/or military uniforms, Germano Celant titled his review "A Gray-Green Biennale."[21]

In the end, however, the Venice Biennale ran its course until October 20. Considering the Biennale's woes, Caramel may have been encouraged by Giancarlo Politi's editorial in his new journal Flash Art. His long tirade is worth quoting not so much for its literary quality as to give a sense of the urgent presentism that went hand in hand with the activism of 1968 in art-critical writing everywhere. As such, its title, "Morte a Venezia," referring to the famous 1912 novella by Thomas Mann, functions as a catchphrase:

> The Biennale is dead. I am not referring to the demonstrations, the presence of the police, the clashes. These things, painful and sad as they are, have nothing to do with the Biennale. I am not saying that the Biennale is dead because the mayor of Venice, in order to save it, has even tried to inaugurate it without works, without artists, and without critics — with only an undersecretary, a ribbon, and a storm of protesting kids. The Biennale is dead because it has become culturally useless, because it is a gigantic ramshackle event for indolent tourists with obligatory itineraries intended to bring money to the gondoliers and the hoteliers. . . . And after the Biennale? Well, after the Biennale, why not an event [*una rassegna*], not necessarily in Venice, but in Bassano del Grappa, or in Cuneo, or in Trevi in Umbria. A selective event, with few participating nations, or no nations at all, only artists. No official ambassadors, no politicians, ideally no government deputies. The event should encompass music, poetry, cinema, and theater. Nothing elaborate is needed. It is only a matter of resolve and clear ideas. But before this, one needs to unyoke culture from tourist interests and political clientele. Which, at least in Italy, is asking for the impossible.[22]

It was upon returning from the 1968 Venice Biennale that Caramel and his friends, the painter Giuliano Collina and the sculptor Francesco Somaini — as though heeding the appeal in Politi's article — began to think about assembling artists for a series of interventions in their hometown.[23]

Caramel's choice of the phrase *campo urbano* rather than *spazio urbano* came from *Teoria del campo: Corso di educazione alla visione* (Field theory: An educational course on vision), a book based on a class taught by the Milanese architect Attilio Marcolli at a technical school in the nearby town of Cantù. There is no doubt that the book appealed to Caramel because its diagrams seemed readily transposable from the page to the ongoing *movimenti di piazza*, the dozens of student and worker demonstrations that were taking place in nearly every city in Italy in the late 1960s. These began in Trento in early 1966, reached the University of Pisa in February 1967, and the University of Milan — called La Cattolica, where Caramel taught — in November 1967, followed by the universities of Naples, Pavia, Cagliari, Salerno, Genoa, and Rome between December 1967 and January 1968. In 1968, the movement reached all the other major university towns across Italy, from Padua, Turin, and Venice in the north, to Florence, all the way down to Palermo. Indeed, while no single movement equaled the intensity and press coverage of the French May 1968, historians Paul Ginsborg and Guido Crainz have recognized the Italian protest movement as the most profound and longest lasting in Europe. Between 1965 and 1968, the number of university students almost doubled in Italy, and the decade from 1959 to 1969 saw a doubling of its school population.[24] The early months of 1969 saw a rash of *assemblee* (meetings) taking place in high schools.[25] In the spring of 1969, student agitation had finally reached even the politically conservative city of Como, sheltered until then by the fact that it had no university. Photos of the demonstrations in Como, published in a supplement to the *Quadrante Lariano*, used the same format as Mulas's photos of *Campo urbano*, which appeared in the same journal several months later.[26]

It is no doubt important in this context that Marcolli's book was intended as a teaching tool in a college class. It was illustrated with myriad diagrams to demonstrate the progression of four types of vision — geometric, gestalt, topological, and phenomenological — and their application to town planning.[27] One of the diagrams (Figure 2.2, left) invites the reader's eye to follow black dots that we may read as figures traversing and dispersing on a town square and yet still recognizable as a distinct group.[28] Marcolli's book was in many ways a throwback to the gestalt experiments of the 1950s, a moment when the organization of experience became the main issue in the redefinition of a socially engaged art. "Urban utopia has now become the refuge of failed revolutions, be they artistic, cultural, social, or political," Marcolli wrote, citing Adorno. And yet, Marcolli argued, urbanism should remain a site of democratic collective endeavor.[29] The section entitled "Urban Nodes" examines a series

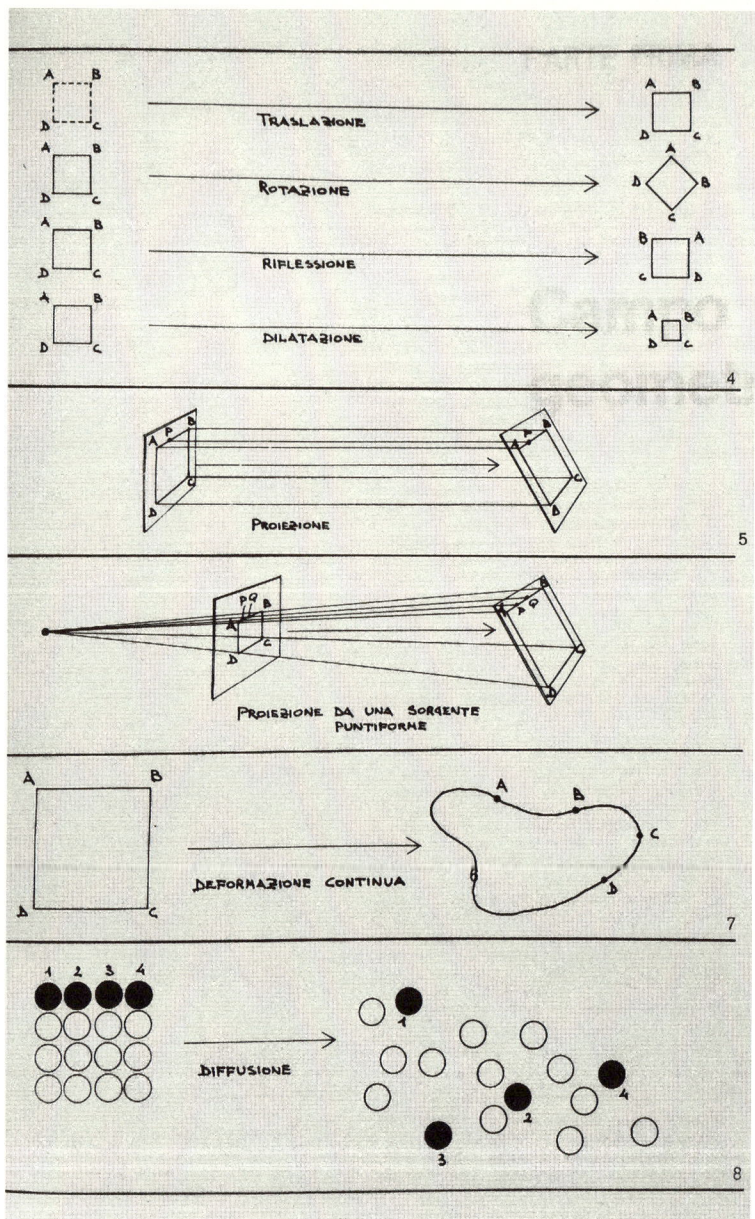

Figure 2.2. Attilio Marcolli, *Teoria del campo: Corso di educazione alla visione* (Florence: Sansoni, 1970).

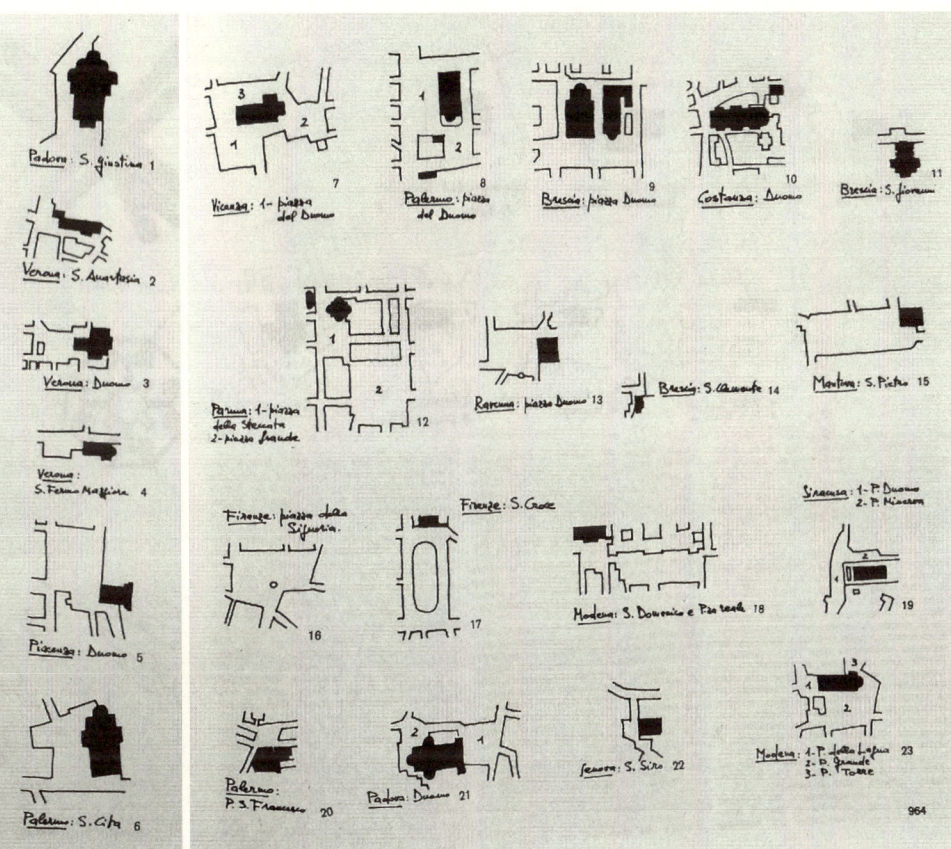

Padova: S. Giustina 1

Verona: S. Anastasia 2

Verona: Duomo 3

Verona: S. Fermo Maggiore 4

Piacenza: Duomo 5

Palermo: S. Cita 6

Vicenza: 1- piazza del Duomo 7

Palermo: piazza del Duomo 8

Brescia: piazza Duomo 9

Costanza: Duomo 10

Brescia: S. Giovanni 11

Parma: 1- piazza della Steccata 2- piazza Grande 12

Ravenna: piazza Duomo 13

Brescia: S. Clemente 14

Mantova: S. Pietro 15

Firenze: piazza della Signoria 16

Firenze: S. Croce 17

Modena: S. Domenico e Pomposa 18

Siracusa: 1- P. Duomo 2- P. Minerva 19

Palermo: P. S. Francesco 20

Padova: Duomo 21

Genova: S. Siro 22

Modena: 1- P. della Legna 2- D. Grande 3- P. Torre 23

964

of twenty-three medieval town squares in Italy and elsewhere in Europe as examples of spaces that are enclosed and overly predetermined, in spite of their generally irregular configurations (Figure 2.2, right).[30] "Vision," he wrote, "should allow one to experience these public squares beyond their surrounding buildings and intuit how they open onto nearby squares or access streets."[31]

Bruno Munari's Photo Book: Episodes from an Unwritten History of Participation

The interventions in Como — some of which will be described here, following the pagination of Caramel's photo book — began simultaneously in different parts of the city. At 3:00 p.m. on Via Tommaso Grossi, a short distance from the center of town, the group Art Terminal performed *Sostituzione di un cancello* (Replacement of a gate), in which they attempted unsuccessfully to remove a derelict iron gate from the city's orphanage, in collaboration with its young occupants. Half an hour later, after the group kicked a soccer ball around with the kids for a few minutes, a number of actions began in different parts of the Piazza del Duomo. Gianni Pettena's uninvited intervention, titled *Come mai quasi tutti hanno scelto la piazza?* (How come almost everyone has picked the main square?), violated Como's most stately square by stringing laundry on clotheslines between two lampposts smack in front of the Duomo (see Figure I.2). This reminder of the working class — unsightly, and yet eternally picturesque — brought an image of Italy's periphery into the city center, metaphorically washing the dirty linen of local and national politics out in the open. Wearing mock uniforms bedecked with medals, the ex-Arte Nucleare (a variant of Pittura Informale) painter Enrico Baj and his collaborators — Ermanno Besozzi, Inse Bonstrat, and Bruno Molli — staged a simulated political coup called *Segnaletica orizzontale* (Horizontal signage) (Figure 2.3). Using a roller designed to paint pedestrian crosswalks, Baj painted a huge Italian flag on the pavement in front of the Broletto, a medieval building adjacent to the cathedral that had been Como's original town hall. Pamphlets were flung from the balconies and tricolored posters distributed to the crowds massed below while a band played mock military tunes. Meanwhile, with *Visualizzazione dell'aria* (Visualization of the air), Munari invited adults and children up to the tower to fold little bits of paper and launch them downward (Figure 2.4). The various shapes circled like toy airplanes, floating at different velocities and along different trajectories, manifesting the resistance of the air.

A few meters away, the architect Mario Di Salvo and the conceptual artist Carlo Ferrario, both from Como, executed an action entitled *Riflessione* (Reflection). They lined a series of mirrors on the ground along the façade of the Duomo, effectively unhinging the edifice via myriad reflections and forcing their fellow citizens to rethink their relation to the town's most iconic monument (Figure 2.5; Plate 6). They also installed a cement sculpture containing a round mirror and resembling a well or baptismal font. The mirror concealed a tape recorder that emitted fragments of music and almost inaudible political slogans recorded during a recent street demonstration. Luciano Fabro, the only Arte Povera artist to participate, declined to perform an action and instead applied — in a letter sent to the town municipality and distributed publicly at 3:30 p.m. — to use the sum of money allotted to him for his intervention to buy property to be used for artistic activities whenever he saw fit.

At 4:20 p.m., the action moved from the square to the adjoining medieval streets with Grazia Varisco's *Dilatazione spazio-temporale di un percorso* (Spatiotemporal dilation of a route). Varisco, formerly a member of the Milanese collective Gruppo T, lined up cardboard boxes on Via delle Cinque Giornate, creating a mock barricade that forced passersby to proceed in a zigzag path down the street. At 4:30 p.m., Attilio Marcolli — the author of *Teoria del Campo* — produced *Colore-Segnale* (Color signal). Offering an alternative to the garish commercial signage of Como's thoroughfares, Marcolli posted color-coded strips of paper on Via Boldoni to identify merchants, as in older times: red for butchers, green for fruit venders. At 4:45 p.m. on the diminutive Piazza San Fedele, Valentina Berardinone unveiled

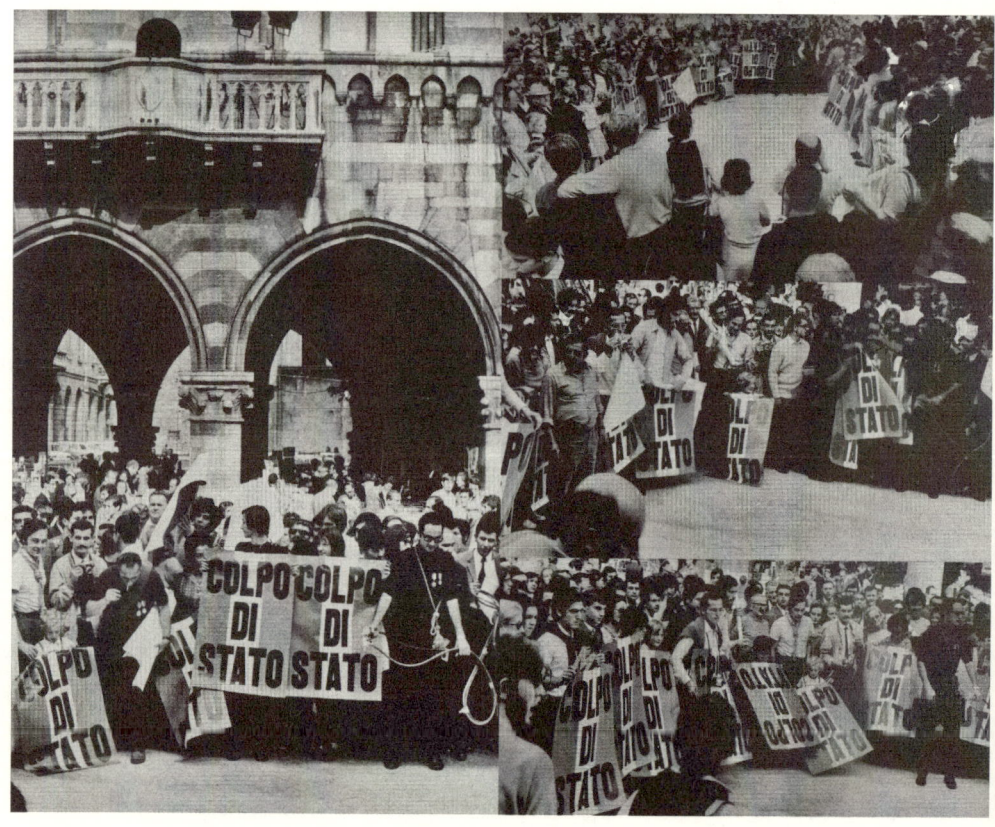

Figure 2.3. Enrico Baj, *Segnaletica orizzontale* (Horizontal signage). *Campo urbano*, 1969. Photography: Ugo Mulas. Design: Bruno Munari.

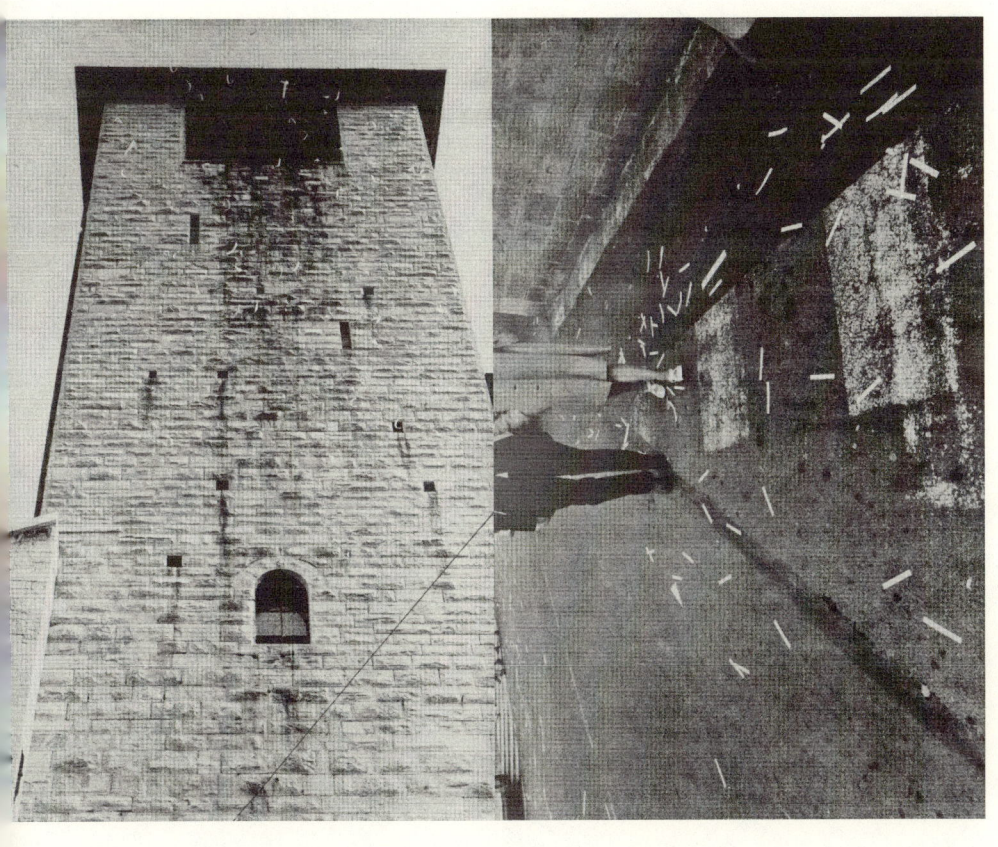

Figure 2.4. Bruno Munari, *Visualizzazione dell'aria* (Visualization of the air). *Campo urbano*, 1969. Photography: Ugo Mulas. Design: Bruno Munari.

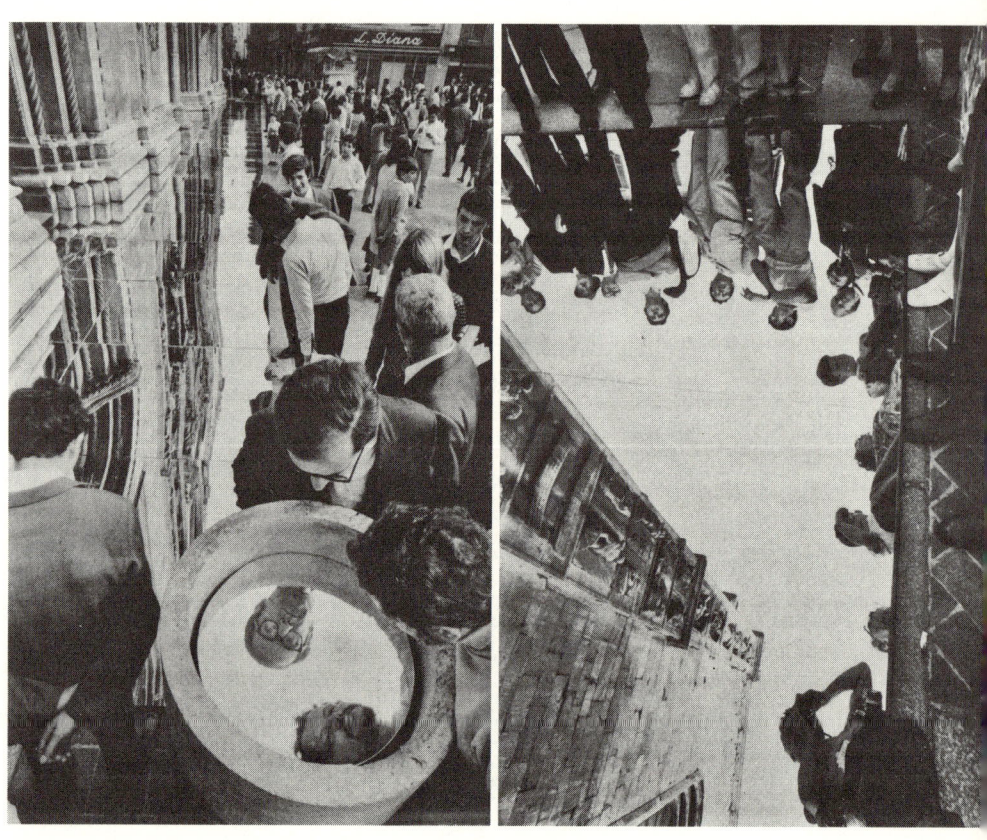

Figure 2.5. Mario Di Salvo and Carlo Ferrario, *Riflessione* (Reflection). *Campo urbano*, 1969. Photography: Ugo Mulas. Design: Bruno Munari.

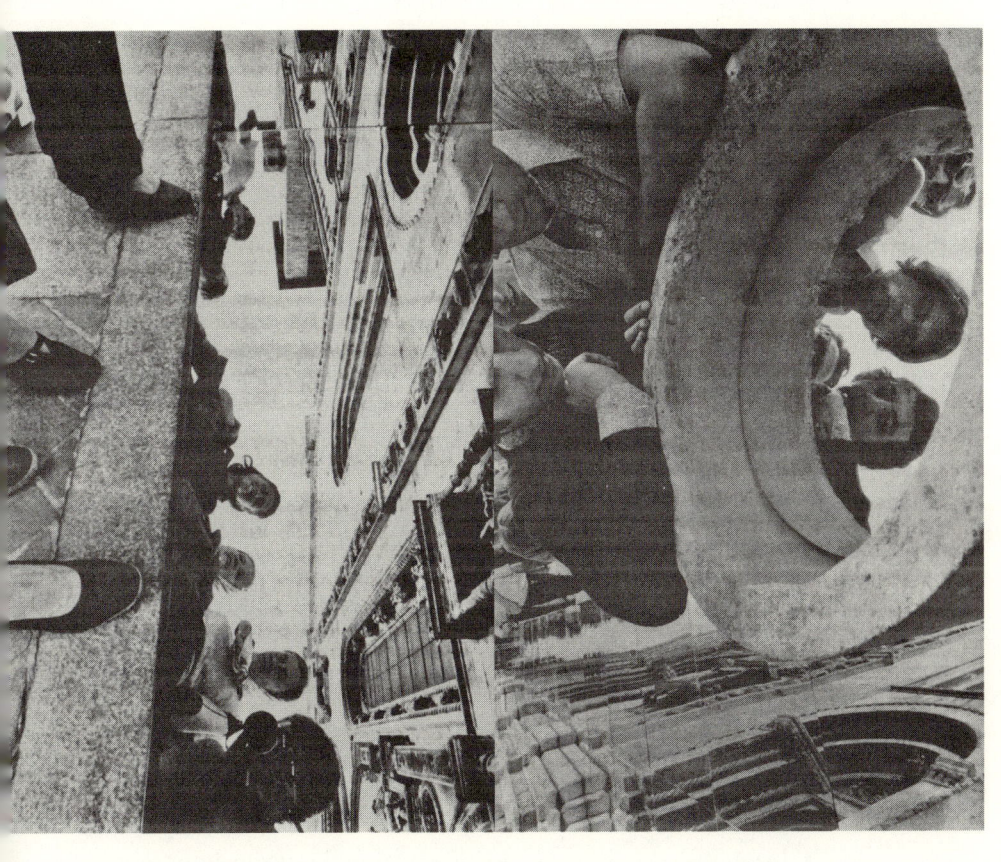

her *Vittoria (antimonumento)* (Victory [antimonument]) to the sound of a band in uniform and the sputtering of engines. In one of the many slapstick touches of the day's events, she painted big red drops of blood running down the side of the stocky papier-mâché cenotaph. Taking a quieter approach, at 5:00 p.m. Giulio Paolini stretched a banner from two balconies across nearby Via Indipendenza. The banner read: "Et quid amabo nisi quod aenigma est?" (And what shall I love, if not the enigma?), a line inscribed by Giorgio de Chirico on the frame of a self-portrait from 1911. At 5:15 p.m., with *Allora: Copro una strada. Ne faccio un'altra. Trasformo gli spazi originari. Cambio le condizioni di comportamento.* (And so: I cover the street. I make another one. I transform the original spaces. I change the conditions of behavior), the Milanese architect/designer Ugo La Pietra "liberated" (as he put it) the city's main commercial artery, Via Vittorio Emanuele II, from its economic compulsion by constructing a wooden tunnel covered with opaque black plastic, blocking the pedestrians' view of the street's shop windows (Figure 2.6). At 6:30 p.m. came an *intermezzo* in musical form called *Suonare la città* (Playing the city). Giuseppe Chiari, a Florentine composer connected to Fluxus, and the mezzo-soprano Franca Sacchi ran electric wires down from the windows of the Broletto and its tower across the Piazza del Duomo to produce a gigantic harp (Figure 2.7). Sound recordings, combined with live music and noise, included car sirens, dishwashers, and a blender. Whistles, tambourines, and harmonicas were distributed to the public (this was the most popular and raucous intervention of the day), and the Comaschi were invited to "play" (*suonare*), quite literally, their city.

The night was reserved for more poetic (in the sense of more dematerialized) interventions by former members of the very recently defunct Paduan and Milanese collectives Gruppo N and Gruppo T, artists who had made their mark with kinetic objects, but had since shifted to creating immersive environments shaped by the manipulation of light. At 9:00 p.m., Dadamaino took Como's inhabitants to the lake — a site largely ignored, as she stated in the photo book, in the everyday life of the city. In *Illuminazione fosforescente auto-motoria sull'acqua* (Phosphorescent automated illumination of water), she dispersed phosphorescent plaques of polystyrene foam across its surface, animating the expanse of water (Figure 2.8; Plate 7). As the night drew on, after long debating what to do to avoid doing anything more than what they called a "maquillage" on the cityscape, "makeup" that would conceal, rather than reveal, the city, Edilio Alpini, Davide Boriani, Gianni Colombo, and Gabriele De Vecchi designated a special perimeter of the Piazza del Duomo at 9:15 p.m. for *Tempo libero: Struttura temporale in uno spazio urbano* (Free time: Temporal structure for an urban space) (Figure 2.9). The title plays on the word *temporale*, which means both "temporal" and "rainstorm" in Italian. The four artists enlisted local firemen, sound technicians, and electricians to commandeer the city's hydrants, producing an artificial storm. Meanwhile, loudspeakers emitted taped sounds of falling rain and projectors cast bluish green lights interrupted by flashes to simulate lightning striking the wet pavement. The synchronized action lasted exactly fifteen minutes. As soon as it was over, Munari began *Proiezione a luce polarizzata su schermi plastici semoventi* (Polarized light projection on moving plastic screens), in which lights were projected onto white umbrellas that had been distributed to the public (Figure 2.10). Last came Franca Sacchi and Paolo Scheggi's *Marcia funebre o della geometria* (March for funerals or geometry), in which actors wearing long robes and pointed hats like penitents in Holy Week processions filed from the Piazza del Duomo into the surrounding streets, accompanied by music written by Sacchi. Dressed in various colors, they carried three-dimensional cardboard effigies of four basic geometric shapes over their shoulders. The day ended with a noisy debate between the artists and the public in a crowded room of Como's town hall, which went on past midnight.

The verdict in the mostly conservative local press the next morning was harsh.[32] While the reviewers in Caorle and San Benedetto del Tronto were ready to be uncritically thrilled by any attention brought to their town by the "marvelous formula" of these summer

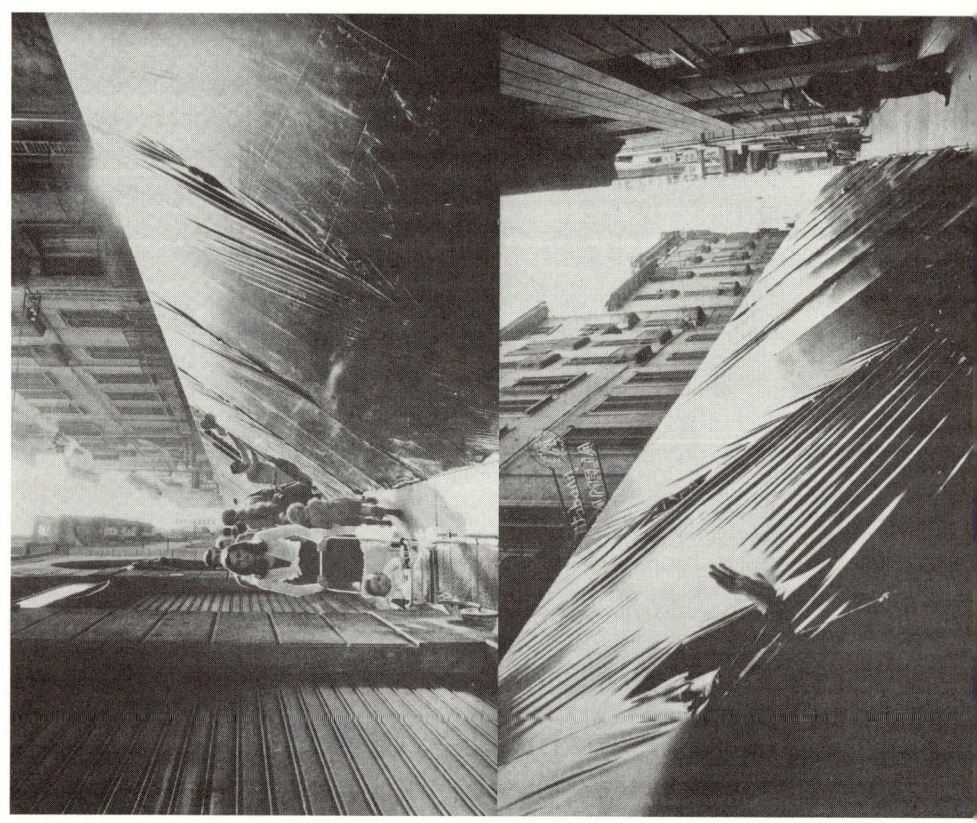

Figure 2.6. Ugo La Pietra, *Allora: Copro una strada. Ne faccio un'altra. Trasformo gli spazi originari. Cambio le condizioni di comportamento.* (And so: I cover the street. I make another one. I transform the original spaces. I change the conditions of behavior.) *Campo urbano,* 1969. Photography: Ugo Mulas. Design: Bruno Munari.

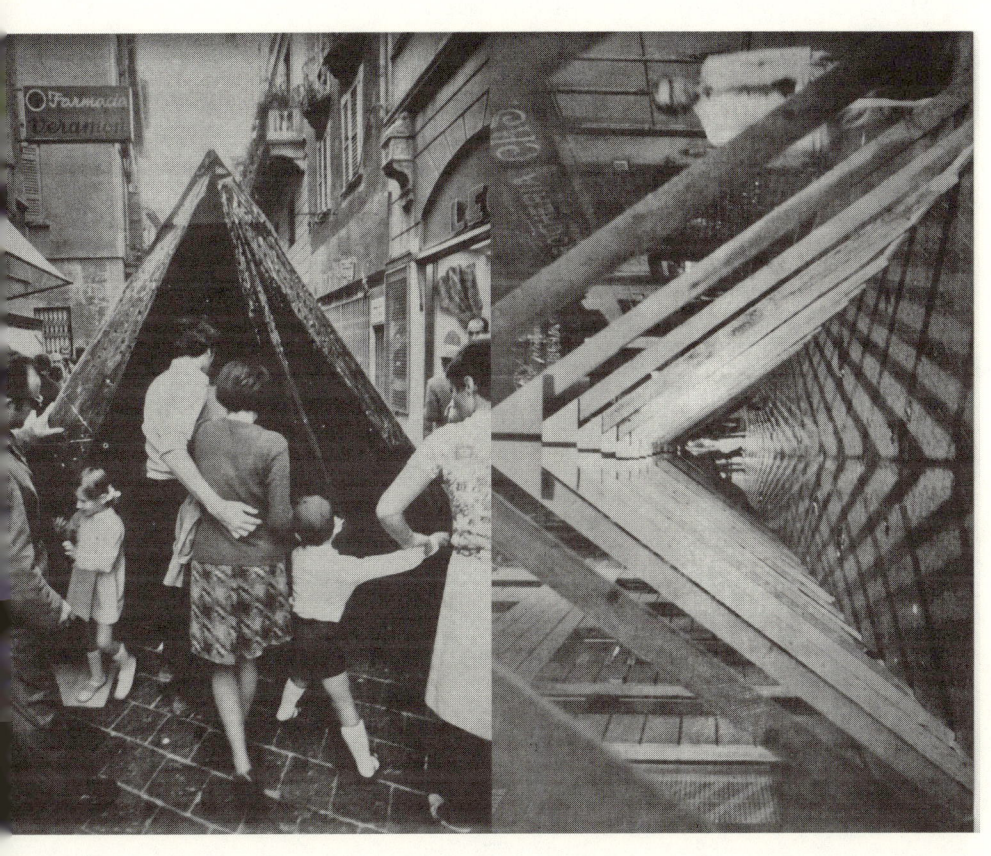

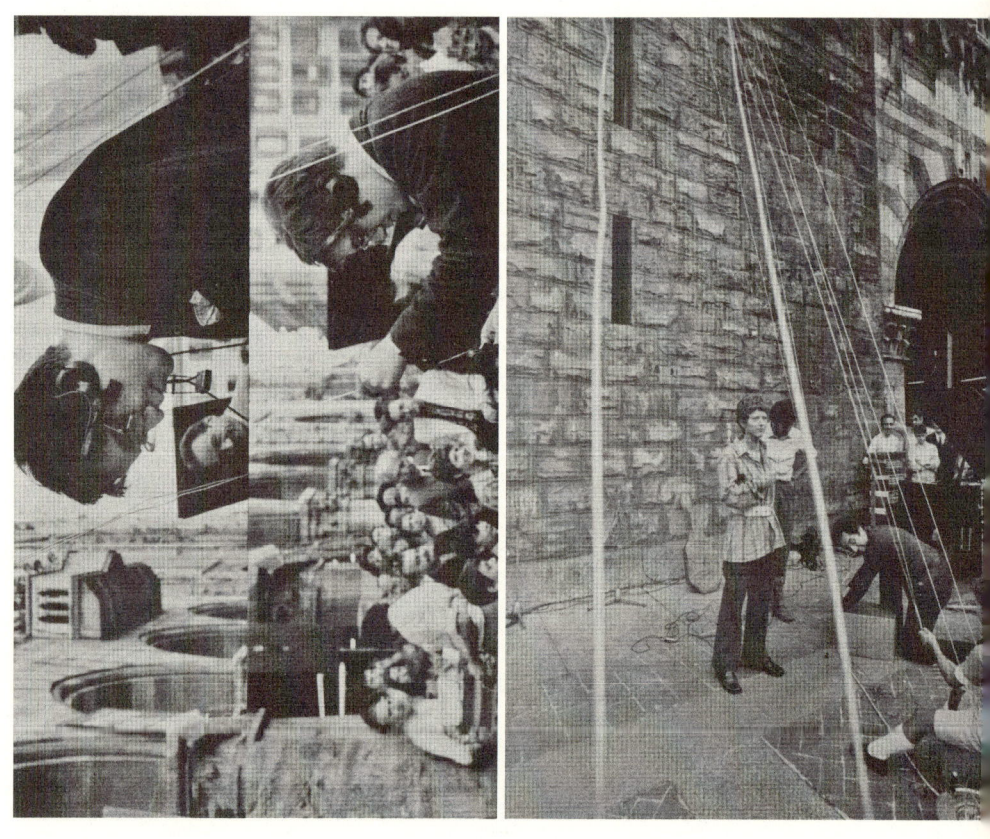

Figure 2.7. Giuseppe Chiari and Franca Sacchi, *Suonare la città* (Playing the city). *Campo urbano*, 1969. Photography: Ugo Mulas. Design: Bruno Munari.

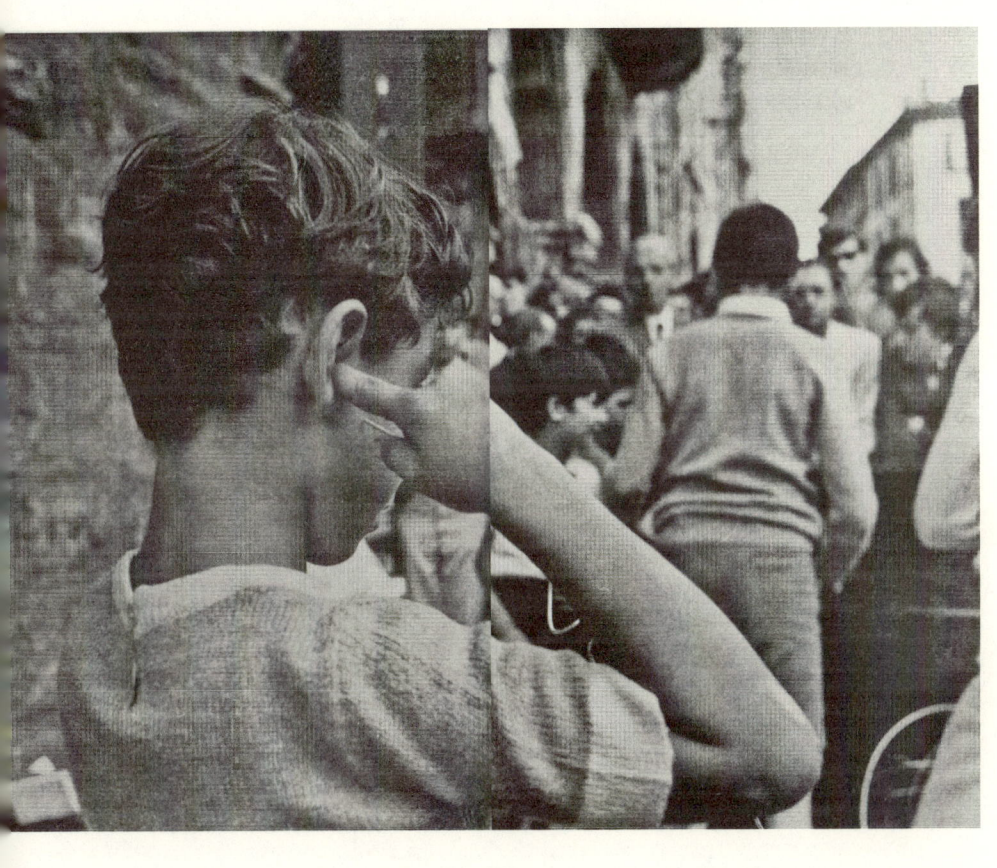

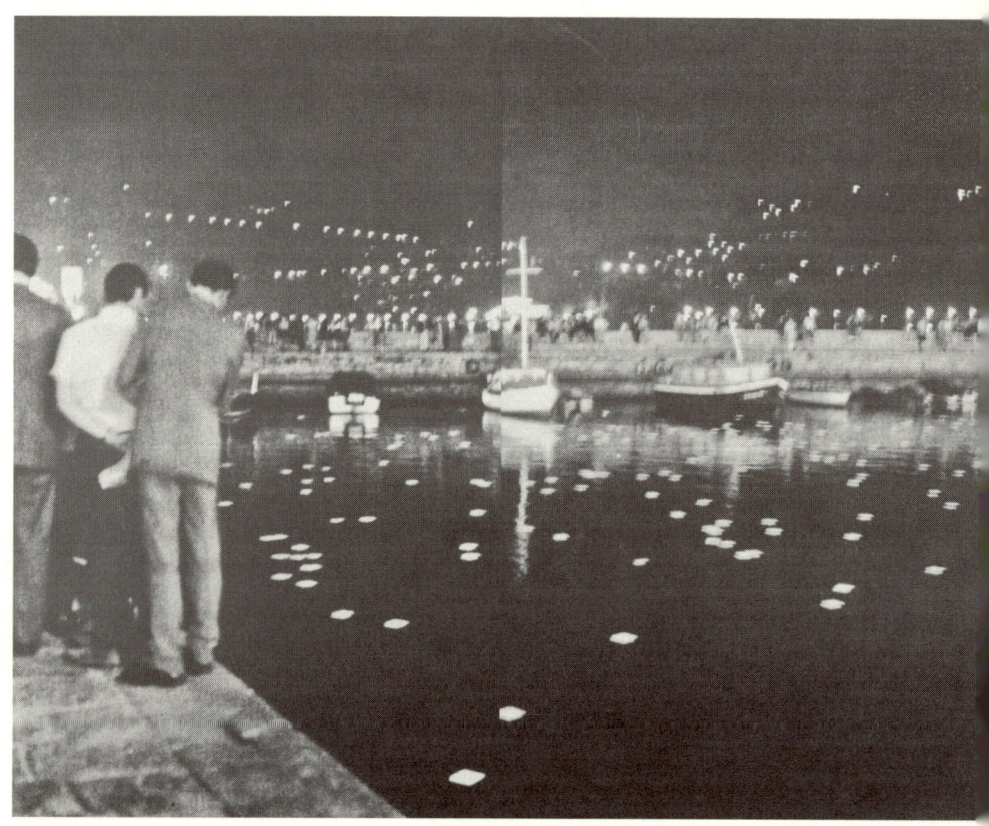

Figure 2.8. Dadamaino, *Illuminazione fosforescente automotoria sull'acqua* (Phosphorescent automated illumination of water). *Campo urbano*, 1969. Photography: Ugo Mulas. Design: Bruno Munari.

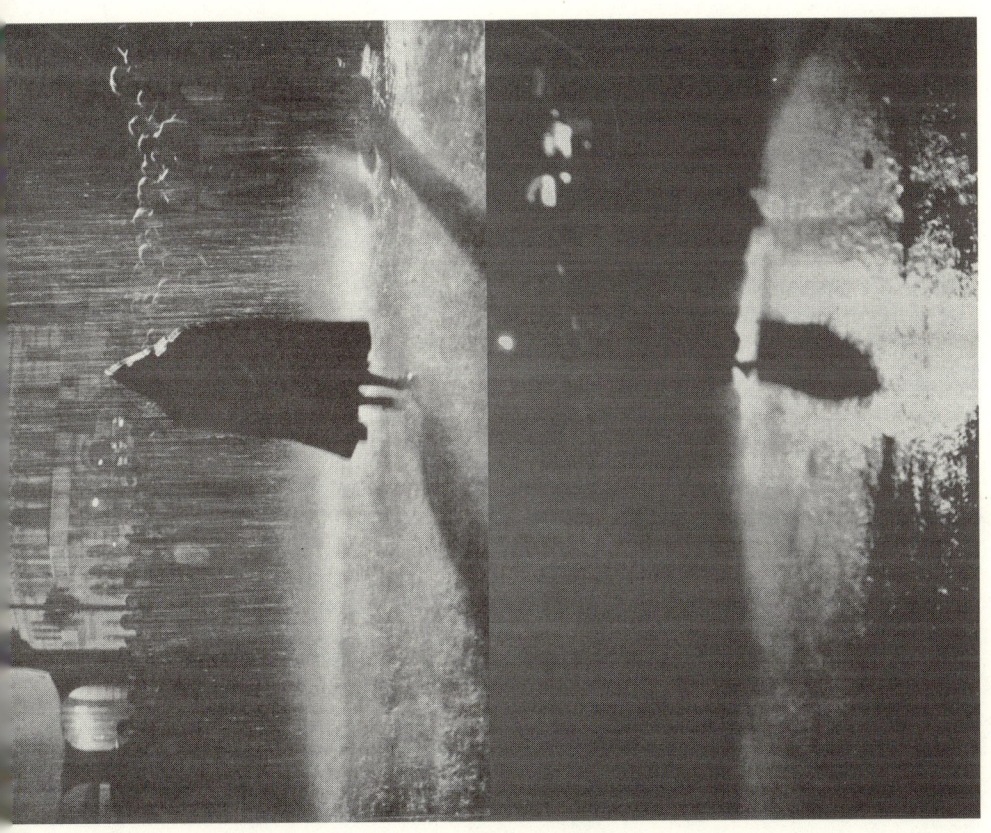

Figure 2.9. Edilio Alpini, Davide Boriani, Gianni Colombo, and Gabriele De Vecchi, *Tempo libero: Struttura temporale in uno spazio urbano* (Free time: Temporal structure for an urban space). *Campo urbano*, 1969. Photography: Ugo Mulas. Design: Bruno Munari.

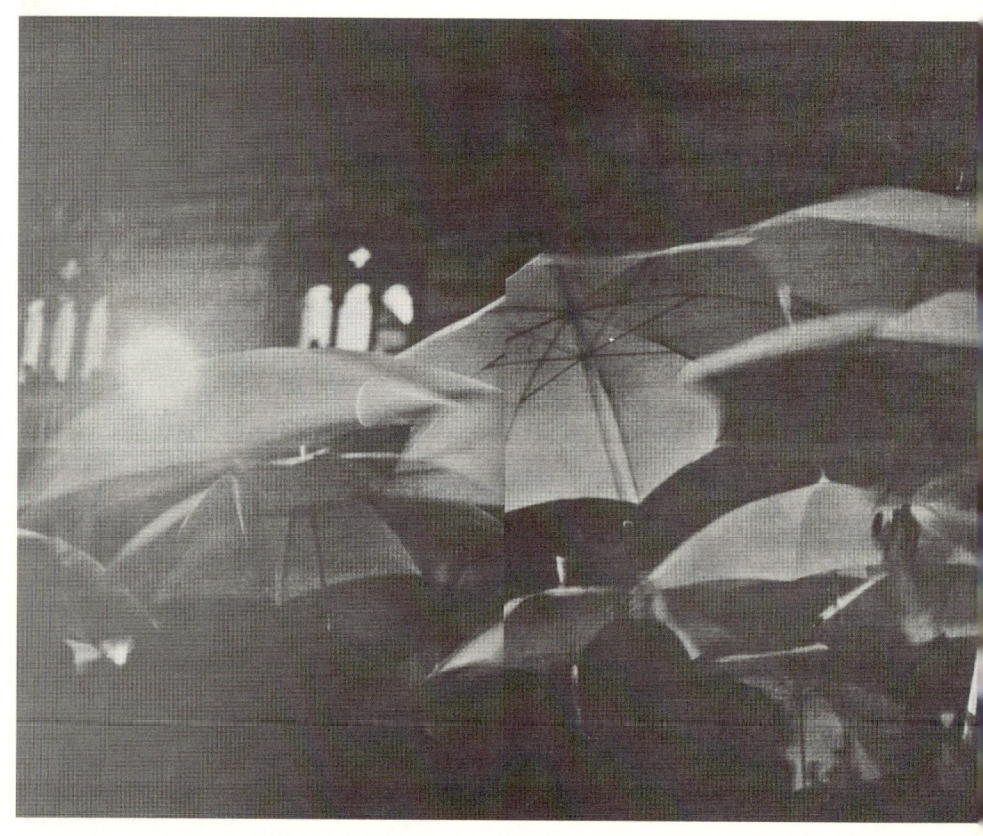

Figure 2.10. Bruno Munari, *Proiezione a luce polarizzata su schermi plastici semoventi* (Polarized light projection on moving plastic screens). *Campo urbano*, 1969. Photography: Ugo Mulas. Design: Bruno Munari.

events, the local press in Como was more defensive, but also more discerning in their critique. "Expensive Games by a Bunch of Artists Yesterday in Town: *Campo Urbano* — Carnival Atmosphere and (Rather Belated) Dada Antics," read the headline in the *Corriere della Provincia*, whose reviewer summarized the event as "a futile and patronizing attempt by a bunch of avant-garde artists to spark electricity in the air of a provincial town on a sleepy Sunday afternoon." "The Futurists fifty years ago and Dadaists forty years ago did a much better job at connecting with the public. . . . The Dada artists had more ideas and imagination and did not ask the public for millions [of lira] in public funds."[33] "A Little Sunday Get-Together by the Artists of *Campo Urbano*," quipped *L'Ordine* in its headline.[34] The *Corriere della Provincia* invited letters of complaint from individual citizens, which tended to focus on the supposed desecration of the Italian flag by Baj and of war memorials by Berardinone. The responses to *Campo urbano* published in the *Corriere* in turn elicited letters of clarification from participating artists: Carlo Ferrario insisted that the soundtrack he and Mario Di Salvo used for *Riflessione* did not include any recognizable (be they right-wing or left-wing) political speeches, and Berardinone protested that the presence of the word "PIGS" (in English) scribbled on her antimonument was not her own doing, but the work of an irate spectator.[35] More generous was a review entitled "*Mostre-Spettacolo* Are Multiplying: We Could Exhibit a Great Downpour. Courtyards, Streets, and Piazzas Have Become Art Galleries," by the critic Marisa Rusconi in *Avvenire*, a new Roman publication founded in the wake of 1968 by the Catholic Church in an attempt to respond to Italy's rapidly changing cultural climate. Yet even she concluded that the only truly participatory event in *Campo urbano* was *Suonare la città*, the concert on the Piazza del Duomo: "Yes, the public was present, sometimes even bewildered or amused, but always as if watching something that didn't really concern them and would be over by the end of the day."[36] In "La Piazza a teatro: Ovvero la scena è 'altrove'" (The piazza as theater: or, the action is "elsewhere"), the theater critic Cesare Sughi spoke of "the extension of the theatrical event" as a way to "recover, often with all its force, an imagination that had often been stifled."[37]

The misgivings expressed in the pages of *NAC* and *Domus* by Trini, a less partisan critic who had actually participated in the event, were more substantial:

> Who was the public, this entity so integral to artistic communication that it has become its ultimate goal? Why is it that art always goes into the squares and the streets on a Sunday for whomever happens to be there? Free time is up for sale. What are they after, those artists who, taking part in such events, affirm either their exhibitionism or spontaneity, or perhaps their impotence toward a productive exercise or an attempt at some overall activation?

And, with a play on words, he wondered if the notion of *campo* had become little more than a *scampo* — that is, a "way out"?[38] As often in *Domus*, the visual layout was key. The full-page photograph of Mario Di Salvo and Carlo Ferrario's *Riflessione* spelled out Trini's theme even before one read his article's title, "L'Estensione teatrale" (translated in the same issue of *Domus* as "Towards theater").[39] His meaning was clear: Como's historical center had been used as a stage set, and some of the actions seemed to have been staged expressly for the camera. And yet Trini had been the only critic to wonder, in the conclusion of his report from Amalfi, published in *Domus* exactly a year before, how such actions could survive the status of sporadic manifestation.[40]

Most disappointing for the participants, and for Caramel especially, was Celant's reporting on *Campo urbano* for the November issue of *Casabella*. Having cast *Arte povera + Azioni povere* as unprecedented, unruly, and subversive, here was a major protagonist of the late 1960s who had the most to lose in the multiplication of similar events.[41] Celant thus dismissed what he saw as Amalfi epigones as examples of "tourist art" (*turistico-culturali*) or worse, what he termed "artistico-balneari," an artsy diversion scheduled to coincide with summer pilgrimages to the beach. Here again, the long tirade is worth quoting not only for its scathing tone, but for a taste of its rapid — doggedly presentist — scanning of the territory:

The tourist season in art, experimental and otherwise, is over. After count-less events in charming beach and alpine locales, it is now time to get back to the cities — their galleries and schools. The summer holidays are over, and the hotshot intellectual has taken off his mask to resume his daily professional , life as an artist or engaged critic. A year of wrangling over the uselessness of exhibitions, prizes, the need to abolish the decrepit Biennale and Triennale, and the impossibility of operating within existing institutions subservient to the market has taken its toll, and the 1969 list of arty summer events and cultural tourism is longer than ever. An epidemic of interventions, delib-erations, actions, catalogues, and manifestos has taken over Italy's cultural scene in an almost orgiastic reaction to the contraction of 1968, the year of the protest movements. The fear of a summer drought is gone thanks to *Al di là della pittura* in San Benedetto del Tronto, *Nuovi materiali nuove tecniche* in Caorle, *Campo urbano* in Como, the Michetti Prize in Francavilla a Mare, and the annual prizes in Gubbio for the Sculpture Biennial, in Fano, Peio, Sassoferrato, Termoli, and so on. Yesterday it was Pop art and Neofiguration, Programmed and Kinetic Art. Today it's situations and environments, Arte Povera or antiform, but the aim remains the same: publicity and tourism. These events take place at the beginning and at the end of the summer, when tourism is down, as with sack races and the festival of the roasted chestnut. Municipal largesse is squandered on invitations, catalogues, installations, and travel expenses. The participants are always the same — one hundred people at most, gathered to dust off the ideas they sell to specialized journals. They wander through the streets, perform in a school turned for the occasion into a museum and in city squares. The whole thing resolves itself into foregone conclusions. If all this is true — and I am speaking here as an insider who has both curated and participated in similar events — it is clear that we have to change the system.[42]

The book that Celant published on *Arte povera + Azioni povere*, like all those accompanying the aforementioned sorties (if there was a publication at all), was not an exhibition catalogue issued prior to the event or a photo book, but explicitly a documentation.[43] Yet even here, Piero Gilardi (who would soon abandon making art altogether) had remarked on the intrusive presence of three photographers and the teams of television reporters who foisted themselves on the actions.[44]

The disruptive role of photography resurfaced during a round-table in San Benedetto del Tronto, which included some of the artists who would participate in *Campo urbano* two months later. Some contended that the use of photography to record an ephemeral event risked commodifying it, as was already the case with performance art, installation art, and Land Art in the United States, once the photograph was signed and exhibited in a gallery. To be avoided, and here everyone agreed, was the unique photograph as autonomous artwork.[45] For Trini, the main objective was the participation of the public. For Ugo La Pietra, however, the most important priority was communication: "We are in San Benedetto del Tronto, and no one knows we are here, producing this event." As such, he went on, "what mattered was not a discussion of the differences between this and that type of kinetic installation or the international tendencies in art, but how to make our interventions more productive to others."[46]

All the debates surrounding *Campo urbano*, including the published reviews of the event, took place in the present tense. And yet different temporalities — the temporality of the flashback and that of the eclipse — inform the photo book produced by Mulas and Munari. Not only does the flashback rearrange narrative order, it introduces an element of intertextuality. As Renate Lachmann writes in *Memory and Literature*, intertextuality can take different forms: cryptic, esoteric, ludic, syncretistic, and carnivalesque. With its focal points of culture, the city provides not only the scaffolding, but also the building material for mnemonic architecture. "The city is a Wunderblock, a mystic writing-pad," she writes.[47]

The quasi-mythical events that shook Paris in May 1968 reverberated long after the fact, and the pages of *Campo urbano's* photo book document one of the first episodes of this afterlife. Photographs of the Paris happenings — showing, for example, burning cars, the police dispersing protesters with tear gas and water cannons in front of iconic monuments such as the Panthéon, and the protestors' sei-zure of the Stock Exchange, which they tried to set on fire — became iconic almost as soon as they were shot (Figure 2.11).[48] In the *Campo urbano* photo book, the sequence of shots documenting *Segnaletica orizzontale*, the simulated coup staged by Enrico Baj and his collab-orators in Como's Piazza del Duomo, recalled the more photoge-nic demonstrations that had taken place the previous summer on another, more famous, *campo* — that of Piazza San Marco in Venice. Mulas himself had shot some of the more memorable images of that violent Biennale.

Framed by famed monuments and arcades, demonstrators occu-pied the piazza with signs reading "Biennale Fascista," "Fuori la polizia dalla Biennale" (Police out of the Biennale), "No all'arte dei padroni" (No to the art of the bosses), and "1964: Pop-Art/1968: Poliz-Art."[49] Titling its report "Biennale under siege," the British magazine *Art and Artists* reproduced a photo by Mulas showing a phalanx of helmeted riot policemen marching through the square a few feet away from tourists sitting at café tables (Figure 2.12).[50] In Venice, as in Paris a few months earlier, clashes with the police led to the arrest of scores of artists and students. In one image, also by Mulas, we see the painter Giangiacomo Spadari being dragged away by the riot police under the porticos of Piazza San Marco in front of the famed Caffè Florian; another shows Trini grappled by two policemen.[51]

Some images in the *Campo urbano* photo book hark back to unreal-ized artistic projects of the past, such as the "constructed situation" entitled *The World as Labyrinth*, which was described by the French and Dutch Situationists in the fourth issue of their journal in 1960, but eventually canned, probably due to misgivings about its excessive spectacularity.[52] The project would have involved a three-day urban Situationist *dérive* or "drift" in the center of Amsterdam in coordi-nation with a *microdérive* in two galleries of the Stedelijk Museum.[53] The latter would have comprised — much like *Tempo libero* by the ex-Gruppo T — a coordinated system of rain, artificial fog, and wind, as well as the passage of the participant artists and the public through

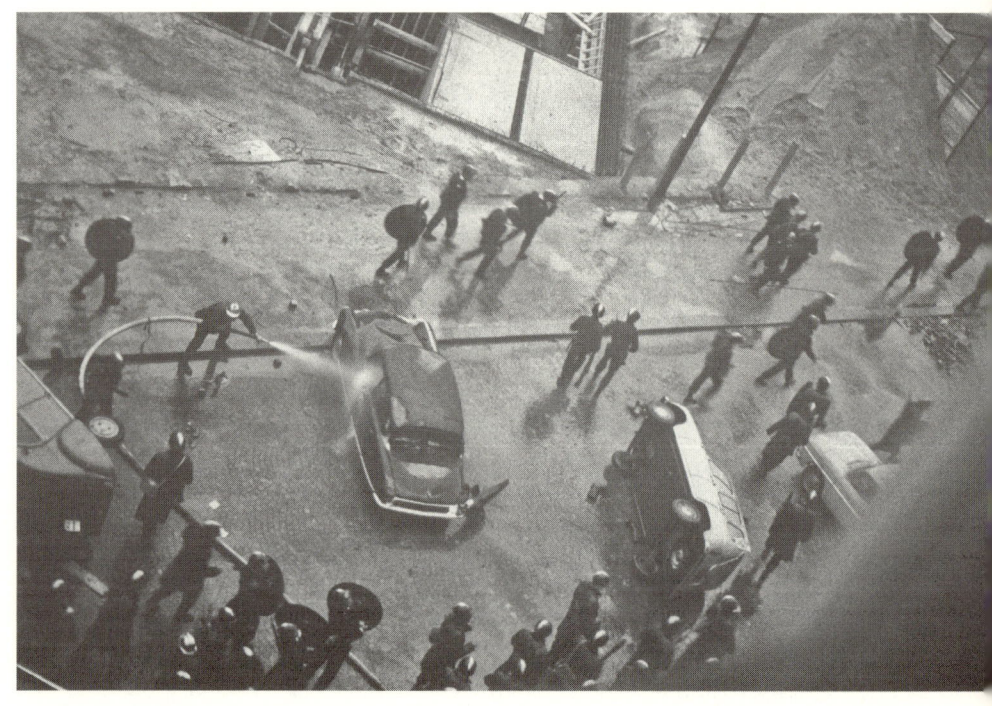

Figure 2.11. May 1968: car burned. © Claude Schwartz/Bridgeman Images.

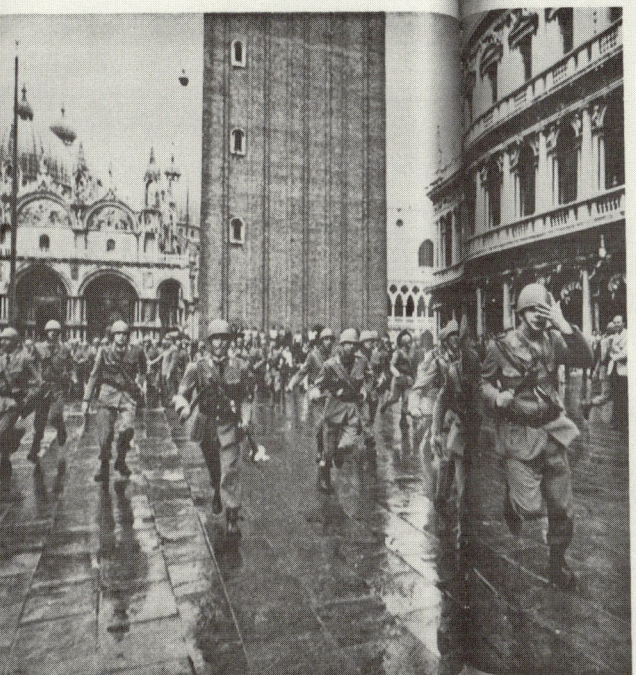

Figure 2.12. Demonstrations at the 1968 Venice Biennale, in *Art and Artists* 3, 1968. Photograph: Ugo Mulas.

different thermal and light zones. It would have included, as in La Pietra's *Allora: Copro una strada*, an obstacle in the form of a tunnel of "Industrial Paintings" made by the Italian Giuseppe Pinot-Gallizio; and as in a number of events in *Campo urbano*, a sound piece involving noises and random words emitted by a battery of megaphones.

Many of Mulas's photographs of *Campo urbano* summon the bonhomie of small-town life in the industrial cities of the Italian North famously cherished by Neorealism: they show a shopkeeper tending to his storefront against the backdrop of *Colore-segnale*, Valentina Berardinone hanging the funereal sheet of her *Antimonumento* as if she were drying laundry, children and teenagers laughing (with Trini) in front of the gates of the orphanage in *Sostituzione di un cancello*, and a boy plugging his ears amidst the racket of *Suonare la città*.

The *Campo urbano* photo book also has a filmic referent, in this case, the rare example of Neorealism that a reviewer termed "a Neorealist fable," or what might be called "fantastical Neorealism." Some photographs evoke, more specifically, the most memorable, if saccharine sequences of Vittorio De Sica's *Miracolo a Milano* (Miracle in Milan), released in 1951 (Figure 2.13), which takes place in the *baraccopoli* (shantytowns) that sprang up as Southern immigrants were expelled to the outskirts of Milan.[54] The *Campo urbano* photo book's sequence of frames showing families — children, parents, and grandparents — peering into La Pietra's tentlike plastic tunnel recalls the film's opening scenes. The sequence documenting *Tempo libero* and Munari's umbrella intervention evokes one of *Miracolo a Milano*'s final scenes, one replete with technical tricks; it shows the migrants protecting themselves from powerful jets of water — pumped from canisters by police at the behest of the capitalist developers — with a canopy of umbrellas, opened and pivoted in unison. As if by magic, the water appears to flow back into the canisters in reverse motion. In the film's final shots, sentimentalist, but iconic, the migrants gather on the Piazza del Duomo and fly over the cathedral's ornate spires and then over the rest of Milan on broomsticks borrowed from the city's sweepers.[55]

In a review entitled "Impossibilità di sintesi trà realtà e favola" (The impossibility of synthesis between reality and fable), one critic saw the surprisingly apolitical nature of *Miracolo a Milano* as a sign of the beginning of the end of Neorealism, its resignation and profound pessimism. The film was dismissed by film critics on the Left for its depoliticization of reality.[56] De Sica's film was itself a flashback to an earlier moment in the history of cinema: that of the magic tricks of Georges Méliès. One is reminded of what the film historian Tom Gunning has described as the "cinema of attractions" at the turn of the twentieth century — a time when audiences went to fairs and expositions to witness demonstrations of the newest technological wonders, such as the phonograph, the X-ray, and film.[57] According to the media/art historian Philippe-Alain Michaud, Méliès's "burlesque fantasies . . . were an apparatus of resistance to the realism of moving images" invented by the Lumière brothers. And the work of Méliès was itself another flashback: his films "perpetuated, through the medium of the cinema, the spirit of the street fair and popular theater that cinema itself was threatening to replace. These filmed fantasies turned nostalgically toward their own past in order to conserve an archive of that past and invent for it a mythology."[58]

It is this early and not necessarily political history of the cinematic medium that Munari recaptured for the 1960s in his photo book. Here we have, however, a disconnect with Mulas's declared views. Asked by the art historian and critic Arturo Quintavalle in another 1973 monograph whether the Neorealist flavor of his 1950s photographs of the Milan periphery came from cinema, Mulas responded: "I never really liked cinema, I never went much," claiming instead that he was more interested in Neorealist painting.[59] At Quintavalle's insistence: "Do you think that Milan was read in a certain way by filmmakers and others, that is to say, do you offer an interpretation of Milan?" Mulas replied:

> By filmmakers, I couldn't say, by the Milan seen in the movies, I don't know. For instance, I never went to see *Miracolo a Milano*. I always felt uncomfortable

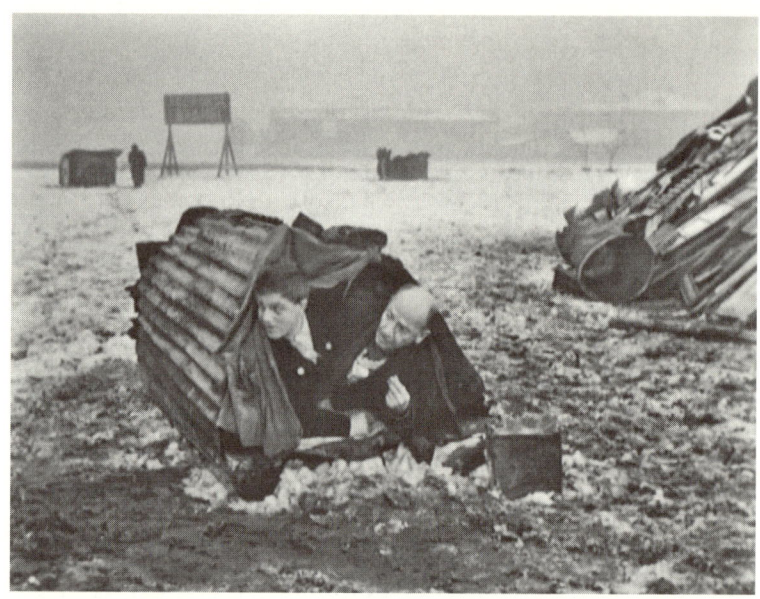

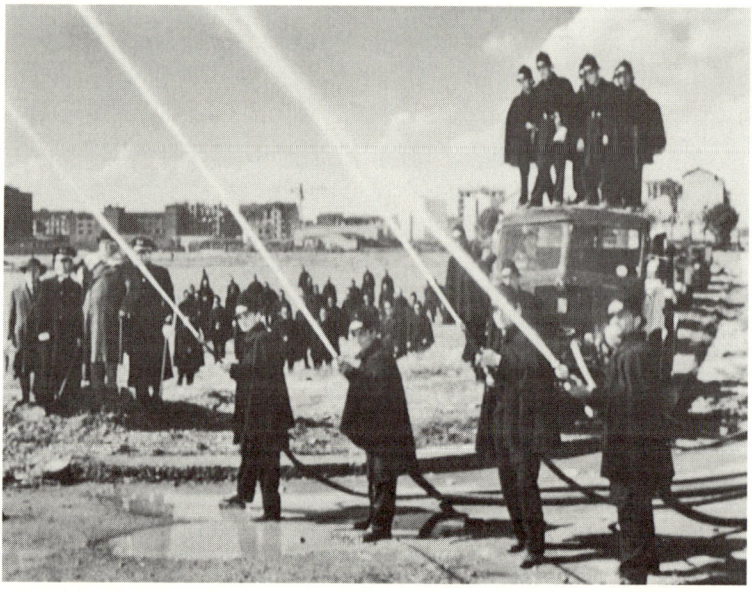

Figure 2.13. Vittorio De Sica, dir., *Miracolo a Milano*, 1951.

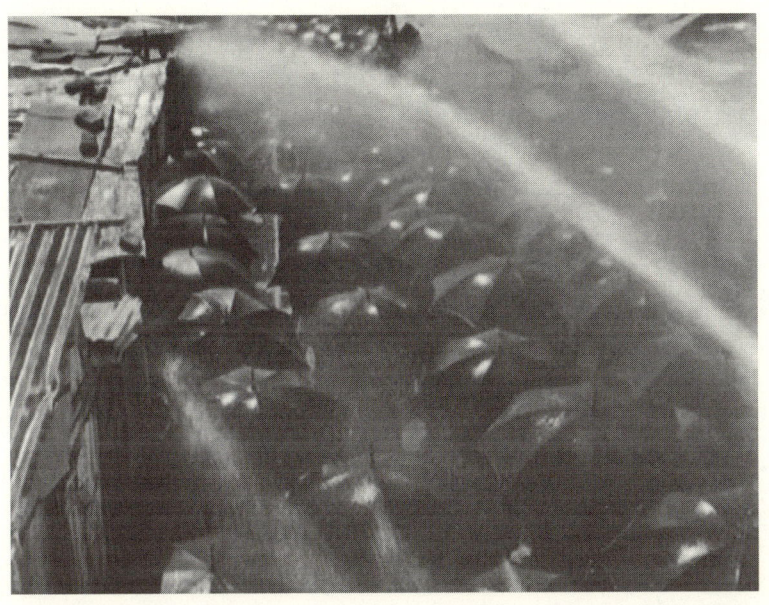

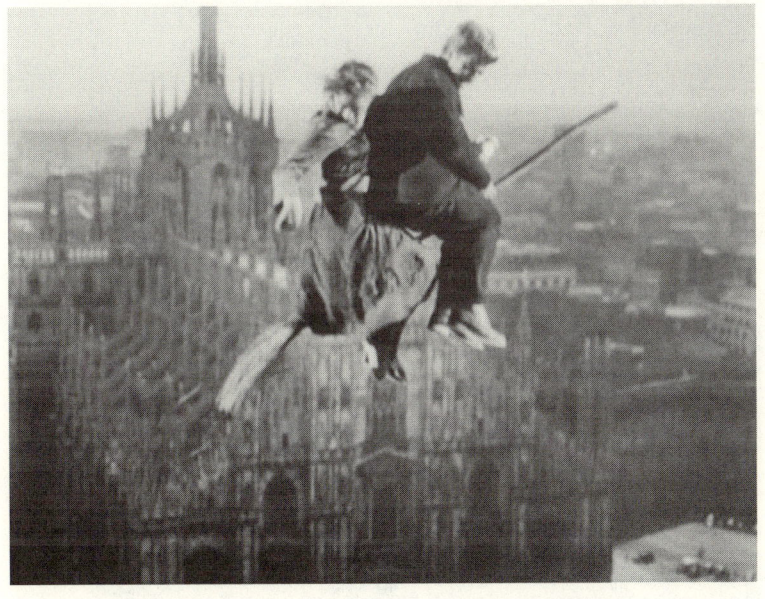

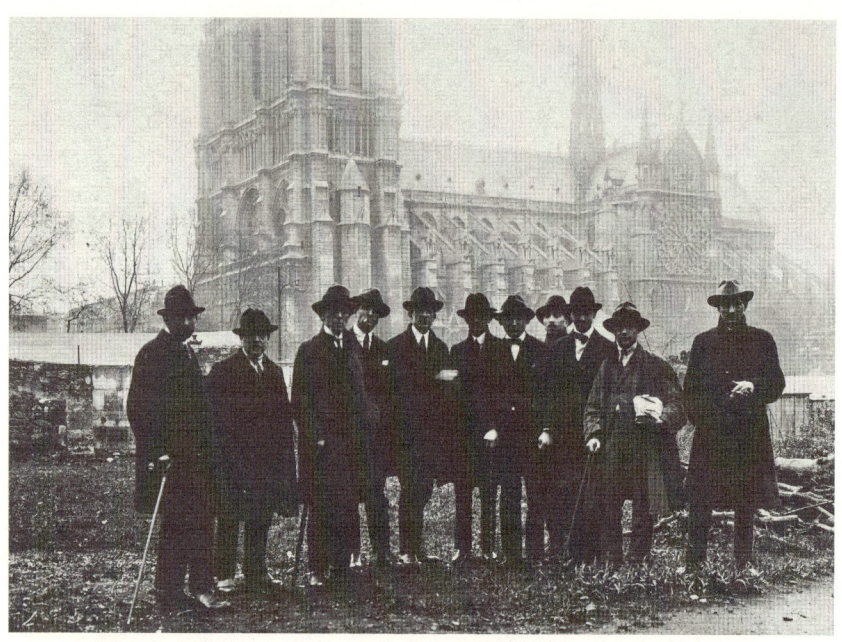

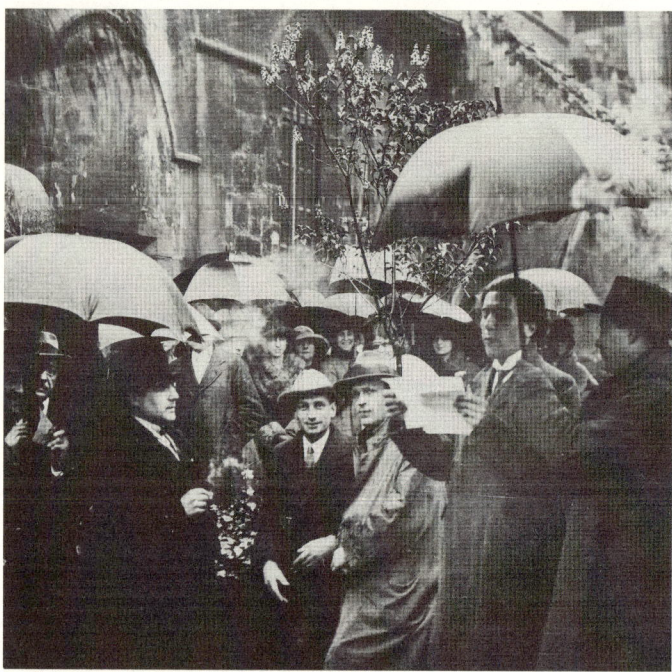

Figure 2.14. Anonymous, The Dada group visit to the Church of Saint-Julien-le-Pauvre in Paris, 1920. ©RMN-Grand Palais/Art Resource, NY.

going to the movies, the reason being that once you are there, you might spend two extraordinary hours, get excited, cry, laugh. The effort I have to go through to regain my mental footing with the city ... it's too disturbing, and thus I only go rarely to the movies.[60]

Structured as a series of flashbacks within flashbacks, a *mise en abyme*, the photographs of the bits of paper that Munari dropped from the Broletto tower in *Visualizzazione dell'aria* and those of the illuminated umbrellas remind the viewer of past events that had taken place in other medieval *campi*, known through extant photographic documentation or by other means. One such event took place in Paris on the afternoon of April 14, 1921, when the poet André Breton launched that year's "Dada Season" by taking his friends on an excursion to a vacant lot between Notre-Dame Cathedral and the Church of Saint-Julien-le-Pauvre in the Latin Quarter, where his anticlerical declamations drew a hundred listeners, in spite of persistent rain. Only two photographs of this event — one showing a small crowd huddled around Breton under umbrellas — seem to have survived (Figure 2.14).

Two of the most beautiful double spreads in the *Campo urbano* photo book are those featuring Dadamaino's plaques of polystyrene foam floating like flotsam on the placid surface of Lake Como at night (the photos "veered" by Munari into cerulean blue) and, a few pages later, the shots of the drenched, luminous pavement of the Piazza del Duomo during *Tempo libero*. These images, along with Mulas's photos of Munari's Broletto action, summon an earlier *campo* event. It took place on July 8, 1910, when, accompanied by a silver trumpet, Filippo Tommaso Marinetti delivered a diatribe through a megaphone while his fellow Futurists hurled some eight hundred thousand leaflets of "Contro Venezia passatista" (Against passéist Venice) from the square's Renaissance clock tower. The pamphlets, which fluttered over the Sunday crowds returning from the Lido, decried La Serenissima as the decrepit queen of the Adriatic, "that great Italian lake" — a city "enfeebled and undone by centuries of worldly pleasure."[61] As Jennifer Scappettone writes in *Killing the Moonlight: Modernism in Venice*, the Futurists' action "symbolically hijacked the timekeeping function of the venerable medieval Campanile," which was then being reconstructed — pathetically, the Futurists thought — following its sudden collapse in 1902.[62] So began the Futurists' three-year campaign against "passéist Venice." A month later, on the evening of August 1, 1910, Marinetti delivered his haranguing "Discorso futurista ai veneziani":

> O Venice, I, too, once loved the sumptuous half shadows of the Grand Canal steeped in exotic voluptuousness, the feverish pallor of your beautiful women who glide down from their balconies on stairways illuminated by lamplight, amid a slanting rain and rays of moonlight, to the tinkling of crossed swords.... But enough! All this absurd, abominable, and irritating stuff makes us sick. And now instead we want electric lamps with a thousand rays of light that can brutally stab and strangle the mysterious shadows — pestiferous, alluring shadows.[63]

By printing their pamphlets simultaneously in Italian, French, and English and having them distributed throughout Europe, the Futurists briefly secured Italy's position at the cutting edge of an international avant-garde. It is such artistically vital moments, shards of a disrupted avant-garde, that Munari allows us to recover. Previously unpublished Futurist texts, edited by Luciano de Maria and Luigi Scrivo, had in fact appeared in 1968, marking a revival of interest in the agitational tactics of Italian Futurism.[64] Mulas's photograph of the dispersed bits of paper strewn by Munari on the pavement at the foot of the Broletto also recalls moments in Italy's Neo-Dada of the 1950s, in this case, a series of small shows mounted by Munari himself in the span of a few months from 1951 to 1952 in an alternative space in Milan, of which no visual record remains. In *Oggetti trovati* (Found objects), Munari scattered stones, tree roots, discarded mechanical tools, and other debris across the gallery floor. In *L'arte e il caso* (Art and chance), he displayed what he termed *sfogliazzi* — sheets of metal recycled by typographers to produce different registers of color — on the floor of the gallery along with rags. In conjunction with these, he published a series of manifestos — "Arte totale" (Total art), "Arte organica" (Organic art), and "Disintegrismo" (Disintegrationism) — in which he called for works that could be alternatively stable or mobile, transparent or opaque.[65]

Giordano Bruno, Patron Saint of the Sixty-Eighters

Of all the photographic sequences in the *Campo urbano* photo book, most phantasmic is that following a spectator seen from the back under the luminous artificial rain produced by Edilio Alpini, Davide Boriani, Gianni Colombo, and Gabriele De Vecchi in *Tempo libero* (Figure 2.15). This figure traverses the gleaming expanse of the Piazza del Duomo as if walking through a ring of fire, wearing a hooded cape made, according to Caramel, of a shiny piece of black plastic torn from La Pietra's tunnel.[66] In the photographs, the paving stones of the piazza appear drenched in oil. The caped silhouette reads like a ghost and triggers multiple flashbacks. The figure looks uncannily like Ettore Ferrari's nineteenth-century bronze monument to the hooded heretical friar Giordano Bruno, which stands in the Campo de' Fiori in Rome, especially when it is seen from the back (Figure 2.16). On February 17, 1600, Bruno was made to walk through the city to this market square to be burned alive before the crowds that customarily gathered for such executions. Bruno was a disciplinary trespasser with a famously speculative mind: his unconventional beliefs and endeavors forced him to live a peripatetic existence, crisscrossing Europe between its university towns, from Naples to Genoa and Venice with many stops in between. Ingrid Rowland, his most recent biographer, describes him as rebellious, inquisitive, thin skinned, precocious, wild minded, and extreme — a professor who hated the standard curriculum and excelled as a performer.[67] The many medieval European cities he visited were among those whose main squares were overrun by demonstrators in 1968.[68] In 1592, Bruno returned to Venice, where he was arrested on May 22, 1593; thereafter, he was sent to Rome and imprisoned for the duration of his trial, which lasted seven years.

147

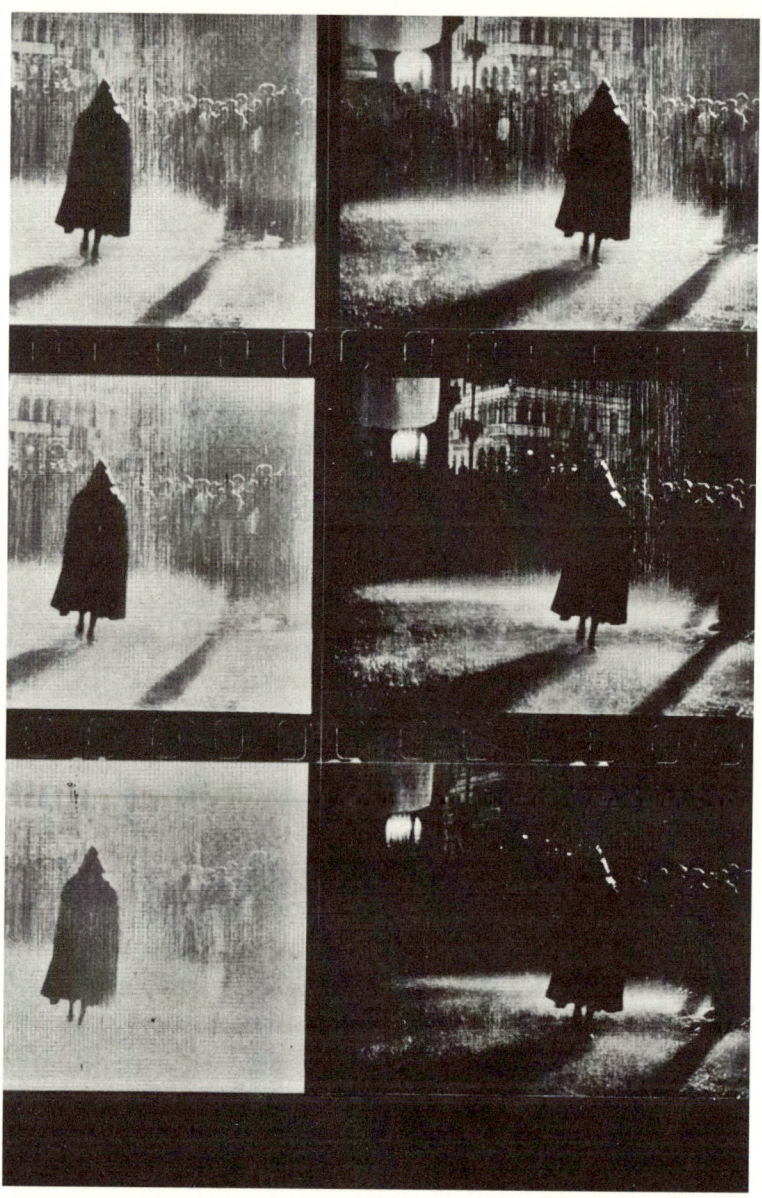

Figure 2.15. Edilio Alpini, Davide Boriani, Gianni Colombo, and Gabriele De Vecchi in *Tempo libero: Struttura temporale in uno spazio urbano* (Free time: Temporal structure for an urban space). *Campo urbano,* 1969. Photography: Ugo Mulas. Design: Bruno Munari.

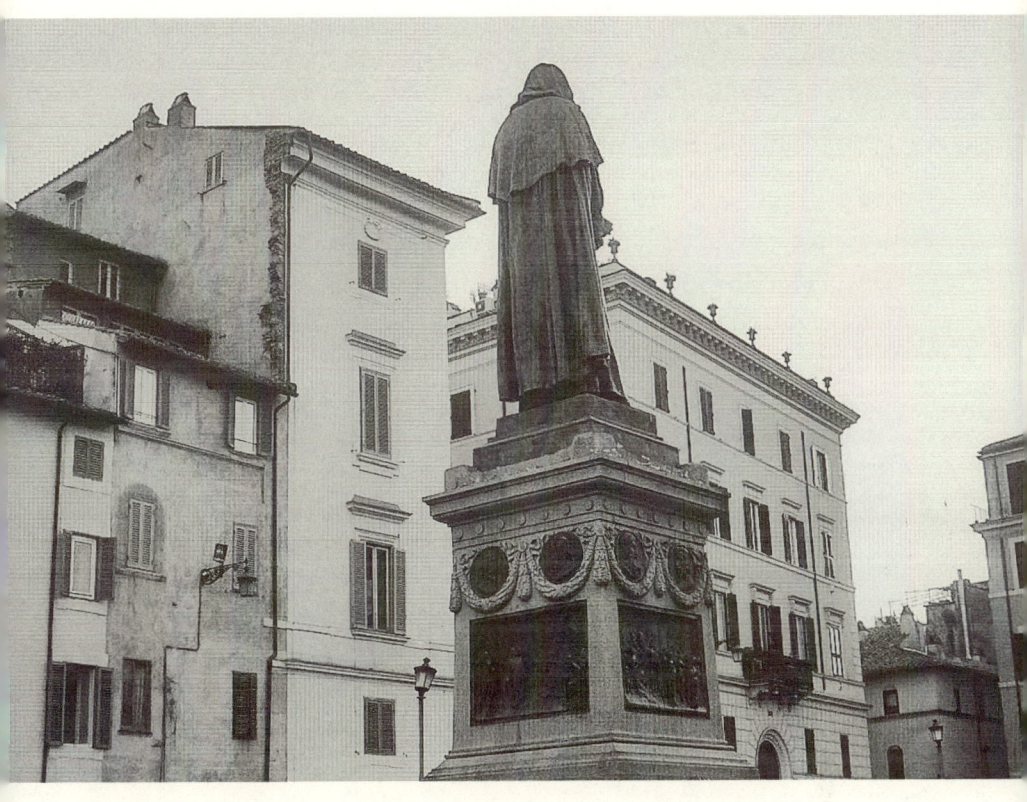

Figure 2.16. Ettore Ferrari, *Monument to Giordano Bruno*, 1889. Campo de' fiori, Rome. Photograph: the author.

An enduringly controversial figure in Italian history, Bruno had all of the prerequisites for becoming the patron saint of the Italian sixty-eighters. Ferrari had made his monument to Bruno, erected in 1889, for free in support of a student initiative that arose in the wake of the Risorgimento, the unification of Italy. The official *resoconto* (report) detailing the sculpture's realization, written by students, sounds amazingly similar to what led to *Campo urbano*. Like the latter, the students' push for a memorial to Bruno, defying centuries of papal suppression in Rome, involved sit-ins, negotiations with local authorities, and the distribution of manifestos and pamphlets, starting in 1876. Like their twentieth-century counterparts, the report declared: "We students mingled among men of letters, journalists, and artists, sharing the same ideas. . . . Our work was feverish."[69]

On May 31, 1968, Roman university students set up barricades on the Campo de' Fiori and in front of the nearby Palazzo Farnese, the French embassy in Rome, in a demonstration of solidarity with their Parisian counterparts. In a violent confrontation with the police, twenty were hurt, four were arrested, and fifty were being held in custody.[70] The wet, caped figure in the Munari/Mulas photo book was an homage to them, as well as to the defiant Bruno.

Aby Warburg in Rome

The 1876 *resoconto* — and this is the truly serendipitous part of the flashback — belongs to the Bibliotheca Bruniana Electronica set up in collaboration with the Warburg Archive. And there we leap to one of the most phenomenal memory machines, *Atlas Mnemosyne*, put together in the late 1920s by the German turn-of-the-century art historian Aby Warburg. In the last years of his life, while assembling his *Atlas*, Warburg also acquired a substantial collection of documents by and pertaining to Bruno, of which the *resoconto* is one. Culled from his archive of twenty-five thousand photographs, *Mnemosyne* consists of assemblages of pictures organized according to certain themes or gestures, displayed on large panels. In his 1975 essay "Warburg and the Nameless Science," the philosopher Giorgio Agamben described the *Atlas* as "a gigantic condenser that gathered together all the energetic currents that had animated and continued to animate Europe's memory, taking form in its ghosts. Mnemonic images that migrate in a culture that is always in a process of transmission, reception, and polarization."[71]

The concept of *Nachleben*, or afterlife, writes the art historian Georges Didi-Huberman, "anachronizes" history and also "disorients" it.[72] For Warburg, he continues, thinking in terms of constellations of images was a business of migrations, of perpetual *Wanderstrassen*. Warburg's *Mnemosyne* is an epistemological tool of disciplinary "deterritorialization."[73] In *Atlas: How to Carry the World on One's Back?* — the book that accompanied the exhibition Didi-Huberman curated at the Reina Sofía in Madrid, which included over one hundred artists — he describes Warburg's *Atlas* as a "time machine" (*machine à remonter le temps*) that allows one to reread the past through the juxtaposition of images.[74] Didi-Huberman's exhibition and previous excursions by Wolfgang Kemp, Werner Hofmann, Kurt Forster, Benjamin Buchloh, and Philippe-Alain Michaud into the so-called "archive aesthetic" have brought Warburg's *Atlas* into the fold of twentieth-century art. It now belongs alongside the *Dadaistischer Handatlas*, Hannah Höch's scrapbook, and the work of El Lissitzky, Kurt Schwitters, Gerhard Richter, Christian Boltanski, Annette Messager, Marcel Broodthaers, John Baldessari, Hanne Darboven, and Lothar Baumgarten. Warburg's method can also be compared to the work of Walter Benjamin, Siegfried Kracauer, and André Malraux.[75] To these we can now add Munari's orchestration and organization of photographic images in the 1930s for the print media in Italy in the 1930s and 1940s.

A more detailed comparison of the work of Warburg and Munari reveals deep and historically specific connections. Like Warburg, Munari imagined past moments — from the Middle Ages through the nineteenth and twentieth centuries — when the hearts of European cities were taken over by crowds. This transhistorical insight results from folding 1929 onto 1969, two particularly volatile years in Italy's history. Munari—a generation older than all the other artists involved in *Campo urbano* and a man whose career deftly and self-consciously bridged Fascism and post-Fascism—was in a perfect position to expose these connections. The year 1966, when students started agitating on the piazzas and campuses of the peninsula, was also the year that the Italians rediscovered Warburg. They were, in fact, the first in Europe to do so: for the centenary of his birth, the Florentine press La Nuova Italia published the first translation of Warburg's *Die Erneuerung der heidnischen Antike* (The renewal of pagan antiquity), a volume of collected writings first published three years after Warburg's death, edited by his lifelong collaborator Gertrude Bing.[76] Bing began her introduction to the volume by thanking Giorgio Pasquali, a professor of philology at the Universities of Florence and Rome, for his obituary of Warburg. (In one of those countless stories of individual compromise, Pasquali, although he penned that obituary in 1930 for the Fascist journal *Pegaso*, had been one of the few signatories of Benedetto Croce's "Manifesto degli intellettuali antifascisti" (Manifesto of the anti-Fascist intellectuals) of 1925.[77] In his review of the Italian translation of Warburg's book in 1966, the historian Carlo Ginzburg insisted on two aspects of Warburg's work: his indifference to aesthetic matters and his interest in "understanding a historical situation."[78] The book's back cover is graced by a black-and-white photograph of an ancient relief of Mnemosyne stepping forward in her flowing drapery. She is traversing the centuries. The image is printed, or "veered," as Munari would do with Mulas's photographs, in cerulean blue. In the *Campo urbano* photo book, the hooded figure traversing the artificial rain of *Tempo libero* on the Piazza del Duomo can be read as an instance of Warburgian *pathosformel*, or "emotive formula," the reappearance of a given posture or gesture from antiquity in later centuries. Harking back to Bruno and the students' *resoconto* of his monument in the years of the Risorgimento, it may also be read as a manifestation of the *Nachleben* (afterlife) of revolution.

Let us return to 1929, when Warburg spent what would turn out to be some of the last months of his life in Rome, obsessing over two things: Giordano Bruno and the signing of the Lateran Treaty on February 11 of that year. The two turn out to be connected. The full historical implications of the Lateran Treaty are still debated to this day. Known as *la Conciliazione*, its signing by Benito Mussolini and Cardinal Pietro Gasparri meant that the Catholic Church would resign its temporal powers and claims to the Italian state, which in return would institute the Catholic faith as the state religion.

While collecting material for his library, Warburg sought as his advisor the philosopher Giovanni Gentile. Gentile was a renowned Bruno scholar and a major exponent of the Fascist regime; he welcomed the Lateran Treaty, seeing it as an act of renunciation on the part of the church. Warburg responded to the event with both excitement and trepidation, as his correspondence reveals. His archive contains many sets of postcards commemorating the event, and a number of letters from his German colleagues acknowledge the receipt of additional such postcards. In one letter, Warburg talks about "a popular Italian photo book" of the event "well worth circulating in Germany."[79]

As the philosopher Ernst Cassirer recalled in his obituary for his friend Warburg: "I had signaled Bruno to him because I believed that he [Warburg] could resolve better than anyone the enigma of this thinker through images. Warburg became immersed in this project, and I noted once again how what was for us a theoretical problem was for him [Warburg] a lived experience that animated and shook him from within. He felt connected to this thinker."[80] Bruno was also renowned as a master of mnemonic techniques, which must have added to his allure for Warburg. As Ingrid Rowland writes in her biography, "Remembering would become Giordano Bruno's chief profession. In his own day, he earned his widest reputation, and often his living, by teaching an ancient technique for the enhancement of memory developed in ancient Greece and called the 'artificial memory' by the ancient Romans, who included memory as a basic element in rhetorical training."[81] The artificial memory would come to be used by Dominicans such as Bruno as a tool for preaching: "The basic principle of the artificial memory was a simple one: to link words with images.... Ancient orators built up their memories by creating imaginary buildings in their minds and stocking these buildings with people and statues that represented individual ideas or parts of a speech."[82]

One of the principal reasons for Warburg's fascination with the Lateran Treaty — one that links him specifically to Bruno — is the way it brought historical memory into the present. On the afternoon of February 11, 1929, Warburg went into the streets to join the crowds celebrating the signing of the treaty. The historian Arnaldo Momigliano relates this escapade, based on the recollections of Warburg's assistant, Gertrude Bing. Warburg had become separated from his companions, including Bing, and reappeared at his hotel only near midnight. "When he was reproached he soberly replied something like this in his picturesque German: 'You know that throughout my life I have been interested in the revival of paganism and pagan festivals. Today I had the chance of my life to be present at the re-paganization of Rome, and you complain that I remained to watch it.'"[83]

In the preceding years, Warburg had been assembling for his archive hundreds of photographs of prints, tapestries, and paintings of secular and sacred festivities spanning the period from 1450 to 1800, which he eventually poured into his *Atlas*. Indeed, as he wrote in 1895: "There is only one way to transform the contemporary narratives, which now strike us at first sight merely as dry or bizarre enumerations, into vividly remembered images: and that is by making the effort to see them in the context of the depictions of festive pageantry in the art of the period."[84] It was only in 1929, however, in the last three panels of the *Atlas Mnemosyne*, that Warburg began to include images from contemporary tabloids, press photographs, and postcards. Our knowledge of these panels' juxtapositions relies on his final arrangement of these in May 1929. One might speculate that had Warburg lived longer, more present-day images would have appeared in his *Atlas*.

As Charlotte Schoell-Glass has convincingly shown in her analysis of these final panels, this coming together of present and past was suffused with a sense of foreboding and political strife.[85] The sense of negative self-fulfilling prophecy is echoed in several pages, namely, in the last scenes going from the hooded figures of *Tempo libero* to the hooded figures of Scheggi's funeral march, in the *Campo urbano* photo book. While panel 77 of Warburg's *Atlas* includes mostly fashion plates, stamps, and travel ads, panels 78 and 79 (Figure 2.17) are dominated by photographic reportage of the signing of the Lateran Treaty and images of the pope blessing the faithful from the loggia of Saint Peter's the following day, with the architecture of the square framing crowds and military troops. On the bottom right of panel 78 is a photograph of Cardinal Pietro Maffi visiting a Fiat factory. As Christopher Johnson has noted, Maffi's "interests in science and astronomy were matched only by his fervent, militant nationalism."[86] In the center of panel 79 is a column with six contiguous photographs showing the Eucharistic procession and parade of the Swiss guards and the state military on Saint Peter's Square on July 25, 1929.[87] Warburg's inclusion of Raphael's *Mass at Bolsena* fresco from the Stanza di Eliodoro in the Vatican (1511), according to Schoell-Glass, is the key to the function of the contemporary images as documents.[88] The fresco depicts a miracle involving a bleeding host in 1263 and is thus a reenactment of the "Hoc est corpus meum" of the Last Supper. After the Fourth Lateran Council of 1215 made the transubstantiation of the host part of the Catholic dogma, reports of bleeding hosts began to multiply. Under Raphael's fresco, Warburg placed an image of Giotto's grisaille figure *Hope* from the Arena Chapel in Padua, while to its right appear photos of the 1929 Eucharistic procession in Rome. On the upper right is an image of Japanese hara-kiri. Below it just on the right is an entire page of the *Hamburger Fremdenblatt* (dated July 29, 1929), intended as a joke about body builders and athletes — what Warburg called "redemption through muscles."[89] The threat of the mob is made explicit by Warburg in his inclusion of two late fifteenth-century woodcuts depicting the desecration of the host,

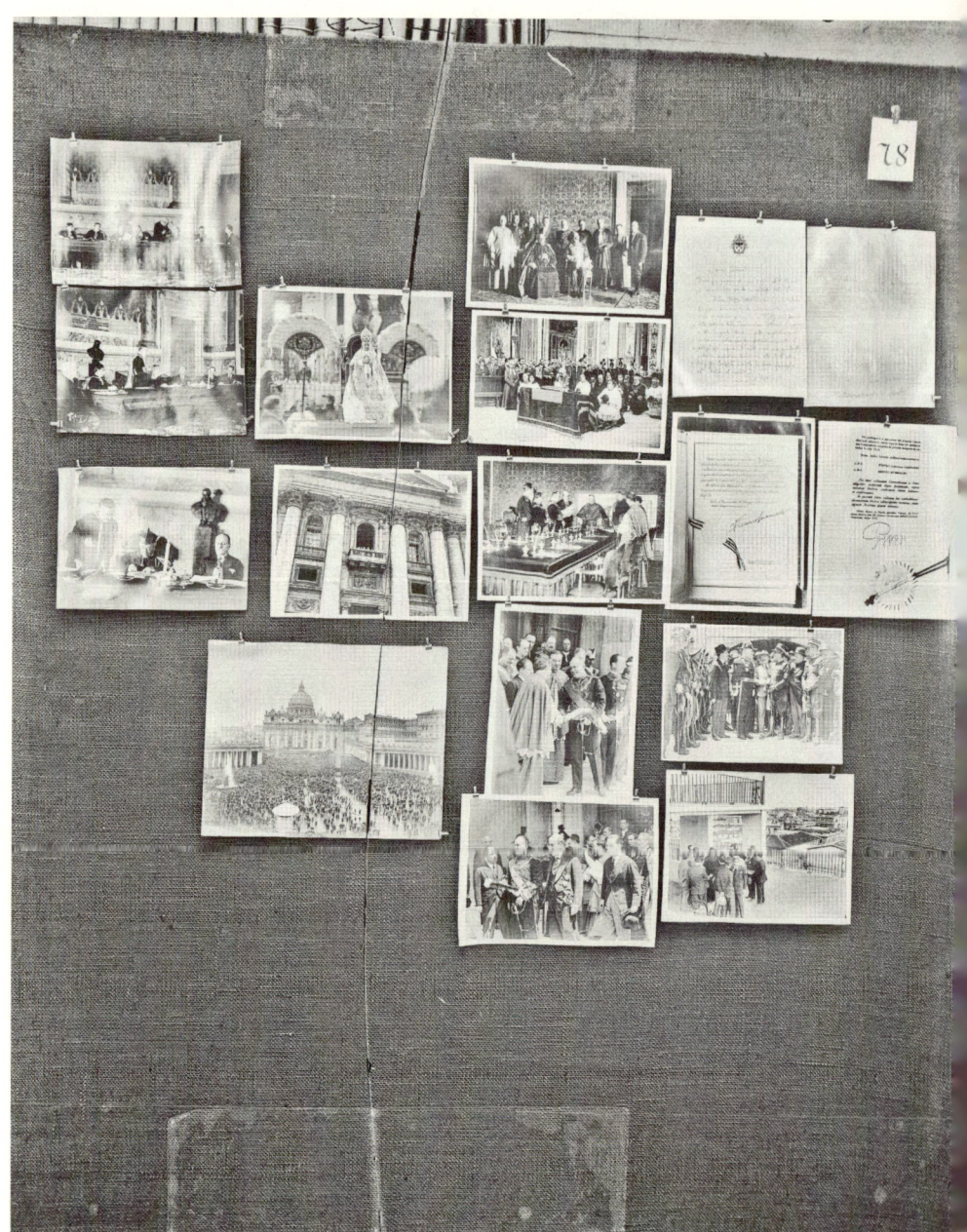

Figure 2.17. Aby Warburg, *Atlas Mnemosyne*, panels 78 and 79. Photograph: The Warburg Institute.

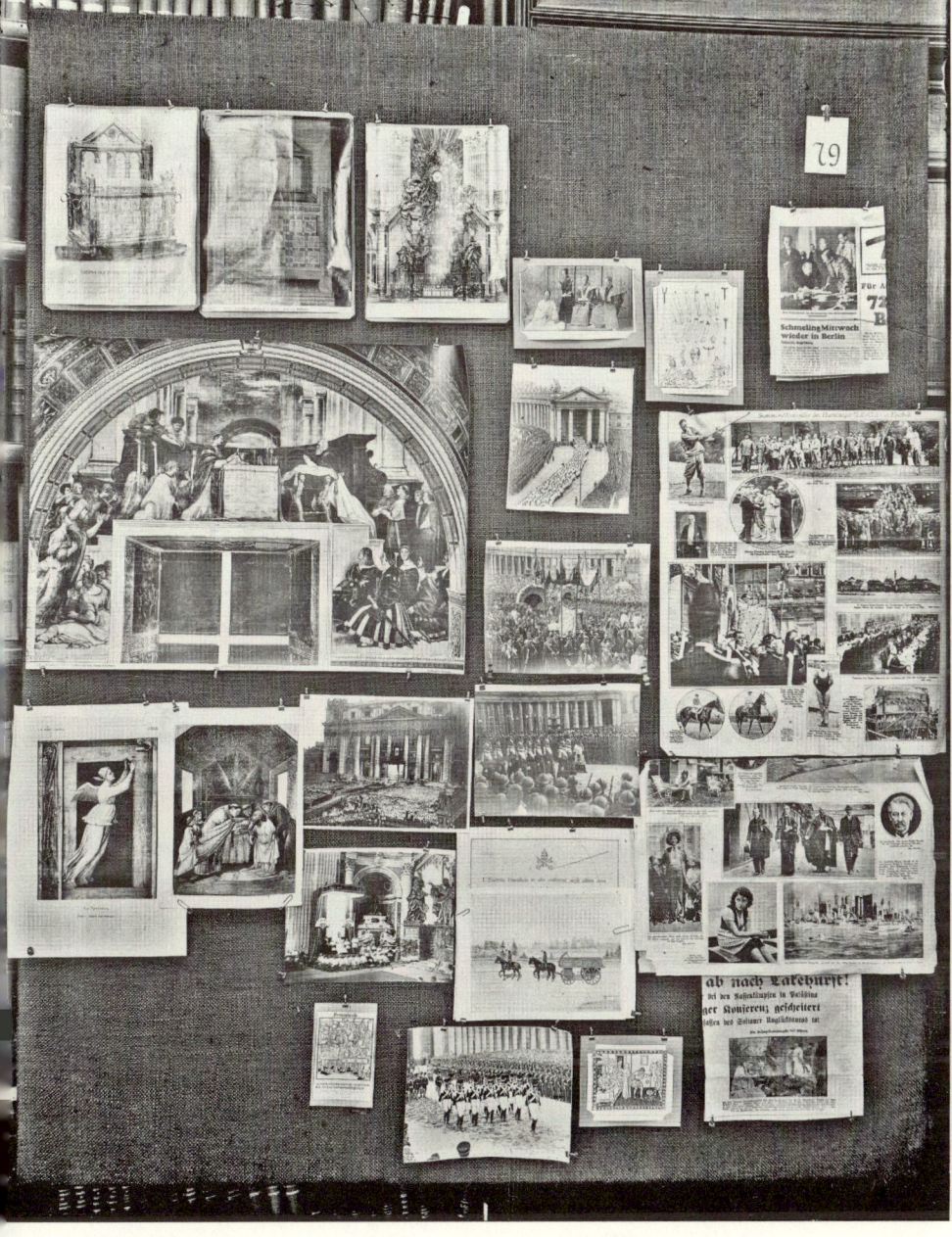

a legend that launched the hunt in Europe against the alleged cul-
prit — Jews — after 1215. In the bottom center, Fascist troops parade
in front of the Vatican.

Eclipsing Giuseppe Terragni's Casa del Fascio

For the artists of *Campo urbano*, turning Como into the ideal city for
a liberatory one-day event meant erasing the footprint of its most
famous architect: Giuseppe Terragni. There was one square just a
few steps from the Piazza del Duomo that all of the participants of
Campo urbano avoided: the Piazza del Popolo — formerly the Piazza
Impero — on which stands Como's principal architectural landmark,
Terragni's Casa del Fascio of 1936, one of the key monuments of Fascist Rationalist architecture and certainly the most photographed.

After the war, the former Fascist headquarters became the center
of operations of the Guardia di Finanza, the state agency combat-
ting financial crime and smuggling. When I interviewed Caramel
and asked why they had avoided this location, he brushed my question aside, claiming that Terragni's building wasn't relevant at that
time: "None of the artists asked to go there. There was no talk about
Rationalist architecture at the time. Also, that space was state property — it could not be used because it belonged to the Finance Ministry. No one would have dreamed of demonstrating there twenty
years after the end of Fascism, except, perhaps, on April 25, the day
of the fall of the regime."[90]

Yet it just so happens that a year before *Campo urbano*, on September 14 and 15, 1968, a large conference on Terragni and his architectural legacy had taken place in Como in which major participants
of *Campo urbano* took part. Organized by Bruno Zevi, it was sponsored by the municipality, the tourism agency, and the chamber of
commerce, the same entities that provided support to *Campo urbano*.
The conference was one of Zevi's many attempts to rehabilitate the
architect; a few months earlier, he had also devoted a special issue of
his magazine, *L'Architettura*, to Terragni.[91] As he stated in his opening
remarks: "This conference represents a necessary and timely homage

on behalf of the city to its son, a great citizen, one of the greatest modernist figures of the last fifty years. And yet nothing has been written on this major figure—the only one with an international reputation between the wars—until now."[92] However, it would be more accurate to say that until then, the story told by Zevi and others of his generation was one of an untainted modernism they characterized as a heroic resistance to the Fascist regime.[93] It was precisely the ambiguity of that history that prompted the ever-lucid Giulio Carlo Argan to state: "The significance of Terragni resides precisely in his inner contradiction between the antique and the modern, Futurism and *Metafisica*, ideology and disengagement."[94]

Both Caramel and Di Salvo spoke at the September 1968 event. Caramel lectured on Terragni and abstract painters from Como, a topic that would continue to occupy him for the rest of his career.[95] Di Salvo spoke on the architect Cesare Cattaneo, one of Terragni's colleagues.[96] In the months prior to *Campo urbano*, Caramel and Di Salvo also contributed articles on Terragni to *Quadrante Lariano*, which published two issues focusing on the architect and his circle in Como, one in advance of the conference and another just after.[97] The architectural historian Giorgio Ciucci has argued in his authoritative monographic volume on Terragni that the 1968 Como conference brought an end to the question of whether Terragni's radical Rationalism was, as Zevi believed, an act of resistance to dictatorship. No longer considered in direct relation to Fascism, Terragni was left, Ciucci writes, "in a sort of political limbo."[98] After that, he maintains, came a more historicist approach to his work. The conference, in his estimation, was a watershed.

Visually, this watershed took the shape of an eclipse (Figure 2.18). The cover of the May–June 1968 issue of *Quadrante Lariano* dedicated to the Casa del Fascio makes an inverted pair with its more famous referent, the October 1936 double issue of the modernist/Fascist architecture journal *Quadrante*, also dedicated to the Casa del Fascio. The silhouette of the building in 1936 set against a black ground is printed in 1968 over a white ground via a solarization

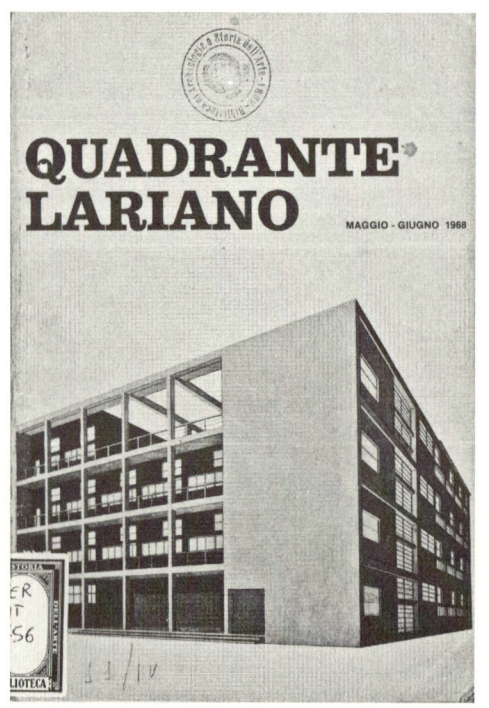 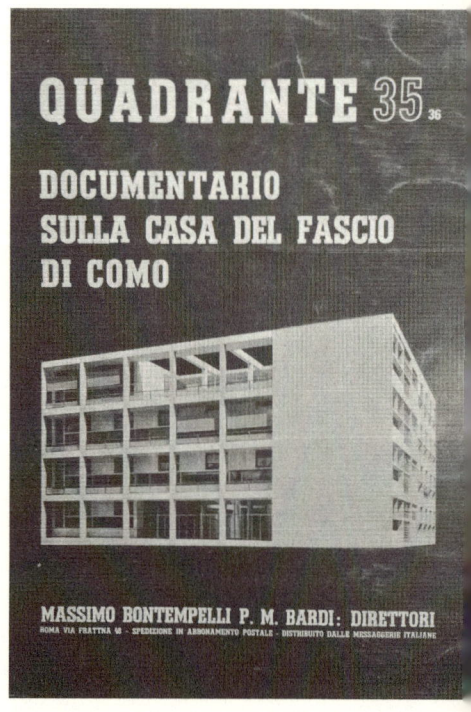

Figure 2.18. Covers of *Quadrante Lariano*, May–June 1968, and *Quadrante* 35–36 (October 1936). Rome: Biblioteca di archeologia e storia dell'arte.

technique in which the tone of a photographic negative or print is reversed, often through overexposure. As if in a solar eclipse, a negative image switches to a positive one: it is *reexposed* (politically), under a new light. As in an eclipse, when the moon covers the sun, it is as if one image of the building had been slipped in front of the other one.

Eclipses can be bad omens. The special double issue on the Casa del Fascio — the most spectacular in *Quadrante*'s three-year run — thus also turned out to be its last. In the meantime, the journal's cover underwent a dramatic graphic makeover. The minimalist, imageless, dust-colored covers of the previous issues were abandoned in favor of a design centered on a dramatic, full-page photograph of the building. The cover's artificial darkness unwittingly signaled the eclipse of Fascist Rationalism encapsulated by Terragni. In 1936, the regime began its shift toward a neo-Roman architectural aesthetic. The stern cubical Casa del Fascio had become, in other words, its own epitaph. In his essay Terragni stated: "With the completion of the Casa del Fascio as foreseen by the city's zoning plan, today it is possible to think of a future when Como will be a 'Fascist city'; an organic and intelligent concentration of the more typical buildings of the Regime in a huge plaza which is the logical and natural continuation of the historic Piazza del Duomo."[99] It is this anointment that the organizers and the artists involved in *Campo urbano* unequivocally strove to revoke.

In 1943, at the end of the war, with Italy now firmly in Allied hands, the Casa del Fascio had already been eclipsed by Bruno Munari himself in a two-page photo-essay for *Domus* entitled "La città ideale" (The ideal city).[100] The article was a call to recognize Rationalism as part of Italy's architectural mix: "We could cite the names of many architects who have contributed to [the rational style]. . . . In Como, for instance, next to the Duomo, we see Terragni's Casa, and that's perfectly fine. From this juxtaposition we can deduce that when a style has reached maturity, it can be set next to the others."[101] Munari's montage featured four photographs along the top of the two pages, showing a medieval castle, the Baptistery of Pisa, a Rationalist apartment building, and Palladio's Villa Rotonda in Vicenza. Along the bottom edge of the pages, in the style of a contact sheet, were arranged ten identical images of a nondescript apartment building. Although cited, the Casa del Fascio was nowhere in the mix.

And yet, perusing the issues of *Quadrante Lariano* from 1968 to 1969, one realizes that there was a continuous back-and-forth between reports on student demonstrations and the history of Como during the *ventennio*. In the March–April 1968 issue, five students who commuted from Como to the University of Milan reported on the agitation across the campuses of the Lombard capital.[102] The May–June 1968 issue with the Casa on its cover featured, in addition to a reprint of Terragni's "Discorso ai Comaschi" (Speech to the people of Como) of March 1940, a spirited article on the flourishing of local student papers such as *La Vasca* (The tub), *La Bomba* (The bomb), and *Como 5*.[103] The issue with the supplement on Como's high school student demonstrations featured an article by Di Salvo on the expropriation of the inhabitants of Cortesella, a working-class neighborhood at the center of town, at the time of the *sventramenti* — the demolition work ordered by Mussolini to clear the ground around Italy's most important monuments.[104] It is again this dialogue between present-day Como and its past that the organizers and artists involved in *Campo urbano* wanted to eclipse. If they had gone to Terragni's piazza, they would have been caught up in it.

Some of the photographs Terragni designed to illustrate his essay would rank among the best-known images of Italy during the *ventennio*. The first was Terragni's typological lineup of Como's medieval tower, the Broletto, the Duomo, and the Casa del Fascio (Figure 2.19).[105] This juxtaposition was used to signal that Terragni's (partly unrealized) project for a total redesign of the Piazza Impero was intended as both an extension of and a substitution for the Piazza del Duomo. The second photograph shows hundreds of Comaschi standing in front of the brand-new Casa on May 5, 1936, awaiting a broadcast of the Duce's speech from the Piazza Venezia in Rome.

The original version of the same photograph reveals that the image published in *Quadrante* was doctored to make the crowd look bigger, more integrated, and univocal. It thus belongs to a distinctly Fascist genre: the *folle oceaniche* (oceanic crowd) images reproduced in publications such as *La Rivista Illustrata del Popolo d'Italia*, the lavish, mass-distributed, official monthly of the regime.[106] Through the printed page and newsreels, Italians were privy to images of spectacular rallies in every city in Italy, from the Piazza del Duomo in Milan, to Piazza Venezia in Rome, to the main squares of Padua, Palermo, and Naples. Tellingly, once again, in 1968 and 1969, neither Zevi's *Architettura* nor Como's *Quadrante Lariano* featured the 1930s Casa-with-crowd photograph. The first monograph on Terragni published by the next generation, Comascho architect Enrico Mantero's in 1969, brought to light previously unpublished archival material, including politically damning speeches delivered by Terragni to his fellow Comaschi.[107] And yet again, visually: an eclipse. The sole image chosen by Mantero to illustrate the Casa was a shot taken from inside the building looking out, through its glass doors and onto a piazza left totally deserted except for a parked Balilla motorcar. No building, no crowds.

Much has been written about glass architecture and transparency.[108] Little has been said, however, about how reflections on public buildings and their furniture can function as political propaganda. The fame of the 1934 Casa issue of *Quadrante* rests largely on the photographs taken by Ico Parisi, a young architect working in Terragni's office who actually took part in *Campo urbano* with his piece *Contenitori umani* (Human containers); it was he who introduced Mulas to Caramel.[109] As evidenced from the photographs, Parisi understood that what made the Casa's doors distinct was not their transparency, which was a feature shared by the doors of other modernist buildings, but the way they functioned like photographic plates, capturing the image of the Duomo in the manner of a palimpsest (Figure 2.19). The same was true for Terragni's office furniture. The first to revisit Parisi's photographs was the architectural historian Kenneth

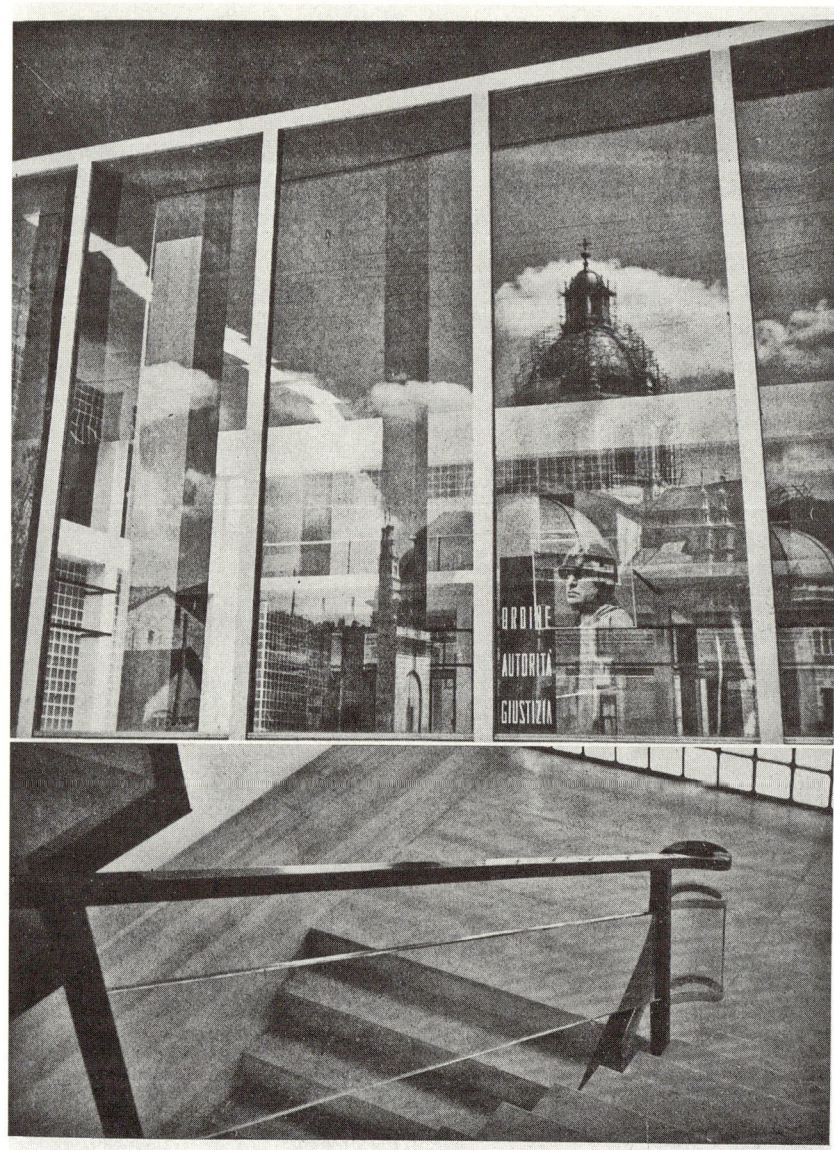

Particolari dell'ingresso e della scala (parapetto in vetro ultraforte). Tutte le lastre di vetro e cristallo sono state fornite e applicate dalla ditta Martelli e Beretta di Como.

Figure 2.19. *Quadrante* 35–36 (October 1936). Rome: Biblioteca di archeologia e storia dell'arte.

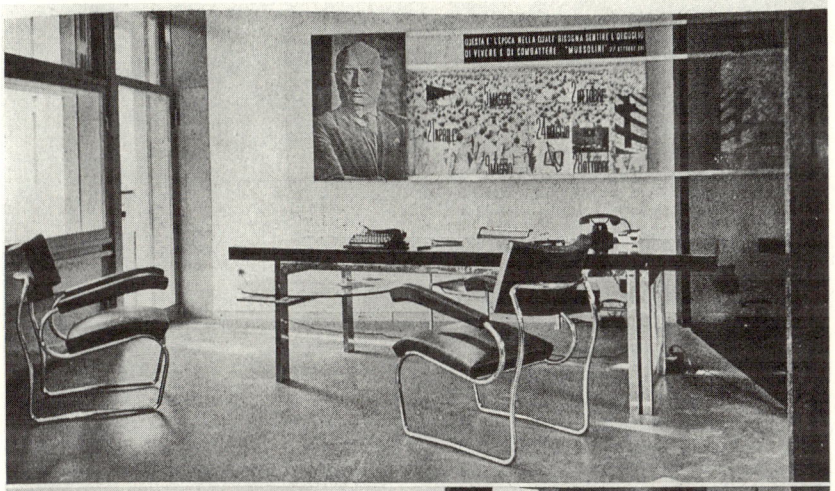

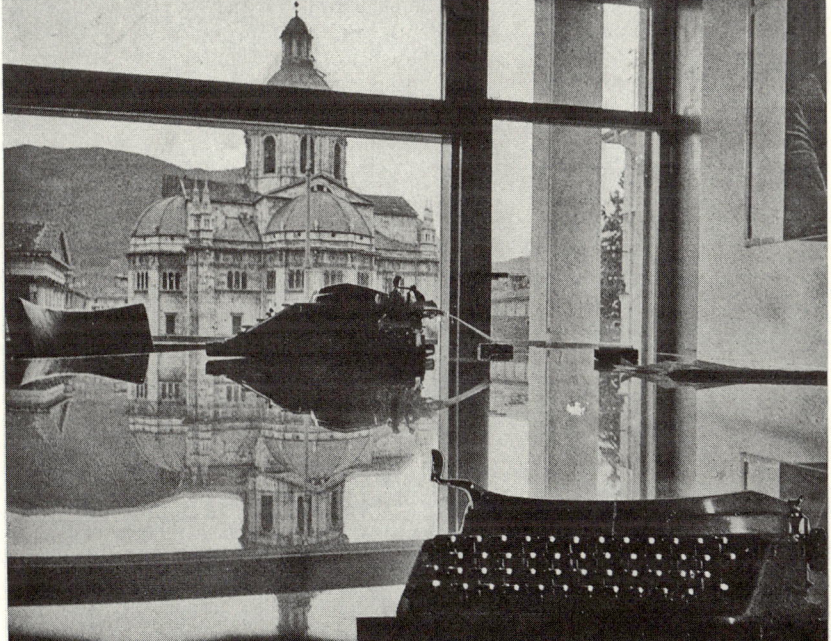

Studio del Federale. Armonia di architettura, d'arredamento, di oggetti (Macchine da scrivere Olivetti.)

Frampton, in "A Note on Photography and Its Influence on Architecture," in 1986.[110] Although he mentions the "metaphorical and isomorphic operations" at work in these photographs, Frampton's account remains a presentist one. A detail in one of these images that interests him is the "ironic parallelism" it constructs between the cathedral and a typewriter, "which are both seen as the origin of the word and of power."[111] But the political implication is far more precise. Seven years after the signing of the Lateran Treaty, the Duomo surges outside the Casa and invades its interior: Catholicism, Fascism, and Rationalism have merged. It is the camera that freezes this symbolism into a lasting image.

Reflection plays a central role in another Parisi photograph, one that was left out of *Quadrante*. The photograph features Massimo Bontempelli, the poet, novelist, and critic who in 1933 cofounded *Quadrante* with the art critic and gallerist Pietro (Pier) Maria Bardi (Figure 2.20).[112] On August 31, 1936, on Terragni's invitation, Bontempelli drove from the Tuscan resort of Forte dei Marmi to Como to tour the building with its architect. Bontempelli voiced his desire to write an editorial about the building, and Terragni had every reason to expect a positive article — all the more so, since Bontempelli was a native of Como. Bontempelli came that day with an entourage that included the writer Paola Masino (his wife), the painter Corrado Cagli, the sculptor Arturo Martini, the architect Alberto Sartoris, and a certain "M.B."[113] Parisi photographed the group during its three-hour tour of the building. In the photograph, we see, from left to right, Masino, Martini, Bontempelli, and Terragni at the head of the immense table Terragni designed for the Sala del Direttorio. Behind them is a mural by the abstract painter Mario Radice, another native of Como. Were it not for the fact that it featured a photomechanical reproduction of a portrait of Mussolini etched on a sheet of white marble, Radice's composition might have been considered an exceptional example of Fascist-era Neoplasticism; instead, the abstract beam motif merely serves as a framing device for the Duce.[114] Parisi's photograph shows the short, yet

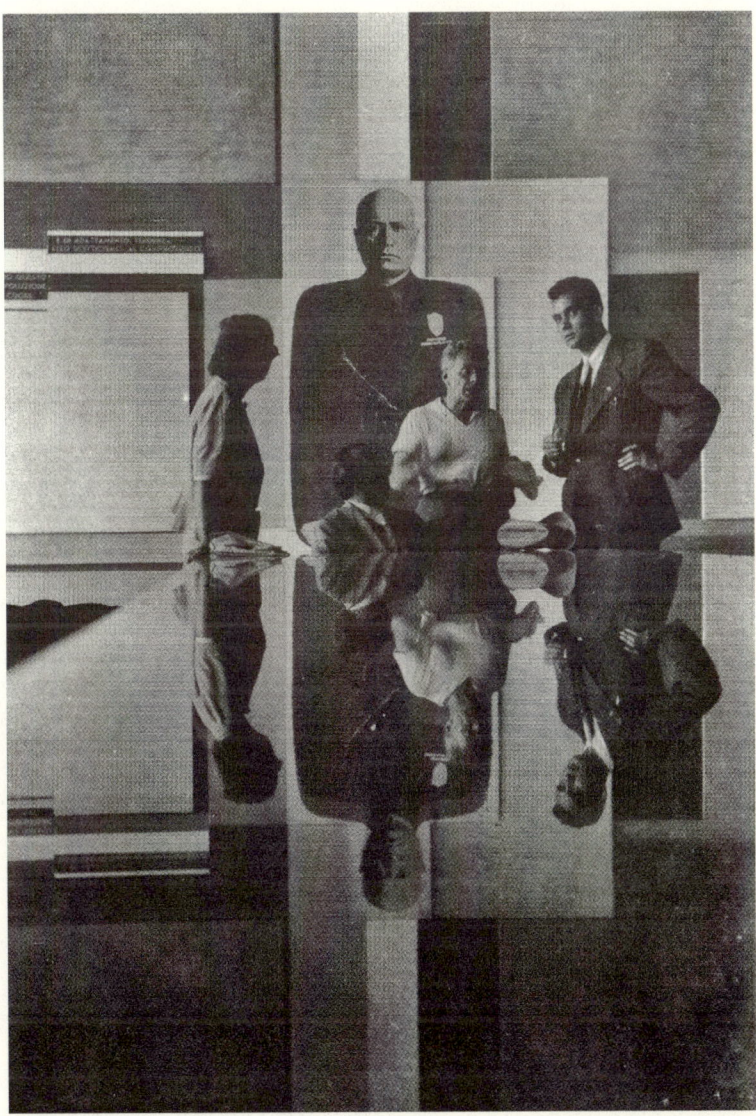

Figure 2.20. Paola Masino, Arturo Martini, Massimo Bontempelli, and Giuseppe Terragni in the Casa del Fascio, August 31, 1936. Photograph: Ico Parisi. Fondo Ico et Luisa Parisi, Pinacoteca Civica di Como.

muscular Bontempelli, wearing a white T-shirt (he is still in vaca-
tion mode), standing just in front of the image of the uniformed
Mussolini, his hair grazing the Duce's insignia. Through the photograph, we realize the degree to which Radice's mural, painted
on a new type of plaster polished to a high sheen, and Terragni's
crystal-topped table constitute a single isomorphic unit.[115] Framed
by the camera and reframed by the grid motif of the mural, the group
reappears, tipped over by the glass, in the bottom half of the photograph. The composition recalls Bontempelli's novella *La scacchi-
era davanti allo specchio* (The chessboard in front of the mirror) of
1922 — his first attempt to convey the uncanny and rarefied atmosphere of de Chirico's Metaphysical paintings through writing.[116] It is
only decades later, via Di Salvo and Ferrario's mirrors in *Riflessione*,
that we come to understand the meaning of covering, polishing,
doubling, and tipping over a building as a means to avoid any real
reckoning.

The photographic sequence of Di Salvo and Ferrario's *Riflessione*
is the only one in the *Campo urbano* photo book where we see Mulas
shooting his pictures (see Figure 2.5). In one of these moments of self-
reflection typical of a *mise en abyme*, we see him standing among the
participants/spectators at the edge of *Riflessione's* mirrors beneath
the soaring corner of the Duomo, holding his camera. The effect is
best described by another photographer, Vera Mutter, about her own
shots of Venice when they were exhibited at the National Gallery in
London in 2016. She was drawn, she says, to the way the city floods
create a still body of water, so that "Piazza San Marco, the space most
prone to flooding, folds into its own image, in a parallel or analogy to
the photographic process which works with reflected light, reflected
image, and the upside down image."[117]

As an architect and as a direct participant in the Terragni conference, Di Salvo must have had the debates over his legacy in mind
when he and Ferrario conceived of *Riflessione* for *Campo urbano*. His
feelings toward the architect are evident in the subtitle of the report
he wrote for *Quadrante Lariano* on Zevi's Terragni conference: "Un

passato che scotta" — a past that burns.[118] This is why he made sure to place his mirrors on the ground *in front* of the Duomo's façade, and not along its nave on Via Maestri Comacini, the street that leads straight to the Casa, or along its apse, which directly faces it (Figure 2.21). Alignment is everything, and here we have the perfect example of an eclipse revealing by omission.

And yet Munari, in one of those humorous gestures that have characterized his work since the beginning, ironizes Mulas's photographs in the double spread that follows (see Figure 2.5). On the left are two men peering into the pseudobaptismal font with the reflective bottom that Di Salvo and Ferrario had placed in front of the building. The font, as we recall, emitted fragments of music and political slogans orchestrated by Ferrario — a comic evocation of the gullible Comaschi who gathered in front of the Casa in 1936 to listen to the harangues of their Duce. The font is being scrutinized like a petri dish in a lab by the two observers, one a bespectacled and the other a bearded (left-wing, for example) intellectual. Meanwhile, on the right, we see Mulas bending down as if to photograph the participants' feet.

After 1968

The one time that Frances Yates — the author of *Giordano Bruno and the Hermetic Tradition* (1964) and *The Art of Memory* (1966) — was invited to step out of the Warburg Institute in London to contribute a piece related to present-day events was for an issue of *AD* (*Architectural Design*) devoted to the 1968 student demonstrations (Figure 2.22, left). In her essay, entitled "Architecture and the Art of Memory" and illustrated with an anodyne photo of a British motorway, one of Guy Debord's psychogeographic maps of Paris, and Giotto's allegorical figures of *Charity* and *Envy* from the Arena Chapel, she sets out to explain mnemonic techniques:

> Architecture may seem the most materially real of all the works of man. It uses solid materials, heavy and lasting, in comparison with the fleeting words of poetry or the fading designs of painting. Nevertheless, great architecture

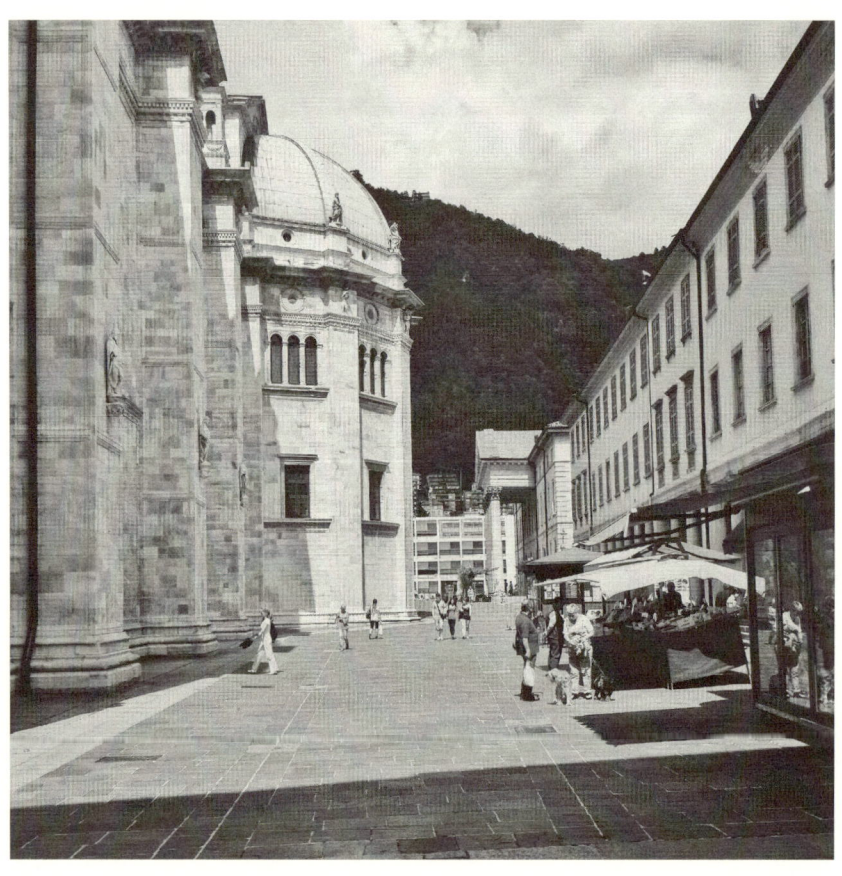

Figure 2.21. Via Maestri Comacini, Como. Photograph: the author.

carries with it a sense of immateriality. . . . If a building has an immaterial existence in the mind of the architect before it is built, it has also many immaterial existences in the memories of those who have seen it. The Roman orators made deliberate use of architectural memory as an aid to memorizing their speeches. This classical mnemonic consisted in fixing in memory a series of places, usually places in a building, or buildings, or in the streets of a city. . . . To these memorized places he fixed, in imagination, signs or images chosen to remind him of the points of his speech. It is a trick which can be practiced by anyone.[119]

Yates's essay was immediately followed by "Cities and Insurrections," by the Marxist historian Eric Hobsbawm (Figure 2.22, right). Hobsbawm asks the reader to imagine "the ideal city for riot and insurrection." He ended his essay — much like Henri Lefebvre and many others that year — wistfully hailing Paris as the great palimpsest city of the revolution, where barricades were erected again and again on the same spots.[120]

In typical Munari spirit, the recording of the *Campo urbano* event in the photo book ends on a charming note with two photographs of kids at play (Figure 2.23). On the left, they are jumping over a pile of flattened cardboard boxes in front of the Duomo, probably those discarded from Varisco's *Dilatazione spazio-temporale di un percorso*. On the right, two boys and a girl face us, smiling, while the adults wend their way home into the night. *Campo urbano*, as contemporary reviewers concurred, aimed to be a carnivalesque, dispersed, and plurivocal event. It flashed back to moments of historical liberation, including Baj's fictional coup against the state, the very antithesis of the Fascist rally illustrated in *Quadrante* in 1936. While by 1969 France had quietly reentered the political order of the so-called *ère pompidolienne*, the Pompidou era, in Italy, the student movement, which began in early 1966 and ended in the fall of 1969, lasted longer than anywhere else in Europe.[121] *Campo urbano* was a late summer festival, a final and in many ways innocent reprieve before the *autunno caldo* — the "hot autumn" of 1969, when the student movement became more

ARCHITECTURE AND THE ART OF MEMORY

Frances A. Yates

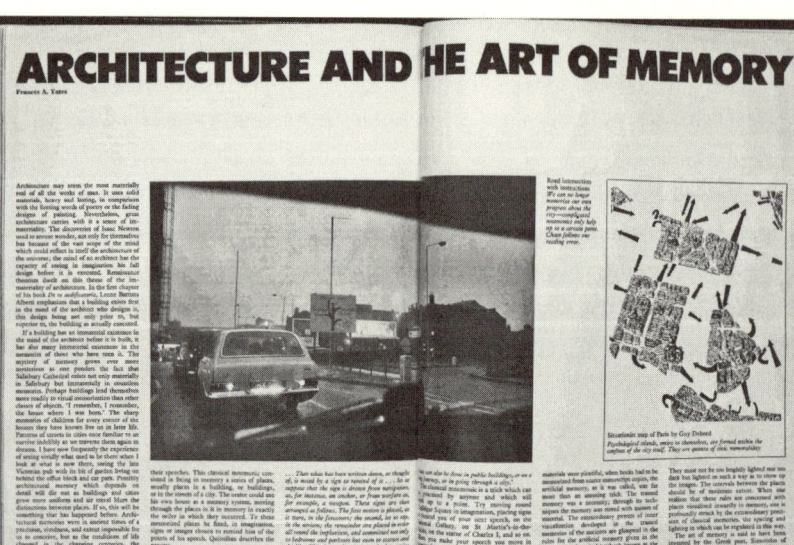

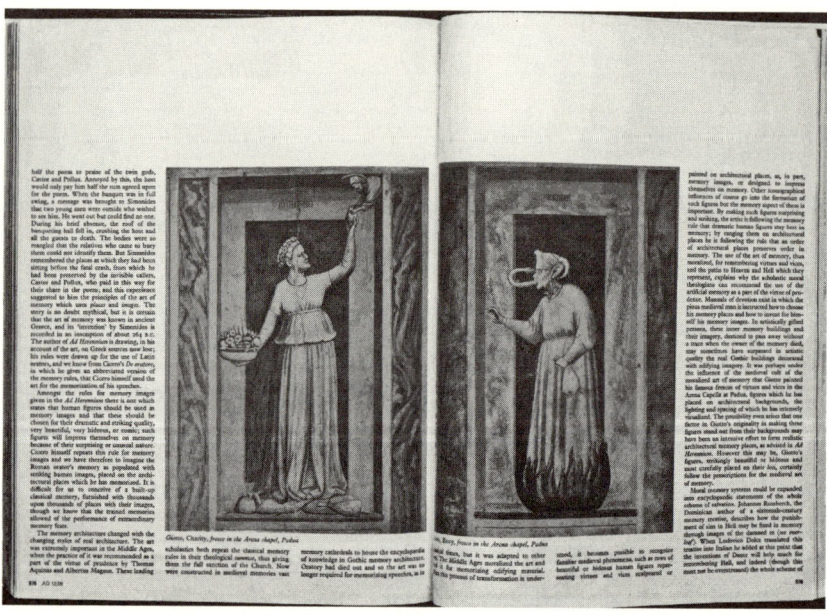

Figure 2.22. *Architectural Design* 7.6 (December 1968). Avery Library, Columbia University.

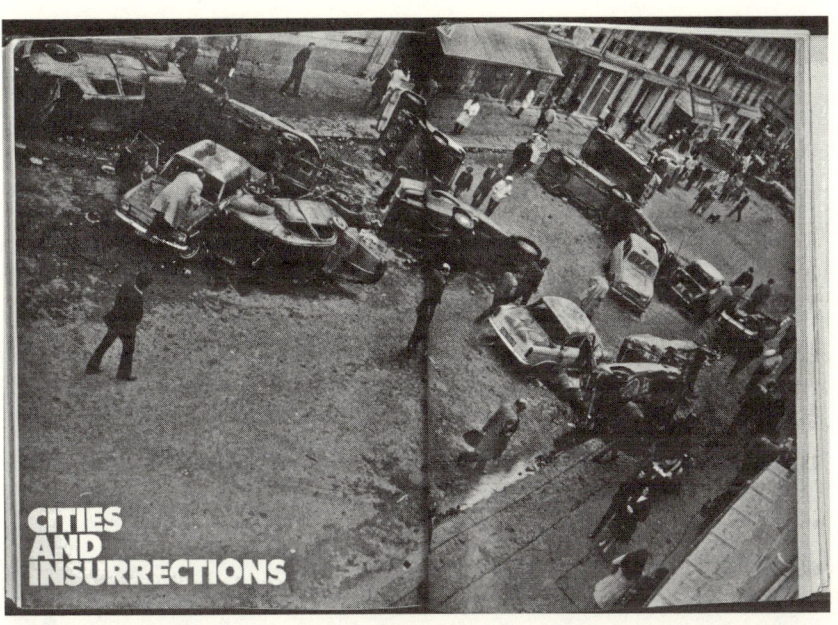

CITIES AND INSURRECTIONS

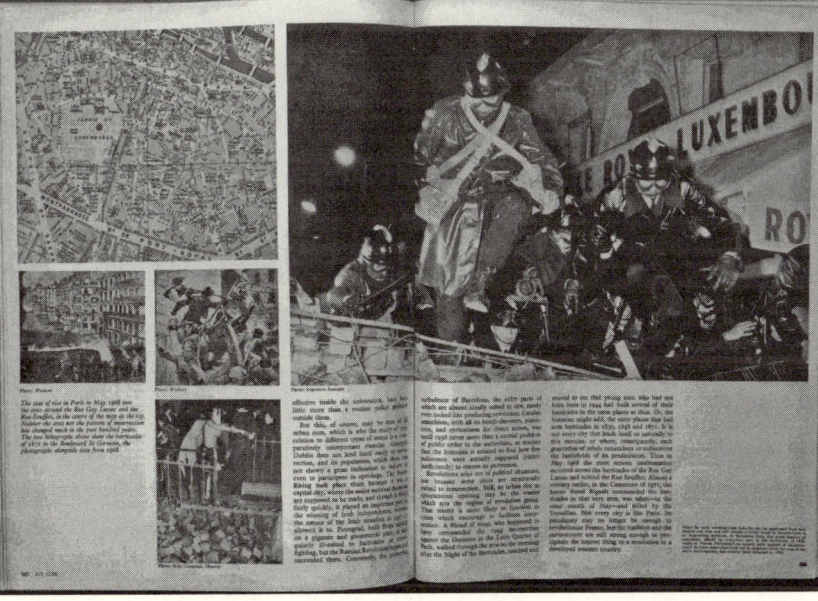

The text of riot in Paris in May 1968 was the area around the Rue Gay Lussac and the Rue Soufflot, in the centre of the map at the top. Number the areas are the pattern of insurrection has changed much in the past hundred years. The two lithographs above show the barricades of 1871 in the Boulevard St Germain, the photographs alongside date from 1968.

Photo: Elsevier

Photo: Viollet

Photo: Jean-Pierre Laffont

Photo: John Campbell, Hornsey

effective inside the universities, but has little more than a routine police problem outside them.

But this, of course, may be true of all urban riots, which is why the study of the relation to different types of terror is a comparatively unimportant exercise. Once the city, and more particularly to urbanisation, and its population, which does not even show a great inclination to move or even to participate in uprisings. The Rising took place then, because it was a capital city, where the entire political power was supposed to be made, and though it fell fairly quickly, it played an important part in the winning of Irish independence, since the nature of the Irish situation in 1916 allowed it to. Petrograd, both then and on a gigantic and grotesque scale, a city greatly devoted to barricade street fighting, but the Russian Revolution succeeded there. Conversely, the great

turbulence of Barcelona, the older part of which are almost ideally suited to riot, rarely even looked like producing revolution. Catalan anarchism, with all its bomb-throwers, punctures, and enthusiasm for direct action, was until 1936 never more than a normal problem of public order in the authorities, in times that the Iberians it seemed to find how few the milestones were actually supposed (many both fronts) to remain on position.

Revolutions who are of political situations, not because some cities are structurally suited to insurrection. Still, an urban riot or spontaneous uprising may be the easier which acts the regime if revolution goes. That counts is more likely to function in cities which encourage it facilitate insurrection. A blend of riots was perhaps to have commanded the 1948 insurrection against the Germans in the Latin Quarter of Paris, walked through the area on the morning after the Night of the Barricades, mused and

moved so, for that young men who had not been born in 1944 had built several of their barricades in the same places as then. Or, the Iberians might add, the same places that had seen barricades in 1830, 1848 and 1871. It is this seventy-year history that is naturally to this revision, or when, consequently, each generation of rebels remembers or rediscovers the barricades of its predecessors. Thus in May 1968 the street seventy combatants occupied across the barricades of the Rue Gay Lussac and behind the Rue Soufflot. Almost a century earlier, in the Commune of 1871, the honest Ernest Rigault commanded the insurrection in that very area, was taken—by the same assault of May—and killed by the Versailles. Not every city is like Paris. Insurrection may no longer be enough in revolutionary France, but the tradition and the prerequisites are still strong enough to impregnate the easiest thing to a revolution in a developed western country.

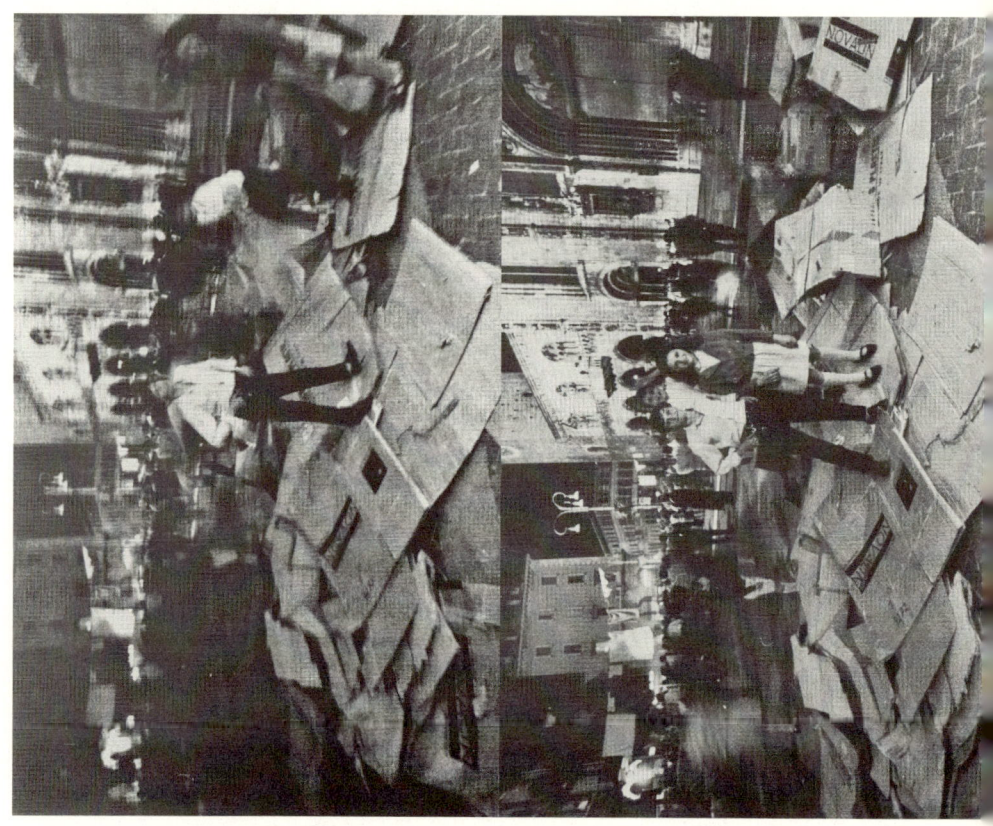

Figure 2.23. *Campo urbano*, 1969. Photography: Ugo Mulas. Design: Bruno Munari.

radicalized on both the Left and the Right, leading to confrontations with the police. On December 12, 1969, a neo-Fascist bombing in the Banca dell'Agricultura on Milan's Piazza Fontana left seventeen dead and eighty-eight injured. By the time Munari embarked on his photo book, Italy had plunged into a decade of turmoil. The ghosts of the *ventennio* had returned.[122]

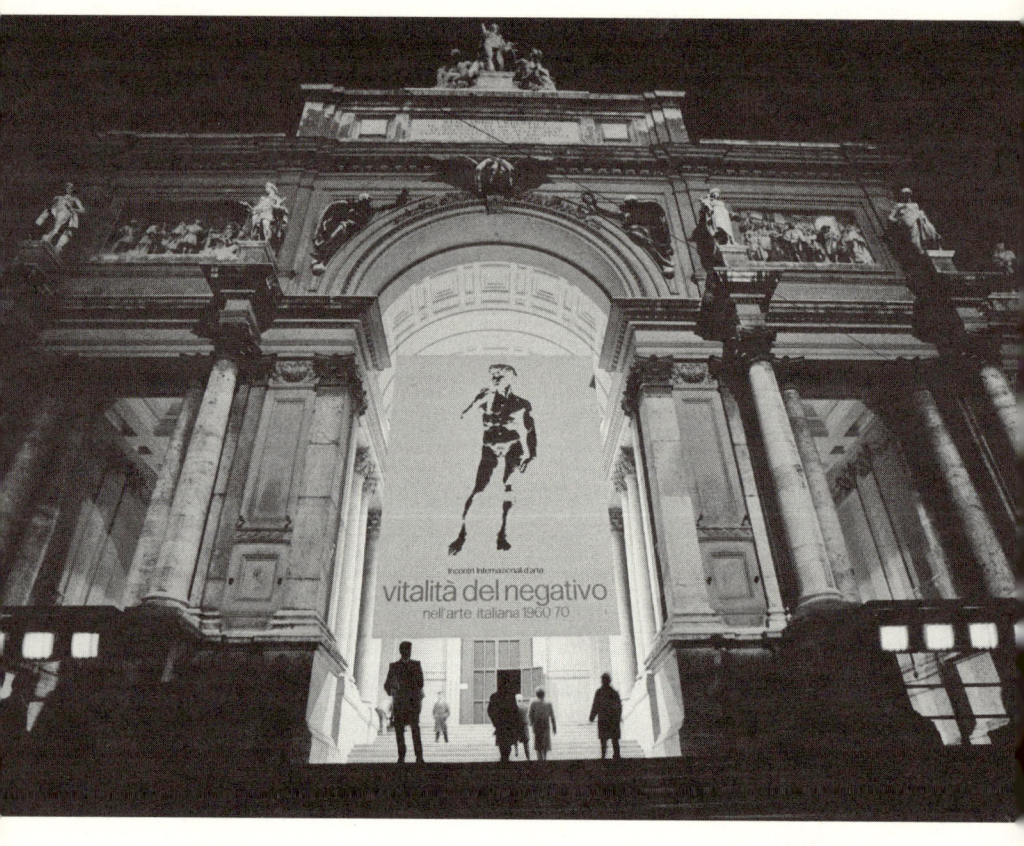

Figure 3.1. *Vitalità del negativo nell'arte Italiana 1960/70* (Vitality of the negative in Italian art 1960/70), façade of Palazzo delle Esposizioni, Rome, 1970. Photograph: Ugo Mulas. Courtesy Ugo Mulas Heirs.

CHAPTER THREE

Vitalità del Negativo:

The Exhibition as Palimpsest

In the Winter of 1970: The Strange World of Vitalità

Reviving an ideologically loaded site under the mantle of contemporary art, *Vitalità del negativo dell'arte Italiana 1960/70* (Vitality of the
negative in Italian art 1960/70), Achille Bonito Oliva's first important
exhibition, was suffused by a somber and politically suspect violence.
Staged in the Palazzo delle Esposizioni on Rome's Via Nazionale in
the winter of 1970–71, it featured thirty-three Italian artists from a
wide range of schools and media: painters from the Scuola di Piazza
del Popolo (the Roman school of Pop), members of the 1960s Milanese
group Azimut; kinetic environments by the Arte Programmata collectives Gruppo N (from Padua) and Gruppo T (from Milan), artists
associated with Arte Povera, and other, more idiosyncratic installation artists.[1] The catalogue included brief comments by its pro-
moter and sponsor, Graziella Lonardi Buontempo, the founder of the
Incontri Internazionali d'Arte, and Palma Bucarelli, the director of
Galleria Nazionale d'Arte Moderna; an introduction by Bonito Oliva;
and an anthology of texts first published in the 1950s and 1960s by the
critics Giulio Carlo Argan, Alberto Boatto, Maurizio Calvesi, Gillo
Dorfles, Filiberto Menna, and Cesare Vivaldi.[2]

Unlike his great competitor, Germano Celant, who put his bona
fide leftist cards on the table with "Appunti per una guerriglia"

(Notes for a guerilla war) in *Flash Art* in response to a surging student movement in 1967,[3] Bonito Oliva's statements in *Vitalità*'s catalogue and his interviews in magazines remained opaque. Although it was entirely dedicated to living artists (except for the recently deceased Pino Pascali), the exhibition prompted a series of flashbacks on the part of its curator, some of its artists, and most fiercely, some of its critics. As these critics correctly perceived, *Vitalità* belonged to a lineage of Italian exhibitions that harkened back, in some ways insistently, to the very spectacular ones of the Fascist *ventennio* housed in that same palazzo.

"Roma come New York" (Rome like New York) announced the capital's official daily, *Il Messaggero*, quoting the French correspondent of *Le Monde*. He had claimed in his review that *Vitalità del negativo nell'arte Italiana 1960/70* was the largest exhibition of its type ever to have been organized in Europe (Figure 3.1).[4] "The Most Beautiful Exhibition in Recent Years," proclaimed a headline in the illustrated weekly *L'Europeo*.[5] "The capital has never hosted a similar event," wrote the art historian and critic Filiberto Menna in Naples's *Il Mattino*, in what would turn out to be one of the few positive reviews of the exhibition. Yet even he concluded: "Bonito Oliva does nothing to clarify the theme of his exhibition. He should have elucidated what is, after all, specifically Italian about it. In this regard, he failed. We don't know what critical discourse subtends it."[6] Another critic, Armando Stefani, wrote:

> The possible meaning of "the negative in art" remains a mystery for the Romans, who began to speculate after seeing posters plastered all over town by November in an unusually ambitious publicity campaign. Some thought it was going to be a photography exhibition in view of the most obvious meaning of "negative." Some put forward a more sophisticated interpretation: this would be an exhibit of the more irreverent, perverse, satanic side of art. Now that it is visible, one needs to register an absolutely peculiar fact: it has managed to arouse the Romans' curiosity.[7]

With *Vitalità*, Bonito Oliva, active until then as a poet and as a critic, was trying out what he would later call his *scrittura espositiva*: "I have always thought that the critic should practice not only essay-istic writing, but also exhibitional writing, that is, a way of laying out critical thinking through an exhibition, in scale with architec-ture and the social body."[8] Partly sponsored by Graziella Lonardi Buontempo's private Incontri Internazionali d'Arte — a controver-sial novelty in Italy, where culture was very much an affair of the state — *Vitalità* introduced Bonito Oliva to the greater public as an independent protagonist of contemporary art who saw his role as one of auteur-curator.[9] The exhibition also recast the role of his col-laborator, the architect Piero Sartogo, who consistently avoided the term *allestimento* — commonly used to describe an architect's work as exhibition designer — to describe his contribution. He insisted instead on calling it *coordinamento dell'immagine* (coordinator of images), thus projecting himself as a strong-minded interpreter of what he called the exhibition's "thesis."[10]

    Vitalità took place at a particularly unstable political juncture. The *secondo biennio rosso* — the red or revolutionary years,[11] 1968 to 1969 — was giving way to the *autunno caldo*, or hot autumn, which witnessed the radicalization of the student and worker movements. Confrontation between protesters and the police became increasingly violent. With the bombing in Milan's Piazza Fontana on December 12, 1969, which killed seventeen people and injured eighty-eight, Italy fell into a decade of turmoil.[12] The bombing, at first attributed to anar-chists, was eventually exposed as a Neofascist plot with connections to the upper echelons of the Christian Democratic government.[13] From that point onward, the Neofascists applied a *strategia della tensione*, generating fear, propaganda, and disinformation in an effort to con-vince the public that order had to be restored, if necessary by force.

    Two violent events bracketed the exhibition itself. On Decem-ber 7, 1970, a week after *Vitalità*'s opening and a week before the first anniversary of the Piazza Fontana bombing, members of the Neo-fascist Fronte Nazionale (founded in 1968) staged an abortive coup d'état in Rome known as the Golpe Borghese.[14] Then, on January 21,

1971, ten days before *Vitalità* closed, firebombs destroyed a number of trucks on the Pirelli tire-testing track in the Lainate neighborhood of Milan, the first action claimed by the leftist Red Brigades.

This climate of uncertainty was registered by *Vitalità* before one even entered the exhibition by the ambiguous inside/outside dynamic of the Palazzo delle Esposizioni's façade. The upbeat banner hung in the entrance archway featured a Pop photographic negative of the familiar figure of Michelangelo's *David*, while a row of ten closed-circuit color television monitors at street level (lent by the Brionvega electronics company) broadcast images of visitors walking through the exhibition, signaling to the passersby along Via Nazionale that the outside world was but a sideshow to the scenario unfolding inside.

Bonito Oliva's exhibition should be understood in the larger historical, political, and cultural context as a turning away from the leftist militant activism of 1968 toward a politically ambiguous reflection on Fascism. At the same time, more specifically, Bonito Oliva was strategically distancing himself from Arte Povera's most vocal spokesman, the critic Germano Celant, the other great protagonist on the Italian art scene at that moment. The latter was conspicuously absent from the roster of Italian critics whose writings from the 1960s were anthologized in the catalogue, and Arte Povera artists played only a minor role in the exhibition. In promoting Arte Povera, especially in the years 1967 and 1968, Celant aligned it with Minimalist and Postminimalist developments taking place simultaneously in the United States, Germany, the Netherlands, and England. Bonito Oliva professed different views. *Vitalità* purported to be a survey of the last ten years of Italian art. But, in his essay in the catalogue, he offered only his own opaque musings on the avant-garde's failure to collapse art into life in the face of an encroaching capitalist system and suggested that art instead might serve as a free zone removed from a "false" world.[15]

What remained obscure in *Vitalità*'s catalogue was (somewhat) clarified elsewhere. In an article published in *Marcatrè* at the beginning of 1970, Bonito Oliva asserted: "The artists are renouncing their extroversion, they reject the public and opt for marginality among their peers. Theirs is a 'concentrated community.'"[16] In a paper delivered at the Incontri Internazionali d'Arte a year after *Vitalità*, entitled "La citazione deviata: L'ideologia" (The diverted citation: Ideology), Bonito Oliva further articulated his preference for an art of re-presentation rather than an art of presentation (read: Arte Povera) and for artists with "an allegorical impulse" who followed what he called "il passo dello strabismo" (the way of the cross-eyed) — by moving laterally and looking sideways and backward, rather than forward.[17] What Bonito Oliva achieved in *Vitalità* was a translation of Italian art in the 1960s — Pop, monochrome, kinetic, as well as Arte Povera, until then always presented by curators and critics in the present tense — into his own scenario. This narrative, I will show, dispensed with a presentist framework in favor of nonlinear forms of temporality — hence its crucial role in this book.

Bonito Oliva's first curatorial move was to counter the cohabitation and cross-pollination of artworks urged by Celant. Arte Povera artists, as we will see, often showed together in a shared space.[18] In *Vitalità*, Bonito Oliva insisted instead on giving each artist what he called a "space of concentration" for their work. Having to contend with that "tomb of Aida," as one critic described the Beaux-Arts Palazzo delle Esposizioni, built by the architect Pio Piacentini (the father of Marcello Piacentini) in 1883, and the "obtuse magniloquence" of its ornate and grandiose enfilades, Sartogo masked the building's soaring vaults and partitioned its space into a sequence of discrete rooms.[19] The preparatory ground plans of the exhibition show that Bonito Oliva aimed, almost systematically, to break down existing artistic movements — and by implication, their communitarian activism — by distributing the works in such a way that the viewer was forced to traverse contrasting atmospheres.[20]

In Black and White

The exhibition's design compelled visitors to move quite suddenly from installations flooded with blinding light to ones plunged into near darkness. In response to the artists' specifications, some rooms were painted white and others gray, while two were black.[21] The dropped ceilings, which were fabricated from either opaque plastic or a semiopaque synthetic fiber called Meraklon, followed a similar color scheme. Among the works installed in the white rooms were Piero Manzoni's *Achromes*; Giulio Paolini's *Quattro immagini uguali* (Four identical images, 1969); Alighiero Boetti's nearly invisible graphite drawings entitled *Cimento dell'armonia e dell'invenzione* (Study of harmony and invention, 1969); Mario Merz's neon sequences of Fibonacci numbers; Enrico Castellani's punctured walls *Spazio ambiente* (Ambient space, 1967) (Figure 3.2); and Jannis Kounellis's sound piece, a passage from Giuseppe Verdi's opera *Nabucco*, played at scheduled times on a grand piano in an otherwise empty room. These spaces alternated with rooms lit only by "black" (ultraviolet) light. Many of the latter were dedicated to Arte Programmata artists such as Carlo Alfano, whose piece *Distanze (della distanze della rappresentazione)* (Distances [The distances from representation], 1969) involved a drop of water falling with implacable regularity (every eight seconds) from the ceiling of a dimmed room into a shallow basin; Gianni Colombo, whose strobe-lit tiled corridors led to *Campo praticabile* (Viable field, 1967), a room cut by thin beams of light filtering through the floor (Figure 3.3); Alberto Biasi, who projected rays of light onto rotating motorized prisms that refracted the rays into pure color; and Arte Povera's Gilberto Zorio, who sent a tenuous stream of incandescent light across his room in which, every four minutes, the space went dark and the word *Confine* (Boundary) appeared on the facing wall. Then came the three most photographed rooms, assigned by Bonito Oliva to some of his favorite idiosyncratic artists: Paolo Scheggi, Vincenzo Agnetti, and Vettor Pisani. Scheggi presented two tombs, which the public was allowed to enter: the *Della metafisica* (On metaphysics, 1970), a claustrophobic white pyramid, and the *Della geometria* (On geometry, 1970), a cubicle lined with metal foil. In Agnetti's *Il deserto con Apocalisse* (Desert with Apocalypse, 1970), one walked on sand past *La macchina drogata* (Drugged

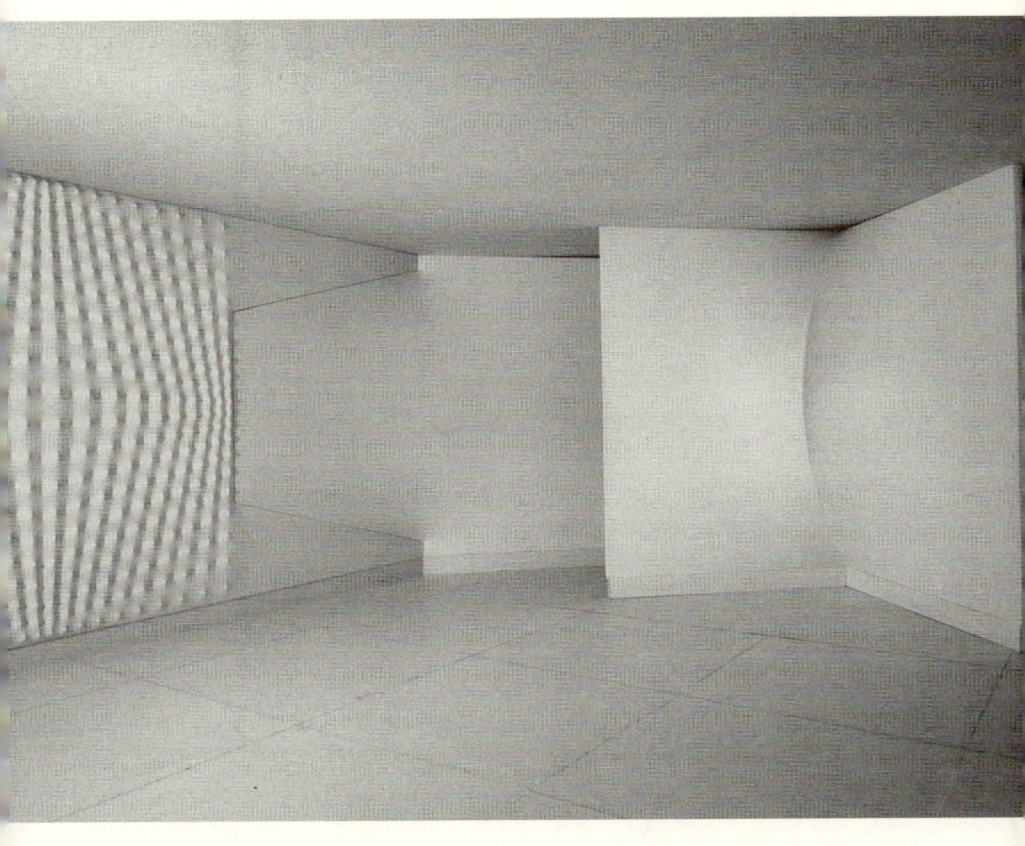

Figure 3.2. Enrico Castellani, *Spazio ambiente* (Ambient space, 1967). View of the installation at *Vitalità del negativo*, Palazzo delle Esposizioni, Rome. Photograph: Ugo Mulas. Courtesy Ugo Mulas Heirs.

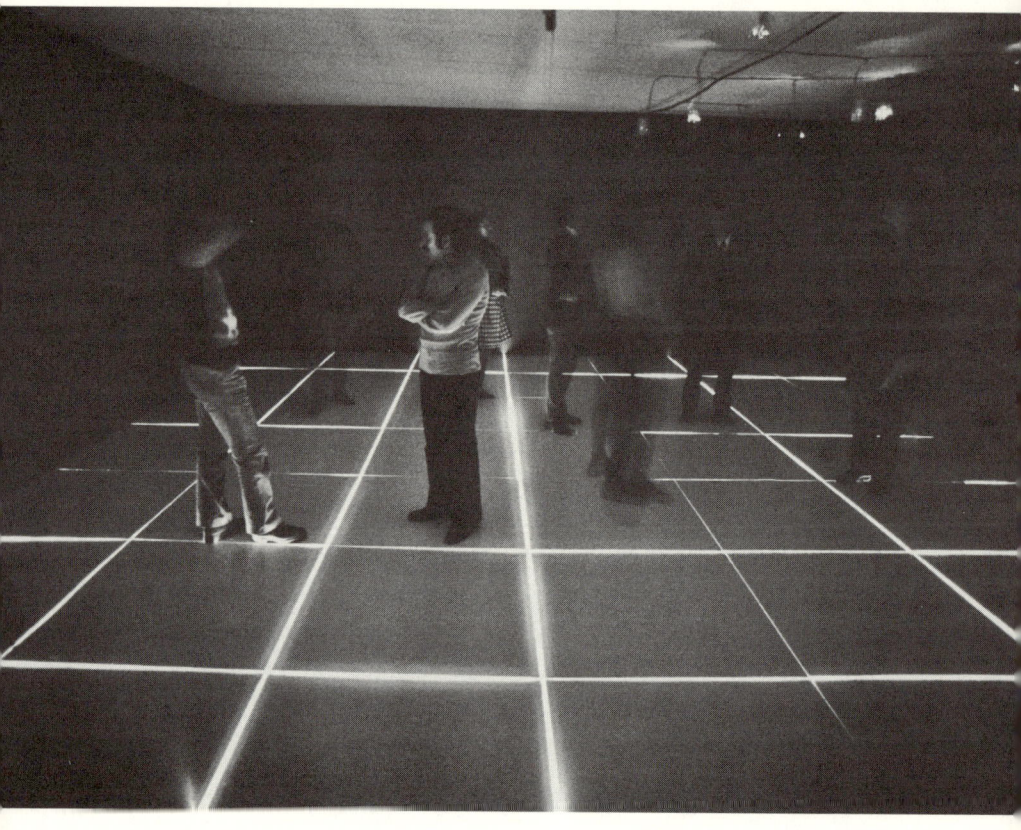

Figure 3.3. Gianni Colombo, *Campo praticabile* (Viable field, 1967). View of the installation at *Vitalità del negativo*, Palazzo delle Esposizioni, Rome. Photograph: Ugo Mulas. Courtesy Ugo Mulas Heirs.

machine, 1969), a broken calculator (an Olivetti Divisumma 24) abandoned in the dark, with quotes from the Book of Revelation inscribed on the adjacent wall. Pisani's installation with *Tavolo caricato a morte* (Table loaded to death, 1970) and *Lo scorrevole* (The slideway, 1970) (Figure 3.4) was bathed in the merciless light of four powerful projectors; in *Tavolo caricato a morte*, a guinea pig was chained to a sliding contraption on an iron table, perhaps awaiting death, while a woman chained in a similar contraption wearing opaque black glasses stood motionless under a ticking clock.[22] The favorite photo op of the more popular illustrated magazines was Fabio Mauri's *La luna* (The moon, 1968). Visitors entered the space through oval openings reminiscent of spaceship hatches and then had to slog through a foot-deep layer of Styrofoam pellets in a dark room that was empty save for the artist's signature monochrome TV-shaped canvases. One such canvas read "The end" (Figure 3.5).

Contemporary reviews are essential for us to recover the disturbing atmosphere of this exhibition. "The Strange World of *Vitalità del negativo*: Art That Ends in an Amusement Park," ran the headline in *Epoca* (the Italian counterpart to *Life* magazine).[23] "Sculptors in Competition with Astronauts: A Salon on the Moon," Bologna's *Il Resto del Carlino* called it.[24] "Magic Eye in the Pop Labyrinth," claimed Rome's Communist daily *Paese Sera*.[25] "Vitality of the Negative in Plexiglas and Polystyrene," announced *Pan*.[26] "Step right up, folks, and come inside! Roll in lunar snow! Listen to Verdi! See real paint strokes made by human hand! Op, pop, funk, junk, kinetic, environmental, conceptual — you name it, we have it!" sneered Edith Schloss in the *International Herald Tribune*:

> You enter womb-like darkness, which in reality is the high, old-fashioned entrance hall (of a Victorian palace) modernized and lowered with simple devices of lighting and black bands. Then you are lured into cubicles, room after room, halls and narrow corridors, distorted or straight, unbearably bright or pitch dark, sometimes too full or so empty you think the fire extinguisher is an exhibit.... It does not matter that the whole ambitious, disproportionately costly project is glossy and gimmicky, that it is a fun fair that is

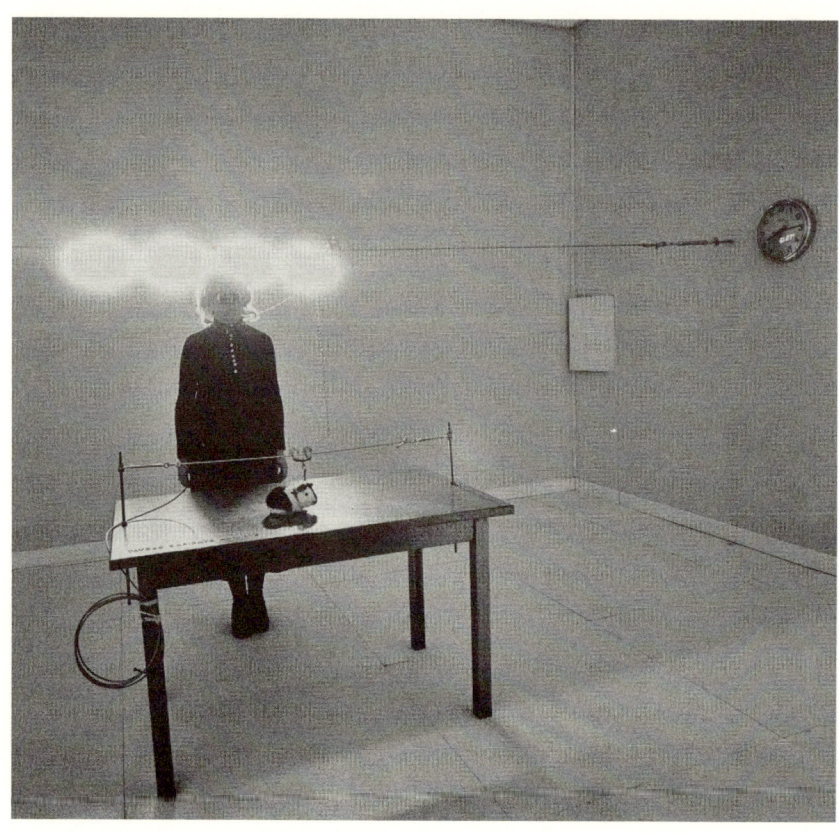

Figure 3.4. Vettor Pisani, *Tavolo caricato a morte* (Table loaded to death, 1970); *Lo scorrevole* (The slideway, 1970), with Mimma Pisani. View of the installation at *Vitalità del negativo*, Palazzo delle Esposizioni, Rome. Photograph: Claudio Abate. © Archivio Claudio Abate.

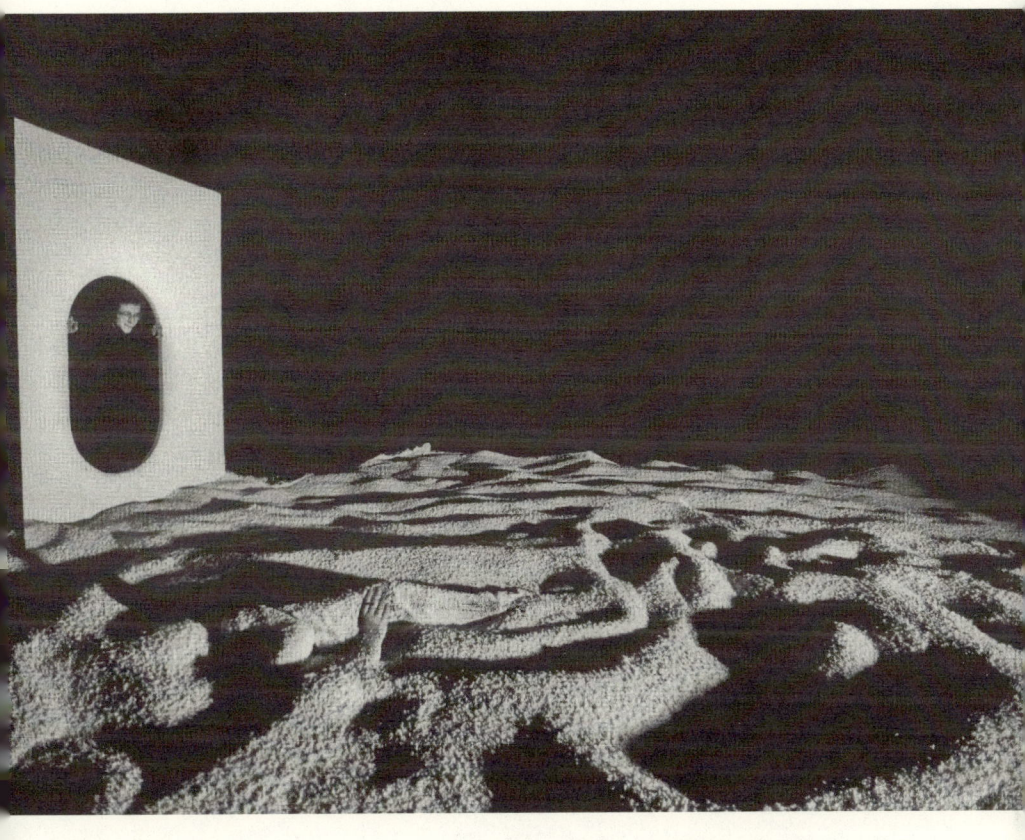

Figure 3.5. Fabio Mauri, *La luna* (The moon, 1968). View of the installation at *Vitalità del negativo*, Palazzo delle Esposizioni, Rome. Photograph: Ugo Mulas. Courtesy Ugo Mulas Heirs.

more fair than fun, that the Roman art world is seething, that some have been unfairly excluded or included, or that the full weight of the establishment is behind the product and that, like Nabucco, they did not heed the writing on the wall. What matters is: it's too late. What is new and different cannot remain new and different. Most things offered here have been done before or elsewhere or by the mass media.[27]

Carlo Laurenzi's review in the *Corriere della Sera* proclaimed a "viewer in crisis" and lamented, as Milanese publications often did, the "scarsissimo aggiornamento del pubblico Romano" — the belatedness of a boorish Roman public, who, having just digested kinetic and Pop art, was now presented with the "stunning symbiosis of the most advanced provisional apparatuses [*macchine*] and the structural curlicues of a boundless building."[28] One critic, identified only as "C. M.," was most perceptive in understanding that the artists' works, isolated as they were in separate rooms, were in façt intended to participate in a larger exhibitional matrix. He or she wrote in the pop music magazine *Ciao 2001*:

> *Vitalità* is not about individual works, but a whole, reminiscent of a hall of mirrors or, rather, a hall of horrors. What hovers is a disquieting atmosphere, a silent drone broken by the noise of the machines, some of them gratuitous, and some not. Judging from the effect on the viewer, rather than the curator's intention, [which is] altogether undecipherable, the aim was to return the viewer to a degree zero of visuality by purging him with lights, plastics, stones and metals, black and white, light and colors.[29]

A chorus of other critics lamented that the exhibition had institutionalized what they saw — *pace* Arte Povera — as an already moribund neo-avant-garde. Sandra Orienti's review in the Roman daily *Il Popolo*, for example, was titled "*Vitalità del negativo*: Exhibition or Museum? What Is Already Dead Is Passed Off as Living."[30] In *La nazione*, Sergio Maldini judged the exhibition to be a "cemetery of the negative," while the review by Giorgio Di Genova in *Mondo nuovo* similarly warned of the "deathliness of the negative."[31] Tullio Catalano nullified the exhibition's punch by upending its title in the headline of his review in *Gala*, "Vitality of the Negative or the Negative of Vitality."[32] Catalano's title echoed that of the review published in *Domus* a few months earlier, written by the French critic Pierre Restany. His "Vitalità del negativo/Negativo della vitalità" introduced to the Milanese magazine the cliché of shadowy Roman deals struck too close to the sources of political power: "This sumptuous event has an ungainly amount of money at its disposal."[33] In fact, Rome's art world had no center at the time: no successor had emerged to replace the aging Giulio Carlo Argan, professor at La Sapienza, art critic, and soon to become the first Communist mayor of Rome. In Restany's view, this exhibition's attempt to fill the city's intellectual power vacuum served only to expose it. The photograph selected for the cover of the *Domus* issue that ran his review recalls the Pop style of *Vitalità*'s poster: it shows the silhouette of three visitors to the exhibition with, in the center, the looming shadow of a fourth, caged in Scheggi's pyramidal tomb, their figures partly or wholly overlaid with blue ink, giving the impression of a bad psychedelic trip.

Similarly snide comments about Roman decadence were voiced in *NAC* by the critic and art historian Enrico Crispolti in his review entitled "The Salon of the Avant-Garde." His comments reflected the longer perspective of an older art critic (born in 1933) who had lived through it all:

> The problem, in short, was this: the new avant-garde wants to legitimize itself, to win over the Roman aristocracy and bourgeoisie, to enter their living rooms — the avant-garde thus intends to create its own "salon," not for nothing in the quintessential site of the Roman "salons" of the Belle Epoque, that of the Quadriennali.... The most glaring proof of [*Vitalità*'s] aspiration to be a "salon" was in the frenzied invitation of officials to attend [the opening]: from President Saragat, to the minister of public education, to the mayor of Rome (enough to provoke the envy of the organizers of the Venice Biennale or the Milan Triennale), plus four ministers, etc. The avant-garde is looking for a home; it might be preparing its candidacy for a seat as senator for life.[34]

And where, Crispolti wondered, did the unlimited funds for the exhibition come from?

The same issue of *NAC* included, back to back with Crispolti's, another review of *Vitalità* by Cesare Vivaldi, a critic who, although mostly identified with the Roman school of Pop, also belonged to the older generation, having been born in 1925. Its title, "The Shrine of the Negative," was even more taunting. Vivaldi wrote: "The 'negativity of language' that, according to our friend Achille Bonito Oliva . . . is the common denominator of the varied artists exhibited here and the justification of the show, cannot offer itself as a model, as a language as such, unless it nullifies itself or turns into academicism. . . . An academicism of horror, of the macabre, just as late *informale* was the academicism of anguish."[35]

Beautiful Season: From Lo spazio dell'immagine to Amore mio

Most interesting in these reviews is the accusation that Bonito Oliva had hijacked Italy's neo-avant-garde for his own private agenda, that is, for a narrative other than its own. In review after review, *Vitalità* was cast as the funereal and ostentatious reprise of a series of smaller avant-garde manifestations that had recently taken place in charming and sunny Italian towns on the margins of official events.[36] Many of the artists, and indeed many of the works shown in *Vitalità*, had been previously shown elsewhere. *Vitalità* was "the last of a series of manifestations previously held in peripheral areas," wrote Gillo Dorfles in *Art International*, listing the names of the artists and describing the installations that had already been shown in Foligno, San Benedetto del Tronto, and Montepulciano. It all seems fatigued, Dorfles concluded, "symptomatic of a lack of creative energy, in Italy as well as abroad."[37] In *Momento-sera*, Lorenza Trucchi wrote: "In art as in politics, revolution is almost always followed by the theoretical crystallization of protest and subversion. . . . The tone of this exhibition is entirely official, with all the solemnity of a salon. An impression accentuated by the restrained elegance of its production." She concluded that it offered nothing new, since most of the works had already been shown, namely, at Foligno and Montepulciano.[38]

"Italian art was shown off beautifully last summer at Foligno, near Spoleto, in an exhibition in a stripped-down Renaissance palazzo, an excellent environment for environments," gushed a reviewer about *Lo spazio dell'immagine* (The space of the image) in *Art in America*.[39] Held from July 2 to October 1, 1967, the exhibition — in contrast to the strongly authorial quality of Celant's and Bonito Oliva's exhibitions — was in today's parlance curated by committee. It was instigated by Dino Gravina, a local entrepreneur, the sculptor Gino Marotta, and four art critics: Umbro Apollonio, Maurizio Calvesi, Giorgio de Marchis, and Gillo Dorfles.[40] It was the first Italian exhibition of works installed in situ around a single theme: the integration of space, color, and the viewer in a total environment. Nineteen individual artists and collectives were each invited to create an installation for the exhibition, which was held at the Palazzo Trinci, a meandering late medieval building with a Renaissance façade near the Duomo that had already served a variety of cultural and educational roles, housing Foligno's Museo Archeologico, Pinacoteca, Museo del Risorgimento, a music room, a library, and a repository for the city's archives.[41] But it now suddenly hosted the first Italian exhibition of contemporary art conceived around a single theme. Although all of *Lo spazio dell'immagine*'s artists were Italian, its bilingual (Italian and English) catalogue conveyed its curators' ambition to broadcast to an international audience.

Foligno was an important railway junction, and its main palazzo had been partly destroyed by Allied bombing in 1944.[42] Having never recovered its position as a commercial hub, the town was experiencing an economic downturn in the 1960s.[43] Even so, the palazzo sustained a number of restoration campaigns. By 1967, many of the splendid frescoes on its second floor were on view.[44] Yet this being an exhibition of installations conceived as immersive, autonomous artworks, the architecture of the palazzo and its decoration were almost entirely occluded by surfaces that were padded, laminated, canvased, perforated, and illuminated in bright monochromatic hues. All traces of the exhibition's historiated container were eclipsed. In the words of one of its organizers, Giuseppe Giorgio Marchiori, "to every present-day problem there corresponds a present-day 'environment.'"[45]

Among the *ambienti* on the first floor were Agostino Bonalumi's *Blu abitabile* (Habitable blue, 1967), a room padded by shaped canvases painted in royal blue; *Interpretazione speculare* (Mirror interpretation, 1965) by Getulio Alviani, who turned his room into a cylinder containing smaller reflective half cylinders in aluminum, rotating on their axes; and Alberto Biasi's *Spazio-ogetto* (Space-object, 1967), in which rays of light hit a prism to transform themselves into pure color. On the second floor was Mario Ceroli's *Gabbia* (Cage, 1967) of wood and chicken wire — humble materials offset by the gold of an ornately framed Renaissance Crucifixion triptych, the only work from the palazzo's Pinacoteca left on view during the show. Crawling along the floor of the Sala dei Giganti, whose frescoes were entirely obscured, was Eliseo Mattiacci's plastic *Tubo* (Tube, 1967), a stumbling giant made of plastic painted Agip yellow; then came *Naturale-artificiale* (Natural-artificial, 1967), a forest of Marotta's signature Plexiglas trees. Enrico Castellani was represented by his *Ambiente bianco* (White environment, 1967), while Pino Pascali contributed *32 mq. di mare circa* (Approximately 32 square meters of sea, 1967), both of which were shown at *Vitalità*. Five rooms were given over to kinetic environments by artists from Arte Programmata collectives.[46] None of these installations were site specific. Restaged for the occasion as the great Italian avant-garde antecedent to installation art was Lucio Fontana's *Ambiente spaziale a luce nera* (Black light spatial environment), originally made in 1949 for Galleria del Naviglio in Milan.[47] Meanwhile, on the exhibition catalogue's cover was a pale blue pixilated photograph of one of the most famous details in Renaissance painting — the ostrich egg that hovers like a pendulum in front of the semicircular niche and over the Madonna's head in Piero della Francesca's

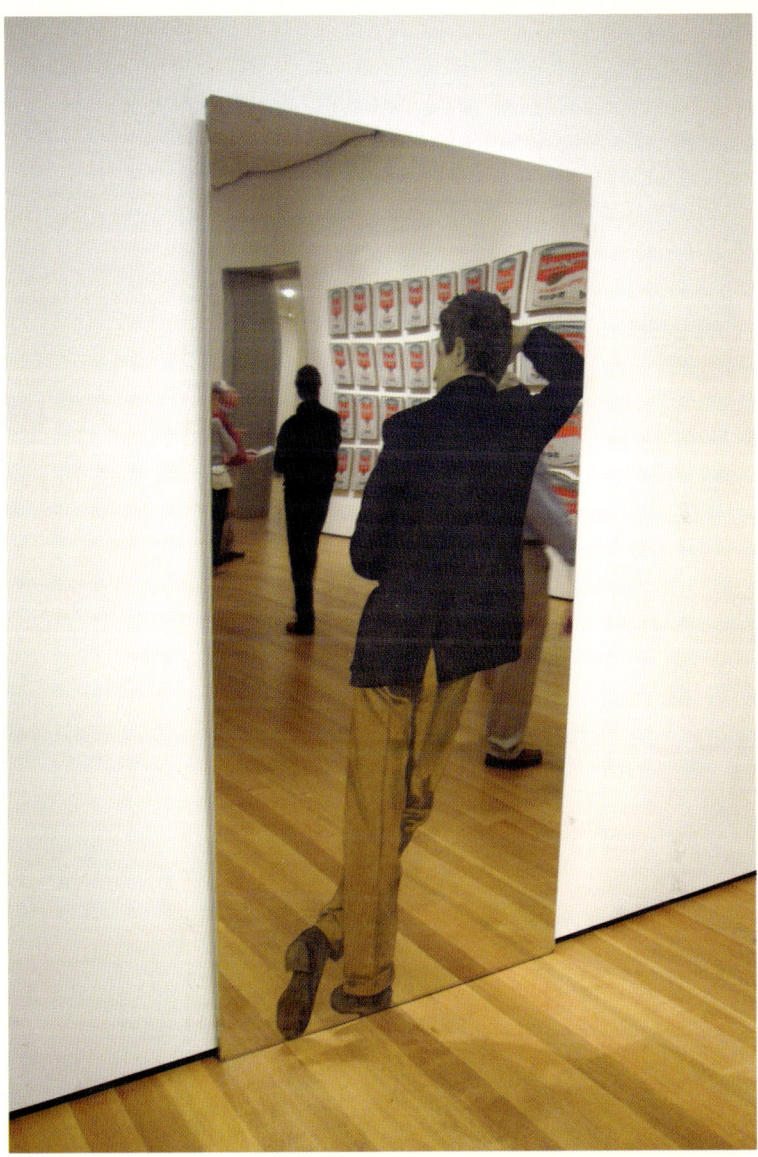

Plate 1. Michelangelo Pistoletto, *Uomo con pantaloni gialli* (Man with yellow pants, 1964). Painted tissue paper on polished stainless steel, 200 × 120 cm. Museum of Modern Art, New York. Photograph: the author.

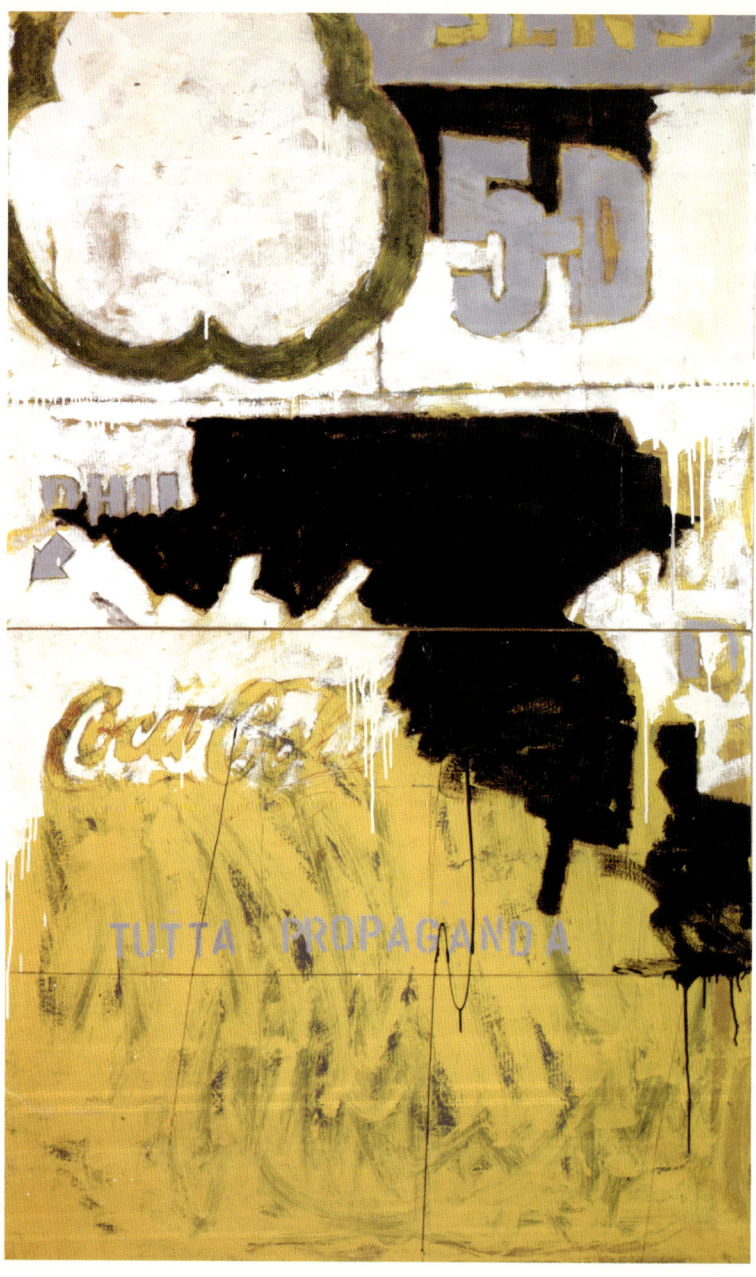

Plate 2. Mario Schifano, *Tutta propaganda* (All propaganda, 1963). Enamel on cardboard mounted on canvas, 198 × 118 cm. Fondazione Marconi, Milan.

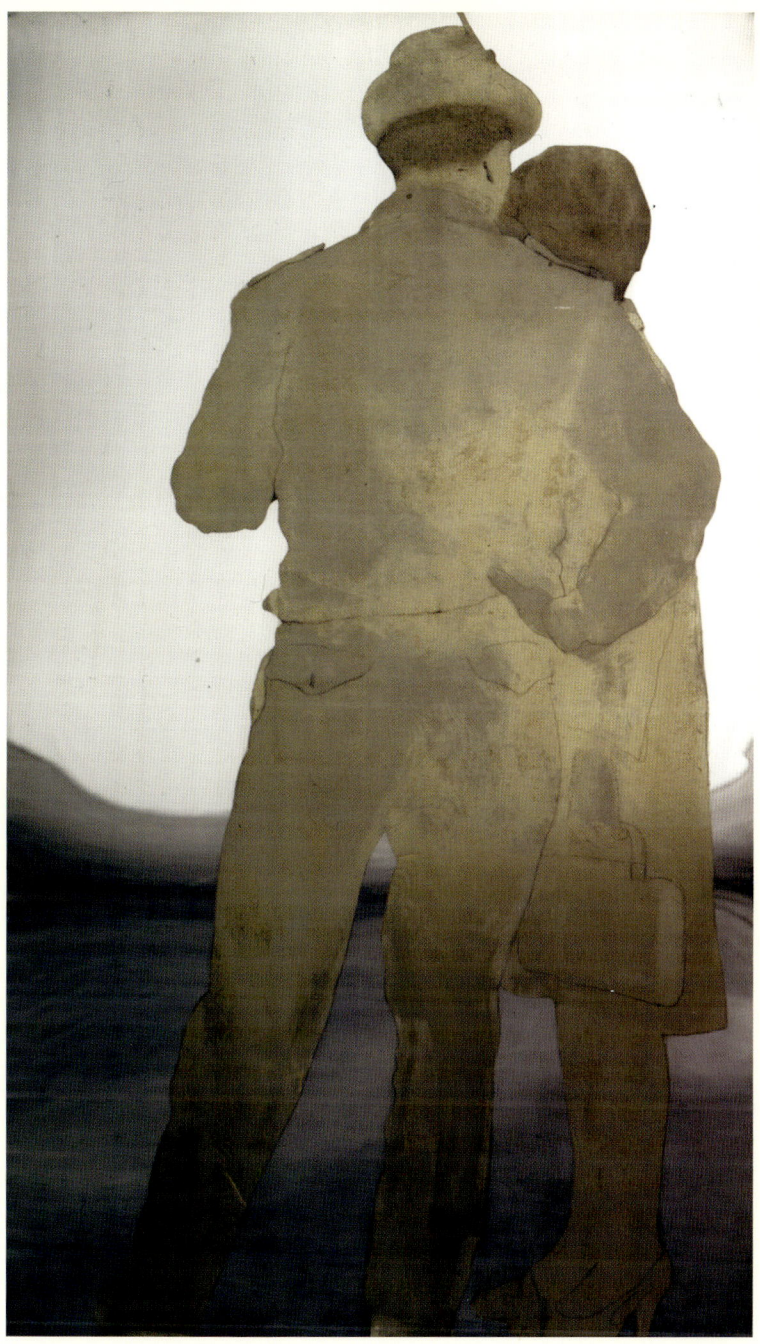

Plate 3. Michelangelo Pistoletto, *Alpino* (Alpine soldier, first version, 1962). Painted tissue paper on polished stainless steel, 200 × 120 cm. Courtesy of the Cittadellarte–Fondazione Pistoletto, Biella, Italy.

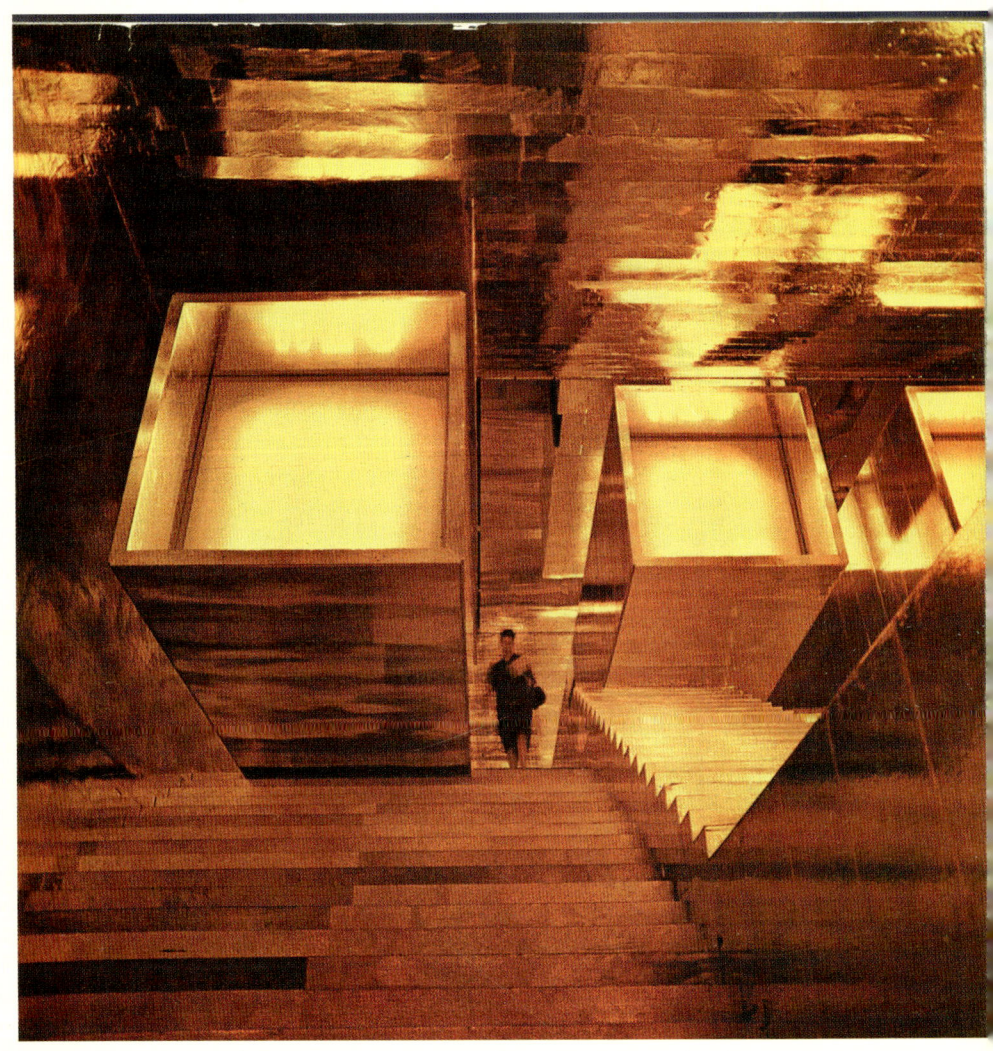

Plate 4. Main staircase of the Milan Triennale, 1964. As reproduced in *Domus*, no. 418, September 1964.

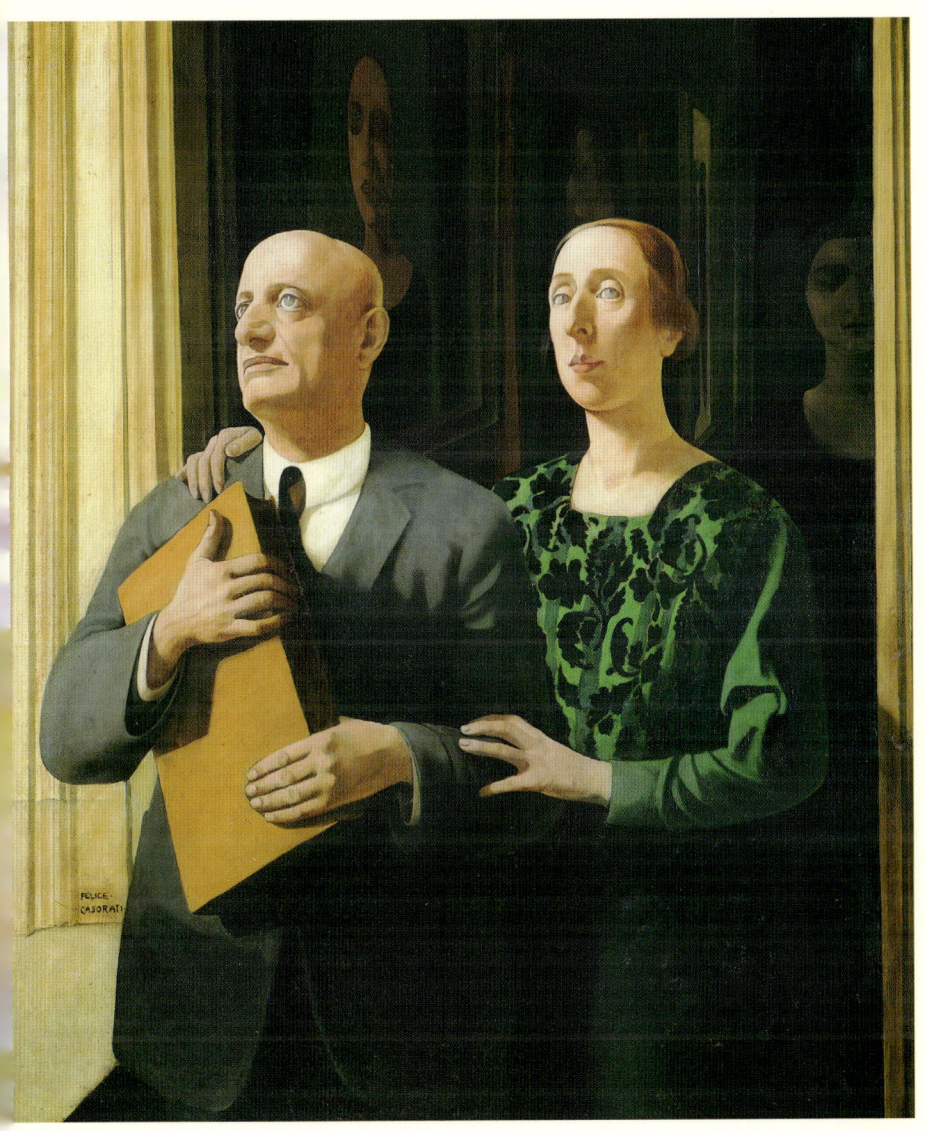

Plate 5. Felice Casorati, *Doppio ritratto* (Double portrait, ca. 1924). Tempera on plywood, 120 × 100 cm. Private collection.

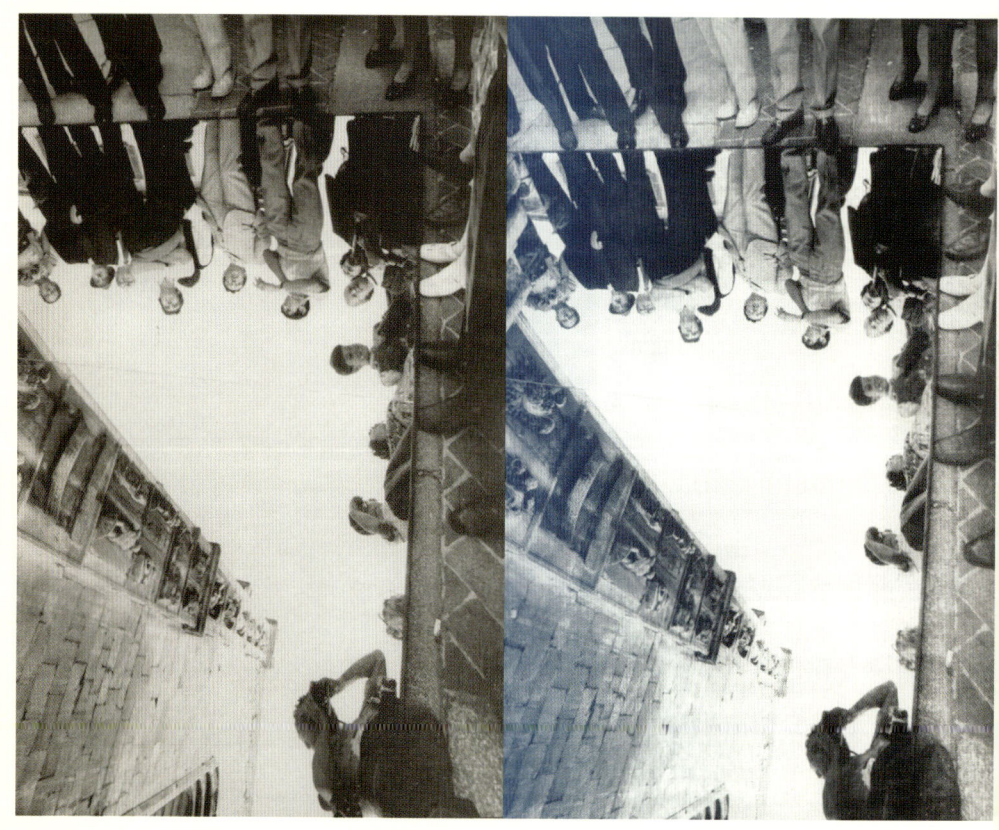

Plate 6. Mario Di Salvo and Carlo Ferrario, *Riflessione* (Reflection). *Campo urbano,* 1969.
Photography: Ugo Mulas. Design: Bruno Munari.

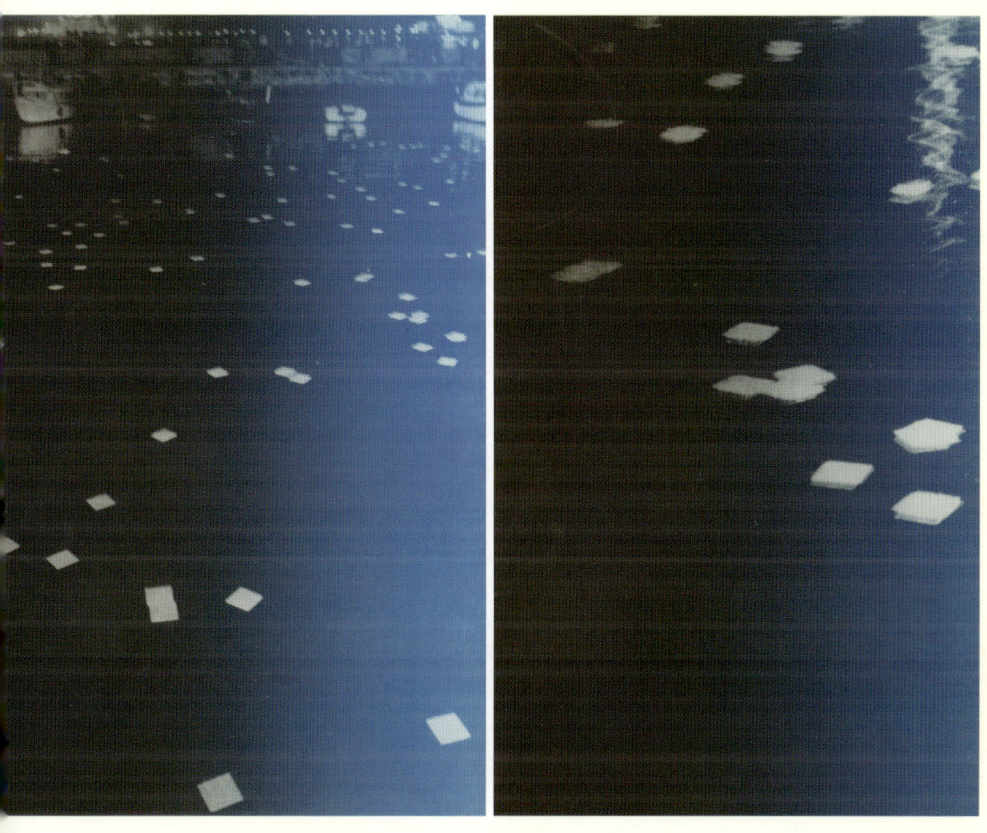

Plate 7. Dadamaino, *Illuminazione fosforescente automotoria sull'acqua* (Phosphorescent automated illumination of water). *Campo urbano,* 1969. Photography: Ugo Mulas. Design: Bruno Munari.

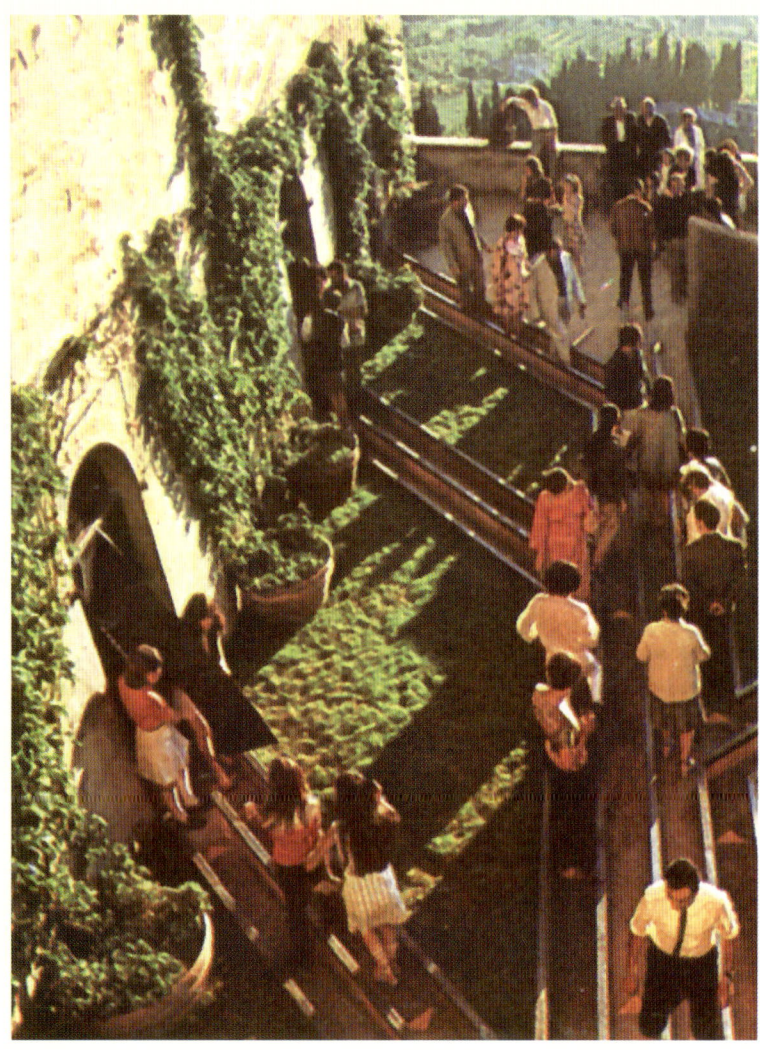

Plate 8. Piero Sartogo, *Percorso* (Path). View of the installation at *Amore mio*, Montepulciano, 1970. Courtesy of the Piero Sartogo Archive.

Brera altarpiece; it asserted a historical claim on Italian art's relation to space via its "invention" of pictorial perspective.

In the exhibition, Pistoletto's *Ambiente* (Environment, 1967) was the only work connected with its site and thus introducing the great past of Italian art (Figure 3.6). In it, five mirror-bottomed cylinders, made of fiber resin painted white on the outside and each a different color on the inside, were installed across the Sala delle arti liberali e dei pianeti, believed to have been frescoed by the Venetian Niccolò di Pietro in 1412. In this room, the most magical in the Palazzo Trinci, the mural's complex decorative program was intended to set in motion a series of correspondences. Painted on one side of the room, overseen by the larger enthroned figure of philosophy, are seven women seated as sibyls on splendid Gothic thrones and introducing young boys to the seven liberal arts. On the other side of the room are seven planets, each next to a scene representing an age of man associated with the different hours of the day, painted in a series of multicolored disks. The visitors who peered in the wells were thus immersed in a wondrous cosmos.

Lo spazio dell'immagine pleased everyone. Celant endorsed it, dubbing it the best event of 1967, the one that could pull Italy out of its provincialism and inferiority to the United States.[48] So did Trini, who marveled at the offerings of the Italian provinces that summer.[49] "After Foligno, in Venice and elsewhere, things will finally change!" exclaimed Giancarlo Politi in his editorial in *Flash Art*. "Here is finally an exhibition able to offer a modest, clear, and courageous response to the prestigious and overblown Venice Biennale. Instead of wanting to be polemical, *Lo spazio dell'immagine* aimed to be innovative."[50]

A year later came the exceptional *R3: "Arte povera + Azioni povere"*— exceptional in the history of 1960s exhibitions for its originality, its poetry, its standing as precedent for Harald Szeemann's *When Attitudes Become Form* in the Kunsthalle in Bern one year later, and for being so splendidly photogenic. It was open for just three days, October 4 through 6, 1968, in the imposing space of the Arsenali of Amalfi, a resort town of a few thousand inhabitants that had been enjoying

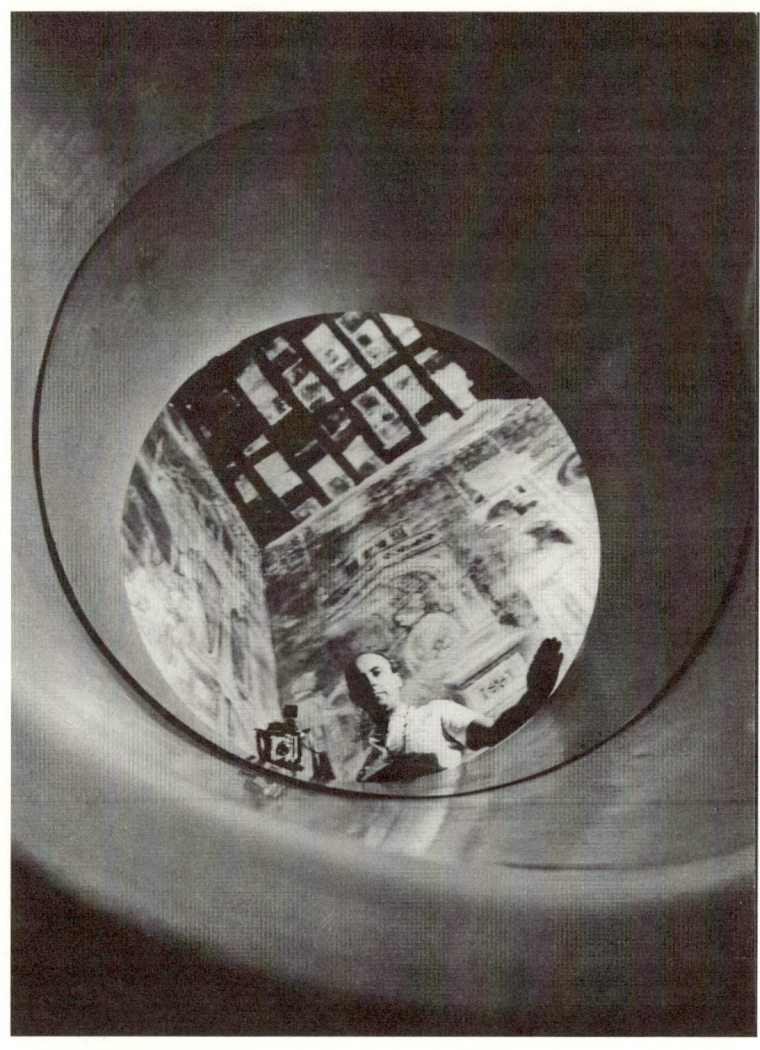

Figure 3.6. Michelangelo Pistoletto, *Ambiente* (Environment, 1967). View of the installation at *Lo spazio dell'immagine*, Foligno. Courtesy of the Cittadellarte – Fondazione Pistoletto, Biella, Italy.

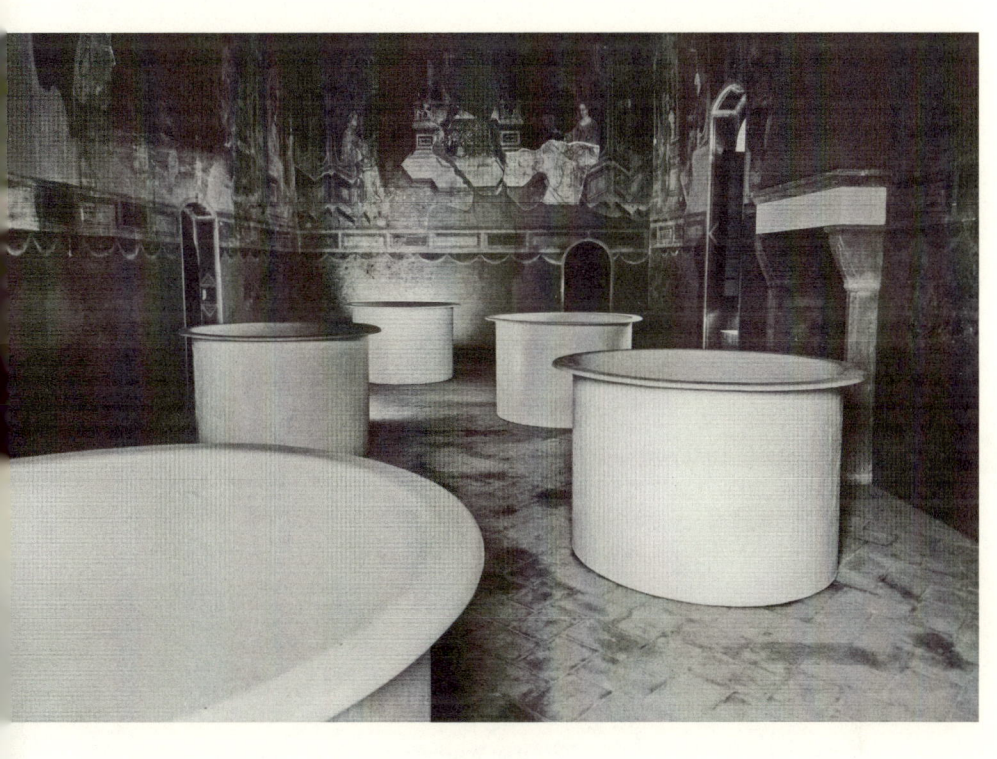

a tourist boom since the years of the economic miracle. A key actor was Marcello Rumma, who from the start was attracted to noninstitutional spaces for the projects he sponsored via the Centro Culturale Colautti di Salerno, with Celant as curator. As its name implies, *R3* was preceded in the formidable cross-vaulted space of the Amalfi arsenals by two exhibitions, *R1* and *R2*, the first and second *Rassegna nazionale di arti figurative* (National review of figurative arts). As we can see in the couple of surviving photographs from *R2*: *L'impatto percettivo* (The perceptual impact, May 19–21, 1967) — and presumably also a year earlier for *R1*: *Aspetti del "ritorno alle cose stesse"* (Aspects of the "return to things themselves," October 8–November 19, 1966) — the works on exhibit in the Arsenali were hung lined up, gallery style, on temporary plywood panels probably painted white (it is difficult to discern from the black-and-white photographs) placed in front of the rusticated walls. Curated by Renato Barilli, *R1* included twenty-seven artists, all of them Italian, many of them women (which was rarely the case), and all of them gravitating toward Pop.[51] Curated by Alberto Boatto and Filiberto Menna, *R2* was, instead, decidedly international. Half of its seventeen artists were from outside Italy. Staged just a year after Sperone's 1965 *Pop* show in his Turin gallery (discussed in Chapter 1), *R2* was the second Italian show to include the nearly complete contingent of American Pop, along with hard-edge and color-field painters such as Ellsworth Kelly and Frank Stella and the Briton Richard Smith, whose work was shown alongside that of their Italian contemporaries. The desired visual effect was, clearly, a dramatic contrast between the colorful punch and immediacy of presentist 1960s painting and the pastness of the rough walls and arches of the Arsenal, the sole remaining monument from Amalfi's great maritime history and the only medieval structure of its kind to have survived in the Mezzogiorno region.

It was only when Celant gathered a roster of artists for three days in Amalfi for *R3*: *"Arte povera + Azioni povere"* that a meaningful solidarity — both material and operational — was established not only among the artists and among the works on view, but also with the space of the Arsenali. With *R3*, container and contained came together. Many of the artists — mostly Arte Poveristi, including Giovanni Anselmo, Alighiero Boetti, Luciano Fabro, Jannis Kounellis, and Pino Pascali, plus Richard Long (British), Jan Dibbets, and Gerhard Van Elk (both Dutch) — brought their materials to Amalfi by truck to execute their works, all of them three-dimensional, in situ. During the Middle Ages, Amalfi had developed an important trade with Asia and Africa, and its large merchant ships and warships — the *sagene* — were built in the Arsenali, dragged to the water's edge, and sent to North Africa and to the East across the most remote seas. This solidarity was captured by Bruno Manconi, in whose photographs of the 1960s artifacts, the rough walls of the Arsenali (most probably laid bare in a twentieth-century restoration campaign), and the odd medieval remnant such as a sarcophagus-shaped receptacle appear as equal protagonists (Figure 3.7). In other photos by Manconi, Pistoletto and Maria Pioppi perform a pseudomedieval orientalizing *tableau vivant* in which the sarcophagus reappears, serving, almost comically, as a theatrical prop: a *mangiatoia* (manger) turned into a crib for a Nativity scene.[52]

In the summer of 1970 came the less beloved, least well known, and yet most captivating of these exhibitions: *Amore mio* (My love), held in Montepulciano from June 30 to September 30. The initial aim of the exhibition — which took place in another frescoed building, the Palazzo Ricci, built by the Renaissance architect Baldassare Peruzzi — was to replicate the success of Foligno. The initiative, which apparently came from the sculptor Marotta and his contact with Maria Russo, an art historian and the wife of a local notary, aimed to upend the format of the exhibitions that had preceded it.[53] Bypassing again the network of galleries, as Bonito Oliva explained in *Domus*, nineteen artists including Bonito Oliva himself and Sartogo organized themselves for the project. The artists — Carlo Alfano, Getulio Alviani, Mario Ceroli, Gianni Colombo, Gabriele De Vecchi, Fabro, Kounellis, Renato Mambor, Gino Marotta, Fabio Mauri, Mario Merz, Mario Nanni, Maurizio Nannucci, Vettor

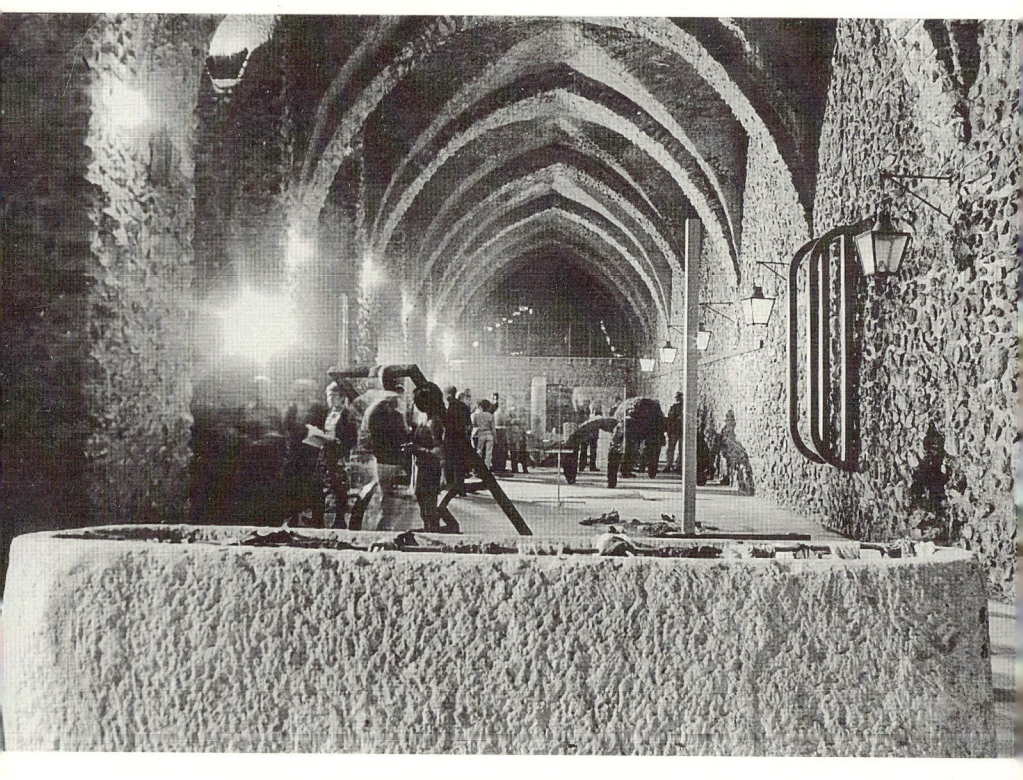

Figure 3.7. *Arte povera + Azioni povere*, Amalfi, 1967. Photograph: Bruno Manconi.

Pisani, Michelangelo Pistoletto, Paolo Scheggi, and Cesare Tacchi — were to occupy their rooms in the Palazzo Ricci without a prestablished theme. In the catalogue — designed and published by the Florentine Centro Di, like those of *Lo spazio dell'immagine* and *Vitalità*, Bonito Oliva and Sartogo appeared among the artists as peers. The artists were told that they could hand over their space in the palazzo as well as their allotted page in the catalogue to another artist of their choice, hence the exhibition's catchy title, *Amore mio*. Bonito Oliva was also asked by the artists ostensibly to disown his role as curator, which gave him cover to work sub rosa as a curator-puppeteer.[54]

The headline of Filiberto Menna's review in *Il Mattino*, playing on the exhibition title, announced that "the artists have brought themselves forward to confess their secret love." Menna described the logic of the exhibition as "a new formula in which artists didn't just present their works, but declared the predilections, the cultural debt, and the affinities that link them to other artists, both past and present: in short, they have openly declared their love."[55] As Fabio Mauri told Giulia Massari, the critic from *Il Mondo*: "In this time of harsh words, *Amore mio* has the title of a summer hit. With these kitschy words we wanted to express our polemic."[56] "This exhibition eludes definition," wrote Lorenza Trucchi in *Momento-sera*. "The title itself — *Amore mio* — is a kind of riddle with multiple solutions, one not without irony, meant to counter the prefabricated and often abstruse titles of many similar events today."[57] As with *Vitalità*, the catalogue clarified nothing; Bonito Oliva used the medium of *Domus* to express, coyly, that the exhibition explored a theme too often ignored by contemporary artists: that of death.[58] "If the spaces look like catacombs," he stated, "it is because of the lucid realization of living a marginal, almost subterranean existence in an alienated everyday life."[59]

Sartogo's *Percorso* (Path) was designed (as the architect would do a few months later for *Vitalità*) to capture the central theme of the exhibition. Set in the sun-drenched courtyard in front of the palazzo and overlooking the splendid Sienese countryside and a cemetery — next to a cement slab carved with the title of the exhibition — *Percorso* forced the visitors to walk single file along narrow metal channels leading to different rooms on the ground floor. The path was just wide enough to put one foot down at a time, catching attendees at the shin — a hint at the entrapment they would soon experience inside (Figure 3.8; Plate 8).

Percolating in the underlit rooms, photographed by Claudio Abate on the opening day, were the marks of an incipient postmodernism: self-referentiality, citationality, and narcissism. The first room, occupied by Ceroli's catafalquelike wooden floor sculptures, set the mood. Next was Marotta's signature Plexiglas tree, placed at the center of a photo history of the tree motif, with examples from the work of Giotto, Carpaccio, Perugino, and Raphael displayed on the surrounding walls. The third room was a prisonlike setting for an action by Kounellis, who lay on a bier under a rough blanket with a blowtorch lit under his naked foot. In the next room, on two free-standing screens, Colombo and De Vecchi projected slides of their own works as well as self-portraits on reproductions of paintings by Giotto, Piero della Francesca, Raphael, and Mantegna — a picaresque flashback through the history of Italian painting. Cesare Tacchi took the love theme to its tautological extreme with *Autovotivo* (Autovotive, 1970; Figure. 3.9). The installation consisted of a heart of stone (a symbol of his own heart, according to the artist's statement) dangling from the ceiling above a funereal casket full of miniature hearts, arrayed at the foot of a column topped with a bust of the artist's head. As a whole, the installation seemed to allude to a heart of stone that is capable only of self-love. More dimly lit spaces followed, such as those containing Alfano's drop of water falling with implacable regularity in *Delle distanze della rappresentazione* and Scheggi's *Della geometria*, both reprised in *Vitalità*. They alternated with more brightly lit installations such as Maurizio Nannucci's homage to his favorite modernists, whose names were spelled out in a neon color most associated with their works: white for Kazimir Malevich, blue for Yves Klein, yellow for Josef Albers, and bright pink for Lucio

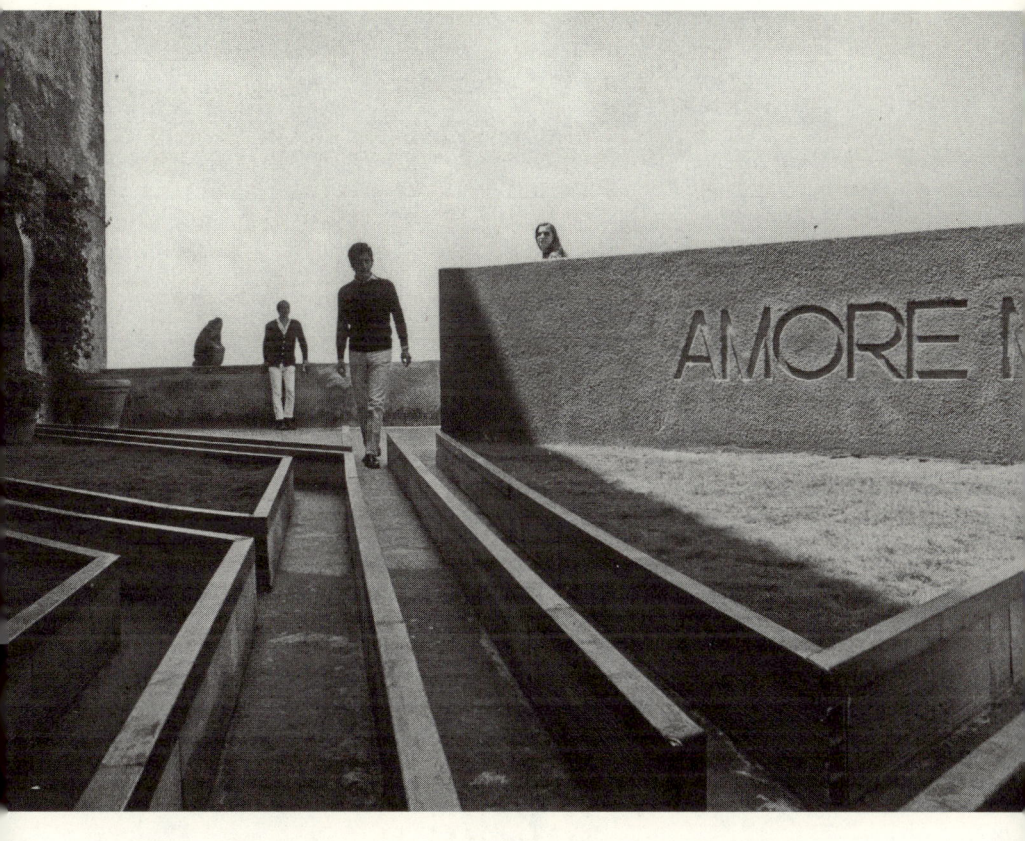

Figure 3.8. Piero Sartogo, *Percorso* (Path). View of the installation at *Amore mio*, Montepulciano, 1970. Courtesy of the Piero Sartogo Archive.

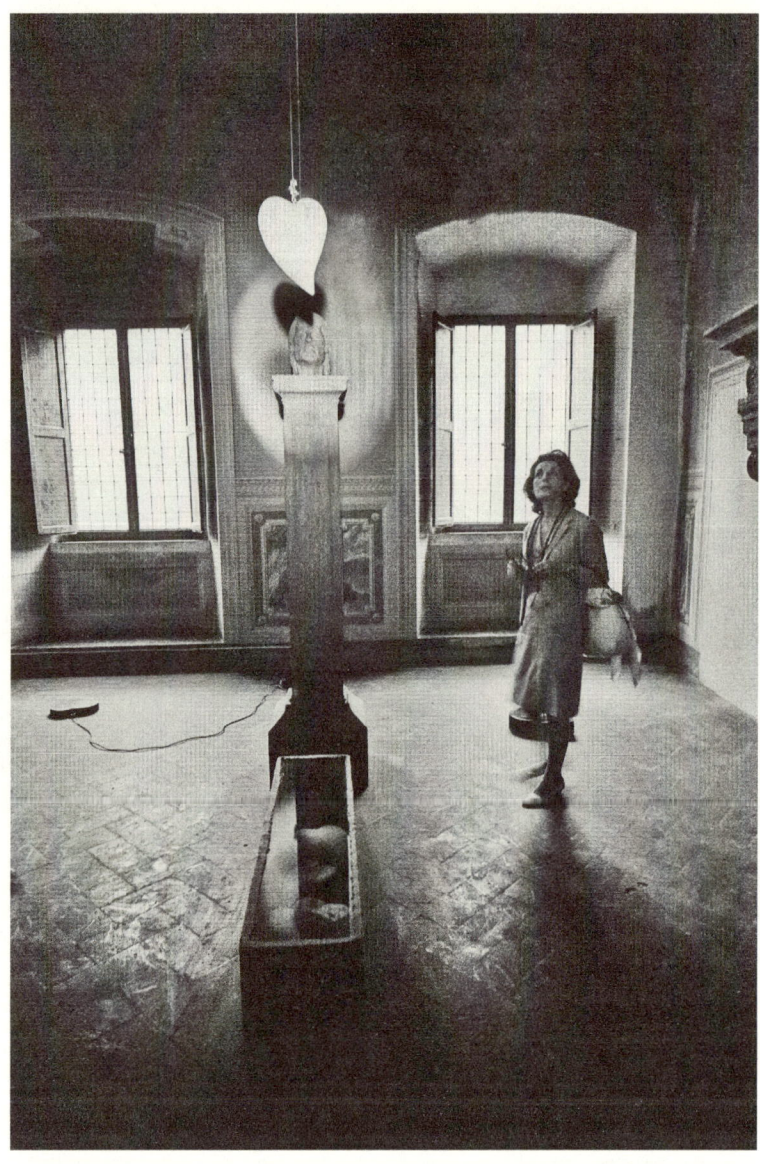

Figure 3.9. Cesare Tacchi, *Autovotivo* (Autovotive, 1970). View of the installation at *Amore mio*, Montepulciano, 1970 (with Palma Bucarelli). Photograph: Claudio Abate. © Archivio Claudio Abate.

Fontana — with the pulsating sound of the artist's heart in the background. The last room, and also the gloomiest, was that given to Mauri, who covered the walls with laminated silk screen reproductions of Andrea Orcagna's *Trionfo della morte* (Triumph of death), a fresco cycle in Pisa's Campo Santo, which had been almost entirely destroyed during the Second World War.

In contrast to the informal, even playful debates that took place surrounding *Al di là della pittura* and *Campo urbano* and a soccer match that occurred between the artists in *Arte povera + Azioni povere* and its critics, the forum that took place in Montepulciano's town hall the day after the opening of *Amore mio* — a meeting promptly dubbed by critics the "Diet of Montepulciano," borrowing the term used for the general assembly of the Imperial Estates of the Holy Roman Empire — was remarkably formal and provided a foretaste of the reputation Bonito Oliva would soon cultivate in Rome.[60] Present were Argan, Boatto, Cesare Brandi (the first director of Rome's Istituto Centrale per il Restauro), Calvesi, Corrado Maltese (professor of art history at the University of Genoa), Marchiori, Menna, the art critic Daniela Palazzoli, and Carlo Ludovico Ragghianti, Lea Vergine, and Marisa Volpi. Notably absent were Celant and Trini, who declined the invitation, but sent an open letter, leading other critics to protest a cultural power shift from Milan to Rome and farther south to Naples and beyond.

Critics immediately detected Bonito Oliva's curatorial stamp: a desire to manipulate the spectator and a penchant for the macabre. As Lara-Vinca Masini, who had just contributed to the catalogue for *Lo spazio dell'immagine*, opined:

> Stunning, upsetting, sometimes, however, poetic (with all the ambiguities that this may entail today), exciting no doubt, this exhibition ends up looking a bit too beautiful, too much of a "memento mori" to be entirely credible. One cannot help thinking that beneath it, something is a little off: too clever, too diplomatic in its alleged independence from art criticism, provocative, yet eager to please, an almost curial organization, a smell of burning incense that

makes one doubt the sincerity of its many peremptory declarations of operative impotence in the face of art.[61]

In "L'Anti-Biennale a Montepulciano," the critic for *La Provincia di Cremona* wrote: "Gestures of passion mixed with irony in the
tableaux created by artists in the rooms of Palazzo Ricci in Montepulciano.... The novelty is that one visits this exhibition like a
sacro monte [pilgrimage site], but its setting is of unspeakable squalor,
the result of the painful disenchantment that affects contemporary
art."[62] The only critic to point out how the *tenerissimo* (very tender)
title of *Amore mio* directly addressed the contemporary political situation was Aurelio Natali in *NAC*, the journal that a few months later
would publish the most trenchant political commentaries on *Vitalità*:

> One thing is clear from the proposals of the participants in Montepulciano,
> and that is that they are patently aware of the involution in our current
> sociopolitical system, which they refuse to endorse, without knowing how-
> ever (but would it be possible?) how to extricate themselves from its way of
> signifying and its mode of communication. The result is an explicit, coldly
> constructed, and determined violence, almost always realized with poor
> materials and verging, at times, on the "nonsensical." It is a response that,
> even if not revolutionary (the only other possibility would be to stop making
> art), manages to underscore a situation of crisis that no longer has a rational
> way out. The only salvation for the artist is an ever greater withdrawal into
> the self, the endpoint of which is soliloquy.[63]

Entrapped in the City of Eternal Return

While *Lo spazio dell'immagine*, *Arte povera + Azioni povere*, and *Amore
mio* all reinvented their historical architectural spaces for novel interventions, *Vitalità* occupied a space specifically designed for expo-
sitional purposes. In Rome, the very same circumstances that had
led organizers to use these exhibitions' appealing provincial locales
led *Vitalità* into an ideologically problematic, toxic building whose
historicist façade and grand interiors had already been overhauled

several times before, most notably during the 1930s. In these years, the Palazzo delle Esposizioni was the favorite venue of the Fascist regime and played a crucial role in its propaganda machine.[64] First came the Quadriennali, inaugurated in 1931 and to this day presented every four years in that building.[65] Then, most spectacularly, came the *Mostra della rivoluzione fascista* (Exhibition of the Fascist Revolution), staged in 1932 to celebrate the tenth anniversary of Mussolini's March on Rome. On this occasion, the Palazzo's entire Beaux-Arts façade was camouflaged, encased in a geometric block, to function as a backdrop to four giant shimmering metal pilasters in the shape of immense *fasci* (literally "bundles" or "sheaves"), exemplifying the "armored modernism" devised by one of Italy's most talented Rationalist architects, Adalberto Libera (Figure 3.10).[66] After the regime turned away from Rationalist architecture, the *Mostra augustea della romanità* (Augustan exhibition of Roman times) of 1937 celebrated the bimillennium of Augustus. This time, the palazzo's façade was refurbished in *stile littorio*, the bombastic Neoclassical style of the late 1930s, with the temporary construction of the ur-Roman motif of the triumphal arch by the lesser-known and less talented architect Alfredo Scalpelli.[67] The last official exhibition of the regime, the highly militarized *Prima mostra degli artisti in armi* (First Exhibition of Artists in Uniform), was held in the palazzo in the summer of 1942.[68]

The palazzo was commandeered by the Allies and used as a military canteen at the end of the war, then by a variety of municipal boards in need of accommodation. By the war's end, it was in a derelict state. The first postwar Quadriennale, that of 1948, thus had to be moved to the Galleria Nazionale d'Arte Moderna in the Villa Borghese. The first major postwar event to take place in the palazzo was, appropriately, the *Mostra della ricostruzione nazionale* (The national reconstruction exhibition) in 1950–51, in which the various government ministries took over both floors of the palazzo to document their new infrastructure projects, including irrigation, aqueducts, railroads, and the restoration of monuments.[69] Run by the Roman municipality, the palazzo continued to limp along in the subsequent

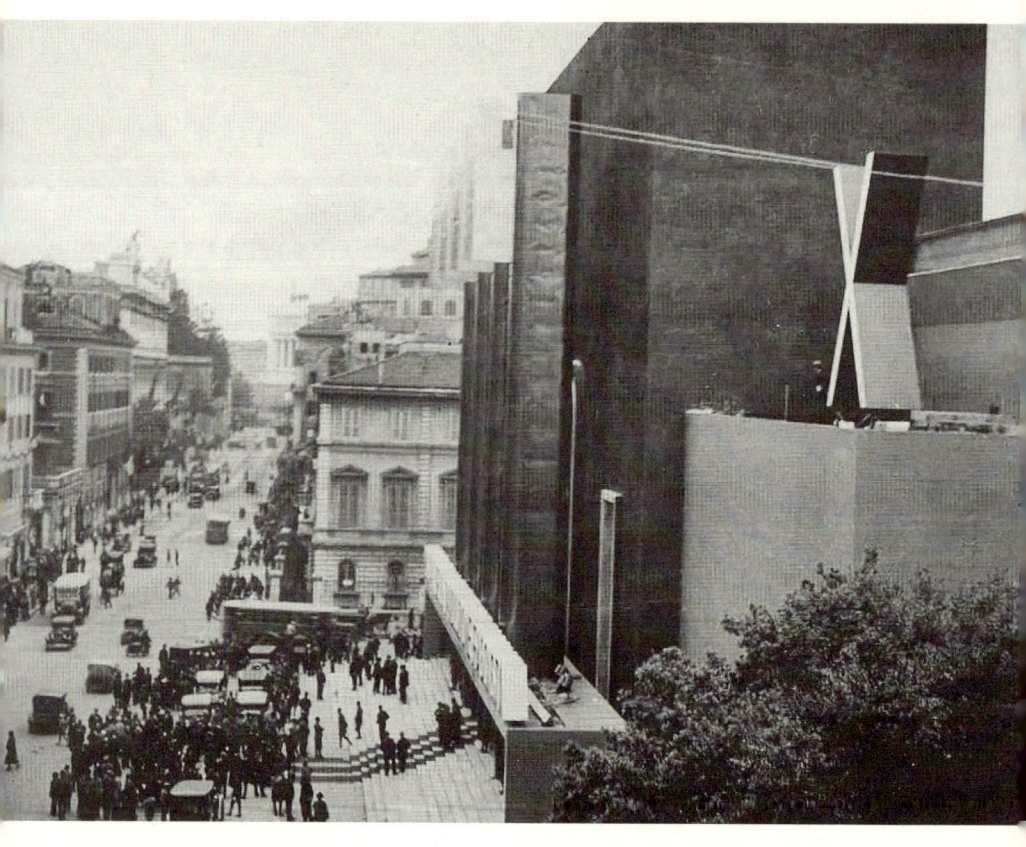

Figure 3.10. Adalberto Libera, façade of *Mostra della rivoluzione fascista*, Palazzo delle Esposizioni, Rome, 1932. Photograph: Archivio Centrale dello Stato, Rome.

years by presenting exhibitions of second-tier art from the provinces, along with exhibitions of paintings by local art teachers or
the employees of the postal ministry. Occasionally, exhibitions were
imported from abroad, such as *Civiltà romana in Romania* (Roman
civilization in Romania) in 1970. And every four years came Rome's
habitually disappointing Quadriennale.[70]

Interviews with Bonito Oliva and Sartogo confirmed that
their choice of the palazzo for *Vitalità del negativo* was quite deliberate. When asked why they chose this venue, Sartogo answered:
"Because this was the only renowned space that looked interesting
to us and wasn't a museum of modern art. We also liked the fact
that it was derelict, almost unsafe [*pericolante*], and out of favor, the
place assigned [since 1931] to those lackluster *quadriennali*." Sartago
acknowledged that they knew the space had been used by the Fascists
in 1932 and added, "but we didn't give a damn."[71] In a climate of political revisionism, when interest in both Rationalist and Neoclassicist
Fascist architecture was being revived through the many studies
published in the late 1960s and early 1970s, such nonchalance remains
unconvincing.[72]

The reviews quoted above by the Roman critics Crispolti and
Vivaldi, published back-to-back in the February 1971 issue of *NAC*
just after *Vitalità*'s closing, made the link back to the *Mostra della
rivoluzione fascista* of 1932 perfectly clear. As Crispolti stated in his
opening lines: "*Vitalità del negativo* is not a problematic exhibition,
it is in fact axiomatic, and in its own way even terroristic (in view
of its performed officialdom), and one may even call it, if somewhat
malignantly, *littoria* [fascist] (without however wanting to push too
far a noxious comparison with a certain exhibition concerning the
revolution, which took place forty years ago in these very rooms)."[73]
Vivaldi's review, a flashback to his childhood, was even more explicit,
its title and content invoking the climactic room of the 1932 *Mostra*,
which was known as the Sacrario dei Martiri, the Shrine of the Mar-
tyrs. This memorial to fallen soldiers of the Fascist Revolution of 1922
designed by Libera and Antonio Valente was a dark, cryptlike space

in which a huge black cross rose from a red-lit floor under a darkened dome and against a striated, backlit wall. On its base were inscribed the names of the fallen *squadristi*:

> The atmosphere of many of the rooms in *Vitalità del negativo* echoes, in one of those curiously vengeful twists of history, the infamous *Mostra della rivoluzione fascista* which also took place, as it happens, in the Palazzo della Esposizioni. I remember (I was a child) a black room, with the word "presente" inscribed countless times in bronze and psychedelic-patriotic music playing in the background, of which Scheggi's room seems a parody; and I remember macabre details, like the wooden bridge stained with the blood of Giovanni Berta (repainted, I suspect, from time to time), which would be the envy of Vettor Pisani. Such coincidences are not random. The Fascist *Mostra* was a shrine, in that it responded to the most profound moral ambitions of the Fascists, which was to be recognized not as flagrant killers so much as vultures and undertakers. *Vitalità del negativo* is also a shrine, for the simple reason that negativity, as soon as it is institutionalized, loses all vitality and becomes its own gravedigger.[74]

It was above all in the rotunda at the building's entrance that *Vitalità* declared itself from the outset a scenographic event of the most spectacular sort by having an architect, Sartogo, upstage the artists (Figure 3.11). Milton Gendel, Rome's correspondent for *ARTnews*, perceptively acknowledged Sartago as the star of the show and remarked: "The interest of the show . . . is in [its] sumptuous Environments, ready to be transposed into a hotel lobby, a nightclub or the equivalent of San Simeon. . . . The larger intention seems to be a final fusion — after Pop's absorption of the media — of art, fashion and display."[75] In the French art magazine *L'Oeil*, Luce Hoctin wrote that "Sartogo immediately plunged the viewer into a paradoxical ambience."[76] Looking for a way to emblematize Bonito Oliva's title for the exhibition — which critics ascribed variously to Hegel, Schopenhauer, Heidegger, Nietzsche, Adorno, or Marcuse — Sartogo strung a black translucent veil that split the palazzo's rotunda horizontally in two, shrouding the dome in darkness. Upon entering this normally

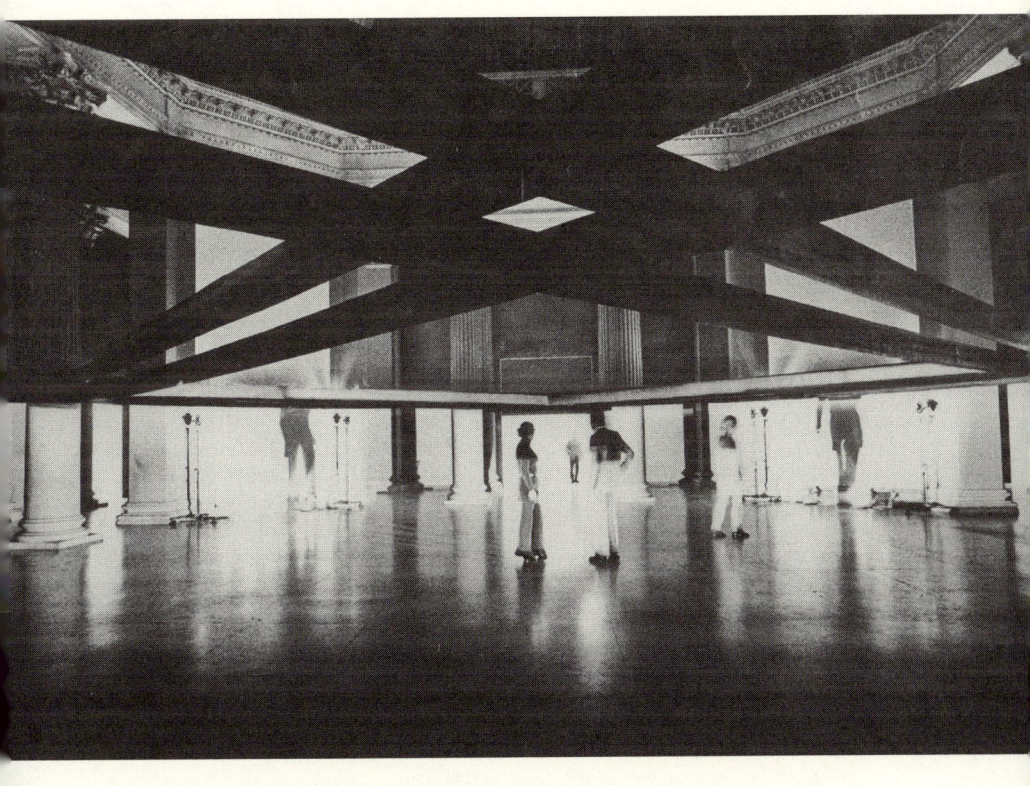

Figure 3.11. Piero Sartogo, entrance to *Vitalità del negativo*, 1970. Photograph: Massimo Pier-santi. Archivio Incontri Internazionale. Courtesy of Fondatione MAXXI, Rome.

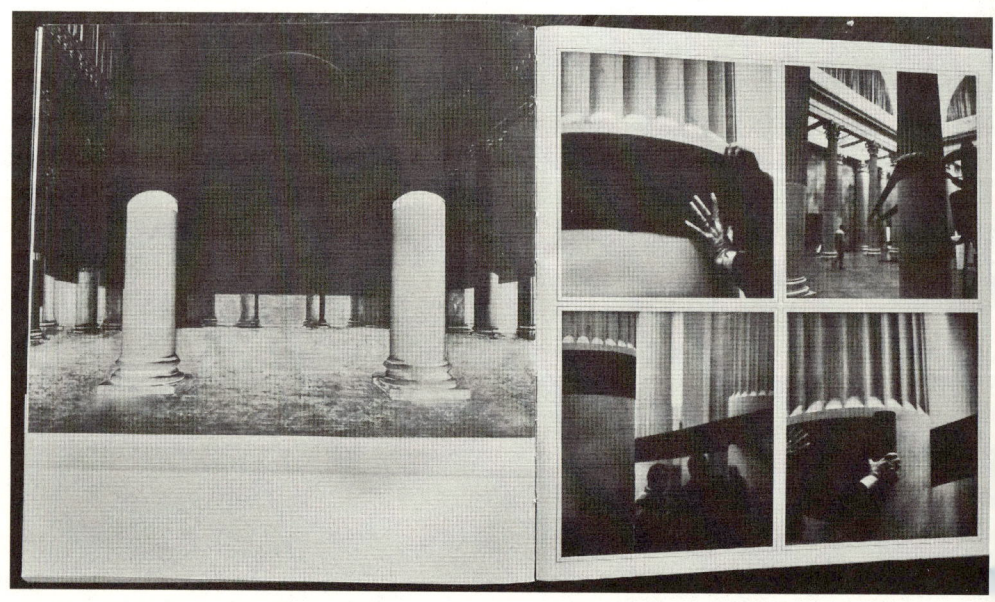

Figure 3.12. Piero Sartogo, entrance to *Vitalità del negativo*, 1970. Palazzo delle Esposizioni, Rome, reproduced in the *Vitalità del negativo* catalogue.

grand, vaulted space, visitors saw their own enlarged silhouettes projected, as in a shadow theater, on four large screens at ground level. The defining gesture was Sartogo's wrapping of the Corinthian columns at the entrance with a black ribbon in the form of intersecting *X*s just above the visitors' heads. These black bands, which Sartogo described with the loaded word *fasci*, amounted to a statement of intent. The intervention in the rotunda was in fact the only element of *Vitalità del negativo* to be photographed in situ and as a work in progress for the catalogue, where it appears in the sequence of five photographs that concludes the book (Figure 3.12).[77] "What emerges from those photographs — I practically theorized the whole affair," Sartogo said, somewhat ambiguously, when I interviewed him. He added, "The ribbon looked like duct tape; it had a demystifying Pop touch to it."[78]

"To cut that space in two was a way to contain its rhetorical emphasis, to punish it," is how Bonito Oliva described Sartogo's intervention.[79] This statement caught my attention, for it sounded less nonchalant and ironic about *Vitalità*'s container than the previous portion of our conversation had led me to assume. It brings us to a particular feature of the exhibitions that took place in the palazzo during its heyday in 1930s: the repeated remodeling of its rotunda entrance, prompting visitors to view them in the form of a palimpsest. As one reviewer of the 1935 Quadriennale wrote: "In reentering the Palazzo delle Esposizioni about to be occupied by the next Quadriennale, one cannot forget the footprint of rooms at the *Mostra della rivoluzione*: here was the rotunda which was its lair (*covo*), and here, where they are now building a fountain, stood the Sacrario dei Martiri."[80] The cupola of what was then called the Salone d'Onore was redesigned in a successive variety of crisp, unadorned, shallow *modernissimi* saucers illuminated by recessed lighting. The Corinthian columns, too, were constantly revised, either encased in streamlined cylindrical shafts, as in 1931 and 1935, creating tall, slightly tapered niches, or, as in 1939 and 1943, hidden by faux walls.[81] Revision had become part of the building's identity.

Not so after the war. It was in the 1950s that a number of architects, including Franco Albini, Ignazio Gardella, Marcello Nizzoli,
Ernesto Rogers, Carlo Scarpa, and others — almost all of whom had
begun their careers in the 1930s — realized some of their most inven-
tive museum and temporary exhibition displays.[82] Yet, in a clear
decision to forgo the spectacular mise-en-scènes of the past, not a
single designer for the Quadriennali from 1952 to 1965 laid hands on
Pio Piacentini's Beaux-Arts building. Attention was paid instead
to the exhibits of individual artists, most of which comprised easel
paintings in the more intimate spaces of the palazzo.[83] In contrast to
the striking architectural photographs of the space reproduced in
Domus and *Casabella* during the *ventennio*, in the postwar years, no
installation shots of the palazzo appeared either in the Quadriennale's official catalogues or in the reviews, and none are kept in the
Quadriennale's archives pertaining to this period. The one exception
is a small photograph in the drastically reduced format of the catalogue of the postregime Quadriennali, this one from 1952. Prostrate
alone on the arid expanse of the marble floor under the unforgiving
monumentality of Pio Piacentini's dome is Arturo Martini's *Il bevi-
tore* (Thirst, or Drinking man) (1933–36), sculpted upon seeing the
plaster casts of the victims of the volcanic eruption during a visit to
Pompei (Figure 3.13).

Made from the porous material of volcanic tufa stone, this survi-
vor of some untold disaster had made a poignant return.[84] Martini,
an enthusiastic Fascist demoted in 1945 from his position as director
of the Accademia di Belle Arti in Venice, died embittered in 1947.
Four years later, however, he was given the entrance room at the
Palazzo's sixth Quadriennale. In Rome, in contrast to Milan, it took
at least until the mid-1950s for bad memories to dissipate. In November 1955, the new Roman illustrated weekly *L'Espresso* published an
article by Mino Guerrini entitled "Quadriennale: Nacque in un Italia
che credeva d'essere fascista mentre era umbertina" (The Quadriennale: Born in an Italy that believed itself to be Fascist while it was
in fact Umbertinian). "Umbertinian," the Italian equivalent of the

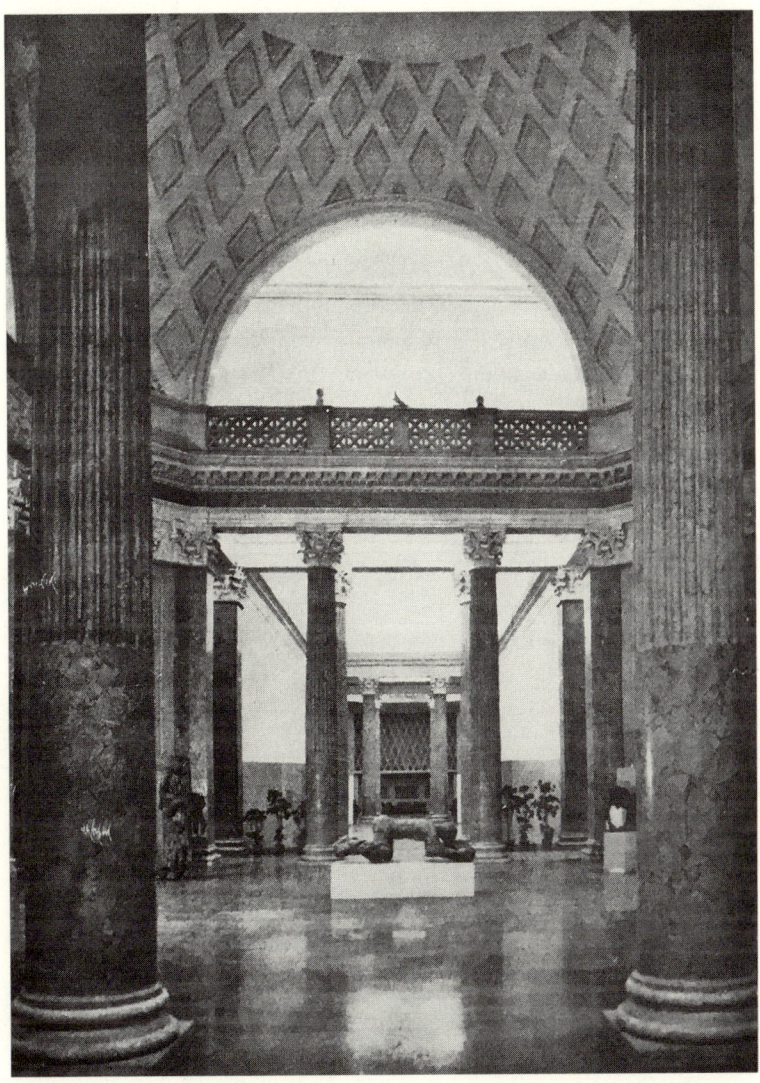

Figure 3.13. View of the installation of Arturo Martini's room, sixth Quadriennale, Palazzo delle Esposizioni, Rome, 1952, reproduced in the official guide.

Belle Epoque, was a perfect description of Italy's spirited mood at the onset of the economic boom. The article was illustrated by a 1931 photograph of King Victor Emmanuel III and his entourage descending the steps of the palazzo on their way out of the Quadriennale. The king wears military, but not Fascist, regalia, while the men standing next to him are in amazingly anachronistic tails and top hats. Guerrini writes:

> Of all the exhibitions originated by Fascism, this is the one that endures the best.... The Quadriennale is more than anything an occasion for Romans to measure the passing of time through the memory of those that preceded it: the wartime one of '43, which was the saddest; that in '48, the most euphoric and pugnacious; and others, such as the first two at the time of the battles between the Scuola Romana and the Novecento and then between the Scuola Romana and the modernists.... The first Quadriennale was held in 1931. At that point, the first signs of a combative and Mussolinian climate, while taking shape, were not yet able to disturb the habits of an Umbertinian Italy. The pomp and circumstance was the same as it ever was.[85]

In the following years, reviewers went on lamenting, in one Quadriennale after another, the sloppiness of the palazzo's staging.[86] In fact it was not until *Vitalità del negativo* that the palazzo regained its cultural stride.

An interesting point of comparison is with the story of another quasi-sacral, photogenic, and much revisited space belonging to the *ventennio*: the entry staircase of the Palazzo dell'Arte in Milan, which we encountered in Chapter 1. Built in 1933 in a Neoclassical style by Giovanni Muzio, a young protégé of the regime's principal architect, Marcello Piacentini (whose father built Rome's Palazzo delle Esposizioni), its function was to host the first Milan Triennale, presented as the great showcase of a Fascist synthesis of the arts. In Milan, the shift from a Fascist to a post-Fascist space was a flight from the solidity of a mural decoration, the favorite Fascist format, to a more unstable, Neobaroque focus on the ceiling. At the eighth Triennale in 1947, visitors accustomed to ascending the staircase toward Mario

Sironi's monumental mosaic *Il lavoro fascista* (Fascist labor, 1936) or Filiberto Sbardella's fresco *Inno alla civiltà fascista* (Hymn to Fascist civilization, 1940), were instead greeted by a room left bare except for a translucent veil hung over the ceiling by thin metal cables. The veil, painted in pale colors by a little-known artist named Leonardo Spreafico, depicted allegorical figures of the various arts. As a way to deflate the heroic quality of that space, the organizers of the Triennale introduced the viewer that year to a new, antimonumental, humility of means.[87] In 1951, at the ninth Triennale, signaling a new-found escapism, Fontana designed a neon whiplash for the ceiling over the grand staircase.[88] In political terms, this was subversive gesture, a clear, yet nonchalant repudiation of Mario Sironi's neo-Roman ceiling of 1933, in which deeply recessed and backlit rectangular coffers emphatically framed the monumental letters "VTM," an acronym for the fifth Triennale held in the then brand-new palazzo. In a flash of neon light, Fontana confronted the updated Romanità of Fascism and eclipsed it.[89] At the 1954 Triennale, as we saw, in an attempt to elicit the excitement that Fontana's ceiling had aroused three years earlier, the ceiling was covered with kinetic multicolored glass disks designed by painter Giuseppe Capogrossi. That ceiling was in turn eclipsed by the *Mostra dell'industrial design* described in Chapter 1. After the unmemorable 1957 and 1961 editions of the Triennale, the space was stripped of all historical connotation in 1964, when Gregotti greeted the visitors with a blazing void.

The Long Life of Symbols: Vitalità's Deposed X

"An obscuring of the cupola and a grazing lighting of the bands of black cloth to obtain a virtual doubling of the space": this is how Bonito Oliva described the entrance to *Vitalità del negativo* at the Palazzo delle Esposizioni in a book that was published on the occasion of the building's second restoration campaign, which took place between 2003 and 2007.[90] The installation he is describing can be read, here again, as a kind of eclipse (see Figure I.3 and 3.11). Ultimately, it was the infamous 1932 *Mostra della rivoluzione fascista* that Bonito

Oliva and Sartogo proceeded to overturn. At that *Mostra*, the letter *X* — which signified the tenth year of the regime while also resonating with the omnipresent word *dux* or *duce*, as well as the Christian cross — had been mounted on the exterior of the building, just inside above the doorway, and elsewhere. In *Vitalità*, the *X* was metaphorically deposed by being rotated ninety degrees in space. While Sartogo's preparatory drawings, some of which were reproduced in the catalogue, show his black ribbons wrapped horizontally around the columns on the perimeter of the entry space, perspectival foreshortening gave the impression that it hung horizontally *over* the entrance hall. In a television report on *Vitalità* made by Michele Gandin for RAI (Radiotelevisione Italiana), the first thing one sees as the camera pans up into the entry space is the giant *X* formed by the black cloth banners suspended overhead, as if crossing out and negating the dome.[91]

Bonito Oliva and Sartogo may have been recognizing an element of negativity in Fascism itself. In the 1932 *Mostra*, the *X* signaled the Fascists' reclaiming of Italy's imperial past, with its Roman numerals. But it also signaled, with a markedly Futurist inflection, a cancellation: a new stage of history that set back the clock to the year zero, negating or, rather, erasing the nation's experience with parliamentarian politics from the time of Italy's unification in 1871 to the March on Rome in 1922.[92] *Vitalità*'s *X* was also a *no*: not only a *no* to Fascism, but also to its revolutionary dimension and so perhaps to revolution in general. Both Sartago and Bonito Oliva were responding to the larger intellectual climate of mid-1960s Italy. Central to Bonito Oliva's thinking at this political juncture was the book *Ideologia e linguaggio* (Ideology and language) published by the poet and academic Edoardo Sanguineti in 1965, one of the earliest and most lucid reflections on the aestheticization of politics as an aspect of the failure of the historical avant-gardes. Most chillingly pertinent in the 1970 reprint of this book was the inclusion of Sanguineti's 1968 essay "La guerra futurista" (Futurist war) in which he called attention to how *interventismo* (militantism) and the marvels of mechanized war became the doctrinal fulcrum of Futurism, crystallizing what had begun as a vaguely anachronistic, vaguely anarchist, vaguely post-Symbolist *paracrepuscolare* (twilight zone) movement into a proper avant-garde.[93]

Equally significant to Bonito Oliva's contentious exhibition might have been *Il fascismo: Le interpretazioni dei contemporanei e degli storici* (published in English as *Interpretations of Fascism*), written by the influential historian Renzo De Felice and published by Laterza, Italy's most reputable academic press. De Felice's book was the first non-Marxist historiographic study of the regime and one of the most controversial publications of 1970, because many found it to be problematically revisionist. Stimulated by postwar Italian and — even more importantly, as De Felice explained — pan-European interpretations of Fascism, it downplayed the role of anti-Fascism in Italy and instead focused on the regime's origins in the 1910s within the ranks of the socialist Left and emphasized what its author repeatedly termed its "revolutionary nature."[94] For Sartogo, a key text was *La struttura assente* (The absent structure, 1968) by Umberto Eco, a member of Gruppo 63. Published after he had spent a year teaching in architecture schools — one of the most politicized fields in Italian academia — this book was Eco's first venture into semiotic theory.[95]

Bernardo Bertolucci's Il conformista and the Exhibition as Cinematic Remake

Reminiscences of Fascism and architecture converged in *Vitalità del negativo* in the silvery mural drawings made by Giosetta Fioroni, which were among the most beautiful works exhibited there (Figure 3.14). While many of the works, including the installations, had already been shown in other contexts, the fragile scenery offered by Fioroni — the only woman among the Roman Pop artists and the only woman artist in *Vitalità* — was made, in contrast to virtually all the other works on view, specifically for the exhibition and was subsequently destroyed.[96]

Fioroni's work had changed around 1966. The turn to black and white and the quality of incompleteness in her images began to suggest temporal flashbacks. *Bambino solo* (Boy alone, 1967), a pencil

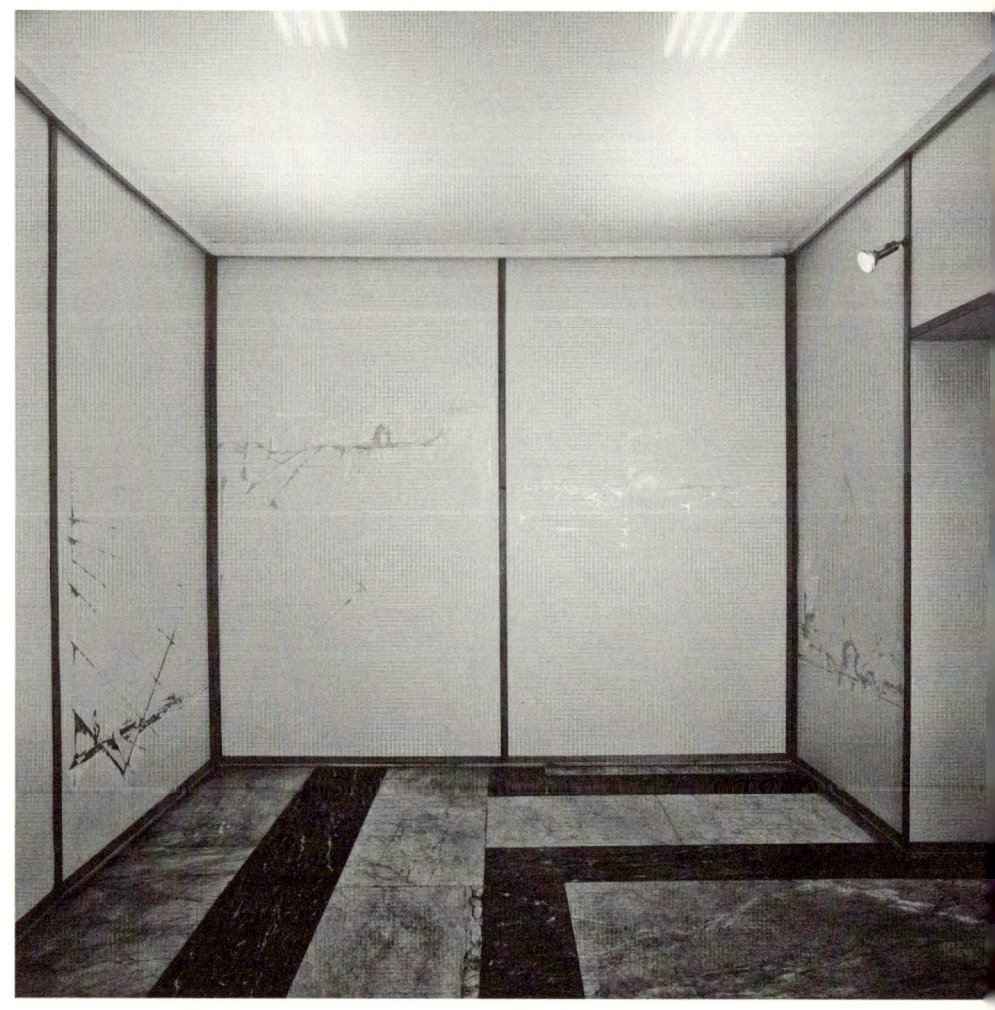

Figure 3.14. Giosetta Fioroni, *Studio per: Stanza dei paesaggi, Villa Valmarana, Vicenza, 17...* (Study for: Landscape room, Villa Valmarana, Vicenza, 17...) (destroyed), *Vitalità del negativo*, 1970. Photograph: Ugo Mulas. Courtesy Ugo Mulas Heirs.

drawing with aluminum paint on paper whose figure stands in one of her signature nondescript spaces, does not convey a specific time frame. Others — such as *Autoritratto a 7 anni* (Self-portrait age seven, 1966) and *Autoritratto di profilo* (Self-portrait in profile, 1969); *Piccola Balilla* (Little Balilla, 1969), which shows a boy in uniform; and *Contemplazione del capo* (Contemplation of the leader, 1969) — made their historical referents perfectly clear. Fioroni first exhibited these works a few months before *Vitalità*, at the Galleria dell'Indiano in Florence. The brochure that accompanied the show featured a work entitled *Obbedienza* (Obedience, 1969): an image of a young girl giving the Fascist salute (Figure 3.15). In this brochure, Fioroni (who was born in 1932) mused about images — some of them family photographs from her childhood — that hover between private thoughts and present-day society: "The point of departure [was] some images of the first years of fascism. The external similarity with the faces, clothes, fashions, and, above all, feelings that circulate — the ghosts of consumption, the funereal 'remake' underway around us."[97] In an interview conducted two decades later, in 1990, in the first extended monograph devoted to her work, Alberto Boatto urged Fioroni to comment again on her works of the late 1960s, which he contrasted with the dogged presentness of American Pop:

> Boatto: At a certain moment you began to detach yourself quite clearly from the present in order to use images of a historical past, albeit a quite recent one. I remember a series of children in uniform, little Balilla, lost, solitary.
>
> Fioroni: Yes, I proposed a series of emblematic 'portraits' of a bygone Italy. A sweet, rural Italy that no longer exists, replaced nowadays by a telegenic one. There were photos of isolated, lost children in the aftermath of the war, photos of the early years of Fascism, ruins, stunned figures.
>
> Boatto: In these figures of children, for the first time you revisit memories that are no longer exclusively personal, but belong to a whole generation.
>
> Fioroni: Yes, a personal visit to a public, collective memory.[98]

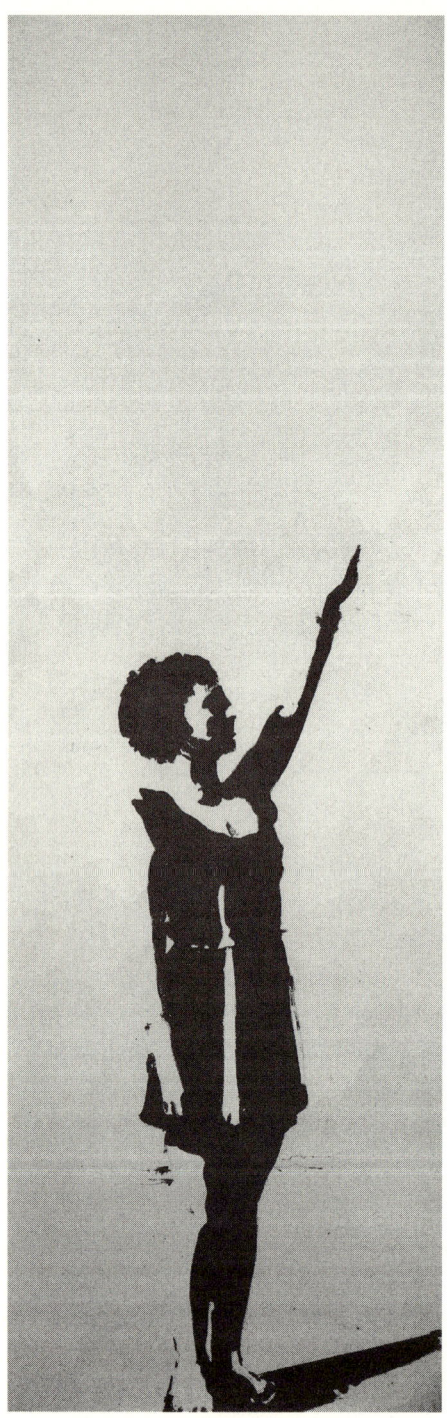

Figure 3.15. Giosetta Fioroni, *Obbedienza*
(Obedience, 1969). Pencil, white and
aluminum enamel on canvas, 180 × 60 cm.
Paola Quesada Collection, Rome.

At the end of 1970, figures had disappeared from Fioroni's work. In the winter of that year, the Galleria La Tartaruga in Rome hosted an exhibition of her work featuring views of palaces along the Grand Canal of Venice, the trapezoidal shape of Piazza San Marco seen from the air, and the Veneto countryside near Pieve di Soligo, all in pencil, highlighted with enamel on cardboard paper.[99] Engulfed in a ubiquitous fog, the silvery silhouettes of buildings and the landforms around them were nearly invisible. Two drawings in particular stand out. One is *La montagna* (The mountain, 1970), a picture of Monte Tomba in the Alps near Belluno, a mountain that owes its name to its pyramidal (tomblike) shape. In an interview, Fioroni explained this site's personal significance for her: "Monte Tomba is where my father fought during the First World War. It was conquered by the Austrians and taken back by the Italians."[100] Another work, entitled *Grande freccia che indica la casa in campagna* (Large arrow pointing to the countryside house, 1970), was also configured like a pyramid.

Similarly recalcitrant and yet daunting images in *Vitalità* are the emblems of totalitarian power exhibited in Franco Angeli's room, painted between 1962 and 1966: the Roman she-wolf (Figure 3.16), eagles taken from the US dollar, red stars from Communist banners, Christian crosses, and Nazi swastikas.[101] In a 1964 interview with Maurizio Calvesi when those paintings with Roman emblems were exhibited as "Frammenti capitolini" at the Galleria Arco d'Alibert in Rome, Angeli explained that he painted his symbols of violence and power with cotton gauze sprayed with enamel "to allow the image to appear, but never too much."[102] It was Pierre Restany, the champion of the French Nouveaux Réalistes, who, in retrospect, most cogently described the climate surrounding Italian Pop by reminding his reader that it was Rome, not Turin or Milan, that was the true "capital" of the movement. In a 1990 interview given on the occasion of the exhibition *Roma anni '60: Al di là della pittura* (Rome in the '60s: Beyond painting) — which was held, as it happens, at the Palazzo delle Esposizioni — Restany said that Italians artists "felt free to look at America from a distance and that gave them operative space. . . .

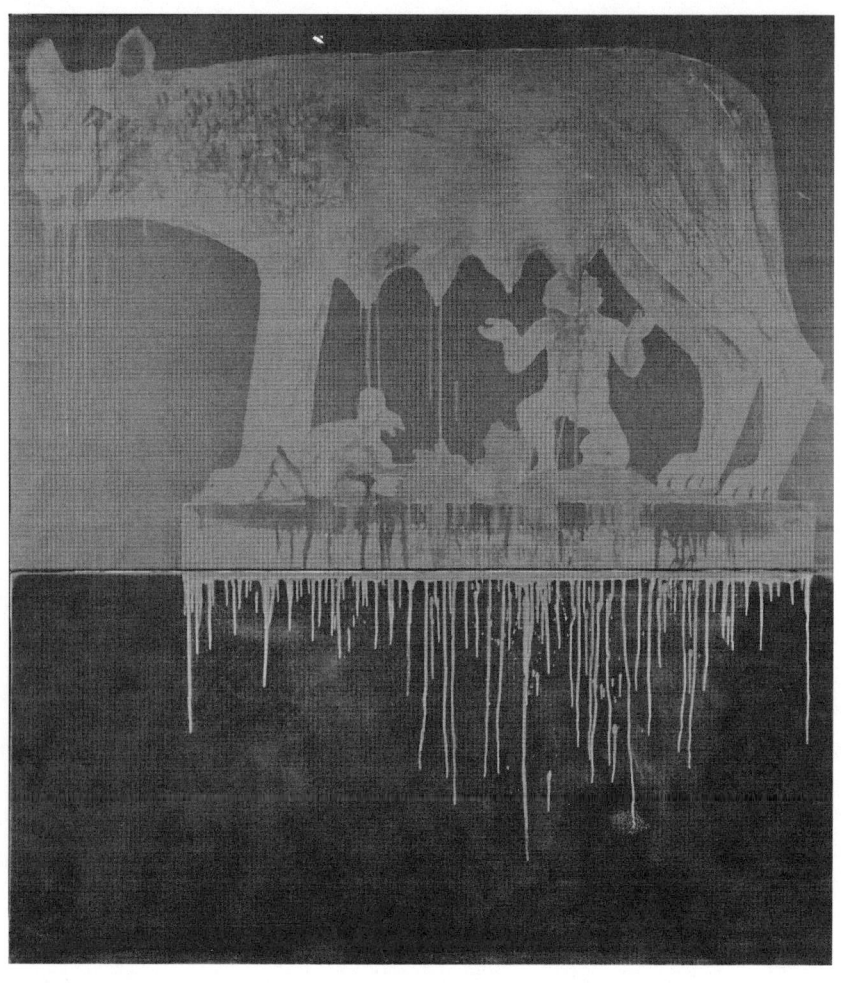

Figure 3.16. Franco Angeli, *Souvenir di Roma* (Souvenir of Rome, 1964). Mixed media on canvas with veil, 170.5 × 150 cm. Courtesy Archivio Franco Angeli, Rome.

One should recall that Rome had been the epicenter of the grand quarrel about Socialist Realism. It was there that the fall of Marxist ideology and its rejection by many artists took place. . . . Rome did not want to force its destiny. It had forced it during the *ventennio*, and maybe that period served as a lesson."[103]

It is no doubt significant in view of Fascist resonances that the first country where Gerhard Richter showed work outside of Germany was Italy and that his first solo show was at the Galleria La Tartaruga — Fioroni's, Angeli's, and Schifano's gallery in Rome in 1966.[104] The selected works included many of his family pictures, such as *Familie Schmidt* (The Schmidt family, 1964), *Drei Geschwister* (Three siblings, 1965), and *Tante Marianne* (Aunt Marianne, 1965), as well as *Motorboot* (Motorboat, 1965), one of Richter's rare images about the euphoric 1960s economic boom. Most interesting to us is *Mutter und Tochter* (Mother and daughter, 1965), in which Richter depicts Brigitte Bardot accompanied by an older woman, presumably her mother (Figure 3.17). Here, as in so many of Richter's German family pictures, we see the parental generation of a collaborationist country, in this case, France. Flashbacks to collaboration created a commonality among France, Italy, and Germany, three nations historically stained by Fascism. Bardot had recently appeared in *Le mépris* (Contempt, 1963), Jean-Luc Godard's most Antonionesque film. It was shot, quite memorably, in the villa built in 1937 by Adalberto Libera for the writer Curzio Malaparte in Capri — one of the most striking examples of Rationalist modernism during Fascism.[105] A year earlier, the group exhibition *Documenti d'arte oggettiva in Europa* (Documents of objective art in Europe), held from April to September 1965 at the Galleria d'Arte Moderna in Palermo, included Richter's *Bomber* (Bombers, 1963), *Familie am Meer* (Family at the seaside, 1964), and a lesser-known work, *Philipp Wilhelm* (1964), based on a seventeenth-century portrait of the Count Palatine of Neuburg. While the first two can be read as comments on the Cuban missile crisis and everyday life in West and East Germany, respectively, they were also redolent of Nazism. In the summer of 1966, Richter had another Italian

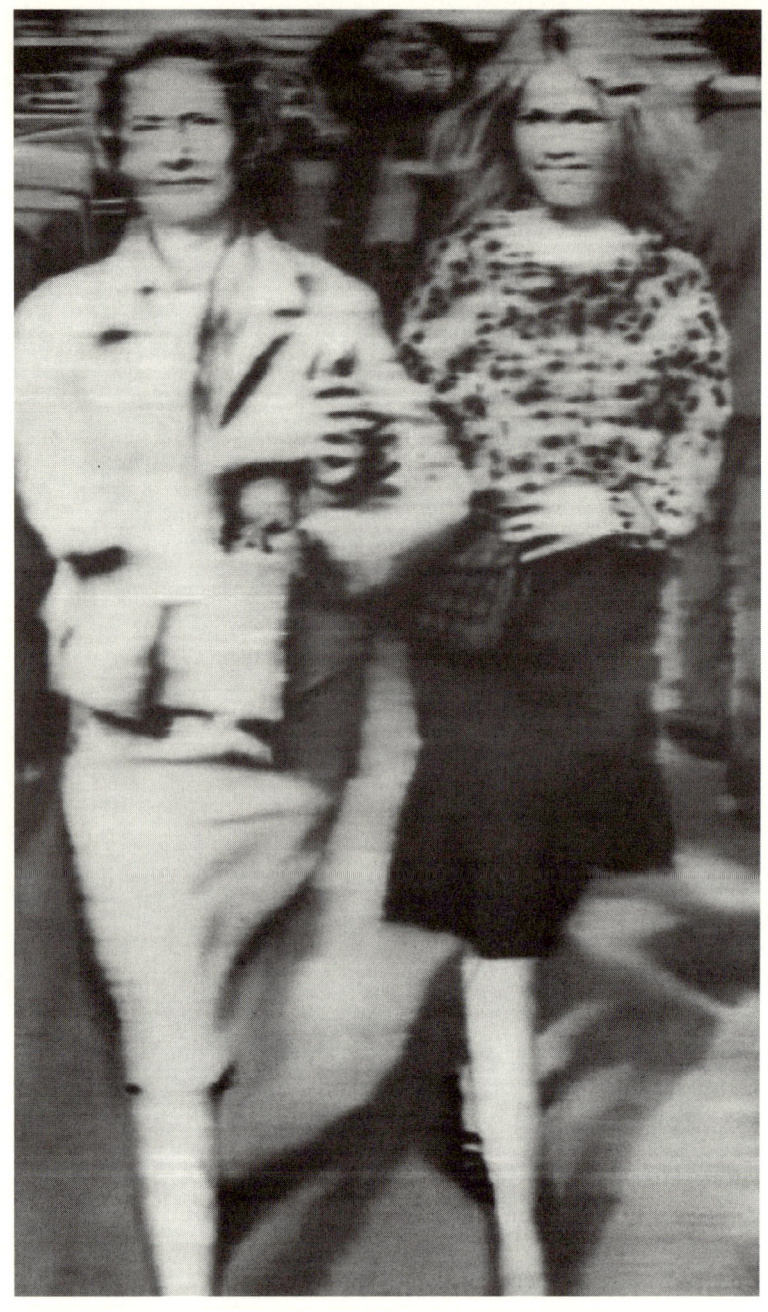

Figure 3.17. Gerhard Richter, *Mutter und Tochter* (Mother and daughter, 1965). Oil on canvas, 180 × 110 cm. Ludwiggalerie, Oberhausen, Germany. ©Gerhard Richter 2020 (0168).

show at the Galleria del Leone in Venice, to coincide with the Biennale. The leaflet's cover featured *Personengruppe* (Group of people, 1965), which was reminiscent of one of the last scenes of Antonioni's *L'eclisse* (The eclipse, 1962). Among the works on show was *Versammlung* (Meeting, 1966), which depicted a crowd with one figure in the foreground striking a salute, possibly Fascist, but perhaps, as in the DDR of Richter's childhood, Communist.[106]

But let us go back to Fioroni's room (Figure 3.14). The title of Fioroni's mural drawings in that room — *Studio per: Stanza dei paesaggi, Villa Valmarana, Vicenza, 17...* (Study for: Landscape room, Villa Valmarana, Vicenza, 17...) — makes reference to the famous Palladian villa in the Veneto whose guest chambers were decorated in the 1750s by Giambattista and Giandomenico Tiepolo. But the ellipsis in the title's reference to the eighteenth-century contains what I believe is an encrypted date that reads as "[19]71" in reverse. In contrast to photographs of the other artists' rooms in *Vitalità*, Fioroni's room shows that the stark geometric design of the travertine and dark-gray peperino marble floor of Piacentini's palazzo has been left visible. The modernist geometries of Fioroni's wall drawings and their relation to the pattern of the floor point us back not to the Tiepolos' wondrous depictions of the end of the ancien régime and the birth of a new world, but to the chilling interior architecture of the Quadriennale of 1935 and indeed to the 1930s. Her use of the word "remake" at the time of her interview with Boatto in 1990 strikes the note that releases her work, and *Vitalità*, from permanent revolution into a more ambiguous temporality.

One of her 1970 drawings featuring a circular platform was entitled *Autunno al Foro Italico* (Autumn at the Foro Italico), referring to the famed Fascist sports arena in Rome. In another, Fioroni penciled the word *autostrada* (highway), while another drawing of 1970 was entitled *Strada per Fregene* (The road to Fregene). This suggests that what we may be seeing in Fioroni's drawings, with their long lines receding toward bleak horizons, are the deserted architectural vistas of EUR (Esposizione Universale Roma), Mussolini's ideal Fascist city: the highway to Fregene, which Fioroni, like most Romans, took to go to the beach, runs right by EUR. Envisioned by Mussolini as a "third Rome," EUR was planned for the World's Fair of 1942, an event that was canceled due to the outbreak of war. The district, which was not completed until the 1950s, became one of the iconic sites of postwar Italian cinema. In Roberto Rossellini's 1945 film *Roma città aperta* (Rome open city), EUR served as a setting for partisan resistance. In Antonioni's *L'eclisse*, it symbolized urban alienation.[107] In Bernardo Bertolucci's *Il conformista* (The conformist) of 1970, a film that premiered in theaters just as *Vitalità* was opening, EUR stood for the relentless mise-en-scène of Fascism.[108]

It was Mulas who captured in his photographs the disquieting and strongly cinematic atmosphere of *Vitalità* better than the critics. Graziella Lonardi Buontempo had invited him to shoot the exhibition both on the night of its opening and in a series of photographs of the spaces bereft of people after it was installed. The two apparently considered producing a photo book and began looking for a publisher. Due to Mulas's declining health and his untimely death in 1973, the project was shelved, but the photographs survive.[109] In one of them, we see the palazzo's neo-Roman coffered ceiling emerging, haunting and remote, through the translucent screen hanging above a painting by Schifano. In another, we find Fioroni in a fur jacket, standing in front of her wall drawings on the opening night of the exhibition (Figure 3.18). Her head is slightly turned to the side, and something appears to have caught her attention from beyond the right edge of the photograph. Another woman faces the opposite direction, examining something — also invisible to us — in one of Fioroni's drawings. As in an earlier photograph by Mulas in which Fioroni appears, shot at the Venice 1964 Biennale, it is as if we have been transported to a film set. The photos recall the architecturally dramatic scene in *Il conformista* in which Marcello Clerici, the turncoat antihero of the story, played by Jean-Louis Trintignant, takes his eccentric mother to an asylum to visit his father, who suffers from dementia. In that scene, filmed on location at EUR, we see the mother, the son, and a doctor standing starkly silhouetted against the chilling whiteness of a marble rooftop. One of the most visually striking moments in the film, it takes the viewer to a rarely visited space: the open-air theater built in 1938 by Libera on the roof of the Palazzo dei Congressi, with its endless rows of benches. At one point, the three figures all face the same direction and stare at something in the distance situated off screen. Marcello's mother, like Fioroni, wears a fur wrapped around her shoulders (Figure 3.19).

In contrast to the linear chronological sequence of the 1951 novel by Alberto Moravia upon which it was based, Bertolucci's film is structured around a series of flashbacks. The film begins where it will end, with Marcello riding in a car to a forest outside of Paris. This is where Luca Quadri, Marcello's philosophy professor in Rome during the early years of the regime, is now in exile as an anti-Fascist in Paris. Marcello had been sent to kill him during his wedding trip to the French capital. Later in the narrative, Quadri and his mysterious young wife, Anna, will be gruesomely assassinated by Marcello's associate Manganiello. The traumatic significance of the site is revealed to us only much later in the film. As film historian T. Jefferson Kline elaborates: "Nothing is explained, and nothing will be explained through traditional narrative exposition. . . . Bertolucci's use of flashbacks is unusual not only for its disregard of chronology but also for the tendency to use flashbacks out of flashbacks. Progression occurs clearly by association rather than logic."[110] And as Maureen Turim maintains, "Many flashback narrations contain an element of philosophical fatalism, coupled with a psychoanalytic fatalism": history as overdetermined repetition.[111]

Vitalità and *Il conformista* — by a curator-auteur and a filmmaker-auteur, respectively, both of whom began as poets — functioned, I believe, in a similar way. For instance, between Alfano's falling drop of water and Pascali's *32 mq. di mare circa*, four shallow containers filled with water dyed in different tints of green and blue, was Franco Angeli's room, with his depictions of past symbols of power. And it was Moravia, the author of the novel *Il conformista*, who wrote the

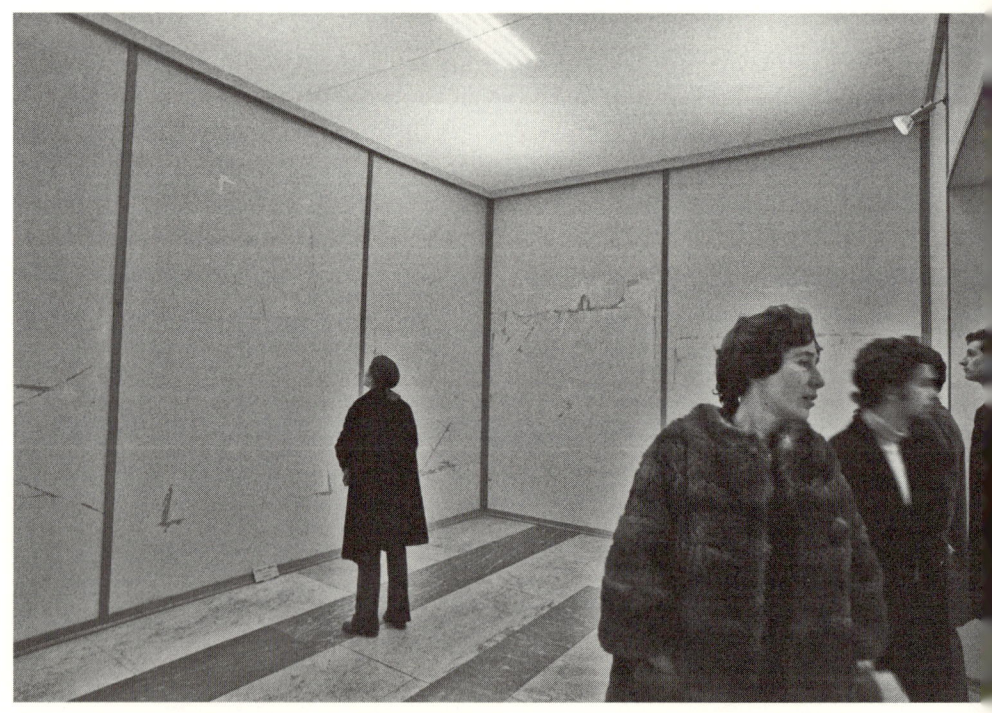

Figure 3.18. Giosetta Fioroni on the opening night of *Vitalità del negativo*, 1970, Palazzo delle Esposizioni, Rome. Photograph: Ugo Mulas. Courtesy Ugo Mulas Heirs.

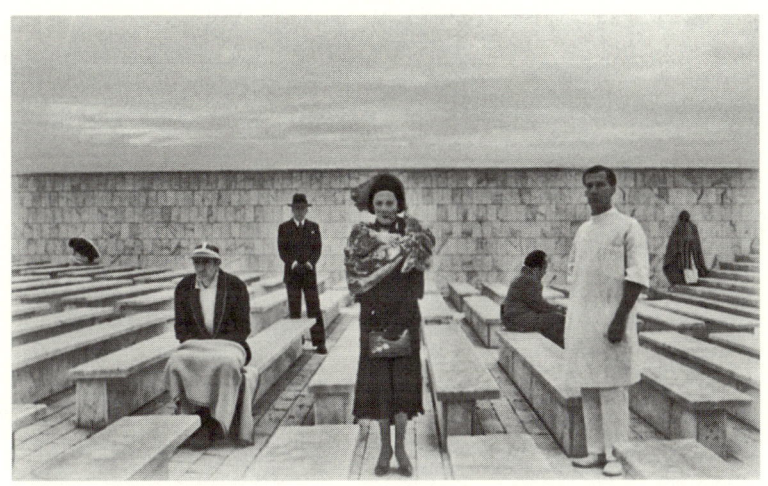

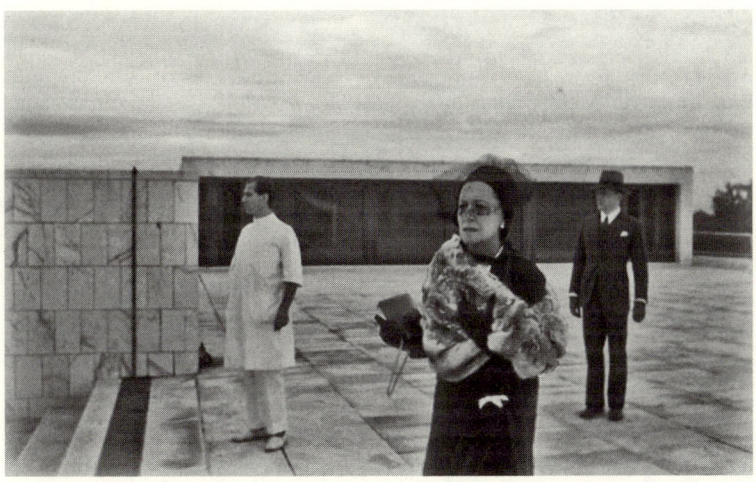

Figure 3.19. Bernardo Bertolucci, dir., *Il conformista* (The conformist, 1970).

brochure for Fioroni's show "*La vita a Roma*": *Luoghi, paesaggi e dimore* ("Life in Rome": Places, landscapes and dwellings) at Milan's Galleria del Naviglio, which opened just weeks after the closing of *Vitalità*. Its opening sentence reprises the theme of eternal recurrence that haunted her work and that of others in those years: "Dear Giosetta, the paths of poetry are few and you can only travel them in one direction. If you set off on a given path, you inevitably end up in places that are foreseeable, though always new." [112]

The oft-noted elegance of *Vitalità del negativo* (and that of its visitors on opening night) was on par with the stylized camerawork of Vittorio Storaro, the lavish set designs by Ferdinando Scarfiotti, and the alluring clothes designed by Gitt Magrini for *Il conformista* — characteristics that would become, soon enough, the defining traits of the postmodern. [113] Throughout the exhibition, the viewer was made to traverse spaces characterized by plunging perspectives and dramatically cast shadows, as in Davide Boriani and Gabriele De Vecchi's manipulations of perspective in *Camera distorta* (Distorted room, 1970), Mulas's photo of which includes, somewhat incongruously, two young men, probably the artists themselves, in military-style coats, overseeing the exhibition; Alberto Biasi's *Movimento continuo di raggi e di colore* (Continuous movement of rays and color, 1967); Gianni Colombo's *Campo praticabile* (Viable field, 1967); and Getulio Alviani's *Rilievo a riflessione ortogonale* (Relief with orthogonal reflection, 1970). Mulas's photographs of these works in *Vitalità* recall different scenes in *Il conformista* (Figure 3.20). One, for instance, when we see Clerici from afar, nervously pacing up and down Libera's interminable halls in EUR's Palazzo dei Congressi, waiting for a meeting with a Fascist government official. In another of Mulas's photographs, a figure, or maybe a couple — the man in an overcoat and Borsalino hat and another figure in reflection — appear trapped as he/they walk, as through a revolving door, into the laminated metal cube of Scheggi's *Della geometria* (Figure 3.21). That photograph echoes the scene in *Il conformista* in which Marcello, wearing, as he does during most of the film, a Borsalino hat, follows Anna (played by Dominique Sanda) as she goes shopping with his wife, Giulia (played by Stefania Sandrelli), along one of Paris's elegant shopping streets.

Most striking is the way the exhibition and the film both relied on the use of light and shadow projected at slanting angles. Asked about this aspect of the film, Bertolucci explained: "*The Conformist* is lighted like a 1930s studio film; even when we were on location, there were a lot of lights and lighting effects . . . this is the first film where I controlled the lighting myself in the old, truly professional classical sense. . . . You can get unbelievable effects which help the psychology, the narrative, the whole language of the film."[114] Sartogo's bisected entrance space has its counterpart in a crucial episode in Bertolucci's film in which Marcello, emerging from a pool of shadow, makes a gesture reminiscent of the Fascist salute during his first encounter with Quadri in his Paris home (Figure 3.22, bottom). In De Vecchi's *Ambiente — strutturazione a parametri virtuali* (Environment — virtual parameters structure, 1969), splendidly photographed, again, by Mulas, a young woman wearing a bouclé coat is trapped by a beam of light in the form of two rotating prisms, as if she were under police interrogation, with the light cutting into her body like a blade (Figure 3.23, top). In the background, looming in the dark, is another, older, woman, wrapped in a cape like a prophetess. Similarly ominous rays cut through Marcello and Giulia, at that point still his fiancée, rays echoed by her striped dress, while they illicitly embrace at her parents' home. However, this somber atmosphere suffusing *Vitalità* was most palpable in Gilberto Zorio's *Confine* (Boundary, 1969): "a boundary," as the artist explained on many occasions, being "an imaginary line that can only be concretized through violence."[115] *Confine* (photographed elsewhere in an earlier iteration) appears in the catalogue next to *Odio* (Hate, 1968), another work by Zorio, in which he hammered the word *odio* into a wall.

To those who may argue that *Vitalità* and *Il conformista* fed off the glamorous frisson of Fascism, I would respond that Bonito Oliva and Bertolucci were both involved in an act of "mimetic subversion," an act that, as I described it in the Introduction, engages the enemy on

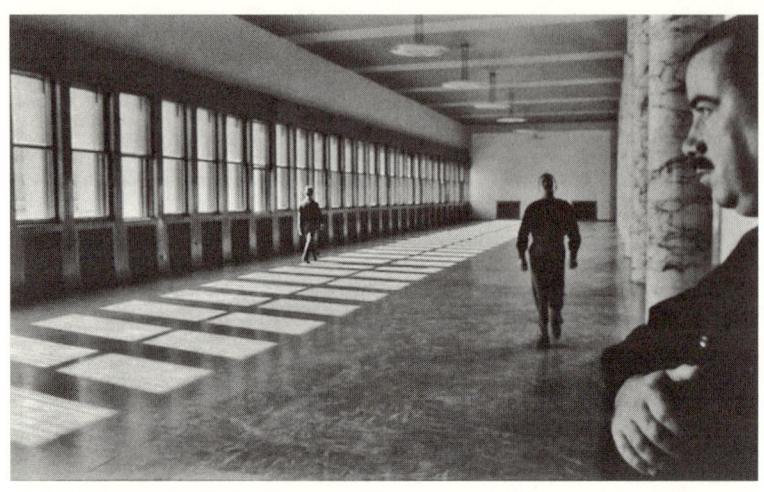

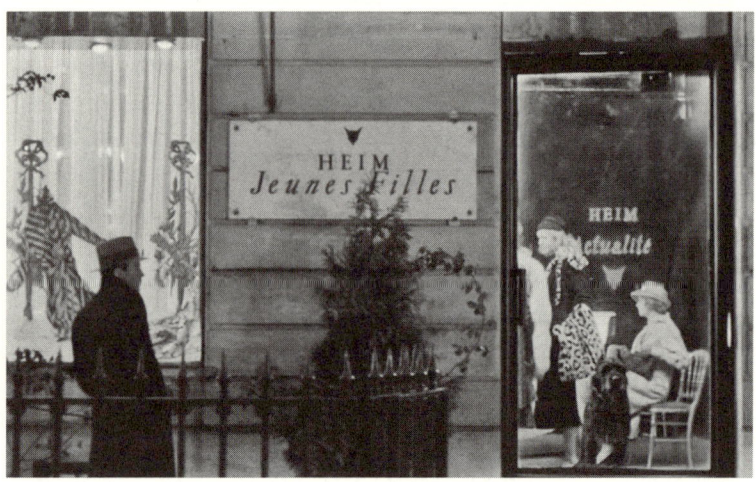

Figure 3.20. Bernardo Bertolucci, dir., *Il conformista* (The conformist, 1970).

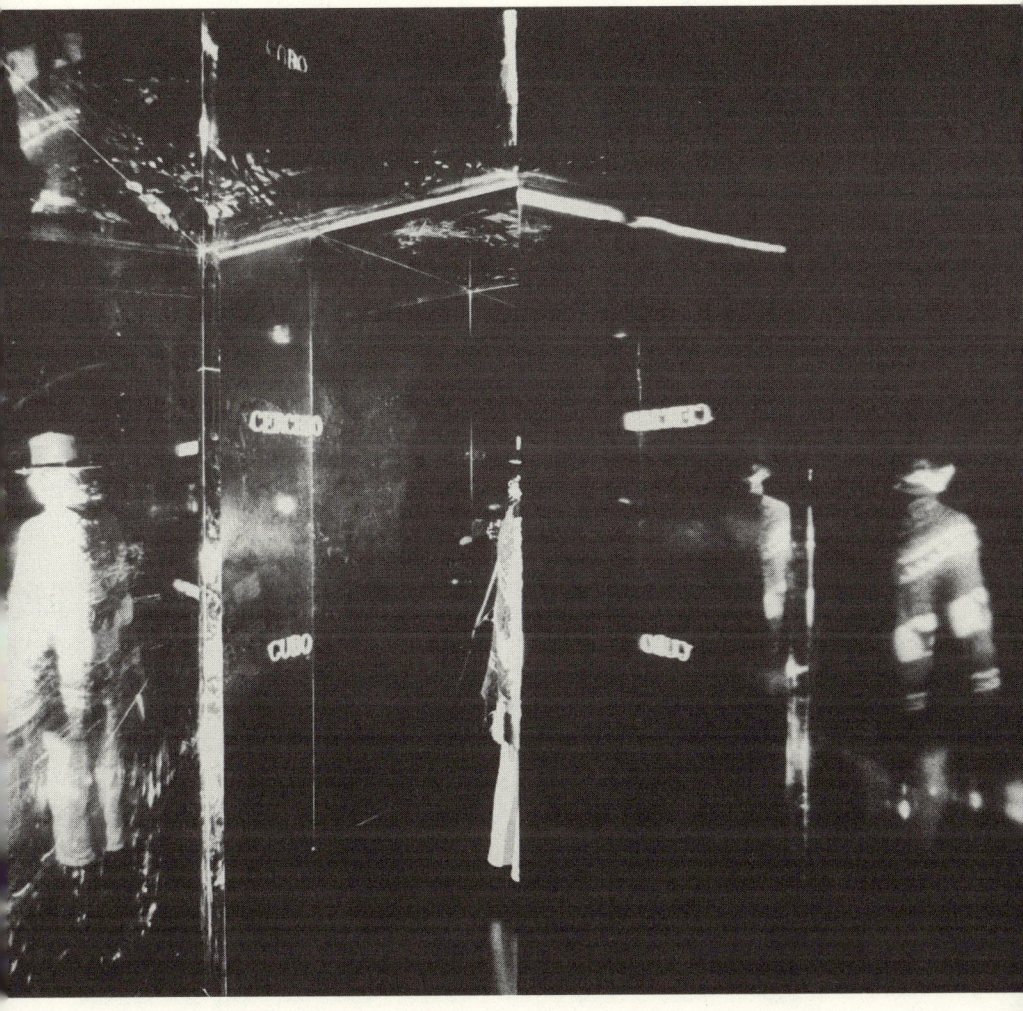

Figure 3.21. Paolo Scheggi, *Della geometria* (On geometry, 1970). View of the installation at *Vitalità del negativo*. Photograph: Ugo Mulas. Courtesy Ugo Mulas Heirs.

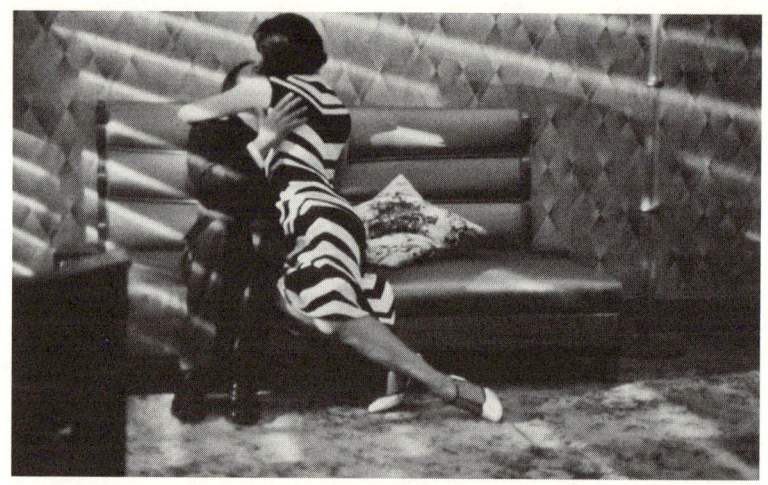

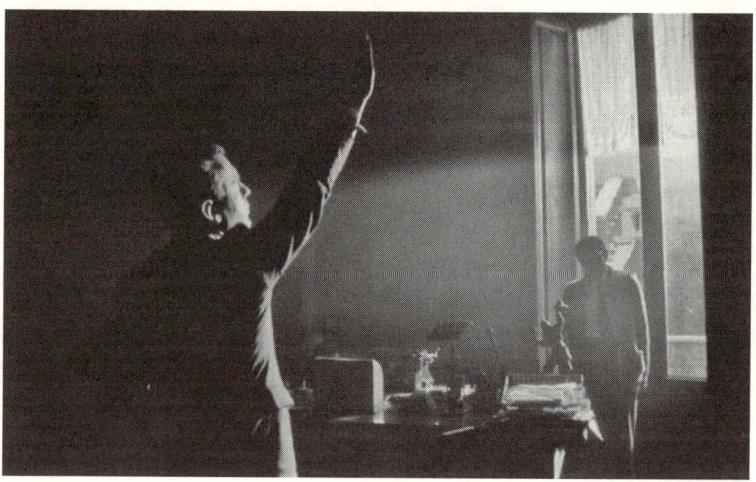

Figure 3.22. Bernardo Bertolucci, dir., *Il conformista* (The conformist, 1970).

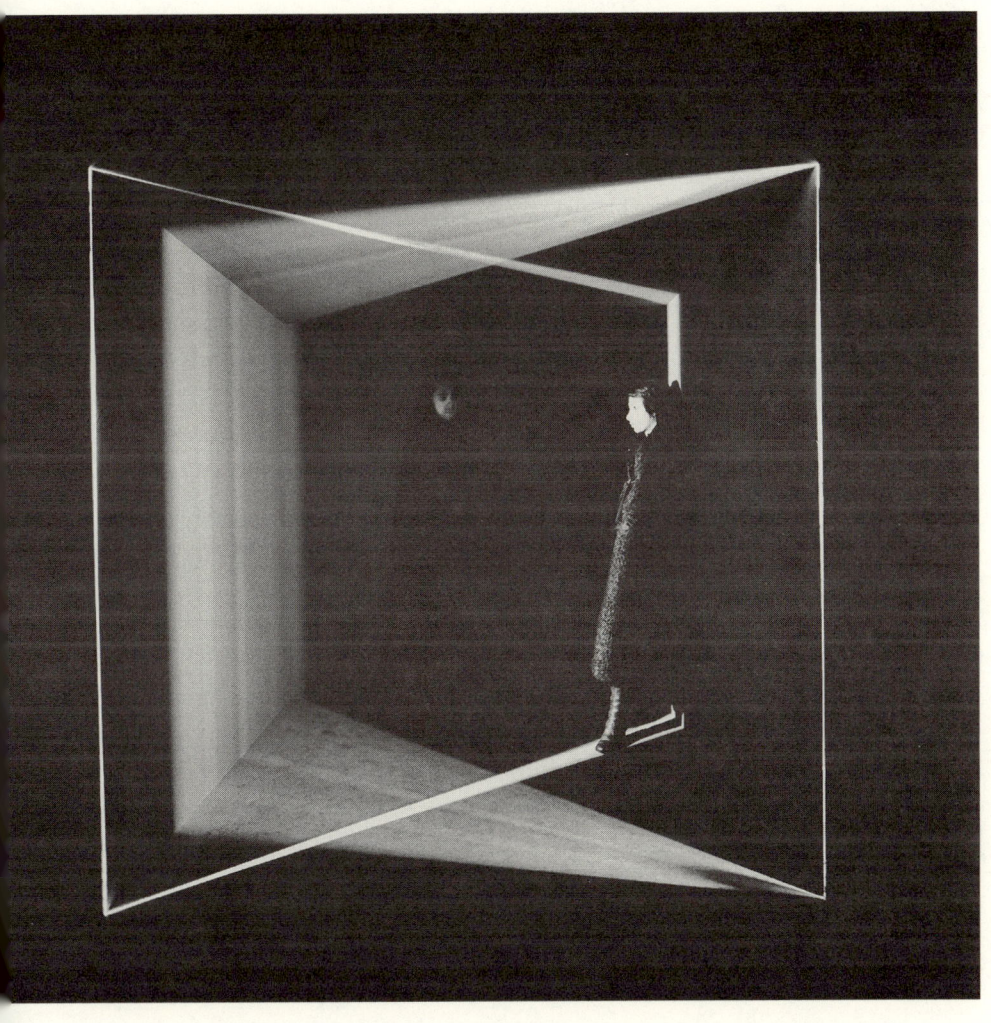

Figure 3.23. Gabriele De Vecchi, *Ambiente—strutturazione a parametri virtuali* (Environ-ment—virtual parameters structure, 1969). View of the installation at *Vitalità del negativo*. Photograph: Ugo Mulas. Courtesy Ugo Mulas Heirs.

its own ground, but obliquely. Pressed in an interview published in 1972 in the British film journal *Sight & Sound* to comment on *Il conformista*'s relation to history, Bertolucci remarked that having failed to make films about the present, he instead made "films that arrive at the present by speaking of the past."[116] When the interviewer, Marilyn Goldin, asked about Italians' nostalgia for Fascism, he responded: "Yes! That's why I say *The Conformist* is a film on the present. And when I say that I want to make the public leave with a sense of malaise, perhaps feeling the presence of something obscurely sinister, it's because I want them to realize that however the world has changed, feelings have remained the same.... For Italy, the film is really very savage."[117] Slightly earlier in the interview, Bertolucci confessed: "*The Conformist* is a story about me and [Jean-Luc] Godard. When I gave the professor Godard's phone number and address, I did it for a joke, but afterwards I said to myself, 'Well, maybe all that has some significance.... I'm Marcello and I make Fascist movies and I want to kill Godard who's a revolutionary, who makes revolutionary movies and who was my teacher.'"[118]

Godard stands in the history of cinema for an intransigent Brechtian avant-gardism. In the 1930s, Bertolt Brecht used his famous concept of *Verfremdungseffekt* (alienation effect) — the rejection of the empathetic, illusion generating, and immersive theater favored by the bourgeoisie — to disambiguate the spellbinding scenarios of Fascism. This said, there was doubtless an element of fascination in Godard's choice of the Casa Malaparte, Fascism's most iconic modernist building along with Terragni's Casa del Fascio, as a setting. Godard needed no less than Brecht himself to play a cameo role in his film. Like Bertolucci's film, Godard's *Le mépris* was based on a novel written by Moravia in 1954, three years after *Il conformista*. There is nevertheless a link between the strategy of mimetic subversion and that of an alienation effect, in that both imply an element of psychological but also political distancing. The difference is that mimetic subversion produces an element of irresolution in the viewer. It is this capacity for irresolution, placing its artists both in and outside of the avant-garde, that allowed *Vitalità del negativo* to comment so effectively on post-1968 politics.[119]

Meanwhile, as Kline elaborates, many betrayals are at work in *Il conformista*:

> Quadri himself is certainly a paternal figure for Clerici, who has "lost" his own father to an insane asylum.... As an anti-Fascist, living in exile in Paris, Quadri is, like Athos's father [in Bertolucci's *Strategia del ragno* (The spider's stratagem), also released in 1970, just a few months before *Il conformista*], a figure of questionable loyalty: Is he traitor or hero? Clerici cannot decide. He ultimately betrays Quadri, his own fascist ideals, and himself, for when it comes time to act he will simply watch from a car as others assassinate Quadri and his wife in the woods of Savoie.[120]

And so it is that with *Il conformista*, a seductive film about the seduction of Fascism, Bertolucci betrayed the cinematic avant-garde epitomized by Godard.

In a 1971 interview coinciding with the film's release, Moravia had the opportunity to return to his 1951 novel. Literary critics had taken him to task for his unsympathetic depiction of the political exiles, the *fuorusciti*, in Paris — the fact, for instance, that he portrayed Professor Quadri surrounded by his disciples in a surprisingly grand flat for a man living underground in Paris — Moravia said that his distaste stemmed from "the strongly bourgeois, meaning strictly ideologizing atmosphere in which they moved." Ultimately, for Moravia, the *fuorusciti* were "renouncers" — that is, passive avoiders of an actively militant action. The only anti-Fascism that made sense, and which he sympathized with at the time, was that of the Communists.[121] In Moravia's description of his position as an author in that book, we perceive the novel's relevance two decades later:

> With *The Conformist*, I wanted to represent Fascism from the point of view of Fascism. I don't consider myself a sectarian. On the contrary, I sometimes feel overcome by a kind of schizoid dissociation so that I do everything to put myself in the shoes of my adversary. In confronting Fascism, I wanted to know

why and how it was born; what it had represented for the Fascists themselves. I asked myself: What is a Fascist intellectual?[122]

Moravia's position is all the more striking in view of the fact that as many recognized and as he himself acknowledged later on, the novel had many autobiographical elements, beginning with the fact that he and Marcello were born in the same year, 1907.[123]

Yet another parallel with Bonito Oliva's exhibition, underscored by the title of Restany's review in *Domus*, "Vitalità del negativo/Negativo della Vitalità," is Moravia's description of the Fascist creed as a series of inversions:

> I understood that negative values on the personal level are converted into positive values at the national level. The misery of the petty bourgeoisie became patriotism. . . . What was in play was the mechanism of conversion. As if by magic, from a sum of negative values emerges a positive value. We witness a total reversal: the reversal happens because inside the person who undergoes it is surely found, even if distorted, what he or she will become.[124]

Toward the end of his 1971 interview, Moravia returned to the main theme of the book, that of betrayal: "Joining Fascism always came at the price of a crime; to begin with, a denunciation. The first thing Mussolini demanded from an intellectual was to write an article against an enemy of his, against Croce, for instance."[125]

Before the Years of Lead:
Achille Bonito Oliva's "Traitor" Strategy

In 1972, Bonito Oliva delivered his lecture "La citazione deviata: L'ideologia," in which he introduced his concept of the "ideologia del traditore" — traitor's ideology.[126] This was the position in which artists (including Bonito Oliva himself), recognizing the collective failure of the avant-garde to collapse art and life, "dissociate themselves from the group."[127] In relation to the tragedy of Piazza Fontana, they recognized the turbid elements contributed by the state apparatus, but a similar strategy of "dissociation" and "desolidarization" was being adopted simultaneously by the Italian Communist Party and other parties on the Left vis-à-vis the violence of the extreme Left.[128]

But betrayal was already there in *Amore mio*. Among the artists involved, only two responded to Bonito Oliva's invitation to surrender their space to another artist. One was Pistoletto, who gave his room to Vettor Pisani, explaining in the catalogue that his idea for whom to invite came to him in the form of a dream, which he set down in longhand in a note reproduced in his allotted pages. In that dream, Duchamp designated Pistoletto as his legatee. By anointing Pisani, an artist who had been plagued for years by an obsession with Duchamp, rather than himself as the legatee, Pistoletto had given him a poisoned gift. It was Pisani who now had to perform his deep anxiety of influence as part of the deal. He responded in kind by turning the gifted room into a lurid vivisection cabinet. Although both artists were in the know, there was an element of cruelty in Pistoletto's choice, which may be read as a betrayal of his artist friend, finding his weak spot and pressing it.[129]

More thought-provoking, because it involves more than one betrayal, and because it implicates a woman in an exhibition that didn't include any women, is the contribution of Luciano Fabro, the most dematerialized of all the works in *Amore mio*.[130] In the Palazzo Ricci's most richly frescoed room, in which cupids (*amoretti*) framed a series of amorous mythological scenes, Fabro placed a loudspeaker that endlessly blared the same phrase: "Cittadini, ritenetemi irresponsabile di quanto succede" — "Citizens, don't consider me responsible for what is happening." For the catalogue, he ceded his allotted pages to the Florentine art critic Carla Lonzi. Lonzi had just published a collection of interviews entitled *Autoritratto* (Self-portrait). Using, like Fabro, the new technology of the portable tape recorder, the book compiled a series of conversations with some of the most important artists of the day — Carla Accardi (the only woman), Mimmo Rotella, Pietro Consagra, Castellani, Kounellis, Fabro, Pascali, Fontana, Paolini, Alviani, and others, fourteen in all — which Lonzi transcribed and reassembled as a montage of overlapping or, rather, a choral assembly of voices.[131]

ci sia nessun pericolo di mercificazione, di mistificazione, nessun pericolo di consumo speculativo. Allora, penso che nascerebbe veramente una comunicazione, un colloquio. Ma se il critico ragiona nel suo tipo di società, lui non mi può capire perché io ho sempre agito come se la mia pittura dovesse appartenere a un altro tipo di società e non a questo. Perciò, ecco perché la discrepanza. Non pensi che sia cosí? Il critico dovrebbe cambiare la sua struttura, dovrebbe mettersi nei panni di una persona che vive in una società ideale, dove non esiste il mestiere del critico, ma esiste il critico... tutti siamo critici. Tutti siamo artisti e tutti siamo critici, in questo mondo, solamente in questa società non siamo tutti critici e tutti artisti, ma in una società ideale lo siamo. È naturale, non è mica che siamo artisti o critici per grazia divina, eh: tutti abbiamo le qualità finché abbiamo la possibilità di amare perché, in fin dei conti, l'arte è una emanazione dell'amore, è una espressione dell'amore. Allora è chiaro che, nello stesso tempo che amiamo, siamo artisti, la migliore arte è l'amore, secondo me. Ma... penso che sia cosí, porca miseria. È cosí, credimi. Questo dei ruoli fissi è la famosa alienazione: se io faccio il mestiere del pittore sono un alienato, se tu fai il mestiere della critica sei una alienata, no? Eh.

Fabro: Bisogna togliere, proprio, questo... questo Potere, togliere le leve del Potere a queste persone. E la cosa è certo difficile... Non so, io credo che questo avvenga naturalmente... se le cose continuano ad andare avanti cosí, ci sarà una tale inadeguatezza... Perché il ritmo sta facendosi, mi sembra, abbastanza... veloce, ecco, non dico frenetico perché è una parola che mi spaventa. Comunque veloce, per cui riesce a star dietro solo chi riesce a stare assieme. È una cosa che ho riscontrato ab-

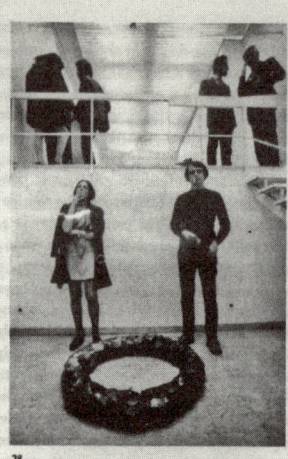

28.

bastanza nella mia esperienza, cosí, vedere come stanchi le persone proprio in quanto metti alla prova il loro fiato, la loro capacità di resistenza. Allora, lí, uno rimane sfiancato e viene tagliato fuori... cioè non viene tagliato fuori perché noi non siamo in grado, non abbiamo questa forza o questa volontà o tale interesse da metterci a fare una azione contro. Secondo me, questo lavoro di eludere continuamente, di scappare da quella che può essere una sistemazione culturale, può essere anche una tattica e la sola tattica che ci porti veramente a... a smantellare la cultura. Anche se avremo magari le stesse per-

114

115

Figure 3.24. Carla Lonzi, with Luciano Fabro at an exhibition, Milan, Galleria de Nieubourg, 1969, in Carla Lonzi, *Autoritratto* (Self-portrait, 1969), pp. 114-15.

Lonzi's text is accompanied by tiny, evocative, captionless black-and-white family snapshots of her and her interlocutors, along with parents and friends, as children, adolescents, and adults; some of the photographs dated back to the 1930s, while others were more recent, such as one in which we see Lonzi standing with Fabro at a gallery opening (Figure 3.24). These gave *Autoritratto* the look of an extended family album, one that spoke to Lonzi's intent, stated in the book's introduction, to approach the artwork as "the possibility for an encounter" and to conflate the personal and the professional.[132]

This, however, was in 1969. By 1970, Lonzi's position had radicalized. For the eight pages given to her by Fabro in the *Amore mio* catalogue, she chose excerpts from the French utopian anarchist Charles Fourier's *Dictionnaire de sociologie phalanstérienne* (Dictionary of phalansterian sociology) on the oppression, degradation, and liberation of women, along with passages from his dictionary entry on plagiarism. Fabro's selection of Lonzi as his collaborator revealed the meaning of his cryptic sound piece, although no one at the time realized the multilayered implication of this choice. By refusing to take responsibility for what was taking place, Fabro had broken ranks with the coterie of male artists convened in *Amore mio*. He introduced a woman—Lonzi—into their midst, implicitly in the palazzo and explicitly in the catalogue, and what is more, a woman who was a critic recently turned feminist.

But there was a twist. As Fabro revealed a few years later in his book *Attaccapanni* (Coat hangers), due to the poor sound quality of his piece, what the visitors heard when entering his space in the Palazzo Ricci, and what Natali quoted in his aforementioned review in *NAC*, was the opposite of what it said. Along with what read like a deposition, Fabro reproduced two small blurred black-and-white photographs of his room during the exhibition, both absent (perforce!) from the pages of the *Amore mio* catalogue (Figure 3.25).

In the summer of 1970, in Montepulciano . . . I hide a tiny loudspeaker on the windowsill of one of the windows that gives onto the square, so that it seemed

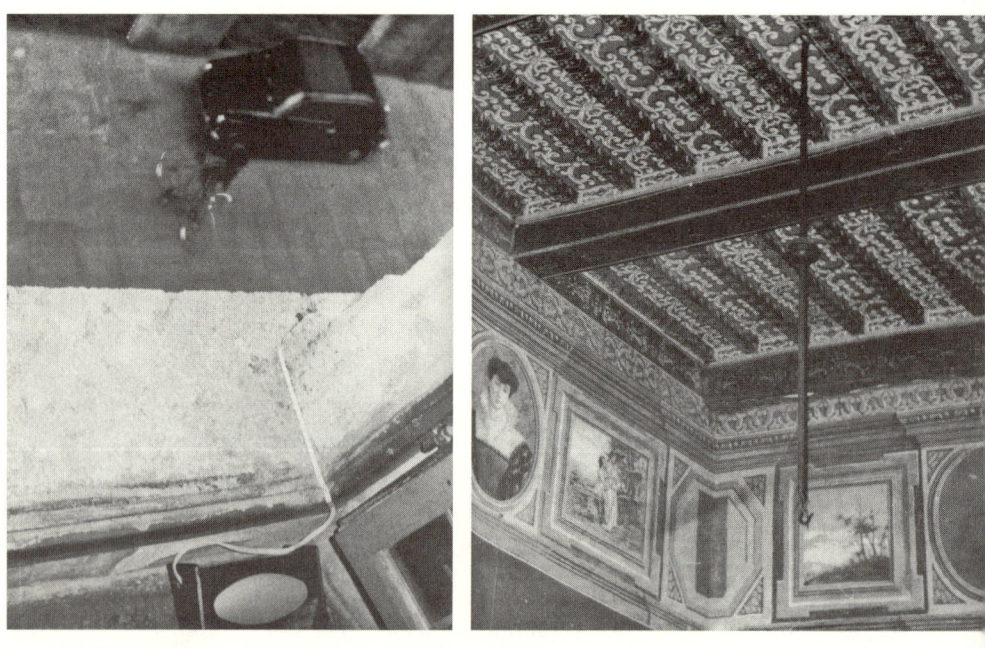

Figure 3.25. Luciano Fabro, *Untitled*, 1970. *Amore mio*. Photograph: Anonymous.

to those in the street that the voice came from within the building, whereas in the room, one heard the voice rising from the square.

The listener was either way excluded and could not understand why the guy kept on repeating, without interruption *"Citizens, don't consider me responsible for what is happening!"* One could hear in the background children's voices repeating those lines, and a moment later the loudspeakers of an electoral rally, various voices and sounds; because the taping was done in many different places: in the car, in the train, in the street, in the family; any opportunity to scream or whisper it.

All the visitors insisted, who knows why, censure on hearing everything in reverse: . . . *"consider me responsible for what is happening!"* . . . It was, I think, inconceivable to them that art would not underwrite the sins of the world, as culture does.[133]

With the serendipitous dropping of two letters — *responsabile* instead of *ir-responsabile* — Fabro's position had thus been reversed. It is as if his intended betrayal of the all-male cast of *Amore mio* had been rescinded. Ironically, the same medium, that of the tape recorder, which Lonzi had chosen in *Autoritratto* to abolish the distance between herself and the artist ended up producing, with Fabro, the exact opposite: seeds of dissension, or what Bonito Oliva called "desolidarization" from the group.

While the artist has pointed us to the political dimension of the work — Belloni even uses the adjective "Jacobin" for it — no reviewer at the time (or since) realized the gendered political dimension of Fabro's cryptic sound piece.[134] With her chosen passages for the pages of *Amore mio*, it was Lonzi who got to perform the desolidarization and the betrayal, with an added tinge of revenge. As the many recent studies on Lonzi have elaborated, 1970 was the year zero of feminism in Italy. Feminism is a way to subtract oneself from paternalistic power relations, and 1968, as many have noted, was very much all male, with its "strutting *leaderini*" (little leaders).[135] Lonzi's second and last performance among artists, this time — significantly — as an artist, rather than a critic, was not in her book

Autoritratto, but as an intruder into less convivial territory: the cast of *Amore mio*.

With "La critica è potere" (Criticism is power), published in *NAC* in December 1970, at the time of the opening of *Vitalità*, Lonzi made her farewell to art criticism.[136] There, she professed her belief in the need of a rapprochement with the artist rather than the art-work — this because the artist had now become the artwork: "The bond with artists was for me, from the start, a sensation of affinity that I chose to trust."[137] Adhesion, affinity, trust: all the good inten-tions that Bonito Oliva set out, not without a touch of humor, to betray. As with Pistoletto and as with Lonzi, this betrayal played itself out not in the show, but on paper, in *Amore mio*'s catalogue. Bonito Oliva's contribution to it was a sequence of eight full-page identical headshots of him by Mulas (Figure 3.26). With moustache and long sideburns, jacket and foulard, and with a deadpan expres-sion, Bonito Oliva appears in the guise of a Neapolitan gangster. Was this, as Lara-Vinca Masini suggested in her review, "the intervention of someone left powerless, with no alternative but to propose, again and again, his own, his own image?"[138] Or was it rather Bonito Oliva as *traditore*, relinquishing, as he had been asked to, responsibility as curator of *Amore mio* and saying: "Citizens, don't consider me respon-sible for what is happening"?

Mulas's photographs are not all that different from those sub-mitted by De Vecchi and Colombo, who also appeared in a series of headshots next to some of the photo collages they projected in their room. They also looked almost comically boggle-eyed, members of a *malavita* (gangland) they might have shared with Bonito Oliva. But Bonito Oliva's face was bisected by light, pointing to the duplicity that characterized his role in *Amore mio* and, just two months later, the entire project and aesthetic of *Vitalità del negativo*. Might we say that like Marcello Clerici in *Il conformista*, infiltrating the clandestine territory of the *fuoriusciti* in Paris, Bonito Oliva, aiming to make mis-chief, infiltrated the convivial group of artists gathered by Marotta in Montepulciano? Once again it took a woman, the critic Sandra

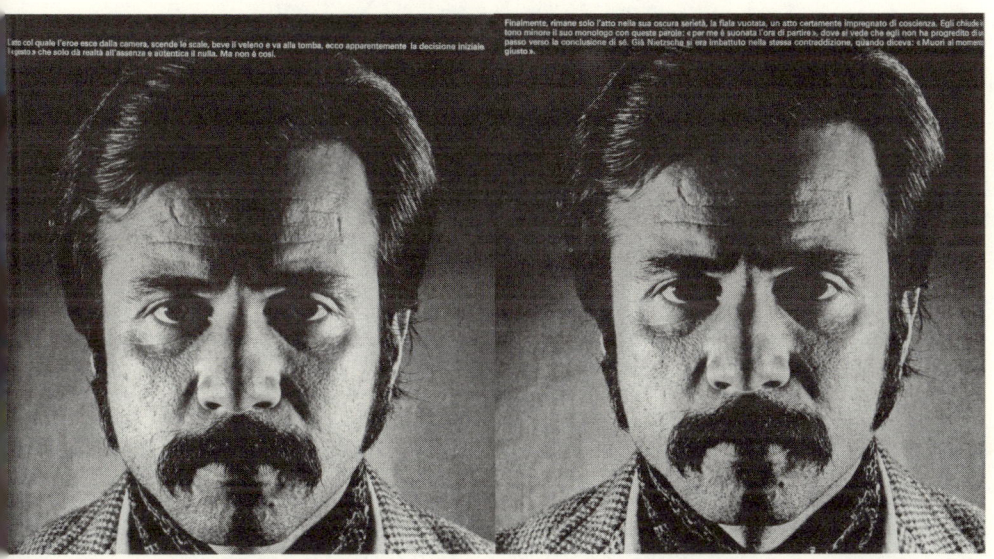

Figure 3.26. Achille Bonito Oliva, in *Amore mio*, exhibition catalogue (Firenze, Centro Di, 1970). Photograph: Ugo Mulas. Courtesy Ugo Mulas Heirs.

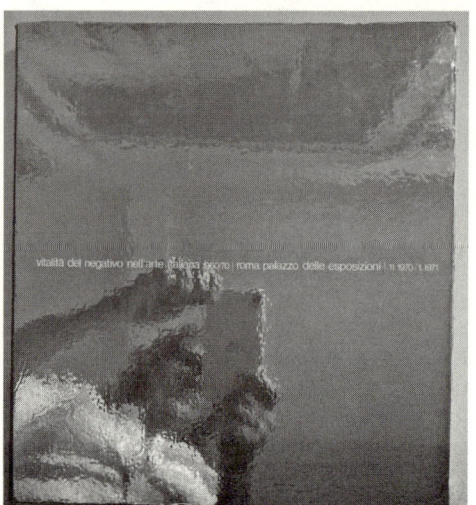 

Figure 3.27. *Vitalità del negativo.* Covers. Photography: the author.

Orienti, to wonder, cannily, in her review: "Might artists and critics feel reciprocally betrayed? Is this an interlocutory experience?"[139] But in contrast with Clerici, Bonito Oliva's betrayal was anything but. His was a counterstrategy to point, again via mimetic subversion, to the impossibility of a curator or critic turning him/herself into an artist. To reveal absolutely nothing, *Amore mio*'s catalogue's cover was, meanwhile, except for the minuscule script of the title, place, and date in the upper corner, left completely white.

A Final Eclipse

Meanwhile, in line with the exhibition's play with doubles, the Centro Di catalogue of *Vitalità del negativo* appeared in two versions (Figure 3.27). The cover of the paperback edition is all black, with the exhibition's title, date, and location running in tiny white script across its midsection. The hardcover edition is a reflective silver, with the white type running almost invisibly across the center.[140] The hardcover version comes with two black sleeves that are slid over the top and bottom halves of the book, allowing only a sliver of the silver — the area with the writing — to appear. The pair follows the format of a solar eclipse. But then again, we may ask: If the negativity of *Vitalità del negativo* is like that of an eclipse, what did its concealment expose? I would submit that it revealed not only the link between Fascism in 1932 and in 1970, but, more problematically, and what was seen on all sides as a betrayal, the link between the violence of 1968 and that of 1970. This is why Bonito Oliva and Sartogo were taken to task by critics from both the political Left and the Right, and therefore its curator's choice of that exhibition's oft-derided and oft-debated exceedingly obscure (*oscurissimo*) title.[141]

Acknowledgments

I wish to thank colleagues and friends who have helped and inspired me in so many ways: Pierpaolo Antonello, Claire Bishop, Benjamin Buchloh, Stefano Collicelli Cagol, Maddalena Carli, John Curley, Valerie da Costa, Paul Davies, Patricia Falguières, Claire Gilman, Gabriele Guercio, Sharon Hecker, Christian Joschke, Daniela Lancioni, Kevin Lotery, Claudia Marfella, Laura Mattioli, Tom McDonough, Matilde Nardelli, Molly Nesbit, Linda Norden, Alina Payne, Maria Antonella Pelizzari, Eeva-Liisa Pelkonen, Vanessa Schwartz, Noa Steimatsky, Martina Tanga, Nicola Trezzi, Federica Vannucchi, and in particular Stefano Chiodi. And Christopher Wood and Raphael Wood, always.

I am ever grateful to those among this book's protagonists whom I have had the chance to interview: Achille Bonito Oliva, Luciano Caramel, Giosetta Fioroni, Michelangelo Pistoletto, Maria Pioppi, and Piero Sartogo.

During my research I benefited from generous fellowships at the Clark Art Institute and the Italian Academy at Columbia University. I wish also to thank Marco Farano at the Cittàdellarte-Fondazione Pistoletto, Assunta Porciani at the Archivio Biblioteca Quadriennale di Roma, as well as Carmela and Valentina Mulas and Alessandra Pozzati at the Archivio Ugo Mulas.

Sections of the chapters have appeared in article form in *Grey Room*, *October*, *Transbordeur*, *Il Confine Evanescente: Arte Italiana*

1960–2010, Giosetta Fioroni: L'Argento, Exhibiting Architecture: A Paradox?, and *Bruno Munari: The Lightness of Art*.

I am indebted to several excellent editors: Shannon Wearing, Robin Ray, and Bud Bynack.

At Zone Books I wish to thank Julie Fry, designer *sans pareil*; Meighan Gale for bringing the book to completion; and of course Jonathan Crary.

Notes

INTRODUCTION

1. See Claire Gilman's excellent "Pistoletto's Staged Subjects," *October* 124 (Spring 2008), pp. 53–74.

2. Interview with the author, Biella, Italy, October 25, 2011.

3. Maureen Turim, *Flashbacks in Film: Memory and History* (New York: Routledge, 1989), pp. 1 and 5.

4. Ibid., p. 247 n.1. Leslie Halliwell, *The Filmgoer's Companion*, 3rd. ed. (New York: Hill and Wang, 1970).

5. Turim, *Flashbacks in Film*, p. 16.

6. In French and Italian the words *histoire* and *storia* usefully encapsulate the double nature of the flashback as both history and story.

7. I would like to thank Kevin Lotery for this observation.

8. Valentina Anker and Lucien Dällenbach, "La réfléxion spéculaire dans la peinture et la littérature récente," *Art International* 12 (February 1975), pp. 28–32 and 45–48. Surveying the mirror effect in multiple forms — including figurative, abstract, video, conceptual, kinetic, and Op art — the article discusses and illustrates works by Michelangelo Pistoletto, Barry Flanagan, Joseph Kosuth, Heinz Mack, Robert Smithson, Jasper Johns, Leonardo Cremonini, Getulio Alviani, and Max Bill. It also considers the writers of the Nouveau Roman: Michel Butor, Nathalie Sarraute, Claude Simon, and Alain Robbe-Grillet.

9. Lucien Dällenbach, *Le récit spéculaire: Essai sur la mise en abyme* (Paris: Le Seuil, 1977); Dällenbach, *The Mirror in the Text*, trans. Jeremy Whiteley with Emma Hughes (Cambridge: Polity, 1989), p. 60.

10. Dällenbach, *The Mirror in the Text*, p. 56.

11. The translations from primary sources throughout are all my own.

12. See Paolo Fossati, *L'immagine sospesa* (Turin: Einaudi, 1971); Emily Braun, *Mario Sironi and Italian Modernism: Art and Politics under Fascism* (Cambridge: Cambridge University Press, 2000); Fabio Benzi, *Arte in Italia tra le due guerre* (Turin: Bollati Boringhieri, 2013).

13. The bibliography is vast. See P. V. Cannistraro, *La fabbrica del consenso: Fascismo e mass media* (Roma-Bari: Laterza, 1975). For a overview of these questions see, most recently, Sileno Salvagnini, "Art in Action: The Organization of Italian Artistic Culture," and Antonello Negri, "Ideas, Questions, Controversies," in Germano Celant, ed., *Post Zang Tumb Tuuum: Art Life Politics Italia 1918–1943* (Prada Foundation: Milan, 2018), pp. 30–45 and 78–87, respectively.

14. See Christopher Duggan, "Italy in the Cold War Years and the Legacy of Fascism," in Christopher Duggan and Christopher Wagstaff, eds., *Italy in the Cold War: Politics, Culture, and Society 1948–1958* (Oxford: Berg, 1995), pp. 1–24.

15. See Nancy Jachec, *Politics and Painting at the Venice Biennale, 1948–64: Italy and the Idea of Europe* (Manchester: Manchester University Press, 2007); *XIV Quadriennale di Roma: Retrospettive 1931/1948*, exhibition catalogue (Milan: Electa, 2005); and Patrizia Rosazza-Ferraris, "La dittatura dell'arte astratta," in Mariastella Margozzi, ed., *Palma Bucarelli: Il museo come avanguardia* (Milan: Electa, 2009), pp. 222–27.

16. Palmiro Togliatti, the head of the Communist Party, directly professed his views — in favor of a Socialist Realism aligned with the Soviet Union — on the occasion of various exhibitions. See Nicoletta Misler, *La via italiana al realismo: La politica culturale artistica del PCI dal 1944 al 1956* (Milan: Mazzotta, 1973).

17. This was the story told by the then-authoritative book on the topic, Roberto Battaglia, *Storia della resistenza* (Turin: Einaudi, 1953). For a different reading recognizing the brevity and history of the resistance in Italy, see Santo Peli, *La resistenza in italia: Storia e critica* (Turin: Einaudi, 2004). See also Henri Rousso, *The Vichy Syndrome: History and Memory in France since 1944* (Cambridge, MA: Harvard University Press, 1991), and Richard J. B. Bosworth and Patrizia Dogliani, eds., *Italian Fascism: History, Memory, and Representation* (New York: St Martin's Press, 1999).

18. See Guido Crainz, *Storia del miracolo italiano: Culture, identità, e trasformazioni frà anni cinquanta e sessanta* (Rome: Donzelli, 1996).

19. The English-language bibliography on Arte Povera is becoming vast. See Germano Celant, *Identité italienne: L'art en Italie depuis 1959*, exhibition catalogue (Paris: Centre

Georges Pompidou, 1981); Celant, *Arte Povera/Art Povera* (Milan: Electa, 1985); Carolyn Christov-Bakargiev, *Arte Povera* (London: Phaidon, 1999); Richard Flood, ed., *Zero to Infinity: Arte Povera 1962–1972* (Minneapolis: Walker Art Center, 2001). See also Robert Lumley's important *States of Emergency: Cultures of Revolt in Italy from 1968 to 1978* (London: Verso, 1990).

20. Sharon Hecker, ed., *Postwar Italian Art History Today: Untying "the Knot"* (New York: Bloomsbury, 2018); Martina Tanga, *Arte Ambientale, Urban Space, and Participatory Art* (New York: Routledge, 2019); and Lindsay Caplan, *Programmed Art: Freedom, Control, and Computation in 1960s Italy* (Minneapolis: University of Minnesota Press, 2020).

21. "Postwar Italian Art," *October* 124 (Spring 2008). The issue was edited by Claire Gilman.

22. François Hartog, *Régimes d'historicité: Présentisme et expériences du temps* (Paris: Le Seuil, 2003); Hartog, *Regimes of Historicity: Presentism and Experiences of Time*, trans. Saskia Brown (New York: Columbia University Press, 2015), p. 112.

23. See Rosella Siligato, ed., *Roma anni '60: Al di là della pittura*, exhibition catalogue, Palazzo delle Esposizioni (Rome: Carte Segrete, 1990), which includes a series of important interviews with the main protagonists.

24. Claudio Crescentini, Costantino d'Orazio, and Federica Pirani, eds., *Roma Pop City 60–67*, exhibition catalogue, Museo d'Arte Contemporanea, Roma (Rome: Manfredi, 2016); Silvana Bignami and Alessandra Pioselli, eds., *Fuori!: Arte e Spazio Urbano 1968–1976*, exhibition catalogue (Milan: Mondadori Electa, 2011); Alessandra Pioselli, *L'arte nello spazio urbano: L'esperienza Italiana dal 1968 a oggi* (Milan: Johan e Levi, 2015); Fabio Belloni, *Militanza artistica in Italia 1968–1972* (Rome: L'Erma di Bretschneider, 2015); Alessandra Acocella, *Avanguardia diffusa: Luoghi di sperimentazione artistica in Italia 1967–70* (Macerata: Quodlibet, 2016); Carlotta Sylos Calò, *Corpo a corpo: Estetica e politica nell'arte italiana degli anni sessanta* (Macerata: Quodlibet, 2018); Paola Nicolin, *Castelli di carte: La XIV Triennale di Milano* (Macerata: Quodlibet, 2011); Luigia Lonardelli, *Dalla sperimentazione alla crisi: Gli incontri internazionali d'Arte a Roma, 1970–1981* (Milan: Doppiozero, 2014). See also Luciano Caramel, Elena Di Raddo, and Ada Lombardi, eds., *Arte in Italia negli anni '70: Verso i settanta (1968–1970)* (Milan: Edizioni Charta, 1996); Adachiara Zevi, *Peripezie del dopoguerra nell'arte italiana* (Turin: Einaudi, 2006); and Gabriele Guercio and Anna Mattirolo, eds., *Il confine evenescente: Arte Italiana 1960–2010* (Milan: Electa, 2010).

25. *I sei anni di Marcello Rumma*, curated by Gabriele Guercio and Andrea Villani, MADRE, Naples, 2019–2020.

26. On the years 1969 and 1970, see Guido Crainz, *Il paese mancato: Dal miracolo economico agli anni ottanta* (Rome: Donzelli, 2003).

27. See Marisa Dalai Emiliani, *Per una critica della museografia del novecento in Italia: Il saper mostrare di Carlo Scarpa* (Venice: Marsilio, 2008).

28. See Jeffrey T. Schnapp, "Epic Demonstrations: Fascist Modernity and the 1932 Exhibition of the Fascist Revolution," in Richard Golsan, ed., *Fascism, Aesthetics, and Culture* (Hanover, NH: University Press of New England, 1992), pp. 1–36; Marla Stone, *The Patron State: Culture and Politics in Fascist Italy* (Princeton: Princeton University Press, 1998); and see my essay, "Monumental Fairytales: Mural Images during the *Ventennio*," in Celant, *Post Zang Tumb Tuuum*, pp. 330–35.

29. Sergio Polano, "L'arte dell'allestimento temporaneo: Mostrario italiano," in *Storia dell'architettura italiana*, vol. 9, *Il secondo novecento* (Milan: Electa, 1997), pp. 421–22. See also Polano, *Mostrare: l'allestimento in Italia dagli anni venti agli anni ottanta* (Milan: Lybra Immagine, 2000).

30. Unwieldy in size, counting at times over a thousand artists, the Fascist exhibitions were reviewed in hundreds of national newspapers. See Claudia Salaris, *La quadriennale: Storia di una rassegna d'arte Italiana dagli anni trenta a oggi* (Venice: Marsilio, 2004); see also Rosella Siligato and Maria Elisa Tittoni, eds., *Il Palazzo delle Esposizioni: Urbanistica e architettura, l'esposizione inaugurale del 1883, le acquisizioni pubbliche, le attività espositive* (Rome: Carte Segrete, 1991).

31. "Mimetic subversion," writes Karen Fiss, "is a means by which one can out 'outstrip' a potential aggressor consciously or unconsciously on his own ground. Resistance through mimetic subversion counterattacks through identification with the aggressor." See Fiss, *Grand Illusion: The Third Reich, the Paris Exposition, and the Cultural Seduction of France* (Chicago: University of Chicago Press, 2009), p. 188. The concept comes from the literary historian Denis Hollier, writing on Georges Bataille.

32. Some passages should be quoted in Italian: "Fotografavo senza nessuna intenzione di capire che cosa stava accadendo, e succedeva sempre qualcosa.... Fotografavo tutto: non solo gli artisti più notevoli o le cose importanti: non che mancasse la volontà di scegliere, ma sentivo chi il mio non poteva essere un atteggiamento da critico, non c'era de capire qualcosa in particolare, non c'era da fare qualcosa quanto da registrare." Ugo Mulas, *La fotografia*, ed. Paolo Fossati (Turin: Einaudi, 1973), p. 130.

33. See Maria Teresa Mori et al., eds., *Di generazione in generazione: Le Italiane dall'Unità ad oggi* (Rome: Viella, 2014).

CHAPTER ONE: INSIDE/OUTSIDE MICHELANGELO
PISTOLETTO'S *MIRROR PAINTINGS*

1. For a detailed analysis of Pistoletto's techniques in the making of these works, see Suzanne Penn, "'The Complicity of the Materials' in Pistoletto's Paintings and Mirror Paintings," in Carlos Basualdo, ed., *Michelangelo Pistoletto: From One to Many, 1956–1974* (Philadelphia: Philadelphia Museum of Art, 2010), pp. 142–67, and my review of that exhibition in *Artforum* 19.6 (February 2011), p. 220.

2. Tommaso Trini, untitled text for Sonnabend Gallery, Paris, 1964. This phenomenological approach has remained dominant as late as the essay by Claire Gilman, "Pistoletto's Staged Subjects," *October* 124 (Spring 2008), pp. 53–74.

3. Tommaso Trini, *Pistoletto*, exhibition foldout, Galleria del Naviglio, Milan, 1967.

4. "Impone di parlare di una *pragmatica* dello specchio.... Lo specchio non si consente neppure questo piccolo artificio volto a favorire la nostra percezione o il nostro giudizio. Esso non 'traduce.' Registra ciò che lo colpisce. Esso dice la verità in modo disumano, come sà chi—allo specchio—perde illusione della propria freschezza.... L'immagine speculare è presente, è in presenza di *un referente che non può essere assente*. Non rinvia mai a conseguenti remoti. Il rapporto tra oggetto e immagine è il rapporto tra due presenze, senza alcuna mediazione. L'immagine è casualmente prodotta dall'oggetto e non si può produrre in assenza del oggetto.... Quindi l'immagine speculare *non può essere usata per mentire*. Si può mentire *sulla e circa* le immagini speculari (facendo passare per speculare fenomeni che non lo sono) ma non si può mentire *con* e *attraverso* l'immagine speculare.... L'immagine speculare *non è interpretabile*. E interpretabile semmai l'oggetto a cui essa rinvia, ovvero il campo stimolante di cui costituisce un doppio." Umberto Eco, "Sugli specchi," in *Sugli specchi e altri saggi: Il segno, la rappresentazione, l'illusione, e l'immagine* (Milan: Bompiani, 1985), pp. 15 and 24–25 (italics in the original).

5. John Ashbery, "Michelangelo Pistoletto," *New York Herald Tribune* (international edition), March 3, 1964, reprinted in John Ashbery, *Reported Sightings: Art Chronicles 1957–1987* (New York: Alfred Knopf, 1989), pp. 158–59.

6. John Ashbery, "Talking of Michelangelo," *ARTnews* 65.4 (Summer 1966), p. 64.

7. Annette Michelson, "Paris Letter," *Art International* 8.3 (April 1964), p. 70.

8. My reference here is to Peter Brooks's *Reading for the Plot: Design and Intention in Narrative* (Cambridge, MA: Harvard University Press, 1984), a book that called for a rejection of the dominant trends of formalism and structuralism in literary theory in favor of a return to a reading driven by the pleasures of the plot, which had been

demeaned as characteristic of popular, mass-consumption literature as opposed to high art.

9. Luigi Carluccio, *Michelangelo Pistoletto: Opere recenti*, exhibition catalogue, Galleria Galatea (Turin, April 27–May 14, 1963), reprinted in *Michelangelo Pistoletto*, exhibition catalogue, Galleria La Bertesca (Genoa, December 1966–January 1967), pp. 17–20. The show included twenty works, sixteen of them *Mirror Paintings*.

10. See Gilles Deleuze, *L'image-temps* (Paris: Edition de Minuit, 1985).

11. Michelangelo Pistoletto, interview with Germano Celant in *Pistoletto: Division and Multiplication of the Mirror*, exhibition catalogue, PS1 (New York: Rizzoli, 1988), p. 32. To complicate things further, film theorist Christian Metz makes an important analogy between the mirror and film in *The Imaginary Signifier: Cinema and Psychoanalysis* (London: Macmillan, 1982), pp. 45–46: "More than the other arts, or in a more unique way, the cinema involves us in the imaginary: it drums up all perception, but to switch it immediately over into its own absence, which is nonetheless the only signifier present. Thus film is like a mirror. But it differs from the primordial mirror in one essential point: although, as in the latter, everything may come to be projected, there is one thing and one thing only that is never reflected in it: the spectator's own body. In a certain emplacement, the mirror suddenly becomes clear glass.... In the cinema, the object remains: fiction or no, there is always something on the screen. But the reflection of [one's] own body has disappeared.... Thus, what *makes possible* the spectator's absence from the screen — or rather the intelligible unfolding of the film despite that absence — is the fact that the spectator has already known the experience of the mirror (of the true mirror), and is thus able to constitute a world of objects without having first to recognize himself within it."

12. Raymond Bellour, "The Film Stilled" (1987), in Bellour, *Between-the-Images* (Dijon: Les Presses du réel, 2012), p. 130.

13. Ibid., p. 132.

14. See Seymour Chatman, *Antonioni, or, The Surface of the World* (Berkeley: University of California Press, 1985), and Carlo Di Carlo, ed., *Michelangelo Antonioni* (Rome: Bianco e nero, 1964).

15. Michelson, "Paris Letter," p. 70.

16. Ettore Sottsass Jr., "Pop e non Pop: A proposito di Michelangelo Pistoletto," *Domus*, no. 414, May 1964, pp. 32–35.

17. I would like to thank Marco Farano, the archivist of Cittadellarte–Fondazione Pistoletto, Biella, for his answers to my many queries.

18. Antonioni's addition of this subplot, which was not present in Cesare Pavese's novel *Tra donne sole* (1949), from which the film is adapted, is intriguing: it may be interpreted as a commentary on his own position between the predominantly artisanal world of Neo-realism and the industrial anomie of the economic boom. See, for instance, the predominance of modern ceramics, majolica, and ironwork in the exhibition *Italy at Work: Her Renaissance in Design Today*, which in 1950 traveled to eleven American venues, including the Art Institute of Chicago and the Brooklyn Museum.

19. See the article by Pierre Restany, the principal art critic for *Domus*, entitled "Le raz de marée réaliste aux USA," *Domus*, no. 399, February 1963, pp. 33–36, which posits that Pop — in contrast to American neo-Dada, which he had attempted to put on the same par as the French Nouveaux Réalistes — derived from a uniquely American sensibility. See also Ettore Sottsass Jr., "Dada, New Dada, New Realists," ibid, pp. 27–32, which clearly favored neo-Dada over what he argued was the academicism of American Pop painting, a charge often made by European critics. On *Domus* and its art critics, from Restany to Trini, see my articles "Restany tout azimut," in Tom Bishop with Coralie Girard, eds., *The Florence Gould Lecture at New York University, vol. 6, 2002–2004* (New York: New York University Center for French Civilization and Culture, 2004), pp. 80–93, and "Point de chute: Restany à *Domus*," in Richard Leeman, ed., *Le demi-siècle de Pierre Restany/The Half Century of Pierre Restany* (Paris: Institut National d'Histoire de l'Art, 2009), pp. 403–14.

20. Mirella Bandini, "Torino 1960/1973: Interviste — Note di lavoro-dichiarazioni," *NAC*, no. 3 (March 1973), pp. 2–28, in particular "4 Domande a un sociologo," interview with Prof. Luciano Gallino, pp. 3–4.

21. "La vecchia Torino era morta e non ne era nata una nuova." Norberto Bobbio, in *Trent'anni di storia della cultura a Torino (1920–1950)*, quoted in Alberto Papuzzi, "Lo scrutatore nella nuvola d'ira (Torino 1950–70)," in *Un'avventura internazionale: Torino e le arti 1950–1970*, exhibition catalogue, Museo Civico, Turin (Milan: Charta, 1993), p. 35.

22. "Mi sono venute tra le mani le foto dei quadri di Pistoletto e mi è stato chiesto di scrivere ... su questo giovane ... che è nato a Biella nel 1933, che ha una faccia robusta e vive a Torino in un appartamento di via Cibrario, vecchia, nera strada 1910, arredato con mobili di serie tipo Rinascente 1958 di tondino di ferro nero con vimini marrone sulle sedie, biblioteca a ripiani lucidi agganciati a tubi di alluminio anodizzato ... lampade faretto e giradischi Braun e dipinge su lastre di acciaio inossidabile, detto inox, ombre o silhouettes di gente, 'persona di schiena' dice il titolo, 'persona in piedi,' 'persona che guarda,' 'persona appoggiata.' Lasciando l'acciaio intatto dove non c'è il personaggio dipinto, l'ambiente e

le persone che circondano il quadro si specchiano nella lastra come attraverso una vaga nebbia. . . . Quei personaggi . . . è come se aspettassero insieme a noi l'arrivo di un treno felice annunciato dal fischio all'orizzonte, un treno felice che in realtà non arriva mai, appesantito com'è dalle malinconie, dai destini, dai cadaveri, dalle migliaia e migliaia di vie Cibrario sparse del mondo, risonanti di vecchi tramvai nei pomeriggi di domenica, di scarpe buone messe il pomeriggio di domenica, di faticose digestioni di cardi, aglio e vino pesante nei pomeriggi di domenica, di western ululanti, odorosi di bucce di arance . . . di chewing-gum nei pomeriggi di domenica al Cinema Statuto. . . . Questo ragazzo che si chiama Michelangelo Pistoletto . . . non si può dire che sia un pittore POP come qualcuno ha detto e se qualcuno non l'ha detto, è meglio sia chiaro che questo ragazzo . . . non c'entra niente coi pittori POP. . . . Sono certo che il POP non c'entra perché a Torino, e forse in tutta l'Italia, non ci sono le premesse per diventare Pittori Pop: non c'è, con quella pressione soffocante e invincibile, il Coca-Cola americano, non c'è il vermouth 'Perlino,' non c'è la corruzione post-gangster, non c'è la violenza post-cowboys, non ci sono le vamps . . . si pratica poco il birth-control . . . si usano poco i deodoranti e invece si gioca ancora alle bocce, ci si mette ancora il pigiama o la camicia da notte per andare a dormire, si cuoce ancora la pasta asciutta, si schiacciano ancora i pomodori, si fanno ancora queste cose. Al Bar Torino, in piazza San Carlo, si beve il Punt e Mes seduti su piccole sedie di stile barocco e si mangia forse molto gelato . . . ma poco ice cream. . . . Così io direi che questo ragazzo di Torino è un poeta sul serio, anche se forse meno preciso e caustico che non siano i ragazzi di New York, i Lichtenstein, i Rosenquist, i Rauschenberg, gli Oldenburg, i Chamberlain nel raccontarci la situazione del nostro dramma, il caso della nostra storia." Sottsass, "Pop e non Pop," pp. 34–35.

Antonioni often reminisced about his own provincial youth in Ferrara. One of the very few scholars to have paid attention to Sottsass's article is Robert Lumley in "Between Pop Art and Arte Povera: American Influences in the Visual Arts in Italy in the 1960s," in Luisa Passerini, ed., *Across the Atlantic: Cultural Exchange between Europe and the United States* (Berlin: Peter Lang, 2000), pp 173–86.

23. Roland Barthes, *La chambre claire* (Paris: Le Seuil, 1980).

24. See my review of Guy Cogeval, ed., *Il Modo Italiano: Italian Design and Avant-Garde in the 20th Century*, Montreal Museum of Fine Arts, *Artforum* 45.2 (October 2006), p. 258.

25. See Dorothy Jean McKetta, "The Leo Castelli Gallery and *Metro* Magazine: American Approaches to Post-Abstract Figuration in an Italian Context," PhD diss., University of Texas at Austin, 2012. Based on the correspondence between Bruno Alfieri, the founder

and chief editor of the magazine, and Leo Castelli, McKetta notes the dominant stamp of Castelli's gallery on the magazine during its first three years, namely, the months leading to the 1964 Venice Biennale. Alfieri hoped that it would provide him with an entrée to the American scene. The articles on the New York scene were published bilingually. See the editorial "A who's who: Tutto il mondo delle arti figurative si avvicina a Venezia per la vernice della trentunesima Biennale," *Metro,* no. 6, December 1962, pp. 12–19.

26. See Laura Iamurri, "Il pennello nell'occhio: La pop art e i sui rotocalchi, prima e dopo la Biennale del 1964," *Studi di Memofonte,* November 2013, pp. 124–44, https://www.academia.edu/5544403/Il_pennello_nell_occhio._La_pop_art_sui_rotocalchi_prima_e_dopo_la_Biennale_del_1964; and Davide Colombo, "L'arte americana dei primi anni sessanta nelle riviste Italiane del periodo," in Flavio Fergonzi and Francesco Tedeschi, eds., *Arte Italiana 1960–1964: Identità culturale, confronti internazionali, modelli america* (Milan: Scalpendi editore, 2017), pp. 165–84.

27. The previously mentioned publication of Pavese's novel *Tra donne sole* along with Antonioni's film script includes two letters from Calvino to Antonioni about his film when *Le amiche* came out.

28. Tellingly, none of the dealers mentioned in the article are French; Sonnabend is thus excluded. In the article, Beatrice Monti states that Americans are much more open and less chauvinistic than the French, citing Betty Parsons, Leo Castelli, Martha Jackson, and Sidney Janis, all New York dealers. Monti emphasizes how she loves traveling all over the United States to see the artists. Editorial, "I mercanti d'arte: Beatrice Monti per la galleria dell'Ariete, Milano; Peppino Palazzoli per la galleria Blu, Milano," *Domus,* no. 398, January 1963, pp. 29–34. The article was part of a series. The other articles were "Carlo Cardazzo per la galleria Il Naviglio, Milano" and "Guido le Noci per la galleria Apollinaire, Milano," *Domus,* no. 395, October 1962, pp. 30–33; "Sidney Janis, New York," *Domus,* no. 403, June 1963, pp. 45–50; and the last in the series, "Mario Tazzoli per la galleria Galatea," *Domus,* no. 411, February 1964, pp. 31–32, which was about Pistoletto's dealer at the time.

29. See Évelyne Sullerot, "Il fotoromanzo mercato comune latino dell'immagine," *Almanacco Letterario Bompiani* (Milan: Bompiani, 1963), p. 121. Exported from Italy to France, Spain, and Latin America, the *fotoromanzo* has been a rich object of study for Italian scholars. See Maria Teresa Anelli et al., *Fotoromanzo: Fascino e pregiudizio. Storia, documenti e immagini di un fenomeno popolare (1946–1978)* (Perugia: Savelli, 1979); Raffaele de Berti, *Dallo schermo alla carta: Romanzi, fotoromanzi, rotocalchi cinematografici. Il film e I suoi paratesti* (Milan: Vita e pensiero, 2000); and Matilde Nardelli, "Leafing through Cinema,"

in Steven Allen and Laura Hubner, eds., *Cinema and the Visual Arts* (Chicago: University of Chicago Press, 2012), pp. 127–48.

30. Cesare Biarese and Aldo Tassone, *I film di Michelangelo Antonioni, un poeta della visione* (Rome: Gremesse, 1985).

31. On Antonioni's interest in contemporary art or what he called "nonpainting" (he cites Alberto Burri, Pietro Consagra, Emilio Vedova, and Lucio Fontana), see his interview "La malattia dei sentimenti," *Bianco e nero* 22.2–3 (February–March 1961), reprinted in Michelangelo Antonioni, *The Architecture of Vision: Writings and Interviews on Cinema*, eds. Carlo di Carlo, Giorgio Tinazzi, and Marga Cottino-Jones (New York: Marsilio, 1996), pp. 21–47.

32. Cesare Pavese, *Tra donne sole: In appendice la sceneggiatura del film "Le amiche" di Michelangelo Antonioni* (Turin: Einaudi, 1998); Pavese, *Among Women Only*, trans. D. D. Paige (London: Peter Owen, 1997).

33. Ashbery, "Michelangelo Pistoletto," pp. 158–59.

34. Ashbery, "Talking of Michelangelo," p. 42. As Antonioni stated: "I have always given a lot of importance to objects. Within a frame, the object can be as important as the characters. What is important is to influence the viewers to become aware of the objects as they are of the characters." "The History of Cinema Is Made on Film," 1979 interview, in Antonioni, *The Architecture of Vision*, p. 213.

35. Tommaso Trini in *L'Egoiste* 1, 1966–67, translated in Trini, *Pistoletto*, p. 48.

36. Ashbery, "Talking of Michelangelo," pp. 42 and 64.

37. This was the kind of hotel room where Pavese would take his own life a year after his novel was published.

38. Editorial, "Un negozio non di oggetti ma di espressioni, di idee," and Gio Ponti, "Espressioni," *Domus*, no. 415, June 1964, pp. 16–19; "Espressioni" *Domus*, no. 423, February 1965, pp. 45–48; Guido Ballo, "Sul concetto di 'spazio attivo': A proposito della sala 'Espressionia' Milano," *Domus*, no. 428, July 1965, pp. 47–58; and Ettore Sottsass Jr., "Corpi plastici," *Domus*, no. 431, October 1965, pp. 50–51. For an overview of the storefront design in Milan in the 1950s and 1960s, see Federica Boragna, "Negozi estrovesi: Non di ogetti ma di idee," in Elena di Rado, ed., *Milano 1945–1980: Mappa e volto di una città* (Milan: Franco Angeli, 2015).

39. "La storia è cominciata con il Trini Castelli che è quello a destra, appoggiato alla balaustra, con la barba e con l'impermeabile nero lucido come li portano i pescatori di merluzzi nei mari del nord. . . . [Egli] venne da me: così i personaggi sono già due e il terzo entrò nella storia quasi subito perché il Trini Castelli mi fece vedere le foto dei quadri di

Pistoletto e mi raccontò la storia del Pistoletto amico suo, che esponeva le sue piastre di acciaio alla Sonnabend di Parigi e che ad ogni modo era, a vedere le foto, un tipo che vedeva li mondo a modo suo, anche lui appoggiato alla balaustra a guardare in un buco, non si sa bene che cosa. La fossa dei serpenti? Una cava di marmo? La partita di calcio? La lezione di anatomia? Il funerale di Marylin Monroe? Il nostro funerale? L'entrata delle truppe? L'uscita delle truppe? Il torero incornato? La consacrazione dei vescovi? Io feci vedere le foto del Pistoletto alla Domus e la Domus le pubblicò. Così le vide il Ponti che disse al Pistoletto di fare la mostra per la vetrina di via Hoepli e allora il Pistoletto venne da me a dire se gli scrivevo, come si dice oggi, la 'presentazione.' Il giro dei personaggi sembra chiuso. Ma nella storia intanto c'era entrata anche altra gente, altri che guardano giù nella fossa, anche lo Sperone, quello della Galleria a Torino che espone i pittori Pop, diciamo così tanto per dire, un ragazzo magro che sembra non trovi mai la soluzione e sembra febbricitante e vive a Carmagnola, un paese vicino a Torino, con la sua mamma molto malata, e lui sarebbe il mercante, un raro mercante che non vende per guadagnare ma soltanto perché si sente personaggio in una storia di personaggi appoggiati alla balaustra che guardano giù nella fossa. E poi ci sono le ragazze. Non so chi sono quelle belle ragazzine col golfino e il palettò, col nastro nei capelli, appoggiate anche loro alla balaustra. Saranno forse le ragazzine di via Cibraio dove abita il Pistoletto o le ragazzine di Carmagnola che la domenica mattina passeggiano su e giù per la strada principale; e la storia qui diventa un po' misteriosa. Chi sono? Com'è che anche loro sono coinvolte in questa storia di personaggi che guardano nella fossa? Mi piacerebbe che le ragazze non ci fossero. . . . Ma Pistoletto ha ragione. Ci devono essere anche le ragazze a guardare giù nella fossa, ragazze col bel vestito della domenica, le belle calze tirate, le belle scarpette del calzaturificio di Varese, le ragazze che aspettano. E ci vuole anche quel tale, certamente, quello che si volta a guardarmi in faccia, che si gira come quel tale che si è girato la mattina che lo dovevano fucilare, che l'avevano fatto sedere sulla sedia faccia al muro e frammenti d'istanti prima che gli sparassero si era girato a guardare da dove veniva la morte. . . . Dovunque, dentro e fuori, da una parte o dall'altra, non c'è altro che un'attesa interessata e attenta per come andrà a finire lo spettacolo, il suspense, che ci lega fino alla fine, l'unica realtà che ci tiene in piedi: l'ha capito Pistoletto maledizione, questa faccenda l'ha capita Pistoletto che se uno lo cerca non sa mai se è di qua o di là dei suoi filtri di acciaio inossidabile e poi è da tutte due le parti." Ettore Sottsass Jr., *"Espressione" di Michelangelo Pistoletto*, Sala Espressioni, Milan, February–March 1965.

I read the manuscript version of the text, which to my knowledge has never been republished, in the *Domus* archives in Milan, and would like to thank Giulia Guzzini, the archivist, for her help. Clino Trini Castelli, a young designer and Sottsass's collaborator, is Tommaso Trini's younger brother. The two other men are Rinaldi and Bressano. The lineup of figures along a balustrade is a visual trope used by Antonioni: we find it in the beach scene of *Le amiche* and in the scenes of the Rome stock exchange in *L'eclisse*.

40. See Marc Ferro, *Cinéma et histoire* (Paris: Denoël, 1977); Ferro, *Cinema and History*, trans. Naomi Greene (Detroit: Wayne State University Press, 1988).

41. Norberto Bobbio, "Intellettuali e vita politica in Italia," *Nuovi argomenti* 7 (1954), reprinted in Bobbio, *Politica e cultura* (Turin: Einaudi, 1955), quoted in Andrea Branzi and Michele De Lucchi, eds., *Il Design italiano negli anni '50* (Milan: IGIS Edizioni, 1981), p. 18.

42. Lucien Dällenbach, *Le récit spéculaire: Essai sur la mise en abyme* (Paris: Le Seuil, 1977); Dällenbach, *The Mirror in the Text*, trans. Jeremy Whiteley with Emma Hughes (Cambridge: Polity, 1989), p. 60.

43. Ballo, "Sul concetto di 'spazio attivo,'" p. 58.

44. They appeared as a double spread on pages 55-56.

45. "Rosenquist: Un nuovo grande dipinto," *Domus*, no. 428, July 1965, pp. 43-44.

46. Ashbery, "Talking of Michelangelo," p. 65.

47. Alberto Boatto, "XXXII Biennale di Venezia: La polemica, la realtà dei consumi, il dialogo Europa-America," *Letteratura*, nos. 69-70-71 (May-October 1964), pp. 151-58. Boatto waited until 1965 to take his own trip to New York; see Boatto, "Manhattan Dada e Pop," *Marcatrè*, nos. 11-12-13 (1965), pp. 293-305.

48. Works by Mimmo Rotella were in a separate room, curated by the French critic Pierre Restany.

49. Boatto, "XXXII Biennale di Venezia," p. 157. See D. Micacchi, "Una neometafisica degli oggetti della città," *L'Unità* (Rome), April 1, 1965; Rossana Bossaglia and Susanna Zatti, *Il pop art e l'Italia*, exhibition catalogue, Castello Visconteo di Pavia (Milan: Mazotta, 1983); and Achille Bonito Oliva, *Tano Festa* (Milan: Electa, 1988).

50. Giorgio de Marchis, "The Significance of the 1964 Venice Biennale," *Art International* 8.9 (November 1964), pp. 21-22 (originally published in *La Fiera Letteraria*, Rome).

51. Cesare Vivaldi, "La giovane scuola di Roma," *Il Verri*, no. 12, 1963, pp. 101-105.

52. On the artist, see Maurizio Calvesi, ed., *Mario Schifano* (Parma: La Nazionale, 1974). See also Flavio Fergonzi, *Una nuova superficie: Jasper Johns e gli artisti Italiani* (Milan: Electa, 2019).

53. Pierre Restany, "Venezia 1964: La Biennale dell'irregolarità," *Domus*, no. 417, August 1964, pp. 27-40. In Antonioni's *L'amorosa menzogna*, as we are shown the slightly grotesque

mise-en-scène of the studio production of the eponymous *fotoromanzo*, the narrator asks: "Are we missing the chalices for the customary scene of the *brindisi?* The interpreters will pretend to hold them in their hands. They will be painted in later in the final photogram." Biarese and Tassone, *Il film di Michelangelo Antonioni*, p. 59.

54. For a detailed account of the facts by Calvin Tomkins reporting for the *International Herald Tribune*, see Calvin Tomkins, *Off the Wall: Robert Rauschenberg and the Art World of Our Time* (New York: Doubleday, 1980), p. 10.

55. One is reminded of the short piece entitled "Ungrab That Gondola" penned a few years earlier by Reyner Banham, a champion of Pop art and keen observer of postwar Italy (a friend of Sottsass's, not surprisingly, who supported him in his Pistoletto review for saying "M il Gusto, W il Pop," that is, down with good taste and hail Pop). The title was taken from the ongoing London musical *Grab Me a Gondola* (1956), which had been inspired by another photograph that, like Mulas's, became famous overnight: that of the British actress Diana Dors who, in a publicity stunt, floated in a gondola on the Grand Canal at the 1955 Venice Film Festival while wearing only a bikini. Banham's article pointed in the most amusing if unforgiving fashion to the dwindling influence of Italy in the "terrible season" when "old Astragal had treated an exhibition of Italian Industrial Design with what sounded like tolerant amusement, instead of the loutish self-abasement required by protocol." Banham quips that Italian influence "has now slipped so far that . . . a copy of *Domus* lasts forever, instead of getting shredded [by use] in a fortnight." Reyner Banham, "Ungrab That Gondola," *Architect's Journal* 126 (August 15, 1957), pp. 233–35, reprinted in Mary Banham et al., eds., *A Critic Writes: Essays by Reyner Banham* (Berkeley: University of California Press, 1996), pp. 24–25.

56. Maurizio Calvesi, "Intervista con i pittori," *Marcatrè*, nos. 8–9–10 (1964), p. 235.

57. Gillo Dorfles, *Giosetta Fioroni* (Venice: Galleria del Cavallino, 1965), reprinted in Germano Celant, *Giosetta Fioroni* (Milan: Skira, 2009), p. 136.

58. Pascal Bonitzer, "Il concetto di scomparsa," in Giorgio Tinazzi, ed., *Michelangelo Antonioni: Identificazione di un autore* (Parma: Società Produzioni Editoriali, 1985); Bonitzer, "The Disappearance (On Antonioni)," in Seymour Chatman and Guido Fink, eds., *L'avventura* (New Brunswick: Rutgers University Press, 1989), pp. 215–18, emphases in the original. I would like to thank Noa Steimatsky for bringing this text to my attention. See also Eyal Peretz, *The Off-Screen: An Investigation of the Cinematic Frame* (Stanford: Stanford University Press, 2017).

59. Tommaso Trini, in Ileana Sonnabend's gallery catalogue, 1964, reprinted in Trini, *Pistoletto*, p. 25.

60. Sottsass, "Dada, New Dada, New Realists."

61. Pierre Restany, "Estate 1964: La 'nuova' figurazione è pop," *Domus*, no. 420, November 1964, pp. 38–39. The catalogue also lists *Due uomini in camicia* (Two men in shirts, 1962), one of Pistoletto's earliest *Mirror Paintings*, featuring the double cutout of Rinaldi. Perhaps because the works belonged to the Sonnabend gallery in Paris, Pistoletto was included in the French contingent. A variant of this show, *Pop art, nouveau réalisme etc.*, went to the Palais des Beaux-Arts in Brussels. The triumph of Pop art at the Biennale also led to a flurry of debates and polls in Italian art magazines, notably, "Cos'è la pop art?: Inchiesta," special double issue, *Arte Oggi*, no. 21 (September 1964), and "Opinioni sulla pop art," *Rivista Italsider* (Milan), nos. 3-4 (1964).

62. Martin Friedman, ed., *Michelangelo Pistoletto: A Reflected World*, exhibition catalogue (Minneapolis: Walker Art Center, 1966).

63. Maurizio Calvesi, "Dine, Oldenburg, Rosenquist, e Segal alla Sidney Janis di New York," *Collage* 2.8 (March 1964). The article was later reprinted as "Dine, Rosenquist, Segal, Pistoletto e Oldenburg," in Calvesi, *Le due avanguardie: Dal futurismo alla pop art* (Bari: Laterza, 1981), pp. 365–67. Calvesi's first long article on the Pop phenomenon was "Ricognizione e reportage," *Collage* 1.7 (December 1963), reprinted in ibid., pp. 280–94.

64. "Pistoletto was key to my initial choices, because through his eyes I intuited what was happening in America, and I did not waste time with local problems." "Intervista con Gian Enzo Sperone," in *Un'avventura internazionale*, p. 169.

65. Other works appear to have been added at the last minute, explaining the unbound, postcard format of the exhibition's brochure.

66. After *Blam*, *Brattata*, and *Takka Takka* of 1962, *Whaam!* was the fourth of Lichtenstein's paintings to make reference to the Futurists' use of onomatopoeia in their wartime poems. See Selena Daly, "The Futurist Mountains: Filippo Marinetti's Experience in Mountain Combat in the First World War," *Modern Italy* 18, no. 4 (2013), pp. 323–38.

67. Paul Ginsborg, *A History of Contemporary Italy: Society and Politics, 1943-1988* (London: Penguin Books, 1990), pp. 66–67; see also Santo Peli, *La Resistenza in Italia: Storia e critica* (Turin: Einaudi, 2004), and *La Torino della liberazione: Dagli scioperi del Marzo 1944 alla festa del 6 Maggio 1945* (Turin: Priuli e Verlucca, 2011).

68. See Roberto Battaglia, *Storia della resistenza italiana (8 settembre 1943 - 25 aprile 1945)* (Turin: Einaudi, 1953).

69. In an interesting parallel with the flashbacks in the present book, in one of the stories, "The Star Jokey," Lieutenant Johnny Cloud, the series' star at the time, relays a story

from his childhood, when a shaman allowed him to foresee a scene where he would fly a fighter plane in a World War II dogfight against the German Luftwaffe. Later in the story, he shoots down an enemy fighter, and it explodes in a brilliant fireball, causing Johnny to remember his earlier vision. See Scott Harris, "The Most Important Comic You've Never Heard Of," *The Vault*, April 7, 2012, http://comicsvault.blogspot.com/2012/04/most-important-comic-youve-never-heard_07.html.

70. Calvesi, *Le due avanguardie*, figures 39 and 40.

71. See Alberto Boatto's *Pistoletto: Dentro/fuori lo specchio* (Rome: Fantini, 1970).

72. For a similar argument, see the splendid analysis of the many lives and possible interpretations of Gerhard Richter's painting *Uncle Rudi* (1964), oscillating between the memory of World War II and the present reality of the Cold War, between Nazism and the Stasi, in John Curley, *A Conspiracy of Images: Andy Warhol, Gerhard Richter, and the Art of the Cold War* (New Haven: Yale University Press, 2013).

73. See Andrea Branzi, "Le luci che cambiano," in Fulvio Ferrari and Napoleone Ferrari, *Luce: Lampade 1968–73. Il nuovo design italiano* (Turin: Allemandi, 2002), p. 14.

74. See Editorial, *Domus*, no. 300, November 1954, pp. 15–17.

75. In Turin, "you save on food for the sake of 'new' consumer goods," wrote Aris Accornero in the Communist daily *L'Unità*. "The discourse of the television in fact is one of those arguments that inspire the insufferable chatter about the misery of the lower classes," wrote Luca Pavolini in another journal of the Left, *Le Vie Nuove*, in 1961, quoted in Guido Crainz, *Storia del miracolo italiano: Culture, identità, trasformazioni fra anni cinquanta e sessanta* (Rome: Donzelli, 1996), pp. 138–40.

76. Italy's industrial productivity surpassed Belgium, Holland, and Sweden and reduced its gap with Britain, England, and France. See the statistics given by Crainz in *Storia del miracolo italiano*, pp. 87–88.

77. Editorial, "Prime immagini della XIII Triennale," *Domus*, no. 417, August 1964, pp. 1–11.

78. "La Triennale di Milano, Intervista con Umberto Eco," *Marcatrè*, nos. 8–9–10 (July–August–September 1964), p. 134, followed by an interview with Gregotti, pp. 135–36. This was the year of Eco's first notorious plunge into the semiotics of mass culture with *Apocalittici e integrati: Comunicazioni di massa e teorie della cultura di massa* (Milan: Bompiani, 1964).

79. *Tredicesima triennale di Milano: Tempo libero; Esposizione internazionale delle arti decorative e industriali modern e dell'architettura moderna, Palazzo dell' Arte al Parco Milano, 12*

Giugno–27 Settembre 1964 (Milan: Arti Grafiche Crespi, 1964), p. 15. The key study of the Triennale is Anty Pansera, *Storia e cronaca della Triennale* (Milan: Longanesi, 1978). The journals were *Abitare* (1961–), *Ambienti* (1965–), *Arredare* (1963–66), *Arte Casa* (1960–65), *Design Italia* (1966–), *Forma Luce* (1967–), *Il mobile in Italia* (one issue in 1967), *Ottagono* (1966), and *Rassegna del mobile italiano* (1965–66).

80. Entirely mirrored, the containers' interiors were designed by the artists Roberto Crippa, Fabio Mauri, Lucio Fontana, Enrico Baj, and Lucio Del Pezzo. See also Federica Vannucchi, "Reflective Thinking: *Il tempo libero* at the XIII Triennale of Milan," *New City Reader: A New Paper of Public Space,* November 10, 2010, p. 5.

81. Leonardo Borghese, *Corriere della Sera,* June 12, 1964, clipping, Achivio Storico, Triennale di Milano.

82. Isa Vercelloni, "Otto ore per giocare: La tredicesima triennale più che una mostra-mercato e un parco di divertimenti—bolle di sapone," *Corriere della Sera,* June 13, 1964.

83. M. Mont, "Cose pazzesche alla Triennale," *Corriere Lombardo,* June 12, 1964.

84. Pierluigi Albertoni, "Triennale Intelletuality," *Italia Moderna Produce,* July 1964, pp. 21–24.

85. Isa Vercelloni, "La triennale caledoscopio," *Bellezza* (Milan), July 1964.

86. *Letture d'italia* (Milan), Archivio della Triennale, clipping.

87. Raffaele de Grada, "La Triennale di Milano," *Sipra* (Turin), September 1964.

88. Franco Gingeri, "Incubi, soffocamenti e deliri nella prigione del tempo libero," *Il Piccolo* (Trieste), October 1, 1964.

89. Ernesto Rogers, "La Triennale uscita dal coma," *Casabella* 290, August 1964, p. 1.

90. Gillo Dorfles, "La XIII Triennale," ibid., pp. 2–18.

91. John Ashbery, "Want a Loudspeaker for Water Music?," *New York Herald Tribune,* August 25, 1964. For an account of the Americans' fascination with the Italians' talent at producing ambience, see Rosalind Pepall, "'Good Design Is Good Business': Promoting Postwar Italian Design in America," in Cogeval, *Il Modo Italiano,* pp. 69–79.

92. Bruno Zevi, "Processo alla XIII Triennale: Il carnevale triste degli architetti," *L'Espresso,* August 16, 1964. See also Zevi, "Sbadigli per divertimento eccessivo," *L'Espresso,* August 23, 1964, and "La Triennale: Una baita per miglionari," *L'Espresso,* August 30, 1964.

93. *Domus,* no. 418. September 1964, n.p.

94. Guido Cannella, Enrico Mantero, and Luigi Semerani, "La triennale dei giovani e l'ora della verità: La lotta di classe vale il mistero del rapporto tra i sessi all' Antonioni," *Casabella* 290, August 1964, p. 46.

95. Michelangelo Antonioni, "Il mio deserto," *L'Europeo*, August 16, 1964. English in Antonioni, *The Architecture of Vision*, p. 82.

96. Gio Ponti, "Domus: Formes Italiennes," *Domus*, no. 450, May 1967, pp. 20–27. Similar events were the design fairs of Eurodomus in Genoa in the summer of 1966 and those in Genoa and Turin the following summer.

97. Germano Celant, "Arte Povera: Appunti per una guerriglia," *Flash Art*, no. 5, November–December 1967, p. 3.

98. For an account of these shows, see Maria Cristina Mundici, "Torino 1963–1968," in Anna Minola et al., *Gian Enzo Sperone: Torino, Roma, New York: 35 Anni di mostre tra Europa e America*, 2 vols. (Turin: Hopefulmonster, 2000), pp. 17–32. One of the few scholars to broach the question of design is Paolo Thea, in *Verso l'arte povera* (Milan: Electa, 1989), p. 38: "Sottsass's contribution takes on a particular relevance, albeit now eclipsed by Arte Povera circles. The phase during which he exhibited in Sperone's space coincides with his remarks on the home, daily objects, and intercontinental travel." See also my review in Cogeval, *Il Modo Italiano*.

99. See Robert Lumley, "Arte Povera in Turin: The Interesting Case of the Deposito d'Arte Presente," in Maria Centonze, Robert Lumley, and Francesco Manacorda, *Marcello Levi: Ritratto di un collezionista* (Turin: Hopefulmonster, 2005), pp. 19–39. For more such interactions, see the series of exhibitions held in 1970 at the Milanese gallery Il Naviglio entitled *Navigli incontri* and the editorial "La Minimal Art entra nell'arredamento," *Le Arti* (Rome), nos. 1–2, February 1971, pp. 60–63.

100. Tommaso Trini, interviewed by Marco di Capua in *Roma anni '60: Al di là della pittura*, exhibition catalogue, Palazzo delle esposizioni, Quadriennale (Rome: Carte Segrete, 1990), pp. 376–79.

101. Tommaso Trini, "No Man's Mirror," *Domus*, no. 449, April 1967, pp. 45–48. For the identification of the gallery and the woman reflected, I would like to thank again Marco Farano. As in the photograph, "Radioattività," the theme song of Antonioni's *L'eclisse*, also known as the "Eclisse Twist," was performed by the Italian pop singer Mina, whom the press loved to describe as Vitti's brunette double.

102. Luigi Carluccio, "Casorati," *Rivista Italsider* (Genoa), no. 2 (April–May 1963), pp. 21–22.

103. Luciano Pistoi, quoted in Franco Fanelli, ed., *Luciano Pistoi: Il mercante d'arte è il consigliere del principe* (Turin: Allemandi, 2005), p. 13.

104. Luigi Carluccio, *Felice Casorati* (Ivrea: Centro Culturale Olivetti, 1958), and

Casorati, Galleria Civica d'Arte Moderna, Turin, April–May 1964. There was also a retrospective at the Galleria La Bussola in Turin, then in Genoa and Milan. It even included an exhibition at the Galleria Colongo in Biella, Pistoletto's hometown. See Luca Massimo Barbero, ed., *Torino Sperimentale 1959–1969: Una cronaca* (Turin: Allemandi, 2010).

105. Editorial, "Il pittore della solitudine metafisica," *La Stampa Sera*, March 2, 1963; Welda Favero, "Il silenzio eloquente di Casorati," *Gazzetta Venezia-Mestre*, December 1964; Leonardo Borgese, "Casorati, il distaccato," *Corriere della Sera*, May 30, 1964.

106. Franz Roh, *Nach-Expressionismus: Magischer Realismus. Probleme der neuesten europäischen Malerei* (Leipzig: Klinkhardt and Biermann, 1925); excerpts translated in Rosemarie Washton-Long, ed., *German Expressionism: Documents from the End of the Wilhelmine Empire to the Rise of National Socialism* (Berkeley: University of California Press, 1993), pp. 292–95.

107. Carlos Basualdo, "Michelangelo Pistoletto: From One to Many, 1956–1974," in *Michelangelo Pistoletto*, p. 7.

108. The show was curated by Lionello Venturi.

109. Carluccio, *Felice Casorati*, n.p.

110. Indeed, Carluccio owned an unfinished oil portrait, painted the year before, of the boy sitting in three-quarter view next to a plant.

111. Carluccio, *Felice Casorati*, n.p.

112. See Maurizio Fagiolo dell'Arco, ed., *Realismo magico: Pittura e scultura in Italia 1919–1925* (Milani Mazzotta, 1988), especially Emily Braun, "Franz Roh: Tra postespressionismo e realismo magico," pp. 57–64.

113. Karl M. Birkmeyer, review of Hartlaub's *Zauber des Spiegels: Geschichte und Bedeutung des Spiegels in der Kunst*, *Art Bulletin* 35.3 (September 1953), p. 254.

114. "Dicendo che l'opera di Pistoletto è sconcertante penso in prima istanza alla sensazione che può suscitare, una sensazione d'urto, la materia da lui usata: la lamiere inossidabile tirata a specchio.... E possibile combaciare, collimare con quei personaggi, e avere la sensazione d'essere al centro di un mondo che rovescia, cioè ribalta, davanti a noi quel che ci sta dietro e rovescia e ribalta noi stessi, mettendoci gli occhi dietro la nuca.... Potremmo infine illuderci che si tratti di un gioco surrealistico, col suo intrico volante di apparizioni e sparizioni, col fiorire abnorme delle immagini su un fondale di cui conosciamo intuitivamente il vuoto.... Tratti in inganno dall'inganno dello specchio, proviamo a parlare ai personaggi di Pistoletto. Non rispondono, non ci ascoltano. Il gioco resta un gioco di specchi,

appunto, che si svolge ai margini, che di se stesso si alimenta e da se si distrugge nel suo medesimo infinito vuoto. . . . Fragilità, solitudine, vuoto, esistenza, nel senso di una 'presenza' effettiva più che di una agitazione esistenziale; motivi di stupore più che di angoscia." Carluccio, *Michelangelo Pistoletto*; reprinted in *Michelangelo Pistoletto*, Galleria La Bertesca, pp. 17–19.

115. Valentina Anker and Lucien Dällenbach, "La réfléxion spéculaire dans la peinture et la littérature récente," *Art International* 19.2 (February 1975), p. 48.

116. Don Morrison, "Mirror, Mirror," *Minneapolis Star*, March 3, 1966, clipping, Pistoletto archive, Cittadellarte–Fondazione Pistoletto, Biella, Italy.

117. "Now You Can Put Yourself . . . in the Picture," *Sunday Pictures Magazine, Minneapolis Tribune*, April 3, 1966, pp. 12–13, Cittadellarte–Fondazione Pistoletto, Biella, Italy.

118. Carluccio, "Casorati," *Rivista Italsider*, clipping, ASAC, Archivio Storico Delle Arti Contemporanee, La Biennale di Venezia. This journal was a bimonthly publication addressed to the investors and employees of the steel conglomerate Italsider, which was based in Lombardy and south of Naples. See also Maria Mimita Lamberti, "I giovani pittori torinesi e la solitudine di Casorati," in Fagiolo dell'Arco, *Realismo Magico*, pp. 65–78.

119. See Bandini, "Torino 1960/1973," p. 4.

120. Piero Gobetti, *Felice Casorati: pittore* (Turin: Piero Gobetti Editore, 1923).

121. Luigi Carluccio, "Gobetti e Casorati," in Umberto Morra, ed., *Per Gobetti: Politica arte cultura a Torino 1918/1926* (Florence: Vallecchi, 1976), pp. 105–14. For a longer discussion of Casorati and politics, see my article, "Is Fascist Realism a Magic Realism?," *RES: Anthropology and Aesthetics* 73–74 (2020).

122. Pistoletto, in conversation with Suzanne Penn, in "'The Complicity of the Materials'," p. 160. The photographs that Pistoletto selected were rephotographed by Paolo Bressano (Pistoletto's second photographer/collaborator) so they could be enlarged; this explains why the final orientation of the figures in the *Mirror Paintings* is the same as that of the figures in the original photos, rather than reversed. See ibid., pp. 158–59.

123. The work is based, as we now know, on a photograph that showed figures demonstrating under a banner showing the name of a new political candidate named Giovanni. See ibid., p. 178.

124. Claudio Petruccioli, "La generazione del Vietnam," *Rinascita*, July 9, 1966; see Crainz, *Storia del miracolo Italiano*, p. 251.

CHAPTER TWO: *CAMPO URBANO*

1. "In fondo ciò che Munari continuamente propone è una sorta di 'dérèglement des procédés'." Enrico Crispolti, "Il caso Munari," *NAC*, no. 25 (November 15, 1969), p. 7; the French phrase is used in the original Italian text.

2. The full list of participating artists in *Campo urbano* is as follows: Edilio Alpini, Enrico Baj, Thereza Bento, Valentina Berardinone, Ermanno Besozzi, Carlo Bonfà, Inse Bonstrat, Davide Boriani, Giuseppe Chiari, Enrico Collina, Gianni Colombo, Annarosa Cotta, Dadamaino, Vincenzo Dazzi, Gabriele De Vecchi, Antonio Dias, Mario Di Salvo, Luciano Fabro, Carlo Ferrario, Giuseppe Giardina, Ugo La Pietra, Renato Maestri, Libico Maraja, Attilio Marcolli, Armando Marrocco, Livio Marzot, Paolo Minoli, Bruno Molli, Bruno Munari, Giulio Paolini, Ico Parisi, Franca Sacchi, Paolo Scheggi, Gianni Emilio Simonetti, Francesco Somaini, Davide Sprengel, Tommaso Trini, Grazia Varisco, Giacomo Veri, and Arnaldo Zanfrini.

3. Luciano Caramel, interview with the author, Venice, July 23, 2013. The interview took place on a memorably scorching hot summer day at Caramel's summer home on the Lido.

4. Tullio Catalano, "Munari alla Serendipity di Roma," *Flash Art*, no. 2, February 1968, n.p. The exhibition subsequently went to the Galleria La Colonna in Como.

5. Camillo Vittani, interview with the author, July 10 2014.

6. Clément Chéroux, *Fautographie: Petite histoire de l'erreur photographique* (Crisnée: Yellow Now, 2003).

7. *Campo urbano*, supplement to *Quadrante Lariano* 2.6 (November–December 1969).

8. Luciano Caramel, "Mostre: Como: Galleria La Colonna: U. Mulas," *NAC*, no. 25 (November 15, 1969), pp. 15–16. His review was published in the same issue as Crispolti's article on Munari.

9. Caramel, interview with the author, Venice, July 23, 2013.

10. About one thousand copies of the book were produced. About fifty were sold and the others distributed as gifts. Camillo Vittani, phone interview with the author, July 10, 2014.

11. Caramel, interview with the author, Venice, July 23, 2013.

12. There has recently been much interest in this phenomenon, the heir of the earlier "mostre all'aperto." For an overview, see Silvana Bignami and Alessandra Pioselli, eds., *Fuori!: Arte e Spazio Urbano 1968–1976* (Milan: Mondadori Electa, 2011); and Pioselli, *L'arte nello spazio urbano: L'esperienza Italiana dal 1968 a oggi* (Milan: Johan e Levi, 2015), and most importantly, Alessandra Acocella, *Avanguardia diffusa: Luoghi di sperimentazione artistica in Italia 1967–70* (Milan: Quodlibet, 2017).

13. The day was organized by Frank Popper. Caramel was the first to give GRAV its historical due, organizing a documentary exhibition on the group in 1975: Luciano Caramel, *Groupe de Recherche d'Art Visuel 1960–1968: Mostra retrospettiva*, Lago di Como (September 20–30, 1975) (Milan: Electa, 1975), and Marco Meneguzzo, "Il GRAV e l'Italia: Storie di gruppi negli anni Sessanta," in Cecilia de Carli and Francesco Tedeschi, eds., *Il presente si fa storia: Scritti in onore di Luciano Caramel* (Milan: V&P, 2008). Caramel's exhibition took place on a barge that toured Lake Como from September 20 until the end of the month. It moored each day at 6:00 p.m. in a different town around Lake Como, stopping in Menaggio, Lecco, Bellano, Colico, Bellagio, Gravedona, Argegno, and, finally, Como.

14. *Con/temp/l'azione* translates as "contemplation" in English. However, the slashes also isolate the words *con* (with), *temp[o]* (time), and *azione* (action), generating an untranslatable pun whereby contemplation is evoked alongside the idea of actions unfolding in time.

15. Pistoletto's action was filmed by Ugo Nespolo, resulting in the short film *Buongiorno Michelangelo* (16 mm).

16. Germano Celant's was the third in a series of exhibitions. The first two, which included mostly paintings, were *Aspetti del "ritorno alle cose stesse": Prima rassegna nazionale di pittura*, curated by Renato Barilli in October 1966, and *L'impatto percettivo: Seconda rassegna internazionale di pittura*, curated by Alberto Boatto and Filiberto Menna in May 1967. They were all partially financed by the city's tourism bureau.

17. See Gillo Dorfles, Luciano Marucci, and Filiberto Menna, eds., *Al di là della pittura: VIII Biennale d'Arte Contemporanea* (Florence: Centro Di, 1969) and Franco Passoni et al., *Nuovi materiali e nuove tecniche* (Cremona: Cremona nuova, 1969). See Mirella Bandini, "Al di là della pittura," *NAC*, no. 21 (September 15, 1969), pp. 8–10, and *Gala* 37, August–September 1969, pp. 36–37; Gillo Dorfles, "Beyond Painting: Afterthoughts on an Exhibition Held Last Year at San Benedetto del Tronto," *Art International* 14.7 (September 1970), pp. 71–73; and Emanuela Mennechella, "Intervista Luciano Marucci," in *Al di là della Pittura*, CD-ROM (Mediatecca delle Marche, 2006) and at http://www.lucianomarucci.it /cms/documenti/pdf2/RotteInediteIntervistaMennechella-Marucci.pdf. See also the two chapters on these events in Acocella, *Avanguardia diffusa*, pp. 123–46 and pp. 147–63.

18. Editorial, "Diecimila visitatori alla VIII Biennale," *Cronaca di Fermo e San Benedetto*, August 28, 1969, p. 7.

19. As can be expected, the student occupations at the 1968 Venice Biennale and Milan Triennale received extensive coverage in all the magazines. They have both attracted much

scholarly attention lately. See editorial, "Milano 14 Triennale," *Domus*, no. 466, September 1968, pp. 14–41; Cristina Casero and Elena di Raddo, eds., *Anni '70: L'arte dell'impegno. I nuovi orizzonti culturali ideologici e sociali nell'arte italiana* (Milan: Silvana Editoriale, 2009); Paolo Nicolin, *Castelli di carte: La XIV Triennale di Milano, 1968* (Macerata: Quodlibet, 2011); and Jacopo Galimberti, "A Third-Worldist Art?: Germano Celant's Invention of Arte Povera," *Art History* 36.2 (April 2013), pp. 418–41.

20. "A Venezia c'erano più poliziotti che opere d'arte." Lea Vergine, "Le ceneri calde," *Almanacco Letterario Bompiani* (Milan: Bompiani, 1969), pp. 163–88. Not every critic sided with the protesters. Pierre Restany's review of the Biennale in *Domus*, which segued directly from the perplexed report on the Triennale cited in the previous footnote, was tellingly entitled "La Biennale poid-plume a raté son suicide," deeming it "a failure in attempted suicide," *Domus*, no. 466, September 1968, pp. 43–54. As Restany made clear, he considered the demonstrations puerile, romantic, and misguided.

21. Germano Celant, "Una Biennale in grigioverde," *Casabella* 327, August 1968, pp. 52–53.

22. Giancarlo Politi, "Morte a Venezia," *Flash Art*, no. 8, September–October 1968, n.p.

23. Caramel, interview with the author, Venice, July 23, 2013. Somaini eventually published a book with a contribution by Enrico Crispolti and photographs by Mulas, *Urgenza nella città: Proposte di intervento* (Milan: Mazzotta, 1972).

24. Paul Ginsborg, *A History of Contemporary Italy: Society and Politics, 1943–1988* (London: Penguin Books, 1990), p. 298.

25. Guido Crainz, *Il paese mancato: Dal miracolo economico agli anni ottanta* (Rome: Donzelli, 2003), pp. 271–72.

26. "Studenti in Piazza a Como," supplement to *Quadrante Lariano* 2.6 (January–February 1969). See also Crainz, *Il paese mancato*.

27. Attilio Marcolli, *Teoria del campo: Corso di educazione alla visione* (Florence: Sansoni, 1970). There was also a second volume: Attilio Marcolli, *Teoria del campo 2: Corso di metodologia della visione* (Florence: Sansoni, 1978). The first volume was reviewed by Luciano Caramel: "Un esperimento a Cantù," *NAC*, no. 3 (December 1970), pp. 10–11.

28. Marcolli, *Teoria del campo*, p. 7.

29. Ibid., p. 341.

30. The towns diagrammed are Padua, Verona, Piacenza, Palermo, Vicenza, Brescia, Parma, Ravenna, Mantua, Florence, Modena, Syracuse, Genoa, Perugia, Copenhagen, Cologne, Kostanz, Hildesheim, Paris, and Rome.

31. Marcolli, *Teoria del campo*, p. 342.

32. Special leaflet supplement to *Quadrante Lariano* 2.7 (November–December 1969).

33. M. S., "Ma il contatto con il pubblico lo realizzavano cinquant'anni fa i futuristi e quarant'anni fa i dadaisti, e in modo ben più brusco di un quanto non sua avvenuto ieri a Como.... Gli artisti dadà avevano più idee e fantasia, e non andavano a chiedere milioni agli enti pubblici." "Il costoso gioco di alcuni artisti ieri in città: *Campo urbano* — aria di sagra e trovate Dada (un pò in ritardo)," *Corriere della Provincia*, September 22, 1969.

34. "Fra striscioni, scatoloni, panni, tunnel e bandiere: La festicciola domenicale degli artisti di *Campo Urbano*," *L'Ordine*, September 23, 1969.

35. *Campo urbano*, supplement, *Quadrante Lariano*, n.p.

36. "Il pubblico era presente sì, talvolta anche sconcertato or divertito, ma come se assistesse a qualcosa che in fondo non lo riguardava e che sarebbe finito con la fine del giorno di festa." Marisa Rusconi, "Si moltiplicano le mostre-spettacolo. Potremmo esporre un bel temporale. Cortili, piazze, vie diventano gallerie d'arte," *Avvenire*, October 11, 1969.

37. "Lo spettacolo...ha riscoperto tutta la forza di un fantastico così spesso soffocato." Cesare Sughi, "La Piazza a teatro: Ovvero la scena è 'altrove'," *Almanacco Letterario Bompiani* (Milan) (1970), p. 197. More dismissive was Lea Vergine in "Costume d'arte: Una mostra in provincia," *Metro*, nos. 16–17, August 1970, pp. 302–303.

38. "*Chi era il publico, questa entità tanto inalienabile ormai alla comunicazione estetica da esserne divenuto il fine, quanto tuttora astratta, equivoca e pure inesistente?* Perché l'arte che scende nelle piazze e nelle strade lo fa sempre di domenica e per chi capita? Il tempo libero è all'asta. Che cosa cercano gli artisti che, partecipando a tali manifestazioni, vi affermano ora il loro esibizionismo ora la loro spontaneità, ora la loro impotenza per un esercizio costruttivo ora i loro tentativi di attivazione globale? Uno scampo urbano alla loro fine?" Tommaso Trini, "Campo urbano: Dubbi," *NAC*, no. 23 (October 15, 1969), p. 7.

39. Tommaso Trini, "L'estensione teatrale. Mostre e azioni collettive in Italia: estate e autunno," *Domus*, no. 480, November 1969, pp. 48–51.

40. Tommaso Trini, "Rapporto da Amalfi/Report from Amalfi," *Domus,* no. 468, November 1968, pp. 50–51.

41. *Arte povera* + *Azioni povere* was extolled as unprecedented, unruly, and subversive in Germano Celant, ed., *Arte Povera più azioni povere* (Salerno: Rumma editore, 1969), the essays by Gillo Dorfles, "Gli incontri di amalfi," pp. 73–75; Piero Gilardi, "L'esperienza di Amalfi," pp. 76–82; and Filiberto Menna, "Un arte di entusiasmo," pp. 85–88.

42. Germano Celant, "Arte turistica," *Casabella* 342, November 1969, pp. 6–7.

43. Celant, *Arte Povera più azioni povere.*

44. Gilardi, "L'esperienza di Amalfi," pp. 76–82.

45. "VIII Biennale d'Arte Contemporanea: Al di là della pittura — San Benedetto del Tronto — Luglio — Agosto 1969," (Milan), no. 16 (September 1969), pp. 83–95.

46. Ibid., p. 94. The soul-searching elicited by participants in *Campo urbano* and similar events echoes arguments made by Claire Bishop in *Artificial Hells: Participatory Art and the Politics of Spectatorship* (London: Verso, 2012).

47. Renate Lachmann, *Memory and Literature: Intertextuality in Russian Modernism* (Minneapolis: University of Minnesota Press, 1997), p. 19.

48. The most memorable are those shot by Bruno Barbey for the photo agency Magnum. See Kristin Ross, *May '68 and Its Afterlives* (Chicago: University of Chicago Press, 2002).

49. Editorial, "Milano 14 Triennale," *Domus*, no. 466, September 1969, pp. 15–18.

50. See also Toni del Renzio, "Biennale under siege," *Art and Artists* 3, 1968, pp. 29–33.

51. Tommaso Trini, *Ugo Mulas: Vent'anni di Biennale* (Milan: Mondadori, 1988), pp. 156–59.

52. "Sur l'empoi du temps libre" and "Die Welt als Labyrinth," *Internationale Situationniste*, no. 4 (1960), pp. 111–15. See also Bishop, *Artificial Hells*, pp. 87–88.

53. "One of the basic situationist practices is the *dérive* [literally, "drifting"], a technique of rapid passage through varied ambiances. Dérives involve playful-constructive behavior and awareness of psychogeographical effects and are thus quite different from the classic notions of journey or stroll." Guy Debord, "Theory of the Dérive," trans. Ken Knabb, *Internationale Situationniste*, no. 2 (December 1958), https://www.cddc.vt.edu/sionline/si/theory.html.

54. The film tells the story of an orphan brought up by an old lady. Upon the woman's death and years in an orphanage, he ends up living with squatters in a shantytown. There he fights against a contractor who wants to destroy their shacks when oil is found beneath the shantytown; the poor are then forced out of their hovels by the police. The boy receives a magical dove with which to perform a miracle: he and his neighbors then steal the brooms of the street cleaners and fly into the sky, over Milan's Duomo, toward a better, more humane world.

55. Maria Carla Cassarini, *Miracolo a Milano di Vittorio De Sica: Storia e preistoria di un film* (Genoa: Mani, 2000).

56. See Luigi Chiarini, "Impossibilità di sintesi trà realtà e favola," *Cinema*, no. 62, May 15, 1951, pp. 254–55.

57. See Tom Gunning, "The Cinema of Attraction: Early Film, Its Spectator and the Avant-Garde," *Wide Angle* 8.3–4 (1986), pp. 63–70.

58. See Philippe-Alain Michaud, "L'appareil du réel: Le cinéma des Lumière," in Michaud, *Sketches: Histoire de l'art, cinéma* (Paris: Kargo & l'Éclat, 2006), p. 69.

59. Arturo Carlo Quintavalle, "Conversazioni con Ugo Mulas," in Arturo Carlo Quintavalle, ed., *Ugo Mulas: Immagine e testi* (Parma: La Nazionale, 1973), p. 18.

60. Ibid., p. 20.

61. Filippo Tommaso Marinetti, Umberto Boccioni, Carlo Carrà, and Luigi Russolo, "Against Passéist Venice," in Lawrence Rainey, Christine Poggi, and Laura Wittman, eds., *Futurism: An Anthology* (New Haven: Yale University Press, 2009), p. 67.

62. Jennifer Scappettone, *Killing the Moonlight: Modernism in Venice* (New York: Columbia University Press, 2014), p. 138. On July 14, 1902, at 9:52 a.m., the tower was reduced to a pile of rubble, crushing Jacobo Sansovino's 1538 Loggetta, the small building at the base of the tower, but resulting in no casualties. The decision to rebuild it on the same site "com'era, dov'era" (as it was, where it was) was made unanimously by the municipality on the same day as the collapse. See Scappettone, *Killing the Moonlight*, pp. 160–61, and Margaret Plant, *Venice: Fragile City, 1797–1997* (New Haven: Yale University Press, 2002), pp. 234 and 261–62. See also Williard Bohn, *The Other Futurism: Futurist Activity in Venice, Padua, and Verona* (Toronto: University of Toronto Press, 2004).

63. Marinetti, Boccioni, Carrà, and Russolo, "Against Passéist Venice," p. 68.

64. Luciano de Maria, ed., *F. T. Marinetti: Teoria e invenzione futurista* (Milan: Mondadori, 1968); Luigi Scrivo, ed., *Sintesi del futurismo: Storia e documenti* (Rome: Bulzoni, 1968).

65. Caramel was among the first art historians to write about these shows. See Luciano Caramel, ed., *MAC: Movimento Arte Concreta, 1948–1958*, 2 vols. (Milan: Electa, 1984), vol. 2. See also my essay "Italy and the Concept of the 'Synthesis of the Arts,'" in Eeva-Liisa Pelkonen and Esa Laaksonen, eds., *Architecture + Art: New Visions, New Strategies* (Helsinki: Alvar Aalto Academy, 2007), pp. 62–81.

66. Caramel, interview with the author, Venice, July 23, 2013.

67. Ingrid D. Rowland, *Giordano Bruno: Philosopher/Heretic* (Chicago: University of Chicago Press, 2008).

68. See Geneviève Dreyfus-Armand and Laurent Gervereau, eds., *Mai 68: Les mouvements étudiants en France et dans le monde* (Paris: Diffusion, Éditions La Découverte, 1988).

69. *Per Giordano Bruno dal 1876 al 1889: Resoconto morale e finanziario del primo Comitato Universitario, costituitosi fra gli studenti dell' Università di Roma il 19 marzo 1876, allo scopo di erigere un monumento a Giordano Bruno in Roma, in Campo de' Fiori, nel luogo dove fu arso vivo il 17 febbraio 1600* (Milan: Giuseppe Civelli, 1889). See also Massimo Bucciantini, *Campo dei Fiori: Storia di un monumento maledetto* (Milan: Einaudi, 2015), n.p.

70. Editorial, "Roma democratica a fianco del popolo francese," *L'Unità*, June 1, 1968, p. 2. See also Dreyfus-Armand and Gervereau, *Mai 68*. The foundational event in the imaginary of 1968 in Italy was the "battaglia di Valle Giulia," a violent demonstration that took place in front of the University of Rome's school of architecture in March 1968, setting off a movement that would go on for eighteen more months.

71. Giorgio Agamben, "Warburg and the Nameless Science," in *Potentialities: Collected Essays in Philosophy*, ed. and trans. Daniel Heller-Roazen (Stanford: Stanford University Press, 1999), p. 95.

72. Georges Didi-Huberman, *The Surviving Image: Phantoms of Time and Time of Phantoms; Aby Warburg's History of Art*, trans. Harvey L. Mendelsohn (University Park: Pennsylvania State University Press, 2017), pp. 202 and 195.

73. Ibid.

74. Georges Didi-Huberman, *Atlas ou le gai savoir inquiet* (Paris: Éditions de Minuit, 2011), pp. 20–23.

75. See Benjamin H. D. Buchloh, "Atlas: Warburg's Paragon?; The End of Collage and Photomontage in Postwar Europe," in *Deep Storage: Collecting, Storing, and Archiving in Art* (Munich: Prestel, 1998), pp. 50–61, and Buchloh "Gerhard Richter's 'Atlas': The Anomic Archive," *October* 88 (Spring 1999), pp. 117–45.

76. Aby Warburg, *La rinascita del paganesimo antico: Contributi alla storia della cultura*, ed. Gertrud Bing, trans. Emma Cantimori (Florence: La Nuova Italia, 1966). Originally published as *Die Erneuerung der heidnischen Antike: Kulturwissenschaftliche Beiträge zur Geschichte der europäischen Renaissance*, ed. Gertrud Bing (Leipzig: Teubner, 1932). English translation in Aby Warburg, *The Renewal of Pagan Antiquity: Contributions to the Cultural History of the European Renaissance* (Los Angeles: Getty Research Institute, 1999).

77. Giorgio Pasquali, "Ricordo di Aby Warburg," *Pegaso* 2.4, April 1930, reprinted in *Vecchie e nuove pagine stravaganti di un filologo* (Turin: de Silva, 1952). See also Helmut Goetz, *Il giuramento rifiutato: I docenti universitari e il regime fascista* (Milan: La Nuova Italia, 2000).

78. Carlo Ginzburg, "Da A. Warburg a E. H. Gombrich (Note su un problema di metodo)," *Studi medievali* 7.2 (1966), p. 1030. In this long essay, Ginzburg assesses the

significance of the recent translation of books by Fritz Saxl, Ernst Gombrich, and War-burg into Italian. Reprinted in Carlo Ginzburg, *Myths, Emblems, Clues* (Baltimore: Johns Hopkins University Press, 1989), pp. 17–59.

79. Letter no. 34, 806, Max Adolph Warburg to Warburg, April 1, 1929; letter no. 22, 517, Warburg to Alice Berend, April 16, 1929; letter no. 30, 784, Kurt Bauch to Warburg, April 4, 1929. In this last letter, Bauch states, clearly in response to Warburg: "The Conciliazione is an enormously important event. The pictures should be circulated in Germany. Catholic countries voted against Germany's application to the League of Nations, while Protestants voted in favor." Two months later, in a letter sent from the Baden-Baden Sanatorium on June 27, 1929, to the publisher Herbert Bittner (letter no. 30, 817), Warburg requested newspaper articles and photographs of the Conciliazione by Eugenio Risi (a photographer working for the Istituto Nazionale LUCE). On July 19, 1929, Warburg wrote again to Bittner, asking him to send him all the photographs he could find relating to Mussolini's relationship to the Holy See (letter no. 22, 594). Finally, on October 7, 1929, three weeks before his death, Warburg wrote to Friedrich Keutgen, a history professor at the University of Hamburg, offering to lecture on a Saturday evening in November on the Conciliazione. References to Mussolini appear in seventy-five letters written by Warburg to his family and colleagues between 1922 and 1929. (English translations from the archive's database.) Box no. 20 includes six postcards of Pope Pius XI blessing the crowds from the loggia of St. Peter's on February 12, 1929, and seven postcards of the signing of the treaty the day before by Foto G. Felici, Rome.

80. Ernst Cassirer, "Aby Warburg," in *Écrits sur l'art* (Paris: Cerf, 1995), pp. 52–59. See also Aby Warburg, *Miroirs de faille: À Rome avec Giordano Bruno et Édouard Manet, 1928–29*, ed. Maurizio Ghelardi (Dijon: Les Presses du réel, 2011).

81. Rowland, *Giordano Bruno*, p. 62.

82. Ibid., pp. 63–64.

83. Arnaldo Momigliano, *On Pagans, Jews, and Christians* (Middletown: Wesleyan University Press, 1987), p. 92, quoted in Christopher D. Johnson, *Memory, Metaphor, and Aby Warburg's Atlas of Images* (Ithaca: Cornell University Press, 2012), p. 186 n.49.

84. Aby Warburg, "The Theatrical Costumes for the Intermedi of 1589: Bernardo Buontalenti's Designs and the Ledger of Emilio de' Cavalieri," in *The Renewal of Pagan Antiquity*, p. 350.

85. See Charlotte Schoell-Glass, "'Serious Issues': The Last Plates of Warburg's Picture Atlas *Mnemosyne*," in Richard Woodfield, ed., *Art History as Cultural History: Warburg's Projects* (Amsterdam: G+B Arts International, 2001), pp. 183–208.

86. Johnson, *Memory, Metaphor, and Aby Warburg's Atlas of Images*, p. 186.

87. Schoell-Glass, "'Serious Issues,'" p. 196.

88. Ibid., p. 194.

89. In a number of letters written soon after the March on Rome, Warburg refers to Mussolini as *muscolini* (little muscles).

90. Caramel, interview with the author, Venice, July 23, 2013. One may also propose that the presence of the train tracks of the Ferrovie Nord—a thorn in Terragni's grand plan that was supposed to be eliminated in accordance with the city's development plan of 1934, but nevertheless remained—functioned as a divider between the area just behind the Duomo and the piazza in front of the southeast "façade." I thank Emilia Terragni for this clarification.

91. "Omaggio a Terragni," special issue of *L'Architettura: Cronache e storia* 14.153 (July 1968).

92. Bruno Zevi, "Atti del convegno di studi: L'eredità di Terragni e l'architettura italiana 1943-1968," *L'Architettura: Cronache e storia* 15.163 (May 1969), p. 5.

93. For a historiographic overview, see Dennis P. Doordan, "Changing Agendas: Architecture and Politics in Contemporary Italy," *Assemblage* 8 (February 1989), pp. 60-77, and Richard A. Etlin, *Modernism in Italian Architecture 1890-1940* (Cambridge, MA: MIT Press, 1991), pp. 119-58.

94. Giulio Carlo Argan, "Relazione," *L'Architettura: Cronache e storia* 15.163 (May 1969), p. 6.

95. Luciano Caramel, "Esperienze d'arte non figurativa a Como negli anni 1933-40," *L'architettura: Cronache e storia* 15.163 (May 1969), pp. 10-12.

96. Mario Di Salvo, "Esperienze del Razionalismo in Italia trà le due guerre," round-table, *L'architettura: Cronache e storia* 15.163 (May 1969), p. 36.

97. Mario Di Salvo, "Cesare Cattaneo: Oltre il razionalismo," *Quadrante Lariano* 1.3 (May-June 1968), pp. 35-42 and 51-55; Luciano Caramel, "Terragni e gli astrattisti comaschi," *Quadrante Lariano* 1.5 (September-October 1968), pp. 43-53. See also Luciano Caramel, "Galleria Martano: Mario Radice," *NAC*, no. 1 (October 15, 1968), p. 20.

98. Giorgio Ciucci, "Terragni e l'architettura," in *Giuseppe Terragni: Opera completa 1925-1943* (Milan: Electa, 1996), p. 24. To the question "Terragni morì da fascista o da antifascista?" (Did Terragni die a Fascist or an anti-Fascist?), Ciucci argues that Terragni remained obstinately Fascist following his return to Como from the eastern front, explaining in part his nervous breakdown. Ibid.

99. "Con la realizzazione della Casa del Fascio, prevista dal piano regolatore della città, è possibile oggi a Como pensare a una non lontana realizzazione della 'città fascista'; accentramento organico e intelligente dei più tipici edifici del Regime in una vastissima piazza che è la logica e naturale prosecuzione della storica piazza del Duomo." Giuseppe Terragni, "La costruzione della Casa del Fascio di Como," *Quadrante* 35–36 (October 1936), p. 16. English translation in Thomas L. Schumacher, *Surface and Symbol: Giuseppe Terragni and the Architecture of Italian Rationalism* (New York: Princeton Architectural Press, 1990), p. 154.

100. Bruno Munari, "La città ideale," *Domus*, no. 197, May 1944, pp. 166–67.

101. Ibid., p. 166.

102. Editorial, "La protesta degli universitari," *Quadrante Lariano* 1.2 (March–April 1968), pp. 35–44.

103. Giuseppe Terragni, "Discorso ai Comaschi," *Quadrante Lariano* 1.3 (May–June 1968), pp. 41–42, and Vittorio Nessi, "I giornali studenteschi," ibid., pp. 70–72.

104. Mario Di Salvo, "Cortesella: Cronaca di un esproprio," *Quadrante Lariano* 2.1 (January–February 1969), pp. 41–47. The article was illustrated with a photograph of a worker shoveling debris in front of a group of men in Fascist uniforms.

105. *Quadrante* 35–36 (October 1936), p. 32.

106. On these images, see Jeffrey Schnapp, "The Mass Panorama," *Modernism/Modernity* 9.2 (2002), pp. 243–81.

107. Enrico Mantero, *Giuseppe Terragni e la città del razionalismo Italiano* (Bari: Dedalo, 1969). The focus of the whole book is indeed on Como. On Mantero, see also Etlin, *Modernism in Italian Architecture 1890–1940*. Mantero's book was reviewed by none other than Caramel in the issue of *Quadrante Lariano* that immediately followed the one with a special supplement on *Campo urbano*, *Quadrante Lariano* 1 (January–March 1970), pp. 81–84.

108. See Anthony Vidler, "Transparency," in *The Architectural Uncanny: Essays in the Modern Unholy* (Cambridge, MA: MIT Press, 1992), pp. 217–26; Jeffrey Schnapp, "The People's Glass House," *South Central Review* 25.3 (Fall 2008), pp 45–56; Emannuel Alloa, "Architectures de la transparence," *Appareil* 1 (2008), pp. 1–17; and Beatrice Colomina, "Beyond Pavilions: Architecture as Machine to See," in Bennet Simpson and Chrissie Iles, eds., *Dan Graham: Beyond* (Cambridge MA: MIT Press, 2009), pp. 191–207.

109. Caramel, interview with the author, Venice, July 23, 2013.

110. Kenneth Frampton, "A Note on Photography and Its Influence on Architecture," *Perspecta* 22 (1986), pp. 38–41.

111. Ibid., p. 39.

112. Fondo Ico et Luisa Parisi, Lombardia Beni Culturali. The photograph, which was not included in *Quadrante* due to the subsequent falling-out between Bontempelli and Bardi over the Casa and the folding of the review, came to my attention while reading Francesco Tentori's essay "Terragni e Bontempelli: Architettura e letteratura," in *Terragni: Opera completa*, p. 211.

113. Ibid.

114. Terragni, "La costruzione della Casa del Fascio di Como," p. 24. See also Mario Radice, "Le decorazioni," *Quadrante* 35–36 (October 1936), p. 33; Luciano Caramel, "Esperienze d'arte non-figurativa a Como negli anni 1933–34," *L'Architettura: Cronache e storia* 15.163 (May 1969), pp. 10–13; and Mario Radice, *Radice: Catalogo generale* (Milan: Electa, 2002).

115. "Un grande tavolo di riunione si compone con una parete completamente affrescata" (A large meeting table falls into arrangement with an entirely frescoed wall), Terragni, "La costruzione della Casa del Fascio di Como," p. 22. To this, as was pointed out by Attilio Terragni (Giuseppe Terragni's brother) in his excellent essay on the Casa, one may add the two glazed lateral walls. Attilio Terragni, "Giuseppe Terragni: Primo architetto del tempo," in *Atlante Terragni: Architetture costruite* (Milan: Skira, 2004), pp. 210–15. See also David Rifkind, "Furnishing the Fascist Interior: Giuseppe Terragni, Mario Radice and the Casa del Fascio," *Architectural Research Quarterly* 10.2 (2006), pp. 157–70.

116. Another photograph from Bontempelli's visit appears, interestingly, in Enrico Mantero and Mario Fosso, eds., *Giuseppe Terragni, 1904–1943* (Como: Tipografia Editrice C. Nani, 1982). The publisher is the same Cesare Nani who financed the *Campo urbano* photo book. On Bontempelli's visit, see also Alberto Longatti, "Così Bontempelli stroncò la Casa del Fascio di Terragni," *La Provincia* (Como), September 24, 2010.

117. Vera Mutter, interview, National Gallery, London, 2016.

118. Mario Di Salvo, "Convegno Terragni: Un passato che scotta," *Quadrante Lariano* 1.5 (September–October 1968), pp. 35–42.

119. Frances A. Yates, "Architecture and the Art of Memory," *Architectural Design* 7.6 (December 1968), pp. 573–74.

120. Eric Hobsbawm, "Cities and Insurrections," *Architectural Design* 7.6 (December 1968), pp. 581–88. So presentist is the magazine that in a typo, the date 1871 for the Paris Commune appears as 1971. The literature on Paris as the ursite for revolution is large; see, for instance, Ross, *May '68 and Its Afterlives*.

121. Pierre Milza, "Italie 1968: Le Mai rampant," in Armand and Gervereau, *Mai 68*, pp. 38–41.

122. Guido Panvini, *Ordine nero, guerriglia rossa: La violenza politica nell'Italia degli anni Sessanta e Settanta (1966–1975)* (Turin: Einaudi, 2009).

CHAPTER THREE: *VITALITÀ DEL NEGATIVO*

1. The participating artists were: Vincenzo Agnetti, Carlo Alfano, Getulio Alviani, Franco Angeli, Giovanni Anselmo, Alberto Biasi, Alighiero Boetti, Agostino Bonalumi, Davide Boriani, Enrico Castellani, Gianni Colombo, Gabriele De Vecchi, Luciano Fabro, Tano Festa, Giosetta Fioroni, Jannis Kounellis, Francesco Lo Savio, Renato Mambor, Piero Manzoni, Gino Marotta, Manfredo Massironi, Fabio Mauri, Mario Merz, Giulio Paolini, Pino Pascali, Vettor Pisani, Michelangelo Pistoletto, Mimmo Rotella, Paolo Scheggi, Mario Schifano, Cesare Tacchi, Giuseppe Uncini, and Gilberto Zorio. Included in the catalogue, which was produced beforehand, are Mario Ceroli, Eliseo Mattiacci, and Maurizio Mochetti, who pulled out just two weeks before the exhibition's opening.

2. *Vitalità del negativo nell'arte Italiana 1960/70*, exhibition catalogue (Florence: Centro Di, 1971).

3. Germano Celant, "Arte povera: Appunti per una guerriglia," *Flash Art*, no. 5, November–December 1967, p. 3.

4. Costanzo Costantini, "Roma come New York," *Il Messaggero*, January 4, 1971, p. 3.

5. Nerio Minuzzo, "La più bella mostra degli ultimi anni," *L'Europeo*, n.p., clipping, archive of Incontri Internazionali d'arte, Museo nationale delle arti del XXI Secolo (MAXXI), Rome.

6. Filiberto Menna, "L'arte italiana negli anni sessanta," *Il Mattino*, January 5, 1971, clipping.

7. Armando Stefani, "Il pomicio dell'avanguardia," *Men*, January 18, 1971, pp. 10–11.

8. Achille Bonito Oliva, interview with the author, Rome, May 27, 2013.

9. For a general account of *Vitalità*, see the catalogue of the exhibition made in homage to Graziella Lonardi Buontempo: Luca Massimo Barbero and Francesca Pola, eds., *A Roma, la nostra era avanguardia: Vitalità del negativo*, exhibition catalogue (Rome: Museo d'Arte Contemporanea, 2010). On the origins and development of the Incontri, see the important study by Luigia Lonardelli, *Dalla sperimentazione alla crisi: Gli Incontri Internazionali d'Arte a Roma, 1970–1981* (Milan: Doppiozero, 2016), a detailed account, based on the Incontri's archive, of eleven years' worth of activities.

10. Piero Sartogo in an interview with Stefano Chiodi and the author, Rome, October 17, 2008.

11. Used by the syndicalist Bruno Trentin, the term *secondo biennio rosso* makes reference to the years 1919 to 1920, when Europe was swept by a wave of revolutionary agitation.

12. See Guido Crainz, *Il paese mancato: Dal miracolo economico agli anni ottanta* (Rome: Donzelli, 2003), and Guido Panvini, *Ordine nero, guerriglia rossa: La violenza politica nell'Italia degli anni Sessanta e Settanta (1966–1975)* (Turin: Einaudi, 2009).

13. To this day, after endless investigations and countless trials, no perpetrators have been brought to justice.

14. The following year, the Borghese coup became public, and in a converse attempt at disassociation from the extreme Right, Arnaldo Forlani, an influential Christian Democrat politician, declared it the most dangerous attempt against the state since the end of the war. See "Le denuncie di Forlani sulle trame nere," *Il Giorno*, November 7, 1972, quoted by Crainz, *Il paese mancato*, p. 386.

15. Achille Bonito Oliva, "Vitalità del negativo," in *Vitalità del negativo nell'arte Italiana 1960/70*, n.p.

16. Achille Bonito Oliva, "Comportamento estetico e comunità concentrata," *Marcatrè*, no. 56, n.d., pp. 72–73.

17. Delivered in the context of a conference series entitled "La critica in atto," it was published in *Quaderni degli Incontri Internazionali d'Arte*, no. 2 (1973) and in *Passo dello strabismo: Sulle arti* (Milan: Feltrinelli, 1978), pp. 153–64.

18. For instance, *Conceptual Art, Arte Povera, Land Art*, curated by Celant at the Galleria Civica d'Arte Moderna e Contemporanea in Turin, June–July 1970.

19. Alberto Arbasino, "Le fanfare della metafora," *Vogue Italia*, January 1971, pp. 72–74.

20. I would like to thank Luigia Lonardelli for showing me the floor plans for *Vitalità* in the Incontri archive recently donated to the Museo nazionale delle arti del XXI secolo (MAXXI) in Rome.

21. A few of the letters written by the artists to Sartogo requesting spatial and other specifications are reproduced in the introductory essay by Luca Massimo Barbero, "*Vitalità del negativo nell'arte italiana 1960/70*: Appunti su un' avanguardia nel presente," in *A Roma, la nostra era avanguardia*, pp. 14–30.

22. For the many lives of this installation, see Stefano Chiodi, "Lo scorrevole: I teatro della crudeltà di Vettor Pisani," *Il Verri*, no. 64 (June 2017), pp. 89–107.

23. Paolo Pietroni, "Lo strano mondo di 'Vitalità del negativo': L'arte che finisce in un luna park," *Epoca*, January 10, 1971, pp. 30–34.

24. Sergio Maldini, "Scultori in concorrenza con gli astronauti: Il salotto sulla luna," *Il Resto del Carlino* (Bologna), January 15, 1971.

25. "L'occhio magico nel labirinto pop," *Paese Sera*, November 6, 1971, clipping.

26. Fabio Cittadini and Renato Tomasino, "Vitalità del negativo in metacrilato e polistirolo," *Pan*, May 1971, pp. 96–98.

27. Edith Schloss, "Art in Rome: An Artistic Fun Fair — More Fair Than Fun," *International Herald Tribune*, December 12–13, 1970, clipping.

28. Carlo Laurenzi, "Vitalità del negativo a Roma: Fruitore in crisi," *Corriere della Sera*, December 6, 1970, clipping.

29. C. M., "Vitalità del negativo," *Ciao 2001*, July 21, 1971.

30. Sandra Orienti, "Vitalità del negativo: Mostra o museo? Si fà passare per vivo quello che è già morto," *Il Popolo*, December 19, 1970. It was followed by another piece, also by Orienti, entitled "Per un bilancio culturale del 1970: Istituzionalizzata la crisi dell'arte," *Il Popolo*, January 15, 1971.

31. Sergio Maldini, "Il cimitero del negativo," *La nazione*, January 15, 1971, p. 3; Giorgio Di Genova, "Mortuarietà del negativo," *Mondo nuovo*, December 27, 1970, p. 11.

32. Tullio Catalano, "Vitalità del negativo o negativo della vitalità," *Gala* 46, March 1971, pp. 37–39.

33. Pierre Restany. "Vitalità del negativo/Negativo della vitalità," *Domus*, no. 494, January 1, 1971, pp. 43–48.

34. "Insomma il problema era questo: la nuova avanguardia intendenva ufficalizzarsi, conquistare aristocrazia e borghesia romane, entratre nei loro salotti, l'avanguardia intendeva creare quindi il proprio 'salon,' non per nulla nella sede tipica dei 'Salon' romani della 'belle époque' alle utlime quadriennali.... La prova la più lampante della vocazione al 'salon'... è nel delirio delle convocazioni ufficali: dal Presidente Saragat, al Ministro della Publica Istruzione, al Sindaco di Roma (c'è da creare invidia nella Biennale veneziana, o nella Triennale milanese), più quattro ministri ecc. L'avanguardia cerca casa, forse prepara qualche candidatura per senatore a vita." Enrico Crispolti, "Il 'salon' dell'avanguardia," *NAC*, no. 2 (February 1971), p. 12. A year later, *NAC* would publish the debate of a roundtable entitled "Arte e fascismo," NAC, no. 4 (April 1972), pp. 5–9.

35. "Il 'negativo del linguaggio' che secondo l'amico Achille Bonito Oliva, prefatore della mostra, sarebble il denominatore comnune ai vari espositori e la giustificazione nella mostra medesima, non può proporsi come modello da esibire, come linguaggio esso stesso, pena la sua vanificazione o il suo volgersi in accademismo.... Un accademismo,

direi, dell'orrore, del macabro, esattamente come il tardo informale è stato l'accademismo dell'angoscia." Cesare Vivaldi, "Il sacrario del negativo," *NAC*, no. 2 (February 1971), p. 11. Meanwhile, *Flash Art*'s review read both in tone and format like a judicial dossier on the machinations surrounding the "terrorist atmosphere" then permeating Italy's cultural institutions. See editorial, "Vitalità del Negativo," *Flash Art*, no. 20, November–December 1970, p. 12.

36. For a rapid overview of these exhibitions, see Paola Nicolin, "Year Zero: On the Canon of Exhibitions in Italy (1967–1968)," *Manifesta Journal*, no. 11 (2010–2011), pp. 28–40.

37. Gillo Dorfles, "Una mostra romana: 'Vitalità del negativo' nell'arte italiana," *Art International* 15.4 (April 20, 1971), p. 15.

38. Lorenza Trucchi, "Vitalità del negativo nell'arte italiana 1960–70," *Momento-sera*, December 18, 1970, p. 11.

39. Nan R. Piene, "How to Stay Home and Help the Balance of Payments," *Art in America* 56.3, May–June 1968, p. 107. Two summers later, *L'Espresso*'s review of *Amore mio* by "G. C." would be titled "Un Palazzo antico per l'avanguardia," *L'Espresso*, August 2, 1970.

40. *Lo spazio dell'immagine*, exhibition catalogue (Venice: Alfieri Edizioni d'Arte, 1967). The essays in the catalogue are by Umbro Apollonio, Giulio Carlo Argan, Palma Bucarelli, Maurizio Calvesi, Germano Celant, Giorgio de Marchis, Gillo Dorfles, Christopher Finch, Udo Kultermann, Giuseppe Marchiori, and Lara-Vinca Masini. The exhibition was also reported on RAI TV: *Amore mio, Arte a Montepulciano*, 1970, directed by E. Flaiano and P. P. Ruggerini (1970, 16 minutes). For a recent revisitation of the exhibition see Italo Tomassoni, ed., *Spazio, tempo, immagine* (Milan: Skira, 2009).

41. For the history of the building, see Giordana Benazzi and Francesco Federico Mancini, *Il Palazzo Trinci di Foligno* (Perugia: Quatroenne, 2001).

42. Ibid.

43. Paola M. Buttaro and Renato Covino, "Le ferrovie in Umbria: realizzazioni e progetti," in Carlo Ceccarelli, ed., *La città di Foligno e gli insediamenti ferroviari* (Città di Castello: Electa/Editori Umbri Associati, 1989), pp. 14–36.

44. See Patrizia Felicetti, "I cicli pittorici di Palazzo Trinci: Le tecniche e il restauro," in ibid., pp. 565–94.

45. Giuseppe Marchiori, *Lo spazio dell'immagine* (Venice: Alfieri edizioni d'arte, 1967), pp. 22–23.

46. These works included Davide Boriani's *Camera stroboscopica multidimensionale* (Multidimensional stroboscopic room, 1965–67), a mirrored cube divided into two

rectangular spaces by a mirror, with a floor of triangles illuminated by nine projectors that emitted pulsating rays of red and green light in forty-six different combinations; *Ambiente stroboscopico programmato* (Programmed stroboscopic environment, 1966) by Gruppo MID, an environment in the three primary colors with a constantly changing light activated by the movement of persons entering the room; Gianni Colombo's *After-structure* (After-structure, 1964–67), a room crisscrossed by a grid in the primary colors; and De Vecchi's *Ambiente — strutturazione a parametri virtuali* (Environment — structuring with virtual parameters, 1969).

47. This was not the first reconstruction of Fontana's *Ambiente spaziale* (Spatial environment), parts of which (probably the mobile) had been salvaged in 1949 to be shown again on later occasions. It was first reexhibited as part of the *Pittura a Milano dal 1945 al 1964* exhibition, held in Milan's Palazzo Reale in 1964, and then once again at the Walker Art Center for the artist's 1966 solo exhibition, *Fontana: The Spatial Concept of Art*, which traveled to Austin, Buenos Aires, Amsterdam, and Eindhoven until just a few weeks before Foligno. See Marina Pugliese, "Pour la première fois en Italie et dans le monde," in Sébastien Gokalp and Choghakate Kazarian, eds., *Lucio Fontana: Retrospective*, exhibition catalogue (Paris: Musée d'Art Moderne de la Ville de Paris, 2014), pp. 165–73.

48. Germano Celant, "A Foligno, lo spazio dell'immagine 1967," *D'Ars*, nos. 36–37, June 1967, pp. 62–69, and Celant, "Im-spazio a Foligno," *Casabella* 318, September 1967, pp. 61–64.

49. Tommaso Trini, "A Foligno," *Domus*, no. 453, August 1967, pp. 41–42. The issue featured Mattiacci's *Tubo* on the magazine's cover.

50. Giancarlo Politi, "Da Foligno una proposta per Venezia," *Flash Art*, no. 2, July 1967, pp. 1–3.

51. Among the women were Giosetta Fioroni, Arabella Giorgi, Laura Grisi, and Titina Maselli.

52. Some of Marconi's photos seemed cribbed from Pier Paolo Pasolini's recent film *Il Vangelo secondo Matteo* (The Gospel according to Matthew) of 1964.

53. The Banca Monte dei Paschi di Siena supplied additional funds. For a detailed archival analysis of this exhibition based on a private (undivulged) local source and the descriptive cards written by Maria Russo to be distributed in the absence of an explanatory catalogue to the visitors, see Fabio Belloni's excellent "Approdi e vedette: *Amore mio* a Montepulciano nel 1970," *Studi di Memofonte* 9 (2012), pp. 121–65.

54. Bonito Oliva, "*Amore mio*: I segni della presenza," *Domus*, no. 490, September 1970, pp. 46–47. As Daniela Lancioni, curator at the Palazzo delle Esposizioni, put it: "In his

exhibitions, Bonito Oliva always initially appears to be ecumenical in his choice of artists, but he then puts his seal." In conversation with the author, Rome, July 9, 2019.

55. Filiberto Menna, "Una originale mostra d'arte a Montepulciano: Gli artisti si sono autoconvocati per confessare il loro 'amore' segreto," *Il Mattino*, August 6, 1970, p. 11.

56. Quoted in Giulia Massari, "Amore mio, una mostra," *Il Mondo*, July 12, 1970, clipped.

57. Lorenza Trucchi, *"Amore mio* a Montepulciano," *Momento-sera*, n.d. (1970), p. 11, clipping, <Archive>.

58. Bonito Oliva, *"Amore mio*: i segni della presenza," pp. 46-47.

59. Achille Bonito Oliva, "Amore mio," *Argomenti e immagini di design*, no. 1 (September–October 1970), p. 96.

60. See Pier Luigi Tazzi, "La dieta di Montepulciano," *NAC*, no. 2 (November 1970), pp. 6-7.

61. Lara-Vinca Masini, "Le mostre di questa estate: *Amore mio* a Montepulciano," *Gala* 7.43, September 1970, pp. 48-49.

62. E. Fezzi, "L'Anti-Biennale a Montepulciano," *La Provincia di Cremona*, clipping, <Archive>. For a critique of pairing *Amore mio* with *Vitalità* as two curatorial swindles see the *Flash Art* editorial "Vitalità del negativo," p. 12.

63. Aurelio Natali, "A Montepulciano: *Amore mio*," *NAC*, no. 1 (October 1, 1970), p. 14.

64. Such events play such a crucial role that the history of the regime can be told through its exhibitions, see: Marla Stone, *The Patron State: Culture and Politics in Fascist Italy* (Princeton: Princeton University Press, 1998); Maddalena Carli, *Vedere il fascismo: arte e politica nelle esposizioni del regime (1928-1942)* (Rome: Carrocci, 2021).

65. See Claudia Salaris, *La quadriennale: Storia di una rassegna d'arte Italiana dagli anni trenta a oggi* (Venice: Marsilio, 2004).

66. The exhibition took over the palazzo's two floors. See Dino Alfieri and Luigi Freddi, *Mostra della rivoluzione fascista* (1933; Milan: Editori del Nuovo Candido, 1982); Giorgio Ciucci, "L'autorappresentazione del fascismo: La mostra del decennale della marcia su Roma," *Rassegna Italiana* 10 (June 1982), pp. 48-55; Jeffrey T. Schnapp, "Epic Demonstrations: Fascist Modernity and the 1932 Exhibition of the Fascist Revolution," in Richard Golsan, ed., *Fascism, Aesthetics, and Culture* (Hanover, NH: University Press of New England, 1992), pp. 1-36; Marla Stone, "Staging Fascism: The Show of the Fascist Revolution," *Journal of Contemporary History* 28.2 (April 1993), pp. 215-43.

67. *Mostra Augustea della Romanità: Bimillenario della nascita di Augusto, 23 settembre 1937-XV - 23 settembre 1938-XVI*, exhibition catalogue (Rome: Colombo, 1938).

68. See Marla Stone, "'Potere e spiritualità': La *Prima mostra degli artisti in armi* del 1942," *Memoria e Ricerca*, no. 33 (January–April 2010), pp. 63–79.

69. See Adolfo Mignemi and Gabriella Solaro, eds., *Un immagine dell'Italia: Resistenza e ricostruzione. Le mostre del dopoguerra in Europa* (Milan: Skira, 2005).

70. For instance *L'Arte nella vita del mezzogiorno d'Italia* (1953), *Premio nazionale di paesaggio: Autostrada del sole* (1961); *Mostra di pittura 'Lazio'* (1963), *Rassegna di arti figurative e di architettura della Venezia Giulia e della Venezia Tridentina* (1968), *Prima rassegna di arti figurative tra artisti romani e napoletani* (1968), and *Mostra interregionale di 'arti figurative'* (1970). For a history of the building, see the essays in Rossella Siligato and Maria Elisa Tittoni, eds., *Il Palazzo delle Esposizioni* (Rome: Palazzo delle Esposizioni, 1990).

71. "Certo che lo sapevamo, ma non ce ne poteva fregare di meno," Sartogo, interview with Stefano Chiodi and the author, Rome, October 17, 2008.

72. See Dennis P. Doordan, "Changing Agendas: Architecture and Politics in Contemporary Italy," *Assemblage* 8 (February 1989), pp. 60–77, and Luciano Patetta, *L'architettura in Italia 1919–1943: Le polemiche* (Milan: Clup, 1972).

73. "*Vitalità* non è una mostra problematica, anzi è assiomatica, e a suo modo terroristica per la sua stessa esibita ufficialità, e malignamente si potrebbe dire persino littoria (senza tuttavia con ciò voler suggerire un confronto, che alla mostra attuale riuscirebbe subito nocivo, con una certa mostra della rivoluzione, di quarant'anni fa in queste stesse sale)." Crispolti, "Il 'salon' dell'avanguardia," p. 12.

74. "Il clima di molte sale di *Vitalità del negativo* riecheggia stranamente, in effetti, per uno di quei curiosi contrappassi della cronaca che ogni tanto si verificano, e certo a insaputa dei giovani e giovanissimi espositori, quello della famigerata *Mostra della Rivoluzione fascista* in altri tempi, guarda caso, ospitata dallo stesso Palazzo delle Esposizioni. Ricordo (ero bambino) una sala nera, con scritta innumeri volte in bronzo la parola 'Presente' e sottofondo di musiche psichedelico-patriottiche, della quale una attuale sala di Scheggi sembra una parodia. Simile coincidenze non sono casuali. La mostra fascista era un sacrario, rispondeva cioè alla vocazione morale più profonda dei fascisti, che era quella di essere non tanto degli scoperti assassini quanto degli avvoltoi e dei vespilloni; un sacrario a sua volta è *Vitalità del negativo*, per il semplice motivo che il negativo, nel momento in cui si istituzionalizza, perde ogni vitalità e diventa il becchino di se stesso." Vivaldi, "Il sacrario del negativo," p. 11. *Contrapasso* refers to the punishment of souls in Dante's *Inferno* wherein for every sinner's crime there must be an equal and fitting punishment.

75. Milton Gendel, "Arte Povera, Amore Mio," *ARTnews* 69.10 (February 1971), p. 70.

76. Luce Hoctin, "Vitalità del negativo," *L'Oeil*, no. 193, January 1971, p. 17.

77. All the other photographs in the catalogue — which were taken by Claudio Abate, Gianni Colombo, Ugo Mulas, and Paolo Mussat Sartor — were garnered from previous publications.

78. Sartogo, interview with Stefano Chiodi and the author, Rome, October 17, 2008.

79. Achille Bonito Oliva, interview with the author, Rome, May 27, 2013.

80. "A rientrare nel palazzo delle Esposizioni ora che gli ambienti dove si dispone la Quadriennale sono quasi ultimati, il pensiero non riesce a dimenticare la Mostra della Rivoluzione e la disposizione che avevano le sue sale a l'andamento delle sue cose, il pensiero ricorda che quì nella rotonda era il covo . . . e, più oltre, dove adesso si lavora a costruire una fontatna, stava il sacrarario dei Martiri." G. C., *La Nazione*, January 25, 1935, quoted in Fabrizio Carli, "L'acceso dibattito sulla mise en scene: L'allestimento espositivo," in Elena Pontiggia, ed., *La grande Quadriennale: 1935, la nuova arte Italiana* (Milan: Electa, 2006), p. 121. See also Mario Quesada, "Palazzo delle esposizioni: Cinquant'anni di allestimenti (1883–1945) in Siligato and Tittoni, eds., *Il Palazzo delle Esposizioni*, pp. 77–87.

81. The first two Quadriennali were designed by the architect Pietro Aschieri — first in collaboration with Enrico Del Debbio, then with Eugenio Montuori — the third in 1939 by Mario Paniconi and Giulio Pediconi, and the fourth in 1943 by Ernesto Puppo and Alessandro Mangione.

82. See Silvia Cecchini, "Musei e mostre d'arte negli anni trenta: L'Italia e la cooperazione intellettuale," in Maria Ida Catalano, ed., *Snodi di critica: Musei, mostre, restaure e diagnostica artistica in Italia (1930–1940)* (Rome: Gangemi, 2013), pp. 57–105; Anna Chiara Cimoli, *Musei Effimeri: Allestimenti di mostre in Italia 1949/53* (Milan: Il Saggiatore, 2007); Dalai Emiliani, *Per una critica della museografia del novecento in Italia:* Il "saper mostrare" di Carlo Scarpa (Venice: Marsilio, 2008); Patricia Falguières, "Politics of the White Cube: The Italian Way," *Grey Room* 64 (Summer 2016), pp. 6–39.

83. See Silvio Pasquarelli, "La quadriennale di Roma: Frà tradizione e innovazione," in the special issue on the Triennali and Quadriennali in *Rassegna* 10 (June 1982), pp. 56–61.

84. See Emily Braun, "Bodies from the Crypt and Other Tales of Italian Sculpture between the World Wars," in Kenneth E. Silver, ed., *Chaos and Classicism: Art in France, Italy, and Germany, 1918–1936* (New York: Guggenheim Museum, 2010), pp. 145–57.

85. Mino Guerrini, "Quadriennale: Nacque in un Italia che credeva d'essere fascista mentre era umbertina," *L'Espresso*, November 27, 1955, clipping, Archivio della Quadriennale, Rome.

86. See, for instance, Maurizio Fagiolo dell'Arco, "La Quadriennale di Roma come un girone dantesco," *Avanti* (Rome), November 23, 1965.

87. See my essay "Chronicle of a Disappearance Foretold," *Art + Architectural Exchanges from East to West*, University of Melbourne, Australia, 2012; Anty Pansera, *Storia e cronaca della Triennale* (Milan: Longanesi, 1978).

88. Gio Ponti, "Insegnamento altrui e fantasia degli italiani," *Domus*, no. 259, June 1951, pp. 10–13.

89. Giò Ponti, "Dalla IX alla X Triennale," *Domus*, no. 264, December 1951, pp. 264–65. See also Romy Golan, *Muralnomad: The Paradox of Wall Painting, Europe 1927–1957* (New Haven: Yale University Press, 2009), pp. 230–31.

90. Achille Bonito Oliva, "L'arte delle mostre," *Il Palazzo delle Esposizioni di Roma* (Rome: Pre Progetti, 2007), p. 65.

91. The documentary, made by Michele Gandin with music by Egisto Macchi, had a running commentary by Bonito Oliva in which the curator noted the violence of the exhibition. Produced by Nexus Film, it was presented at the Incontri Internazionali d'Arte in the Palazzo Taverna on November 11, 1971, and is kept in the archive of the Incontri.

92. On the double temporality of the *X* and its centrality within the "surfeit of fascist signs, images, slogans, books, and buildings" that aimed "to compensate for, fill in, and cover up its forever unstable ideological core," see Schnapp, "Epic Demonstrations," p. 3.

93. Originally published in Rome's new and influential *Quindici*, a literary journal identified with Gruppo 63, the essay reflected the internal polemics between the old (i.e., Communist) Left, to which Sanguineti adhered, and the rise of a new, radical, extra-parliamentary Left, leading to the demise of the journal only two years after its founding. Edoardo Sanguineti, "La guerra futurista," *Quindici* (Milan) 14 (December 1968), pp. 35–38, and Sanguineti, *Ideologia e linguaggio* (Milan: Feltrinelli, 1970).

94. Renzo De Felice, *Il fascismo: Le interpretazioni dei contemporanei e degli storici* (Bari: Laterza, 1970); De Felice, *Interpretations of Fascism*, trans. Brenda Huff Everett (Cambridge, MA: Harvard University Press, 1977). See also De Felice, *Intervista sul fascismo* (Bari: Laterza, 1975).

95. Umberto Eco, *La struttura assente: Introduzione alla ricerca semiologica* (Milan: Bompiani, 1968).

96. See Romy Golan, "The Scene of a Disappearance," in Giosetta Fioroni, *L'argento* (New York: The Drawing Center, 2013), pp. 87–102. I also interviewed Fioroni in Rome on June 1, 2013.

97. "Il punto di partenza sono state alcune immagini dei primi anni del fascismo. La coincidenza figurativa con la visita esterna nella nostra società di volti, vestiti, mode, e sopprattutto sentimenti che si aggirano, spesso fantasmi del consumo, del 'remake' funebre intorno a noi." *Giosetta Fioroni*, Galleria dell'Indiano (Florence, 1970). The brochure is reproduced in Germano Celant, *Giosetta Fioroni* (Turin: Skira, 2009), p. 184.

98. "Dialogo con Alberto Boatto," in Alberto Boatto, Anne-Marie Sauzeau, and Andrea Carancini, eds., *Giosetta Fioroni* (Ravenna: Essegni, 1990), p. 16.

99. *Giosetta Fioroni: "Laguna" smalto bianco e luce su tela*, La Tartaruga, November–December, 1970.

100. Fioroni, interview with the author, Rome, June 1, 2013.

101. One of his she-wolves is entitled *Natale di Roma* (The Christmas of Rome), the first festivity introduced by Mussolini after his takeover to celebrate, every April 21, the mythical founding of Rome.

102. Maurizio Calvesi, "Intervista con i pittori," *Marcatrè*, nos. 8–9-10 (1964), p. 220.

103. Roberto Lambarelli, "Intervista a Pierre Restany," in Rosella Siligato, ed., *Roma anni '60: Al di là della pittura*, exhibition catalogue, Palazzo delle Esposizioni (Rome: Carte Segrete, 1990), pp. 364 and 366. See also *Roma Pop City 1960–1967*, MACRO, Museo d'arte contemporanea, Rome, July 13 – November 27, 2016.

104. For a fascinating reading of Richter's ambivalence toward the relation between politics and modernism having experienced Fascism, Communism, and capitalism (in that order) by the mid-1960s, see John Curley, *A Conspiracy of Images: Andy Warhol, Gerhard Richter, and the Art of the Cold War* (New Haven: Yale University Press, 2013). Curley's reading of Richter's *Uncle Rudi* (1965) can also be seen in relation to my reading of Pistoletto's *Alpino* in Chapter 1.

105. *Gerhard Richter*, Galleria La Tartaruga, Rome, January 20 – February 20, 1966.

106. Galleria del Leone, Venice, 1966. Interestingly, these exhibitions go unmentioned in the literature on Richter and on Italian Pop. The artist had one more solo show abroad that year in between the two Italian ones, at Galerie Bruno Bischofberger in Zurich, in March and April 1966.

107. See John David Rhodes, "The Eclipse of Place: Rome's EUR from Rossellini to Antonioni," in John David Rhodes and Elena Gorfinkel, eds., *Taking Place: Location and the Moving Image* (Minneapolis: University of Minnesota Press, 2011), pp. 31–54.

108. The film opened simultaneously in Italy and the United States on October 22, 1970.

109. Although the maquette for the book was lost, the photos have been published in

book form thanks to the priceless initiative of Giuliano Sergio: Giuliano Sergio, ed., *Ugo Mulas: Vitalità del Negativo* (Milan: Johan & Levi, 2010). Other photographs of the exhibition, lacking the suggestiveness of Mulas's, were shot in the following weeks by Cristina Ghergo and Massimo Piersanti; many of these are kept in the Incontri's archive.

110. T. Jefferson Kline, *Bertolucci's Dream Loom: A Psychoanalytic Study of Cinema* (Amherst: University of Massachusetts Press, 1987), pp. 91–92. See also Millicent Marcus's chapter on *The Conformist* in *Italian Film in the Light of Neorealism* (Princeton: Princeton University Press, 1986), pp. 285–312.

111. Maureen Turim, *Flashbacks in Film: Memory and History* (New York: Routledge, 1989), p. 17.

112. *"La vita a Roma": Luoghi, paesaggi e dimore*, Milan, Galleria del Naviglio, March–April 1971. Translation based on that in Celant, *Giosetta Fioroni*, p. 202.

113. Gitt Magrini was also the costume designer for Antonioni's *La notte* and *L'eclisse*.

114. "Bertolucci on *The Conformist*," interview with Marilyn Goldin, *Sight & Sound* 40.2 (Spring 1972), reprinted in Fabien S. Gerard, T. Jefferson Kline, and Bruce Sklarew, eds., *Bernardo Bertolucci: Interviews* (Jackson: University of Mississippi Press, 2000), pp. 64–65. On the parallels between *Il conformista* and Fascist cinema, see Lino Miccichè, *Il cinema del riflusso: Film e cineasti italiani degli anni '70* (Venice: Marsilio, 1980), and Angela Dalle Vacche, *The Body in the Mirror: Shapes of History in Italian Cinema* (Princeton: Princeton University Press, 1992).

115. Gilberto Zorio in the *Vitalità* catalogue, n.p.; and "Gilberto Zorio, Corpo di energia," interview with Jole de Sanna, *Data* 2.3 (April 1972), pp. 16–23.

116. "Bertolucci on *The Conformist*," p. 66.

117. Ibid., p. 68.

118. Ibid., p. 66.

119. One may argue, as I have elsewhere, that there is a degree of irresolution in the magical effect created by Brecht's alienation effect, as well, making the distinction more problematic.

120. Kline, *Bertolucci's Dream Loom*, pp. 82–83.

121. Enzo Siciliano, "Moravia parla del 'Conformista'," *Moravia* (Milan: Longanesi, 1971), republished in the introduction to the novel, *Il conformista* (Milan: Bompiani, 1975), pp. xix-xxii.

122. "Con *Il Conformista* volevo rappresentare il fascismo dalla parte del fascismo. Non mi sento un uomo settario. Anzi, certe volte mi sento dominato da una specie di dissociazione schizoide per cui faccio tutto per trasferirmi nei panni del mio avversario. Di fronte al

fascismo, volevo sapere come e perchè era nato; che cosa aveva rapresentato per I fascisti stessi. Mi chiedevo: che cosa è un intellettuale fascista?" Ibid., p. xix.

123. The dates of the events related in the book coincided, albeit with poetic license, with the assassination of his famous Jewish anti-Fascist cousins — the journalist and historian Carlo Rosselli and his brother, the Socialist leader and historian Sabatino ("Nello") Rosselli. Both were murdered on June 9, 1937, by a militant of La Cagoule, a French ultrafascist group, in the woods of the resort town of Bagnoles de l'Orne. See Alberto Moravia, *Vita di Moravia* (Milan: Bompiani, 1990), and Tonino Tornitore's introduction to a recent reprint of the novel (Florence: Giunti, 2018), pp. 5–11.

124. "Capii che i valori negativi a livello personale, si capovolgevano in valori positivi a livello nazionale. La miseria, la meschinità della piccola borghesia diventavano pattriotismo.... Quel che agiva era il meccanismo della conversione. Come per incanto, da una somma di valori negativi, viene fuori un valore positivo. Assistiamo a un capovolgimento completo: il capovolgimento avviene perche la persona che lo subisce ha certamente già in sé, anche se in forma deviata, quello che diventerà." Siciliano, "Moravia parla del 'Conformista'," p. xx.

125. "L'integrazione al fascismo si pagava sempre con un delitto; per cominciare una delazione. La prima cosa che Mussolini chiedeva ad un intellettuale era di scrivere un articolo conto un suo nemico, contro Croce ad esempio." Ibid., p. xxi.

126. Bonito Oliva, *Passo dello strabismo*, pp. 153–64. See also Bonito Oliva's interview with Stefano Chiodi in the reprint of *Il territorio magico: Comportamenti alternativi nell'arte* (Florence: Le lettere, 2009), pp. 247–66, a book he wrote a year before *Vitalità*, although it was published in 1971. This essay became the kernel for the ideas developed in his book *L'ideologia del traditore: Arte, maniera, manierismo* (1976; Milan: Feltrinelli, 2012); Achille Bonito Oliva, *The Ideology of the Traitor: Art, Manner and Mannerism*, trans. Mark Eaton and Paul Metcalfe (Milan: Electa, 1998). For an account of how the 1970s lead to *Transavanguardia*, see Stefano Chiodi, *Genius loci: Anatomia di un mito italiano* (Macerata: Quodlibet, 2021).

127. Bonito Oliva, *Passo dello strabismo*, p. 154.

128. Crainz, *Il paese mancato*, p. 382.

129. On Pistoletto's collaboration with Pisani, centered on Duchamp and appropriately entitled *Plagio* (Plagiarism), see Vettor Pisani and Michelangelo Pistoletto, *Plagio* (Rome: Malborough Gallery, 1973), and Marco Farano, Maria Cristina Mundici, and Maria Teresa Roberto, *Michelangelo Pistoletto: Il varco dello specchio: Azioni e collaborazioni, 1967–2004* (Turin: Fondazione Torino Musei, 1985).

130. Natali, "A Montepulciano: *Amore mio*," p. 14

131. Carla Lonzi, *Autoritratto* (Milan: De Donato, 1969). The book was recently republished along with interviews edited by Laura Conte, Laura Iamurri, and Vanessa Martini (Rome: Et al., 2010). There has been much attention to Lonzi in the last few years: see Lara Conte, Vinzia Fiorino, and Vanessa Martini, eds., *Carla Lonzi: La duplice radicalità; Dalla critica militante al feminismo di rivolta* (Pisa: ETS, 2011), and Laura Iamurri, *Un immagine che sfugge: Carla Lonzi e l'arte in Italia 1955–1970* (Macerata: Quodlibet, 2016).

132. Lonzi, *Autoritratto*, pp. 3–4.

133. "Nell'estate del settanta, a Montepulciano. . . . Nascondo un minuscolo altoparlante nel vano di una delle finestre che da sulla piazza, sicché sembrò a chi stata in strada che la voce venisse da dentro il palazzo, mentre, in quella stanza, si sentiva l voce salire dalla piazza. L'ascoltatore in ogni caso veniva escluso e non poteva capire dove e perché quell'altro continuava a ripetere, ininterrottamente: *cittadini, consideratemi irresponsabile di quanto succede!* . . . Sentiva in sottofondo voci di bambini che rifacevano il verso, ed un momento dopo gli altoparlanti di un comizio elettorale, voci e rumori diversi; perché la registrazione fu fatta in tanti luoghi: in automobile, in treno, in strada, in famiglia; ogni occasione fu buona per gridarlo o sussurrarlo. Tutti i visitatori si ostinarono, chissà? Per censura? A sentire tutto capovolto: . . . *consideratemi il responsabile di quanto succede!* . . . Era, credo, inconcepibile che l'arte non si assumesse i peccati del mondo come fa la cultura. Luciano Fabro, *Attaccapanni* (Turin: Einaudi, 1978), p. 88. Italics in the original.

134. Belloni, "Approdi e vedette," p. 127.

135. For an extensively feminist account of Lonzi, see Giovanna Zapperi, *Carla Lonzi: Un'arte della vita* (Rome: DeriveApprodi, 2017).

136. Carla Lonzi, "La critica è potere," *NAC*, no. 3 (December 1970), pp. 5–6. This essay belongs to a series of articles in *NAC* on the crisis of art criticism. See Germano Celant, "Per una critica acritica," *NAC*, n.s., no. 1 (October 1970), pp. 29–30; Aurelio Natali "Se la critica tace," *NAC*, no. 2 (November 1970), p. 4; Tommaso Trini, "Critica e identità," and Luciano Caramel, "Critica come cooperazione," *NAC*, n.s., no. 1 (January 1971), pp. 4 and 5; Marisa Volpi, "Critici si nasce," *NAC*, no. 2 (February 1971), p. 4. For an excellent overview, see Lara Conte, "La critica è potere: Percorsi e momenti della critica Italiana negli anni sessanta," in *Carla Lonzi: La duplice radicalità*, pp. 87–110.

137. "L'adesione agli artisti è stata per me fin dal'inizio una sensazione di affinità al cui ho dato fiducia," Lonzi, "La critica è potere," p. 6.

138. Masini, "Le mostre di questa estate," p. 49.

139. "Artisti e critici si sentono forse, vicendevolmente traditi: è un esperienza inter-locutoria?" Sandra Orienti, "L'amore mio è il futuro," *Il Popolo*, July 7, 1970, clipping, <Archive>.

140. As with Pistoletto's *Mirror Paintings*, it is almost impossible to edit the photographer out — hence my reflection in it.

141. "Il titolo oscurissimo: ma oscurità rimane oscurità, sempre" — "The very obscure title: but obscurity remains obscurity, always" — wrote Goffredo Parise, a novelist and the husband of Giosetta Fioroni in his review of the exhibition entitled "Una baracca molto spettacolare," untitled and unpaginated clip, Incontri archive.

Index

Dreyer Carl Theodor, 49.
Duchamp, Marcel, 239, 292 n.129.

ECLIPSES: in Antonioni's films, 14, 65; avoid-
ance of Como's Casa del Fascio as, 24, 162,
163, 169, 279 n.107; in *Campo urbano* photo
book, 136; conference on Terragni as,
159–61; of Fascist Palazzo dell'Arte, 215; of
Palazzo Trinci in Foligno, 191–92; photographic nature of, 14, 89; relationship to
flashback, 11, 13, 14–16; solar, 14, 53, 161, 247;
Vitalità as, 215–16, 247. See also *Eclisse, L'*.
Eclisse, L' (Antonioni, 1962): Ashbery on, 48;
and eclipses, 14; EUR in, 226; figures lined
up along balustrade trope, 262 n.39; final
freeze-frames, 52–53; lamps, 56, 79–80;
parallels with Pistoletto, 18, 37, 39, 47, 52,
54; and Richter's *Personengruppe* (1965),
225; Rome cityscape suggesting painting
by Balla, 55; theme song "Radioattività,"
267 n.101.
Eco, Umberto, 32, 81, 86, 265 n.78; *La struttura
assente* (1968), 217.
École du regard, 48.
Eliot, T. S., "Love Song of J. Alfred
Prufrock," 47.
Environments by 4 New Realists exhibition
(1964), 72.
Epoca, 45, 185.
Esposizione Universale Roma (EUR), 53,
225–27, 236.
Espresso, L', 45, 85, 212.
Europeo, L', 45, 178.
Eurodomus (Genoa), 267 n.96.
Exhibitions: and architecture, 26; design of,
26; under Fascism, 27, 205, 206, 207–208, 211,
214, 225–26, 254 n.30, 286 nn.64,66.

FABRO, LUCIANO: at *Amore Mio*, 239, 241–43,
242; and Arte Povera, 119, 197; *Attaccapanni*, 241; and *Campo urbano*, 119; with
Carla Lonzi at an exhibition, *240*, 241;
ceded catalogue pages to Lonzi, 239, 241;
and *Vitalità*, 281 n.1.
Factories, 87, 101, 103, 107, 155.
Fascism: allusions and flashbacks to, 11, 52,
217, 223–25, 236; and architecture, 158–61,
217, 236; and art, 16, 49, 80, 89–93, 166, 168,

214, 217; and Bertolucci's *Conformist*, 226,
227, 230–31, 236, 237; collaboration with and
resistance to, 17, 52, 76, 101, 152, 159, 223, 252
n.17; De Felice on, 217; exhibitions under,
27, 205, 206, 207–208, 211, 214, 225–26, 254
n.30, 286 nn.64,66; genre of oceanic crowd
images, 163; Moravia's portrayal of, 237–38;
Neofascism, 175, 179, 238, 282 n.13; nostalgia
for, 236; rallies and parades, 155, 158, 171;
in Spain, 53; and *Vitalità*, 179–80, 217–19, 231,
247; in works of Fioroni, 217–19. See also
Casa del Fascio; Lateran Treaty; Musso-
lini, Benito.
Fellini, Federico, 48, 60.
Feminism, 241, 243.
Ferrari, Ettore, *Monument to Giordano Bruno*
(1889), 147–50, *149*.
Ferrario, Carlo, *Riflessione* (*Campo urbano*,
1969), 119, *122–23*, 133, 134, 168–69, plate 6.
Ferzetti, Gabriele, 41.
Festa, Tano, 58, 59, 281 n.1; at the 1964
Venice Biennale, 63, 64, *66*.
Fiat factory, 87, 101, 103, 107, 155.
Figuration Narrative movement, 69.
Figurative art, 17, 93, 251 n.8; Neofiguration,
135.
Finch, Christopher, 284 n.40.
Fioroni, Giosetta; *Autoritratto a 7 anni* (1966),
219; *Autoritratto di profilo* (1969), 219;
Autunno al Foro Italico (1970), 225; *Bambino
solo* (1967), 217–19; cityscapes of, 64; compared with Antonioni, 65–66; compared
with *Mirror Paintings*, 64–65; *Contemplazione del capo* (1969), 219; exhibitions of, 219,
221, 230, 285 n.51, 290 n.97; family pictures,
223; *La fidanzata* (1961), 64; *Grande freccia
che indica la casa in campagna* (1970), 221;
husband of, 294 n.141; *L'immagine del silenzio* (1964), 63–64, 66; interviews with, 27,
63, 219, 225; *La montagna* (1970), 221; *Obbedienza* (1969), 219, *220*; photographed at the
1964 Venice Biennale, 28, 63–64, *66*, 226;
Piccola Balilla (1969), 219; as protagonist, 12;
La ragazza sulla spiaggia (1966), 64; *Strada
per Fregene* (1970), 225; *Studio per*, *218*, 225; at
Vitalità, 28, 217, *218*, 225–27, *228*, 281 n.1.
Fiss, Karen, 254 n.31.
Flanagan, Barry, 251 n.8.

Piazza San Marco (Venice), 137, 168, 221.

Picasso, Pablo, *Guernica*, 52, 53, 56.

Piccolo, Il (Trieste), 84.

Piedmont, liberation of, 76.

Piero della Francesca, 192–93, 200.

Piersanti, Massimo, 291 n.109.

Pieve di Soligo, 221.

Pino-Gallizio, Giuseppe, "Industrial Paintings," 140.

Pioppi, Maria, 197.

Pisani, Mimma, 186.

Pisani, Vettor: *Plagio* with Pistoletto, 292 n.129;
room at *Amore mio*, 197–99, 239; *Lo scorrevole*
(1970), 185, 186; *Tavolo caricato a morte* (1970),
185, 186; and *Vitalità*, 182, 208, 281 n.1.

Pistoi, Luciano, 93.

Pistoletto, Michelangelo: at *Amore mio*, 199,
239; apartment and studio of, 40–41,
44, 87; at *Arte povera + azioni povere*, 197;
curation of *Arte abitabile* exhibition, 88;
dealer of, 259 n.28; family of, 76; home and
archive in Biella, 76, 89, 97, 112, 268 n.104;
and the Left, 53; and 1964 Biennale, 68;
parallels with Antonioni, 37–40, 41, 47,
52–53, 262 n.39; participation in street
events, 112, 271 n.15; and Pop, 41–45, 68–69;
in *Pozzo* photograph, 89, 92; as protagonist, 12, 27; *A Reflected World* exhibition
(Walker Art Center, 1966), 19, *30*; refusal
strategy, 87–88; reviews and essays on,
31–34, 40–52, 57–58, 68–69, 72, 89, 251 n.8, 255
n.2; in Sala Espressioni, *50*; self-portraits,
99, *100*; Sottsass on, 40–47, 49–52, 57, 68;
and *Vitalità*, 281 n.1. See also Mirror Paintings; Pistoletto, Michelangelo (works).

Pistoletto, Michelangelo (works): *Alpino*
(1962/1963), 72–79, *73*, *78*, 101, plate 3; *Ambiente* (1967), 193, *194–95*; *Autoritratto argento*
(1960), *100*; *Bandiera rossa (comizio 1)* (1965),
103; *Bottiglia sul pavimento* (1963), 40–41,
42–43; *Comizzi* series (1965), 103; *Deposizione*
(1973), *106*, 107; *Donna in verde e due personaggi* (1963), 40, *42–43*; *Donna seduta di spalle*
(1963), *33*, 69; *Due persone* (1963–64), 35, 41,
42–43; *Due persone che passano* (1965), 103;
Due uomini in camicia (1962), 264 n.61; *Ficus*
(1965), 87; *Lampadina* (1964), 79; *Marzia con
bambino* (1963), 37, *38*; *No all' aumento del*

Tram (1965), 103, 107; *Oggetti in meno* (1966),
52, 87–88, 89, 112, 271 n.15; *Paesaggio* (1965/
1966), 87; *Persona appoggiata* (1964), 69, *71*;
Persona di schiena (1962), 40, *42–43*; *Persone
alla balconata* (1964), 49, 57; *Plagio with
Pisani*, 292 n.129; *Pozzo* (1965), 52, *54*, 87, 89,
91–92; *Quadro da pranzo* (1965/1966), 87;
Ragazze alla balconata (1964), 28; *Ragazzo*
(1965), 103–107; *Riflettore* (1964), 79, 89, *90*;
Tre ragazze alla balconata, *58*; *Uomo con
pantaloni gialli* (1964), *10*, 19–20, 69, plate 1;
Uomo seduto (1962), 34–35, *36*, 69, *70*, 87;
Vietnam (1965), *105*, 107, 269 n.123. See also
Mirror Paintings.

Pittura a Milano dal 1945 al 1964 (Milan, 1964),
285 n.47.

Pittura Informale, 40, 47, 93, 118, 190.

Pius, XI, Pope, 277 n.79.

Pocket films, 47.

Polano, Sergio, *Storia dell'architettura Italiana*,
26.

Politi, Giancarlo, 113–14, 193.

Political activism, 20, 113, 115, 150, 169, 171–75,
179–81. *See also* Student movements.

Pompei, 212.

Pompidou era, 171.

Ponti, Gio, 49, 51, 80, 87, 88.

Pop: American sensibility of, 44–45, 257 n. 19;
British, 69; debates in Italian art magazines, 257 n.19, 264 n.61; domestication of,
in New York, 41; elements of, at *Vitalità*,
180, 188, 189, 208, 211; exhibitions, 69, 72–76,
74–75, 196, 264 nn.61,63 290 n.106; and
Fioroni's works of late 1960s, 219; galleries
representing, 63; geopolitics of, 18–20,
58, 79; Italian and American, 44–45, 57,
58–60, 72, 221; Italian photography of, 45;
at Milan Triennale (1964), 81, 85; *Mirror
Paintings* and, 17, 18, 34, 69, 72, 264 n.61;
"Pop e non Pop" by Sottsass, 40–47, 57,
68, 258 n.22; Roman, 21, 63, 177, 190, 217, 221;
and tourism, 135; at Venice Biennale (1964),
58, *59*, 79.

Pop art, nouveau réalisme etc. (Brussels),
264 n.61.

Pop etc. (Vienna, 1964), 69.

Pop gallery show (Turin, 1965), 72–76, *74–75*,
196, 264 n.63.

307

Zone Books series design by Bruce Mau

Typesetting by Meighan Gale

Image placement and production by Julie Fry

Printed and bound by Maple Press